INGMAR BERGMAN

Ingmar Bergman
An enduring legacy

EDITED BY ERIK HEDLING

Lund University Press

Copyright © Lund University Press 2021

While copyright in the volume as a whole is vested in Lund University Press, copyright in individual chapters belongs to their respective authors, and no chapter may be reproduced wholly or in part without the express permission in writing of both author and publisher.

An electronic version of this book is also available under a Creative Commons (CC-BY-NC-ND) licence, thanks to the support of Lund University, which permits non-commercial use, distribution and reproduction provided the author(s) and Lund University Press are fully cited and no modifications or adaptations are made. Details of the licence can be viewed at https://creativecommons.org/licenses/by-nc-nd/4.0/

Lund University Press
The Joint Faculties of Humanities and Theology

LUND
UNIVERSITY
PRESS

P.O. Box 192
SE-221 00 LUND
Sweden
http://lunduniversitypress.lu.se

Lund University Press books are published in collaboration with Manchester University Press.

British Library Cataloguing-in-Publication Data
A catalogue record for this book is available from the British Library

Lund University Press gratefully acknowledges publication assistance from the Thora Ohlsson Foundation (*Thora Ohlssons stiftelse*)

ISBN   978-91-985577-0-1   hardback

First published 2021

The publisher has no responsibility for the persistence or accuracy of URLs for any external or third-party internet websites referred to in this book, and does not guarantee that any content on such websites is, or will remain, accurate or appropriate.

Typeset by
Servis Filmsetting Ltd, Stockport, Cheshire

Contents

List of figures vii
Notes on contributors viii
Acknowledgements xiv

Ingmar Bergman at 100: an introduction
Erik Hedling 1
1 Ingmar Bergman on the international scene
  Peter Cowie 17
2 Bergman transnational: Munich–Rome–Los Angeles, or 'The last temptation of Ingmar Bergman'
  Thomas Elsaesser 30
3 Bergman and the business: notes on the director's 'worth in the market'
  Olof Hedling 42
4 Bergman, writing, and photographs: the auteur as an ekphrastic ghost
  Maaret Koskinen 56
5 The playfulness of Ingmar Bergman: screenwriting from notebooks to screenplays
  Anna Sofia Rossholm 70
6 Cinema as a detour: Ingmar Bergman, writer
  Jan Holmberg 90
7 Laughing through tears: the soundscape of Ingmar Bergman's *Smiles of a Summer Night*
  Alexis Luko 107
8 Sound, act, presence: classical music in the films of Ingmar Bergman—a lecture-recital
  Anyssa Neumann 136
9 Film-musical moments in Ingmar Bergman's films
  Ann-Kristin Wallengren 151

10 Where does music come from? Musical meaning and
    musical discourse in Ingmar Bergman's films
    Per F. Broman   167
11 Bergman, Janov, and *Autumn Sonata*
    Paisley Livingston   185
12 *Persona*'s penis
    Daniel Humphrey   197
13 Battlefield family: Ingmar Bergman, Henrik Ibsen, and
    television
    Michael Tapper   211
14 Bergman/Birdman/Vogler: an ecocritical examination of
    the birds of Bergman
    Linda Haverty Rugg   224
15 Visionaries and charlatans: Ingmar Bergman's
    filmmaking
    Laura Hubner   236
16 Imagined without dialogue: *Sawdust and Tinsel* and
    Dreams
    Dan Williams   249
17 The ghost in the machine: *Saraband*
    Lars Gustaf Andersson   261
18 Return to the bourgeoisie: *Fanny and Alexander* in
    Swedish politics
    Erik Hedling   270

Index   285

List of figures

7.1–7.13	Excerpts from the soundtrack of *Smiles of a Summer Night* (1955). Music by Erik Nordgren. Reproduced by permission of the estate of Erik Nordgren	112–133
10.1	Bergman's director's script (document B:010). Used with permission from The Ingmar Bergman Archives	172
10.2	Chopin, daguerreotype by Louis-Auguste Bisson (*c.* 1849)	176
10.3	Hindemith Sonata for Cello op. 25 No. 3	179
12.1	*Persona*'s penis, *Persona* (1966)	198
12.2	The carbon rod, *Persona* (1966)	200
15.1	Sara beckons Isak from the other side, *Wild Strawberries* (1957)	241
15.2	Sara walks into Isak's world, *Wild Strawberries* (1957)	242

Notes on contributors

Lars Gustaf Andersson is a Professor of Film Studies at Lund University, Sweden. His research has mainly focused on issues concerning minor cinema cultures such as experimental filmmaking, and he is co-author of *A History of Swedish Experimental Film Culture* (2010) and *A Historical Dictionary of Scandinavian Cinema* (2012). Together with Professor John Sundholm of Stockholm University, he has co-authored several articles on immigrants in Swedish film culture as well as the book-length study *The Cultural Practice of Immigrant Filmmaking* (2019).

Per F. Broman is Professor of Music Theory and Associate Dean of the College of Musical Arts, Bowling Green State University, Ohio, USA. He holds degrees from the Royal College of Music in Stockholm, McGill University, and Gothenburg University. His research interests include twentieth-century analytical techniques, Scandinavian music, aesthetics, and film music. Broman was editor-in-chief of *What Kind of Theory Is Music Theory?* (2008) and has contributed to numerous journals. He published a chapter on Ingmar Bergman's use of music in his films in James Wierzbicki (ed.), *Sound and Filmmakers: Sonic Style in Cinema* (2012).

Peter Cowie received his MA in History from Cambridge University, UK. He began writing about Ingmar Bergman while still an undergraduate, and his first pamphlet devoted to the director appeared in 1961. His *Ingmar Bergman: A Critical Biography* appeared in 1982. In the early 1980s, Cowie was a Regents' Lecturer at the University of California Santa Barbara, and he has lectured on Bergman in the USA, the UK, France, Germany, Italy, Sweden, China, and Australia. In 1989 he received the Royal Order of the Polar Star from the King of Sweden in recognition of his services to

Swedish culture. Cowie has also written commentaries for numerous Bergman films, published on DVD and Blu-ray by the Criterion Collection in New York. He is the author of over thirty books on cinema.

Thomas Elsaesser, who died in 2019, was Professor Emeritus at the Department of Media and Culture, University of Amsterdam. In 2006–2007 he was the Ingmar Bergman Professor at the University of Stockholm, and from 2006 to 2012 he was a Visiting Professor at Yale University. His recent books include *The Persistence of Hollywood* (2012), *German Cinema – Terror and Trauma: Cultural Memory since 1945* (2013), *Film Theory – An Introduction through the Senses* (with Malte Hagener, 2015), *Körper, Tod und Technik* (with Michael Wedel, 2016), and *Film History as Media Archaeology* (2016). His final book was *European Cinema and Continental Philosophy: Film as Thought Experiment* (2018).

Linda Haverty Rugg is the Associate Vice Chancellor for Research and a Professor in the Scandinavian Department at the University of California, Berkeley, USA. She has taught Berkeley's undergraduate course on the films of Ingmar Bergman ten times since arriving on campus in 1999, and she delivered the Bergman centennial lecture series held at the University of California Berkeley Pacific Film Archive in 2018. She has written and published on Ingmar Bergman in articles and in her second book, *Self-Projection: The Director's Image in Art Cinema* (2014). This was a sequel to her first book, *Picturing Ourselves: Photography and Autobiography* (1997). Her current focus on environmental humanities takes her in new directions. Her earlier scholarship includes writing on August Strindberg, Mark Twain, Rainer Maria Rilke, and Kerstin Ekman, and she has been active as a translator of Hans Magnus Enzensberger, Sven Lindqvist, and Ingmar Bergman.

Erik Hedling is a Professor of Film Studies at Lund University, Sweden. He is the author, editor, or co-editor of more than fifteen books and has written more than 150 scholarly articles in English or Swedish on film. Among his publications are, as author, *Lindsay Anderson: Maverick Film-Maker* (1998) and, as co-editor, *Lindsay Anderson Revisited: Unknown Aspects of a Film Director* (2016). He has taught and written about the films of Ingmar Bergman in the USA and Sweden for more than twenty-five years. His latest book-length study was published in 2015 as 'The Battle of Dybbøl

Revisited: The Danish Press Reception of the TV-Series *1864*', which may be accessed electronically at Kosmorama.org.

Olof Hedling, who died in 2020, was an Associate Professor in Film Studies at the Centre for Languages and Literature, Lund University, Sweden. In the last few years, his scholarly activities dealt with queries located at the intersection between several scholarly fields, including Scandinavian film history, film production studies, economics, critical film policy review, and regional development. Between 1994 and 2001, he co-taught a summer course on Bergman at the local college on the Baltic island of Gotland, very close to Fårö where Bergman had his main residence for the last forty years of his life.

Jan Holmberg is CEO of the Ingmar Bergman Foundation and Head Curator of the Ingmar Bergman Archives. Holding a PhD in cinema studies from Stockholm University, Sweden, Holmberg has taught film history and cultural studies at Stockholm University, Linnaeus University and Malmö University. He is the author of three books, *Förtätade bilder: Filmens närbilder i historisk och teoretisk belysning* (Tight frames: The history and theory of cinematic close-ups, 2000); *Slutet på filmen: O.s.v.* ('The end of cinema: Etc.', 2011); and *Författaren Ingmar Bergman* ('Ingmar Bergman, the writer', 2018). Holmberg was editor-in-chief of the forty-volume book series *Ingmar Bergmans skrifter* ('The writings of Ingmar Bergman', 2018), and has written numerous articles on Ingmar Bergman, early cinema, film aesthetics, and the digital turn in scholarly journals and popular press alike.

Laura Hubner is Professor in Film and Media at the University of Winchester, UK. She is author of *The Films of Ingmar Bergman: Illusions of Light and Darkness* (2007) and *Fairytale and Gothic Horror: Uncanny Transformations in Film* (2018), editor of *Valuing Films: Shifting Perceptions of Worth* (2011) and co-editor of *Framing Film: Cinema and the Visual Arts* (2012) and *The Zombie Renaissance in Popular Culture* (2014). She recently contributed an article to *Ingmar Bergman's Cinema* (2018). Her next monograph on Bergman launches the book series she is editing, *Iconic Movie Images* (forthcoming).

Daniel Humphrey is an Associate Professor of Film Studies and Women's and Gender Studies as well as the Coordinator of the

Film Studies Program at Texas A&M University, Texas, USA. He is the author of the monograph *Queer Bergman: Gender, Sexuality and the European Art Film* (2013), two previous articles on Ingmar Bergman's cinema published in *Post Script*, and other essays published in *Criticism*, *Screen*, *GLQ*, *Invisible Culture*, and *A Companion to the Horror Film*. Recently, he contributed an essay, 'Sex, fladdermöss och utropstecken—när Bergman kom till Amerika', included in a DVD boxset, 'Ingmar Bergman: 100 år' (released in 2018 by Studio S Entertainment).

Maaret Koskinen is a Professor Emerita at the Department of Media Studies of Stockholm University, Sweden. She was the first scholar to be given access to Ingmar Bergman's private papers, which led to the formation of the Bergman Foundation, and was appointed Honorary Bergman Professor by Stockholm University and the Bergman Foundation jointly in 2009. Her publications include *Ingmar Bergman Revisited: Cinema, Performance and the Arts* (2008), *Ingmar Bergman's The Silence: Pictures in the Typewriter, Writings on the Screen* (2010), and *Ingmar Bergman y sus primeros escritos: En el principio era la palabra* (2018). Recent publications include the chapter, 'The Capital of Scandinavia? Imaginary Cinescapes and the art of Creating an Appetite for Nordic Cinematic Spaces' in *Companion to Nordic Cinema* (2016), and the article 'Time, Memory and Actors: Representation of Ageing in Recent Swedish Feature Film', which appeared in the *Journal of Scandinavian Cinema* (2019).

Paisley Livingston is Emeritus Professor of Philosophy at Lingnan University, Hong Kong, and Visiting Professor in Philosophy at Uppsala University, Sweden. He previously held teaching or research positions at McGill University, the University of Copenhagen, l'Ecole Polytechnique, Paris, and Aarhus University. His books include *Cinema, Philosophy, Bergman: On Film as Philosophy* (2009) and *Art and Intention: A Philosophical Study* (2005). He has published in a variety of academic journals and reference works.

Alexis Luko is an Associate Professor of Music in the School for Studies in Art and Culture and College of the Humanities at Carleton University, Ottawa, Canada. She holds a PhD from McGill and previously worked as a Visiting Professor at the Eastman School of Music and the College Department of Music at the

University of Rochester. Her articles have appeared in the *Journal of Film Music*, *Tijdschrift van de Vereniging voor Nederlandse Muziekgeschiedenis*, *The Journal of Plainsong and Medieval Music*, *Early Music History*, and *The Journal of Music History Pedagogy*, and she has contributed chapters to *The Cambridge Wagner Encyclopedia*, *The Oxford Handbook of Music and Medievalism*, and *Music and Auteur Filmmakers in European Arthouse Cinema*. Her book *Sonatas, Screams, and Silence: Music and Sound in the Films of Ingmar Bergman* was published in 2015.

Anyssa Neumann is a concert pianist and musicologist currently based in Sweden, where she holds a postdoctoral research position in the Engaging Vulnerability programme at Uppsala University, Sweden. She earned her PhD in musicology from King's College London, UK, in 2017, focusing on pre-existing music in the films of Ingmar Bergman, and subsequently toured a lecture-recital based on this work, with appearances at TIFF (Canada), Filmoteca Española (Spain), Blackheath Halls (UK), the Helsingborg Classical Music Festival (Sweden), and Bowdoin College (USA). She has published on the aesthetics of Glenn Gould, written liner notes for Naxos International Records, and taught music history at the University of Oxford. As a solo and collaborative pianist, she performs frequently in North America and Europe with a repertoire that spans the Baroque to the twenty-first century.

Anna Sofia Rossholm is an Associate Professor in Cinema Studies at Stockholm University, Sweden. Her research focuses on the relation between film and other media. She has published numerous articles and book chapters in the fields of adaptation studies and screenwriting studies. Her latest book, *Ingmar Bergman och den lekfulla skriften: studier av anteckningar, utkast och filmidéer i arkivets samlingar* (2017), examines the process of screenwriting in Ingmar Bergman's filmmaking.

Michael Tapper is an Assistant Professor in Cinema Studies at Lund University, Sweden, and has an MA in journalism. He is an affiliated researcher at Lund University, has taught at a number of Swedish universities, and has worked as a film critic for over twenty years. From 1998 to 2002 he was the chief editor of the film journal *Filmhäftet*, and from 2003 to 2005 he edited its English successor *Film International*. In 2011 he published the biography/monograph *Clint Eastwood* and the doctoral dissertation 'Snuten i skymningslandet: Svenska polisberättelser i roman och film 1965–2010'. The latter was published in a revised and updated English edition in 2014 as *Swedish Cops: From Sjöwall and Wahlöö to Stieg Larsson*. His most recent book is *Ingmar Bergman's Face to Face* (2017).

Ann-Kristin Wallengren is a Professor in Film Studies at Lund University, Sweden. Her research embraces questions about film and national and cultural identity, representation, ideology, and transnationality, as well as different aspects of film music. Her publications include (co-edited with Erik Hedling) *Den nya svenska filmen: kultur, kriminalitet, kakofoni* ('New Swedish Cinema: Culture, Criminality, Cacophony', 2014). Her *Welcome Home Mr Swanson: Swedish Emigrants and Swedishness in Film* was also published in 2014. Together with K.J. Donnelly, she has edited a special issue of *Music and the Moving Image* about the psychology of film music (2015) and the anthology *Today's Sounds for Yesterday's Films: Making Music for Silent Cinema* (2016).

Dan Williams has taught film studies in adult, sixth-form, and higher education, including work at Brunel University, UK and City, University of London, UK, Department of Continuing Education. He currently teaches for the Workers' Educational Association and at Collingham College, UK. He also teaches Philosophy and English Language in adult education. Williams's publications include *Citizen Kane* (2000) and *North by Northwest* (2001) in the York Notes series, and *Klein, Sartre and Imagination in the Films of Ingmar Bergman* (2015). The latter was developed from a PhD at Brunel University, UK.

Acknowledgements

First of all, my thanks go to all the contributors to this book. I am also grateful to the financial supporters behind this project: Riksbankens Jubileumsfond, Allhemsstiftelsen (the Allhem Foundation) in Malmö, and Kungliga Humanistiska Vetenskapssamfundet i Lund (the Royal Society of Letters at Lund). Thanks are due to NECSUS for permission to reprint Anna Sofia Rossholm's chapter. I also wish to mention assistance provided by Jan Holmberg and the Ingmar Bergman Foundation in Stockholm. Finally, my thanks go to Professor Marianne Thormählen, Publishing Director of Lund University Press, for her tireless work on getting this volume into print.

The book is dedicated to the memory of our friends and co-workers Thomas Elsaesser and Olof Hedling, who are sadly no longer with us.

Lund, in June 2021
Erik Hedling

Ingmar Bergman at 100: an introduction

Erik Hedling

The year 2018 marked the centenary of an event that was to have a great impact on cinema and theatre history: the birth of Ingmar Bergman in Uppsala, Sweden, on 14 July 1918. In honour of the occasion, celebrations were held around the world to commemorate Bergman's achievements as a prolific filmmaker and theatre director. From the 1930s until his death in 2007, Bergman wrote and directed many classic works, from the films *Sawdust and Tinsel* (1953) and *Winter Light* (1963) to the television series *Scenes from a Marriage* (1973).

These centenary celebrations included retrospective screenings of Bergman's films, theatrical productions based on his scripts, the release of various documentary films, museum exhibitions, and the publication of a number of new scholarly and other books.[1] An international seminar was also held at Lund University in southern Sweden with the explicit aim of producing a new research anthology that summarizes modern trends within scholarship on Bergman. Many of the world's prominent Bergman scholars were invited to contribute to both the seminar and the resulting anthology, which you are now reading.

---

1 For instance, Swedish publishing house Norstedts published several Bergman film scripts, hitherto unavailable in their original Swedish, as well as edited volumes of the director's own workbooks and a collection of his various literary works. They also published a new scholarly book in Swedish on Bergman's writings by Jan Holmberg: *Författaren Ingmar Bergman* (Stockholm: Norstedts, 2018). Two more scholarly books were published on Bergman during the previous year: Anna Sofia Rossholm's *Ingmar Bergman och den lekfulla skriften: studier av anteckningar, utkast och filmidéer i arkivets samlingar* (Gothenburg: Makadam, 2017) and Michael Tapper's *Ingmar Bergman's Face to Face*, written in English by a Swede (London and New York: Wallflower Press, 2017).

The Lund University project was also launched as a follow-up to the major symposium organized by Bergman scholar Maaret Koskinen at Stockholm University in 2005, an event that ultimately produced the anthology *Ingmar Bergman Revisited*.[2] This publication introduced new aspects; and to a large degree, its contributors went on to speak at the 2018 event at Lund and to contribute to this book. Some new faces were also invited to participate. Scholarship on Bergman—his films, his work in the theatre, and now also his writings—has a long tradition that this present volume both upholds and hopes to extend, although it concentrates on Bergman's films— and, to a certain extent, also his writings—though unfortunately not on his accomplishments in the theatre.[3] It aims to display what is happening in Bergman scholarship at the present time: methods, research angles, new archival material consulted, and so forth. Regarding the latter, many of this volume's chapters make liberal use of material held at the Ingmar Bergman Archive at Stockholm, a research resource that has only been available to scholars for the past two decades. Naturally, this book cannot address all kinds of Bergman scholarship, nor can it include all Bergman scholars. Nevertheless, it is hoped that it will succeed in showcasing something of the current state of the art.

Previous research on Bergman

Bergman is one of the world's most celebrated filmmakers. After being hailed as one of the great auteurs by Parisian film magazine *Cahiers du Cinéma*'s famous critics François Truffaut and Jean-Luc Godard and his breakthrough at the Cannes festival in 1956, scholarly writings on Bergman's films became commonplace. The very

---

2 Maaret Koskinen, ed., *Ingmar Bergman Revisited: Performance, Cinema and the Arts* (London and New York: Wallflower Press, 2008).

3 Only a fraction of the massive corpus of academic writing published on Bergman's works has been devoted to his groundbreaking theatre productions at Malmö, Stockholm, and Munich. This is probably largely due to the broader world of international scholarship's limited access to Swedish-language—and even German-language—theatre. Only one theatre scholar, Rikard Loman, an expert on Bergman directing Shakespeare in Sweden, participated in the seminar at Lund. Loman has not contributed to this book, however. Most writings on Bergman's theatrical work are in Swedish. The classic English-language work on the subject is *Ingmar Bergman: Four Decades in the Theater* by Lise-Lone Marker and Frederick J. Marker (Cambridge and New York: Cambridge University Press, 1982).

first books on Bergman, by Jean Béranger and Jacques Siclier, were published in French in the late 1950s.[4] However, the most influential piece of writing published on Bergman at this time was aspiring filmmaker Godard's celebration of Bergman's art in *Cahiers*, in which, in the spirit of the auteur theory, he hailed Bergman as a cinematic Marcel Proust.[5] Godard's piece set the tone for much Bergman criticism to follow—criticism concerning the exposition of the filmmaker's world-view, or *Weltanschauung*, as expressed in the aesthetics of his films. Many subsequent monographs on Bergman have been conceived in this spirit, such as those by Philip Mosley, Laura Hubner, and Robin Wood.[6]

Bergman's world-view has sometimes been approached in philosophical terms, and a strong tradition of philosophical investigation into his work has emerged, with contributions from scholars such as Paisley Livingston, Irving Singer, and Dan Williams.[7] Investigation through the lens of psychoanalysis has been another trend, including work by world-famous psychoanalyst and Harvard professor Erik H. Erikson, who used Bergman's classic film *Wild Strawberries* (1957) in an influential and much-cited study of developmental psychology.[8] General psychoanalysis has featured prominently in Bergman studies

---

4 Jean Béranger, *Ingmar Bergman et ses films* (Paris: Le Terrain Vague, 1959) and Jacques Siclier, *Ingmar Bergman*, Collection Encyclopedique du Cinéma: Les Grandes Createurs du Cinéma 12–13 (Brussels: Club de Livre de Cinéma, 1958).

5 Jean-Luc Godard, 'Bergmanorama', *Cahiers du Cinéma* 15:85 (1958), 1–5.

6 Philip Mosley, *Ingmar Bergman: The Cinema as Mistress* (London and Boston, MA: Marion Boyars, 1981), Laura Hubner, *The Films of Ingmar Bergman: Illusions of Light and Darkness* (Basingstoke: Palgrave Macmillan, 2007), and Robin Wood, *Ingmar Bergman*, rev edn., ed. Barry Keith Grant (Detroit, MI: Wayne State University Press, 2012). Wood's highly readable book was originally published in 1969. The new edition, however, was published posthumously and well after Wood's transition to a Marxist-feminist-gay liberation position. It incorporated new chapters with a different methodological outlook than before.

7 Paisley Livingston, *Ingmar Bergman and the Rituals of Art* (Ithaca, NY: Cornell University Press, 1982); Paisley Livingston, *Cinema, Philosophy, Bergman: On Film as Philosophy* (Oxford: Oxford University Press, 2009); Irving Singer, *Ingmar Bergman, Cinematic Philosopher: Reflections on His Creativity* (Cambridge, MA: MIT, 2007); Dan Williams, *Klein, Sartre and Imagination in the Films of Ingmar Bergman* (Basingstoke: Palgrave Macmillan, 2015).

8 Erik H. Erikson, 'Reflections on Dr. Borg's Life Cycle', *Dædalus* 105:2 (1976), 1–28.

in works by, for instance, Frank Gado, alongside more specific works, such as Don Fredericksen's study of Jungian dimensions in Bergman's classic tour de force *Persona* (1966) and Michael Tapper's recent study of Arthur Janov's influence on Bergman.[9] Of course, Bergman's dark, brooding cinematic style has also been understood and interpreted in religious terms, with Bergman cast as the critical challenger of the Lutheran position that characterized his own strict upbringing. It is therefore hardly surprising that some of the many theological studies of Bergman's films were written by Roman Catholic priests. Prominent examples include monographs by Richard Aloysius Blake, Marc Gervais, and Robert E. Lauder.[10] Whereas the religious intent in Bergman might be open to debate, most scholars agree that his films do address urgent religious questions, particularly those films that express and problematize the silence of God, such as *The Seventh Seal* (1957), *Through a Glass Darkly* (1961), and *Winter Light* (1963). It goes without saying that Bergman's films have been very favourably received in countries where religion is strongly entrenched, such as France and the USA. Conversely, their popularity in Sweden (a far more secularized country) has very little to do with religion, although theological studies on Bergman have been published in Sweden as well.[11]

Journalists in Bergman's native Sweden also produced a few early monographs on his works, as did Finnish-Swedish author Jörn Donner, whose book was translated into English. As head of the Swedish Film Institute, Donner later produced Bergman's farewell to cinema: *Fanny and Alexander* (1982).[12] Most early Swedish books

---

9 Frank Gado, *The Passion of Ingmar Bergman* (Durham, NC: Duke University Press, 1986); Don Fredericksen, *Bergman's Persona*, Klasyka Kina (Poznań: Adam Mickiewicz University, 2005); Tapper, *Ingmar Bergman's Face to Face*.

10 Richard Aloysius Blake, *Lutheran Milieu in the Films of Ingmar Bergman*, Arno Press Cinema Program (New York: Arno, 1978); Marc Gervais, *Ingmar Bergman: Magician and Prophet* (Montreal: McGill-Queens University Press, 1999); Robert E. Lauder, *God, Death, Art and Love: The Philosophical Vision of Ingmar Bergman* (Mahwah, NJ: Paulist, 1989).

11 For example, theology lecturer Hans Nystedt, *Ingmar Bergman och kristen tro* (Stockholm: Verbum, 1989) and former Stockholm bishop Caroline Krook, *Rastlös sökare och troende tvivlare: Existentiella frågor i filmer av Ingmar Bergman* (Stockholm: Verbum, 2017).

12 Jörn Donner, *The Personal Vision of Ingmar Bergman*, translated from Swedish by Holger Lundbergh (Bloomington, IN: Indiana University Press, 1964).

on Bergman were biographies of the life-and-works kind. The definitive biography among them to date was published a year after Bergman's passing in 2007 and was written by Mikael Timm, an experienced arts journalist who had followed Bergman's work closely since the 1970s.[13] Bergman himself participated in this huge project, providing Timm with extensive interview time. Timm also had access to the huge archive of Bergman's papers administered by the Ingmar Bergman Foundation in Stockholm, the Ingmar Bergman Archive, which had only been available to scholars for a few years at that time. It was here that Timm examined Bergman's own workbooks, the diaries he kept regarding the process of writing most of his scripts. Naturally, these workbooks have proved extremely valuable to modern scholarship on Bergman. Thanks to the availability of this material, Timm's meticulously recorded biographical details on Bergman are complemented by careful analyses of all of Bergman's films and theatre productions. It is a great pity that Timm's work still does not exist in an English translation. On the other hand, Bergman's own contributions on the subject, as contained in his two autobiographical works *The Magic Lantern* and *Images*, are readily available in English.[14] These indispensable volumes remain important resources for serious researchers.

While neither Timm's nor Bergman's books are academic works, academic research on Bergman in Sweden has been prolific since the 1990s. Two scholars deserve special mention in this regard: the first is Birgitta Steene, the second Maaret Koskinen. Although Swedish by birth, Steene spent most of her career as a professor of Scandinavian studies in the USA and has published several books and articles on Bergman, most of them in English. She was the first to draw attention to Bergman's films' reliance on a long-standing Swedish literary tradition, a tradition especially manifest in August Strindberg's groundbreaking work at the turn of the twentieth century.[15] However, Steene's most outstanding contribution to Bergman scholarship is the exhaustive work (more than 1,000 pages

---

13 Mikael Timm, *Lusten och dämonerna: Boken om Bergman* (Stockholm: Norstedts, 2008).
14 Ingmar Bergman, *The Magic Lantern: An Autobiography*, translated from Swedish by Joan Tate (New York and London: Penguin, 1988) and Ingmar Bergman, *Images: My Life in Film*, translated from Swedish by Marianne Ruuth (New York: Arcade, 1990).
15 Birgitta Steene, *Ingmar Bergman*, Twayne's World Authors 32 (Boston, MA: Twayne, 1968).

long) *Ingmar Bergman: A Reference Guide*.[16] This work is the most sophisticated research tool available to any serious investigator of all aspects of Bergman's nearly sixty-year-long career in films, theatre, and publishing. It contains an extensive filmography, a detailed bibliography (including lists of thousands of reviews and other items printed in the Swedish and international press), and an index of stage productions and television and radio programmes. The volume also includes comprehensive analyses of Bergman's work by the author herself.

Following the Steene tradition, Maaret Koskinen has also published a number of books and articles on Bergman, characteristically employing a film-theoretical and intermedial approach. Her doctoral thesis was the first work produced on Bergman at this level in Sweden and was published as a book.[17] Here Koskinen applied insights from new Anglo-Saxon and French film theory to the formal traits of Bergman's aesthetics. In a later study, she thoroughly analysed the interrelations between Bergman's film and theatre practices, drawing on her deep knowledge of his cinematic works, but also on having personally attended all of Bergman's theatre productions at the Royal Dramatic Theatre in Stockholm from the 1980s onwards.[18] Koskinen's latest book on Bergman, published in English, is a theoretical analysis of his classic film *The Silence* (1963).[19] It should be noted that owing to her personal acquaintance with Bergman, Koskinen was also instrumental in the founding of the Ingmar Bergman Archive at Stockholm. A generation of young Swedish scholars has since followed in her footsteps and published learned books on Bergman. My notes on this chapter mention some of these scholars: Jan Holmberg, current director of the Ingmar Bergman Foundation; Michael Tapper; and Anna Sofia Rossholm. Another figure of note is Christo Burman, who has published a thesis on Bergman in book form in Sweden. In it, he employs the

---

16 Birgitta Steene, *Ingmar Bergman: A Reference Guide* (Amsterdam: Amsterdam University Press, 2005).
17 Maaret Koskinen, *Spel och speglingar: En studie i Ingmar Bergmans filmiska estetik* (PhD dissertation Stockholm University, Department of Theatre and Cinema Studies, 1993).
18 Maaret Koskinen, *Ingmar Bergman: 'Allting föreställer, ingenting är'; Filmen och teatern, en tvärestetisk studie* (Nora: Nya Doxa, 2001).
19 Maaret Koskinen, *Ingmar Bergman's* The Silence: *Pictures in the Typewriter, Writings on the Screen*, Nordic Film Classics (Seattle, WA: University of Washington Press, 2010).

concept of 'theatricality' as a theoretical tool for understanding the centrality of the viewer's gaze in Bergman's films.[20]

I have paid extra attention to Swedish writings on Bergman here, since this book has been produced in a Swedish context (despite being written in English). Even so, Bergman studies are most certainly not restricted to Sweden. As has always been the case, international contributions to Bergman scholarship are equally significant. Several new non-Swedish Bergman scholars have emerged in Britons Laura Hubner and Dan Williams (both of whom are mentioned in the notes on this chapter), American Daniel Humphrey, and Canadian Alexis Luko. Humphrey's study of Bergman's impact on American queer culture has opened up a whole new horizon in Bergman studies;[21] meanwhile, Luko's analysis of Bergman's use of music and other soundscapes is, to date, the most prominent book-length study of how Bergman's filmmaking was inspired by music.[22]

The present study

Many of the aforementioned scholars have contributed to this book. Other contributors not yet mentioned have been equally important in its development. The book contains eighteen chapters in all, in addition to this introductory chapter. Some of these develop earlier trends in Bergman scholarship, while others enter hitherto uncharted territory. The first half of the book is geared towards new fields within Bergman studies: production studies (which have been notably absent to date), studies of Bergman as a writer, and studies of Bergman's use of music. The book's latter half adheres to a more traditional—though no less significant—line of analysis, addressing psychology, thematic criticism, and politics. The combination of familiar and innovative angles of approach enabled the book to cover as many aspects of his work as possible.

---

20 Christo Burman, *I teatralitetens brännvidd: Om Ingmar Bergmans filmkonst* (Umeå: Atrium, 2010).
21 Daniel Humphrey, *Queer Bergman: Sexuality, Gender, and the European Art Cinema* (Austin, TX: University of Texas Press, 2013).
22 Alexis Luko, *Sonatas, Screams, and Silence: Music and Sound in the Films of Ingmar Bergman* (New York and London: Routledge, 2016).

Production

The book's first three chapters—Chapters 1, 2, and 3—focus on Bergman's standing in the world of film criticism and film production. The first chapter is written by Peter Cowie, a veteran Bergman scholar and specialist on Nordic cinema. Cowie wrote the first English-language biography on Bergman in the early 1980s.[23] He also provided the commentary for several Bergman films released by the Criterion Collection, first on laser disc and later on DVD and Blu-ray. Cowie's chapter provides an overview of Bergman's entire career in terms of production, distribution, and critical reception. Cowie also emphasizes Bergman's strong reputation among other filmmakers and his artistic influence on directors from Stanley Kubrick to Catherine Breillat. He focuses on Bergman as a truly international artist, a standing made possible by the filmmaker's tapping into the zeitgeist of the Cold War era while exploring the new age of sexual liberation during the 1950s and 1960s.

During his 2006–2007 tenure as Ingmar Bergman Professor at Stockholm University, film historian and theorist Thomas Elsaesser conducted research in the Bergman Archive on Bergman's contact with Hollywood, which yielded a fascinating story. Bergman primarily had contact with transnational film producer Dino De Laurentiis and Hollywood talent agent Paul Kohner, with whom he discussed film projects over the years; De Laurentiis would eventually produce Bergman's film *The Serpent's Egg* (1977). However, Bergman's most notorious correspondence with Hollywood was with Kohner regarding the filming of Franz Lehár's operetta *The Merry Widow* starring American actress Barbra Streisand. Although Bergman's and Kohner's discussions on the subject came to nothing in the end, Elsaesser's research charts previously unknown territory.

Olof Hedling's chapter follows a similar trajectory, discussing Bergman's potential worth in the commercial film market on the basis of the director's own correspondence. Hedling first addresses Bergman's correspondence with Carl Anders Dymling, head of the Swedish production company Svensk Filmindustri, regarding Bergman's potential turn to the more profitable colour-film format in the early 1960s, and then turns to his correspondence with New York agent Bernhard L. Wilens regarding a film adaptation of Albert

---

23 Peter Cowie, *Ingmar Bergman: A Critical Biography* (New York: Charles Scribner, 1982).

Camus's short novel *The Fall* (*La Chute*, 1956). Third, Hedling explores Bergman's correspondence with his American distributors Janus Films, who specialized in the art-house market, represented by Cyrus Harvey. Bergman never made a colour film during Dymling's reign at Svensk Filmindustri, nor did he ever direct a film based on Camus's novel. He did have a lengthy relationship with Janus Films, however. Hedling demonstrates how Bergman's conception of himself as an artist conflicted with Hollywood, especially with regard to filmmaking practices.

Writing

The subsequent chapters—Chapters 4, 5, and 6—concern Bergman as a writer. Bergman was a prolific author throughout his lifetime. Having begun by writing unpublished novellas, short stories, and plays, he went on to write a multitude of screenplays. In his later life, Bergman wrote many literary works that were published as such in their own right.

Maaret Koskinen presents a highly elaborate theoretical analysis of Bergman's intermedial play, particularly in some of his later literary works, such as *The Best Intentions* and *Sunday's Children*. Bergman often used the textual ekphrasis tool in his written works; that is, he created verbal representations of visual representations, such as linguistic descriptions of photographs and paintings. Included in texts that Bergman was fully aware that he would not direct on film himself, these ekphrases served (among other things) as subtle stage directions for future filmmakers, thus turning Bergman into something of an invisible presence, directing unseen from the written manuscript. This aesthetic device also constituted a sophisticated play between different media, often giving rise to ambiguity and other new clusters of meaning.

Anna Sofia Rossholm digs deep into the Bergman Archive in her investigation of his writing process, carefully studying his workbooks in minute detail. Rossholm cites what is now known as 'genetic criticism' as her theoretical point of departure. This approach focuses on the movement of writing, that is, on evidence of the actual writing process, such as notes, proofs, drafts, corrections, revisions, and so forth. Her chapter emphasizes Bergman's general playfulness, as he clearly experiments, adds new dimensions, and develops his ideas, leaving tangible developmental traces behind him. Finally, Rossholm discusses the finished screenplays themselves, with a certain emphasis on Bergman's story 'The Cannibals', which some years later became the film *Hour of the Wolf* (1968).

Jan Holmberg is eager to prove Bergman's worth as a literary author, despite the fact that Bergman himself always denied aspiring to be described in such terms. Holmberg's chapter focuses on Bergman's screenplays, drawing attention to their literary qualities. He characterizes these not simply as written words intended for cinematic adaptation, but as words in and of themselves—as literature. With regard to *Hour of the Wolf*, Holmberg goes so far as to suggest that the printed screenplay rightly belongs to the dream-play genre, and that it is more artistically refined than the film itself. He also studies a handful of other Bergman screenplays in some detail, including *Autumn Sonata* (1978), *The Seventh Seal*, and *Persona*, in making his case for designating Bergman a great literary author.

Music and soundscapes

The next part of the book (Chapters 7–10) makes a strong contribution to a fairly recent phenomenon in Bergman studies: detailed analyses of how his films employ music. While Bergman's love of classical music is well known, the fact that he integrated music into his films with great imagination and subtlety is somewhat less well documented, at least in terms of solid academic accounts. According to most new Bergman scholarship on this subject, their musical scores add hitherto uncharted layers of meaning to some Bergman classics.

Alexis Luko, author of one of the first monographs entirely devoted to Bergman's use of sound and music, close-reads Bergman's highly imaginative use of music in his comedy *Smiles of a Summer Night* (1955). Luko's point of departure involves exploring theories of humour, since Bergman creates comedic moments with the aid of Erik Nordgren's original score and little classical melodies (by Schumann, Mozart, Chopin, Liszt, and a traditional Swedish hymn) performed on the piano, hummed by the actors, or—in the case of the hymn—played by a clock. Structurally, the film resembles a Mozart opera, with four couples getting entangled in various amorous predicaments. Of course, the film also includes a touch of Shakespeare's *A Midsummer Night's Dream*, thanks to the inclusion of music with magical powers. Luko examines all these facets in great analytical detail.

American concert pianist Anyssa Neumann, who is also a film and musical scholar, provides a comprehensive overview of Bergman's employment of classical music in his films from the outset of his career. In nearly half of his films, Bergman did not employ specially composed scores but relied on pre-existing music, which he used with great narrative precision. Some Bergman films are completely devoid of music. In others, Bergman let composed music interact with classical music, as in *The Seventh Seal* with the use of Carl Orff's 'Dies Iræ' in Erik Nordgren's underscore. Famously, Bergman's favourite composer was Johann Sebastian Bach, whose music appears in several Bergman films. Neumann also studies the large number of musicians among Bergman's characters as well as those of his films that deal directly with music and musicians, such as *Music in Darkness* (1948), *To Joy* (1950), and *Autumn Sonata*.

Film-music specialist Ann-Kristin Wallengren employs musical theory to account for musically charged scenes found in Bergman's films. Referring to these scenes as 'film-musical moments', she claims that they provide an especially heightened sense of experience. Examples include composer Karl-Birger Blomdahl's weird modernist music in the prologue to *Sawdust and Tinsel* and the Chopin piano 'duel' between mother and daughter in *Autumn Sonata*. Wallengren studies these scenes in terms of different kinds of 'film-musical moments', providing a detailed analysis of Bergman's uses of music with the aid of a highly complex theoretical line of reasoning.

Musicologist Per F. Broman reflects on Bergman's participation in the Swedish radio talk-show *Sommar* (Summer) in 2004, where he was given nearly two hours to contemplate any topic he liked, as long as his speech was accompanied by musical numbers of his own choosing. Bergman chose to devote the entire programme to his musical interests, selecting works by composers including Bach, Wagner, and Beethoven. Pointing to the fact that Bergman so often used pre-existing music in his films, Broman goes on to analyse the interaction between classical music and dialogue in Bergman films such as *To Joy* and *Autumn Sonata* (obviously a favourite among film-music scholars), *Saraband* (2003), and *In the Presence of a Clown* (1997). Broman concludes by claiming that Bergman challenges a traditional understanding of classical music.

Psychology

The next three chapters (11–13) return to more familiar territory in the field of Bergman research. They examine Bergman's keen interest in psychology and neurosis, particularly in relation to family, albeit from very different angles. Paisley Livingston studies *Autumn Sonata*, the story of a deeply troubled relationship between a mother, who is a famous concert pianist, and her daughter, who has lost her young son in an accident. These two main roles are played by Ingrid Bergman and Liv Ullmann. At this time, according to Bergman himself, he was studying influential American psychologist, psychotherapist, and writer Arthur Janov, whose book *The Primal Scream* had caught Bergman's interest.[24] The two men even met in Los Angeles. Livingston then presents a detailed analysis in which he asks whether *Autumn Sonata* can rightly be labelled a Janovian film and, if not, on what grounds such a claim can be rejected. Livingston's philosophically inclined argument culminates in a tantalizing review of the various possibilities, in which he ultimately concludes that even if Janov influenced the story of the film, its narrative does not contain particularly Janovian solutions.

Daniel Humphrey provides a highly theoretically orientated analysis of Bergman's 1960s cult movie *Persona*, which has elicited many different interpretations over the years since its release. Humphrey's take on the film is grounded in post-structuralist psychoanalysis, particularly the psycholinguistic theories developed by Frenchman Jacques Lacan. As his point of departure, Humphrey analyses the very briefly exposed (one-eighth of a second, according to the author) photographic image of an erect penis hidden in the famous opening montage, where the penis replaces the number 6, an element that Humphrey contemplates in some detail. Although Bergman never allows his female couple—played by Bibi Andersson and Liv Ullmann—to come out as lesbians, the film contains a potential queerness which makes it into the subversive classic it is.

Michael Tapper analyses various family troubles in his study of Bergman's TV movie *The Lie* (1970), one of the few works by Bergman to receive very little critical attention owing to its inaccessibility (it was only shown on Swedish television once). Jan Molander directed the work and not Bergman, although Bergman wrote the script. *The Lie* is the first of three Bergman works made for television and set in the upper-class Stockholm district of Djursholm in which he penetrates traditional, bourgeois family values, the other works being *Scenes from a Marriage* and *Face to Face* (1976). Tapper refers to these works as the 'Djursholm trilogy'.

---

24 Arthur Janov, *The Primal Scream. Primal Therapy: The Cure for Neurosis* (New York: Dell Publishing, 1970).

Many critics have labelled Bergman a bourgeois filmmaker, sometimes opposed to the Swedish Social Democratic welfare state in which he worked. By contrast, Tapper maintains that Bergman was himself a Social Democrat and that his films, including the Djursholm trilogy, were in fact deeply critical of the bourgeoisie, all in the radical spirit of Strindberg and Ibsen.

Thematics

The analyses in chapters 14–17 focus on various recurring thematic aspects of Bergman's films that are not discussed in the preceding chapters. While not performing a musical analysis, Linda Haverty Rugg presents a pioneering investigation of another aspect of Bergman's soundtracks, namely ambience—here in the form of various bird sounds included in his works. Haverty Rugg's conception of ambience is influenced by British ecocritic Timothy Morton's book *Ecology without Nature* and his notion of *ecomimesis*, that is, a 'representational practice in literature and art [and film, of course,] that attempts to recreate the experience of nature'.[25] Accordingly, this is an aesthetic strategy and not an unintentional inclusion that occurred during filming. Haverty Rugg demonstrates Bergman's use of an abundance of ambience created by birds in his films. She also provides a detailed thematic analysis of the function of this ambient noise in Bergman's films, drawing lucid examples from *The Virgin Spring* (1959), *Summer Interlude* (1950), *Hour of the Wolf, Wild Strawberries,* and *The Seventh Seal*.

Laura Hubner investigates Bergman's application of the themes of vision and charlatanism. She carefully examines famous Bergman scenes, such as Jof's godly visions in *The Seventh Seal*, Professor Borg's painful encounter with the examiner in his dream in *Wild Strawberries*, Dr Vogler's various tricks in *The Magician*, and, finally, the matriarch Emilie's visions of her dead son in *Fanny and Alexander*. In some instances, the visionary is fearful of being exposed as a charlatan, as in the cases of Isak Borg and Dr Vogler. In others, he is unperturbed, as in the case of Jof. Hubner provides a fresh perspective on some of Bergman's most frequently analysed individual scenes.

Dan Williams bases his chapter on a close reading of scenes from two Bergman films, *Sawdust and Tinsel* and *Dreams* (1955).

---

25 Timothy Morton, *Ecology without Nature* (Cambridge, MA, and London: Harvard University Press, 2007).

He supplies an account of Bergman's strong relationship to silent cinema, as evidenced by his deep admiration for E.A. Dupont's *Variety* (1925), as well as Victor Sjöström's *The Phantom Carriage* (1921) and subsequent Hollywood movie *He Who Gets Slapped* (1924). Williams goes on to posit that Bergman incorporated techniques from these silent classics in his own works to express complex psychological processes, whereupon he analyses these in terms of the psychological theories developed by Austrian-British psychoanalyst Melanie Klein. Among other scenes, he cites both the famous prologue and the conclusion to *Sawdust and Tinsel* in support of his claim.

Next, Lars Gustaf Andersson analyses *Saraband* as a Strindbergian chamber play, carefully staged in ten distinct scenes. *Saraband* was Bergman's last work made for television and was first broadcast in Sweden in December 2003. The film also proved to be Bergman's final work, concluding a career in moving images that began in 1944 with the script for Alf Sjöberg's film *Frenzy* and spanned fifty-eight years in total. Nominally, the film was intended as a continuation of the family saga depicted in *Scenes from a Marriage*; but in fact, as Andersson demonstrates, it constitutes a virtual anthology of dramatic situations depicted by Bergman in some of his most famous films. It is also a tribute to the classical music which Bergman loved and which features prominently in the film, particularly works by Bach. Andersson also contemplates other aspects of *Saraband*, including the influence of Swedish philosopher and mystic Emanuel Swedenborg (1653–1735) and the film's focus on different kinds of liminality.

Politics

Finally, in Chapter 18, Erik Hedling argues that Bergman deviated from his highly critical depictions of bourgeois life in the 1960s and 1970s with *Fanny and Alexander*. Bergman came from a bourgeois background, and by his own account he did not take an interest in politics until the mid-1960s. He sided with Sweden's ruling Social Democratic party at that time, which certainly represented a sort of break with his family background. However, Bergman temporarily broke off with Sweden in the aftermath of his being charged with tax evasion in 1976. Hedling argues that Bergman's return to Sweden with *Fanny and Alexander* in the early 1980s coincided with a new zeitgeist, in which the country's Socialist past came under much critical scrutiny. It was in this political climate that

Bergman chose to celebrate the bourgeois society in which he was raised.

Some thoughts on future directions

Despite the enormous volume of research on Bergman, a number of avenues of investigation remain unexplored. One such avenue pertains to Bergman's role in post-war Swedish society as well as to the political role of the artist in society in general. Bergman became a very powerful figure within the Swedish cultural establishment during his lifetime, playing a dominant role in theatre culture, particularly in Stockholm, and in the Swedish film and television industry from 1960 onwards. Bergman made—and probably also unmade—the professional careers of many people. While accounts attesting to this fact remain in common circulation today, they are far from systematized. One possible research project might involve interviewing the many first-hand witnesses to Bergman's influence while they are still alive.

Regarding production studies (concerning which this volume contains some exemplary chapters), much remains to be uncovered with respect to Bergman's international and other industry contacts. Any such studies would need to make use of the Ingmar Bergman Archive, an undertaking that requires either some degree of proficiency in the Swedish language or access to a translator. Of course, this fact does not exclude other kinds of studies; new insights within the fields of philosophy and psychology, for example, would stimulate people to continue to use Bergman's films as empirical material. In this respect, the potential for further enquiry is equally great for international scholars.

Another obvious and expanding field is, of course, intermedial studies, with Bergman material becoming the subject for other forms of expression. In reality, this phenomenon began decades ago in the form of musicals, operas, theatrical productions, documentary films, concerts, novelizations, and so on. The trend has continued to gain momentum over the years, reaching its peak in 2018. Regarding the cultural output during this centenary year, Ingmar Bergman Foundation director Jan Holmberg writes:

> As the year began, we publicly announced our goal of Bergman 100 becoming the largest commemoration of a single filmmaker ever. The outcome exceeded our highest expectations. With thousands of events (screenings of his films, stage performances of his works, documentaries,

concerts, book releases, conferences, exhibitions, etc.) held in eighty-odd countries all over the planet, Bergman 100 was an absolutely remarkable success.[26]

This intermedial explosion will undoubtedly trigger much academic activity.

Finally, there is still something to be said about the aesthetic merit of Bergman's work. Even if the general tenor of this book tends to favour hailing Bergman as a great and original artist, there is always room for diverging opinions, such as have been articulated elsewhere.[27] Whatever the case, his is an enduring legacy.

---

26 Jan Holmberg, '2018: The Year of Bergman', *1918–2018 Bergman: A Summary of the Ingmar Bergman Year*, chronicle produced and published by the Ingmar Bergman Foundation, Stockholm, 2019, p. 1.
27 One of the most notorious pieces of criticism of Bergman as a filmmaker was published by the well-known American critic Jonathan Rosenbaum just a few days after Bergman's passing. See 'Scenes from an Overrated Career', *The New York Times*, 4 August 2007.

1
Ingmar Bergman on the international scene

Peter Cowie

Few Scandinavian artists, among them Ibsen, Strindberg, and Sibelius, have achieved an international renown as great as that of Ingmar Bergman. Victor Sjöström, Mauritz Stiller, and to a lesser degree Georg af Klercker established Sweden in the forefront of the silent cinema, but during an era without television, without air travel, and when films were released only in the 'civilized' countries of Western Europe and North America. Admittedly, both Sjöström and Stiller had the courage to take up residence in Hollywood, but neither man was truly at ease in America. Like Fellini, Bergman acquired his worldwide fame despite not succumbing to the siren call of the studios in Los Angeles.

Bergman's conquest of the international art-house scene must be accounted all the more remarkable because he was working in Sweden. Firstly, the Swedish language prevented him from penetrating the mainstream French or Anglo-Saxon marketplace. Secondly, as the local industry counted fewer than 10 million Swedes as the domestic audience, this meant that budgets were strictly controlled (Bergman's own salary rarely surpassed 200,000 crowns or some $35,000 in the 1960s). Thirdly, the star system has never existed in Scandinavia; and thus, while Godard could rely on Brigitte Bardot in *Le mépris* (1963), Kurosawa could count on the box-office appeal of Toshiro Mifune, and Fellini on that of Marcello Mastroianni, Ingmar Bergman was obliged to nurture his own team of gifted actors and gradually impose them on international audiences.

Fellini compared him to a medieval troubadour, who

> can sit in the middle of the room and hold his audience by telling stories, doing sleight of hand. Even if you're not in full agreement with what he says, you enjoy the way he says it, his way of seeing

the world with such intensity. He is one of the most complete cinematographic creators I have ever seen.[1]

Throughout the 1940s, Bergman's work was sent diligently to festivals by Svensk Filmindustri. *Frenzy* (1944) screened at the Mostra in Venice in 1947, while *Music in Darkness* featured there in 1948, *Summer Interlude* (1951) in 1952, and *Waiting Women* (1952) in 1953. *A Ship Bound for India* was presented at Cannes in 1947.

In September 1947, *A Ship Bound for India* opened in Paris, and the influential critic André Bazin wrote in *Le Film Français* of his admiration for the young Bergman's 'creating a world of blinding cinematic purity'.[2] The next year Peter Ustinov directed a stage version of *Torment* (the American title of *Frenzy*) in London, and the same text was produced for the stage in Oslo. In the autumn of 1948, David O. Selznick, still one of the most powerful moguls in Hollywood, approached Bergman's producer Lorens Marmstedt and suggested that together they should make a screen version of Ibsen's *A Doll's House*, to be scripted by Bergman and directed by Alf Sjöberg. The project fell through, because Sjöberg had too many ideas, recalled Bergman, but the handsome fee enabled him to buy a high-quality 9.5mm projector and prints of several Chaplin movies.

In 1952, Forsyth Hardy, the Scottish critic, wrote in his book *Scandinavian Film* that '[Bergman] can see and feel in film. What he decides to see and feel will greatly influence the future of the Swedish film.'[3]

In the wake of his successes in Italy, France, and the UK, Bergman began to receive offers from abroad, from the United States, West Germany, and even from Russia. The Americans urged him to come to Hollywood to make a screen version of Turgenev's *First Love*. The Germans wanted to place him under contract to make *A Doll's House*, from the play by Ibsen. But he declined all these approaches and continued to shoot his films in Sweden.[4]

When *Sawdust and Tinsel* (1953) was given a market screening during the Cannes Festival of 1954, a South American distributor

---

1 Interview in *Playboy* magazine, February 1966.
2 Peter Cowie, *Ingmar Bergman: A Critical Biography*, rev. edn (London: André Deutsch, 1992), p. 59.
3 H. Forsyth Hardy, *Scandinavian Film* (London: Falcon Press, 1952).
4 Jean Béranger, 'Rencontre avec Ingmar Bergman', *Cahiers du Cinéma* 15:88 (1958), 12–20.

was impressed, and promptly flew to Stockholm to acquire it and various other Swedish titles. Two years later Bergman achieved his first major breakthrough, when *Smiles of a Summer Night* won the Special Jury Prize at Cannes in 1956 for 'Best Poetic Humour'. The following year he won the same award for *The Seventh Seal* (1957); and in 1958 *Wild Strawberries* (1957) was given the Golden Bear at the Berlin Film Festival, while *So Close to Life* (1958) brought Bergman the Best Director prize at Cannes and the three actresses in the film, Eva Dahlbeck, Ingrid Thulin, and Bibi Andersson, were given a joint award as Best Actress.

In the mid-1950s, Cyrus Harvey, president of Janus Films in New York, flew to Sweden and bought the US rights to *The Seventh Seal* and *Wild Strawberries*, establishing a relationship with Svensk Filmindustri that continues to this day. Both films attracted long queues at art houses across America, and indeed *The Seventh Seal* became the single most booked film on 16mm at universities in the United States.

By 1959, Bergman's reputation was almost at its peak, both in the Anglo-Saxon territories and in France and Italy. Perhaps the first truly significant retrospective was the work of the British programmer and historian John Gillett who, in the summer of 1959, presented a vast series of Swedish films under the title 'The Passionate Cinema' at the National Film Theatre in London. This featured not only most of Bergman's work, but also the best films of Alf Sjöberg, Arne Mattsson, and other directors, enabling audiences to see Bergman in the context of his country's cinema. Also in 1959, *The Magician* (1958) or, as it was called more appropriately in Swedish, *The Face (Ansiktet)*, won the Jury Prize for Best Direction, and it was given the Pasinetti Award by the Italian press for 'the best foreign film of 1959'.

The Academy Award for Best Foreign-language Picture went in the early months of 1960 to *The Virgin Spring* (1960), and the following year, *Through a Glass Darkly* (1961) brought Bergman his second successive Oscar in that category. The singer Harry Belafonte even declared that he wanted Bergman to make a film on the life of the Russian poet Pushkin, with Belafonte himself playing Pushkin![5]

At home in Sweden, recognition was accorded Bergman by the father against whom he had reacted so violently in youth. In 1963, after seeing *Winter Light*, Pastor Erik Bergman wrote to him in

---

5 Cited in *Time*, 14 March 1960.

fulsome terms: 'You will give more, far more, than what I have been capable of, reach deeper and further. This is clear to me. In grateful and humble joy.'[6]

The Silence, released in 1963, became Bergman's most notorious film, attracting the ire of censors in various countries. In France, the censors at first declined to issue the film with the obligatory visa. The minister responsible, Alain Peyrefitte, requested certain cuts in the cabaret sequence and in the lovers' rendezvous in the hotel room. The official magazine *Soviet Screen* attacked Bergman sharply for the 'latent Fascism and hatred of mankind' displayed by *The Silence*. In West Germany, debate over the film reached the Parliament; millions of Germans queued up to see the film, making a fortune for the distributors, Atlas Film.[7] This commercial success seemed to compensate for the moral opprobrium, and it may well have prompted United Artists to snap up the rights to *Persona* in 1966, as well as to three subsequent films, *Hour of the Wolf* (1968), *Shame* (1968), and *The Passion of Anna* (1969), none of which performed as well as the Americans had expected at the international box office.

Nevertheless, in 1970, ABC Pictures offered Bergman $1 million to make *The Touch* (1971). He agreed to shoot it in English, but dismissed any notions of making the film in Hollywood. Once again, American investment seemed inevitably to lead to a flop. Despite this failure, in 1971 Bergman won the Irving Thalberg Award, and he sent Liv Ullmann to accept it on his behalf during the Oscar ceremony.

Bergman's successful foray into television brought him a new audience from among those who were deserting the traditional cinemas in favour of staying at home and watching the small screen. *The Rite* was made for television in 1969, and then, three years later, came *Scenes from a Marriage*. This mini-series was screened over a six-week period from 11 April to 16 May 1973 on Swedish television and subsequently on foreign channels and networks. Dubbed versions were commissioned by PBS in the United States and by the BBC in the UK, but neither proved successful. Subsequently, the series was shown in Britain with subtitles and proved more

---

6 Letter on display in exhibition devoted to Bergman at the Berlin Film Festival of 2011.
7 Gert H. Theunissen, *Das Schweigen und sein Publikum* (Cologne: Du Mont Schauberg, 1964).

popular to home audiences. A theatrical release for a feature-length version also did well. There is little doubt that from an economic and artistic viewpoint, *Scenes from a Marriage* revived Bergman's reputation on both sides of the Atlantic. Indeed the torrent of revenues accruing to Bergman's production company, AB Cinematograph, enabled him to give the green light to independent film productions such as Gunnel Lindblom's *Paradise Place* (1977) and Kjell Grede's TV series, *En dåres försvarstal (A Fake Defensive Figure*, 1976). In 1974 Bergman was asked by Magnus Enhörning, the head of the music department at Sveriges Radio (SR), to direct a version of Mozart's *The Magic Flute* (1975), which would be aired as a premiere on television to celebrate the golden jubilee of SR. Sven Nykvist shot the film on 16mm, and this was then blown up to 35mm for worldwide theatrical distribution.

Dino De Laurentiis, who had established his reputation and his shrewdness as a producer with the early films of Fellini, notably *La strada* in 1954 and *Cabiria* in 1957, had tried to woo Bergman and Svensk Filmindustri as early as 1973. Their proposed screen version of *The Merry Widow*, starring Barbra Streisand, impressed De Laurentiis so much that he was willing to offer $4 million, on condition that the film be made entirely in Sweden and that Svensk Filmindustri should assume responsibility for any increase in the budget. The project fell through, not to Bergman's chagrin. But De Laurentiis, undeterred, met secretly with Bergman in New York in February 1975 and arranged to finance the TV series *Face to Face* (1976). 'It's a wonderful, strong story', he declared, 'and I visualize an ideal relationship with this brilliant filmmaker. I recognize that as a creative artist Ingmar is unexcelled, and I consider myself, above all, as a showman.'[8]

Face to Face fell to earth with a resounding thud, however, when it was shown soon after Bergman's humiliating confrontation with the Swedish tax authorities, and during the same period when, in the spring of 1976, he went into exile. This setback did not diminish Dino De Laurentiis' commitment to Bergman. Later that year, he joined Germany's Rialto Film in financing *The Serpent's Egg* (1977). The budget was by far the highest ever required by a Bergman production—$3,266,000.[9] Again, however, the reception from both

---

8 Quoted in brochure issued by Cinema International Corporation (CIC) at Cannes for *Face to Face* in 1975.
9 Cowie, *Ingmar Bergman*, p. 314.

critics and audiences was disappointing and, had it not been for a large number of locked-in pre-sales internationally, almost disastrous.

On 7 June 1976, Bergman made the cover of *Time* magazine yet again, but for the wrong reasons—'Sweden's Surrealistic Socialism' was the headline. Inside, there was a long article about the income tax situation. 'Says Ulrika Rosenberg, 23, a secretary in Botkyrka: "Bergman does not mean anything to the average Swede. He is too much above us. His films are not the films that the average Swede goes to the movies to see."'[10]

By the mid-1970s Bergman was attracting the attention of more producers outside Sweden. Lew Grade, the founder of ATV in the UK and a familiar, cigar-chomping figure at Cannes and other major events, would become a principal financier of both *Autumn Sonata* (1978) in 1977 and *From the Life of the Marionettes* in 1980. And yet if one looks back at Bergman's career between 1975 and 1981, it is clear that his public was deserting him. In the United States, *From the Life of the Marionettes* proved a flop at the box-office, perhaps all the more so because Bergman had cancelled a visit to New York, Chicago, and Los Angeles which was to have supported a campaign on behalf of Scandinavian film. Back in Sweden, the average attendance at each cinema on the film's first run was a mere sixty-four persons. In Malmö, only twelve tickets were sold at one performance.[11]

And this makes his renaissance with *Fanny and Alexander* in 1982 especially remarkable. With a massive budget of $6 million, *Fanny and Alexander* could so easily have become a disaster. Instead, it enchanted audiences throughout the world, both on television and in cinemas. It grossed $6,763,000 in the United States alone, and was rewarded with six Academy Award nominations. The film won Oscars in four categories: Cinematography, Art Direction, Costume Design, and Best Foreign-Language Film. Bergman was nominated for Best Director and for Best Original Screenplay. (He had previously been nominated as Best Director for *Autumn Sonata* and *Face to Face*.) Bergman despatched his wife Ingrid to join producer Jörn Donner on stage at the awards ceremony in Hollywood.

Serene in self-styled 'retirement', Bergman could now look back on his career with satisfaction. Rights in his memoirs, entitled *The*

---

10 *Time* magazine (international edition), 7 June 1976.
11 See *Film og Kino* (Oslo) 1 (1981).

Magic Lantern, were sold to the United States for $500,000, to the UK for £90,000, and to West Germany for DM400,000. The book proved a huge popular success in the Nordic countries, with 15,000 copies sold in Denmark, 48,000 in Norway, and 60,000 in Sweden, plus a further 50,000 for the Book of the Month Club in Sweden.[12]

On 26 November 1988, Bergman was given the European Film Academy's Lifetime Award. In his acceptance speech, he declared: 'I hope we shall never leave behind all the shadows on the screen for all these big electronic gadgets. I hope we'll never forget the mystery of those 24 frames a second. I hope we shall never deny the magic of our dreams. Long live the cinematographic art!'[13]

In 1997 at the Cannes Festival he was given the Palme of Palmes, voted by the thirty-five living directors who had won the Palme d'Or.

By the time of his international breakthrough in the mid-1950s, Ingmar Bergman had been directing films for a full decade. Even then, not all critics shared in the applause. When *Wild Strawberries* appeared in the United States, Bosley Crowther, the long-established movie critic of *The New York Times*, wrote: 'This one is so thoroughly mystifying that we wonder whether Mr. Bergman himself knew what he was trying to say.'[14] Dilys Powell, the esteemed critic of the *Sunday Times* in London, had the temerity to write:

> Mr. Bergman, I am sure, has a midnight, Arctic-winter sincerity: the violence of my dislike of his film is probably evidence of that. Did I say *The Seventh Seal* was sobering? On me, it has the impact of one of those spiked iron balls chained to a club, so popular in films about goodwill in the Middle Ages.[15]

So why was he such a godhead in the eyes of an entire generation of cinéastes and intellectuals? Why was he so successful, when many other auteurs who shared the limelight with him in the 1950s and 1960s have retreated into obscurity?

His work tapped into the zeitgeist. *The Seventh Seal* and *Wild Strawberries* emerged at the height of the Cold War. There was fear

---

12 See *Veckans Affärer* 41 (8 October 1987).
13 See www.europeanfilmawards.eu/en_EN/archive/1988 (accessed 11 March 2021).
14 *The New York Times*, 23 June 1959.
15 See *The Sunday Times*, 9 March 1958.

of imminent nuclear annihilation, which is of course expressed metaphorically in *The Seventh Seal* and quite openly in *Winter Light*, where Max von Sydow's fisherman believes that the Chinese will develop the atom bomb and then wreak havoc on the enshrined values of our Western civilization.

The artist (or in the eyes of the down-to-earth Bergman, the entertainer) is the victim of persecution. He is regarded as subversive, a danger to established society. This was a theme that recurred in the great Bergman works of the 1960s—the humiliation of the clown Frost in *Sawdust and Tinsel* or of the mesmerist Vogler in *The Face*, not forgetting snide remarks like that of Madame Armfeldt in *Smiles of a Summer Night*, who says dismissively that the actors 'can sleep in the stables'. Ironically, some of these fears were revived in the year of Bergman's centenary—the fear of nuclear weapons, the sense that despite the wondrous achievements of science there is the danger of our being controlled by gigantic corporations and authorities.

All this struck a chord in those growing up in the late 1950s and early 1960s, taught as they were in the Eisenhower years, in the Erlander years, in the De Gaulle years, to wear the grey flannel suit of convention and to place order above inventiveness. A work like *Summer with Monika* carried a powerful charge of sexual liberation. Monika lives for each passing day and does not count the cost. One cannot help but speculate if Roger Vadim was influenced by Bergman when he made *And God Created Woman* (1956) just two years after *Summer with Monika* (1953) was released in France?

The Virgin Spring, with its graphic account of a rape in the forests of medieval Sweden, and *The Silence*, which showed sex in a strikingly candid way, continued to keep Bergman in the headlines and aroused the wrath of the conservative press, not to mention the censors in various countries, notably the UK and USA. When Bergman agreed to give an interview to *Playboy* magazine in 1964, he was simply endorsing the Anglo-Saxon view of him as a controversial and provocative auteur.

Another factor helped to establish Bergman. With the close of the 1950s, a profound intellectual revolution came into play. The French New Wave, the emergence of Fellini, Antonioni, and Visconti from Italy, the British proletarian cinema of Anderson, Schlesinger, Richardson, and Reisz, Saura in Spain, Cassavetes in New York—all this created a climate of talking and experiencing film among intellectuals and bourgeoisie alike throughout Europe and the USA. The Beatles were just around the corner. John F. Kennedy swept like a fresh wind into the White House. 'Art' was 'in' for the first time since the Second World War.

Bergman's influence on filmmakers was and remains considerable. Young directors envy the lucidity of his technique. Max von Sydow once said to him in print that '[f]ew directors have shown such trust in their actors, simplified the machinery around them and emphasised the human being as well as you have'.[16] In 1960, Stanley Kubrick wrote in a letter to Bergman: 'Your vision of life has moved me deeply, much more deeply than I have ever been moved by any films. I believe you are the greatest film-maker at work today.'[17]

Krzysztof Zanussi remarked that 'Bergman was for me a god. I only came to film-making because I discovered Bergman.'[18] Paul Verhoeven has noted that *The Seventh Seal* 'made me realize that films can be art. It inspired me to become a film director. This is one of the most powerful and significant films ever made.'[19] Bertrand Tavernier said that he 'did not miss a single film by Bergman', and Jean-Luc Godard wrote ecstatically about Bergman in the pages of *Cahiers du Cinéma*: '*Summer with Monika* is the most original film of the most original of directors. It is to the cinema today what *Birth of a Nation* is to the classical cinema.'[20] Ecstatic, he sent *Cahiers* a telegram from the Berlinale in 1958: 'GOLDEN BEAR WILD STRAWBERRIES PROVES INGMAR GREATEST STOP SCRIPT FANTASTIC ABOUT FLASH CONSCIENCE VICTOR SJOSTROM DAZZLED BEAUTY BIBI ANDERSSON STOP MULTIPLY HEIDEGGER BY GIRAUDOUX GET BERGMAN STOP.'[21] Arnaud Desplechin, who paid tribute to Bergman's close-ups in his film *A Christmas Tale* (2008), has commented: 'While making a film, he is the only one whom I forbid myself to think of, otherwise I would stop everything.'[22] Claire Denis remembers what she felt when she saw *Summer with Monika* for the first time: 'I felt physically

---

16 See Max von Sydow, 'Vi byggde många broar', *Chaplin* 30:2/3 (1988), 120.
17 Letter dated 9 February 1960, lodged in the Bergman Foundation Archives, Stockholm.
18 Peter Cowie, *Revolution! The Explosion of World Cinema in the '60s* (London: Faber & Faber, 2004).
19 See www.ingmarbergman.se/en/universe/bergmans-legacy (accessed 11 March 2021).
20 Quoted in *Godard on Godard*, translation and commentary by Tom Milne (London: Secker and Warburg, London, 1972), p. 84.
21 *Godard on Godard*, p. 89.
22 www.ingmarbergman.se/en/universe/bergmans-legacy (accessed 11 March 2021).

what it is to be a young woman, this feeling of summer, youth, to be in the present.'[23]

When directors refer to Bergman, they do not do so in terms of narrative or editing. Either it is a reference to character, as in *The Right Stuff* (1980) where the minister, played by Royal Dano, who trudges up to front doors to announce the death of pilots, very much evokes Bergman's humanization of Death in *The Seventh Seal*. Or a tribute to a particular kind of framing, like the profile shot of Lindsay Crouse in David Mamet's *House of Games* (1987), which is identical to that of Bibi Andersson in *Persona*. David Lynch also referred to Bergman's figure of Death in *Lost Highway*, even to the point of whitening his face.

Bergman's most devoted disciple, Woody Allen, modelled *A Midsummer Night's Sex Comedy* (1982) as much on *Smiles of a Summer Night* as on *A Midsummer Night's Dream*. His earlier film *Interiors* (1978) seemed like a re-tread of *Through a Glass Darkly*. Allen elaborated on his admiration for Bergman:

> It was a combination of three things. It was the fact that thematically, the material resonated with me so strongly. Secondly, his cinematic technique, his style, was so interesting, so intense, and so riveting to me. And the third was that his approach was poetic. It wasn't prose; it was a poetic approach. *The Seventh Seal*, *Wild Strawberries*, *The Magician* were really poetic films in the same sense as that, when years went by, you see in a film like *Cries and Whispers* – there is really very little dialogue in it.[24]

Other directors of different generations, from Andrei Tarkovsky to Park Chan-wook, and from John Boorman to Terry Gilliam, have acknowledged a debt to Bergman. Catherine Breillat, now celebrated for her candid studies of sexual *moeurs*, remembers seeing *Sawdust and Tinsel* at the age of twelve in Paris. 'There and then', she has written, 'I decided to become a film-maker.'[25]

In 1988, one of Bergman's most iconic actresses, Eva Dahlbeck, wrote: 'In recent years Ingmar Bergman has attracted a level of interest that few living individuals ever experience. [...] Like his

---

23 Quoted in *Trespassing Bergman*, film by Jane Magnusson and Hynek Pallas (2013).
24 Gregg Kilday, 'Woody Allen Pays Tribute to Ingmar Bergman: "His Approach Was Poetic"', *The Hollywood Reporter*, 9 February 2011.
25 See www.criterion.com/current/posts/619-sawdust-and-tinsel-awakening (accessed 11 March 2021).

works, in the end Ingmar Bergman has come to be regarded as a unique phenomenon, many-faceted and impenetrable, sometimes debatable, always controversial.'[26]

We should not ignore the remarkable legacy Bergman gave to the cinema through the actors and technicians whom he cherished, and who were eagerly employed by directors in other countries: Sven Nykvist, who would work with filmmakers like Tarkovsky, Woody Allen, Phil Kaufman, Bob Rafelson, and Louis Malle. Then Max von Sydow. Or Liv Ullmann, Bibi Andersson, Harriet Andersson, Ingrid Thulin, Erland Josephson, and so many others.

It is a curious paradox that Bergman had yearned to be a playwright in his youth, and failed almost completely. Not a single one of his early plays is known to audiences today. So there is a certain irony in the fact that in the decade since his death, his dramatic writing has been revived and disseminated throughout the world. Yet his finest comedy of manners, *Smiles of a Summer Night*, was resurrected as a musical on the Broadway stage under the title *A Little Night Music* as long ago as 1973, with music and lyrics by Stephen Sondheim and with Len Cariou playing the role created by Gunnar Björnstrand in the movie. After 601 performances in New York, it travelled across the United States and around the globe, becoming a staple of the repertory scene. *A Little Night Music* became a film, starring none other than Elizabeth Taylor, directed by Harold Prince in 1977. This leads to a further paradox: Bergman's stage productions were memorable events in the Swedish cultural landscape, but only a handful ever travelled abroad (*Urfaust*, *Hedda Gabler*, and *Hamlet* to London, for example, and *Hamlet* and *Miss Julie* to New York); theatres around the world have programmed stage versions of his films and screenplays, such as *Scenes from a Marriage* and even *Persona*.

Bergman's status as an international phenomenon may have reached its zenith with the release of *Fanny and Alexander*; but in the quarter of a century between that film and his death in 2007, he was seldom left in obscurity. He continued to make films for television until 2002, and the faithful trekked to his beloved island of Fårö to pay their respects during 'Bergman Week', launched in 2004. His major films were constantly reissued in home-video formats, from VHS to laser disc, from DVD to Blu-ray. The final accolade

---

26 Eva Dahlbeck, 'Några funderingar kring en arbetskamrat på väg att kanoniseras', *Chaplin* 30:2/3 (1988), 116.

came in the centennial year of his birth on 14 July 1918, with a vast array of events, screenings, and stage productions. Bergman still seems capable of beguiling foreign directors, as witnessed by Margarethe von Trotta's *Searching for Ingmar Bergman* (2018) and Mia Hansen-Løve's *Bergman Island* (2021), featuring Tim Roth, Vicky Krieps, and Mia Wasikowska.

Alejandro González Iñárittu, director of the Academy Award-winning *Birdman* (2014) and *The Revenant* (2015), has commented about Bergman's island of Fårö, albeit somewhat extravagantly, '[i]f cinema was a religion, this would be Mecca, the Vatican. This is the centre of it all.'[27]

How, finally, did his international fame affect Bergman and his work? He certainly took more risks in terms of form and, on occasion, of content. He could afford to live on Fårö and make his films almost without telling Svensk Filmindustri what they would be like, other than a quick call to the president, Kenne Fant. Often the title of the film would be decided only at the last moment.

Two months after his passing in 2007, the number of references to 'Bergman and film' on Google amounted to 2.80 million. For Fellini, it was 2.10 million, for Kurosawa 2.08 million, for Welles 2.06 million, for Antonioni 2.05 million, and for Godard 1.70 million. A random exercise, no doubt, but one that suggested that Bergman was not about to fade from sight. True, revisionist articles had begun to appear, at first in august magazines like *Sight and Sound* and then, brutally, in the days following Bergman's death, in *The New York Times*. There Jonathan Rosenbaum savaged his reputation in a piece entitled 'Scenes from an Overrated Career'. Rosenbaum accused Bergman of being theatrical instead of cinematic and, bizarrely, of having the power to entertain, which directors like Bresson and Dreyer lacked. Therefore, according to Rosenbaum, Bergman failed to challenge 'conventional film-going habits'.[28]

The fact remains that, as the critic Mikael Timm has acknowledged,

> audience reactions and reviews show that Bergman's work has an impact on people from other cultures in an apparently straightforward way. Bergman stands with both feet in the mainstream European cultural tradition, and this is a common platform for many

---

27 Quoted in *Trespassing Bergman*.
28 Quoted in *The New York Times*, 4 August 2007.

people – regardless of what language they speak. [...] Like Shakespeare's England, Bergman's Sweden is a stage.[29]

And over a period of almost sixty years, Bergman enveloped cultural thinking to the point that his Swedish stage became, in effect, that of the world.

---

29 Mikael Timm, 'A Filmmaker in the Borderland: Bergman and Cultural Traditions', *Chaplin* 30:2/3 (1988), 95.

2

Bergman transnational: Munich–Rome–Los Angeles, or 'The last temptation of Ingmar Bergman'

Thomas Elsaesser

With this chapter I am essentially revisiting my experience during 2006–2007 when I was the Ingmar Bergman Professor. I was attached to Stockholm University but was appointed by the Ingmar Bergman Foundation, and it was the year that turned out to be the final one of Bergman's life. Among the official aims of the appointment was that I should work in the newly housed Ingmar Bergman Archives at the Swedish Film Institute, and open up the holdings to fresh areas of research, including for international scholars.

As I had written about *The Serpent's Egg* (1977) for another Bergman conference—one also attended by several of the authors in this volume—this to my mind under-appreciated film seemed like a good place to start. And while going through the various papers and files of the Munich years, I made some notes from the letters, telegrams, and business correspondence which Bergman exchanged with Dino De Laurentiis in Rome, and with Paul Kohner in Los Angeles. Thus, when Erik Hedling invited me to write this chapter, I first remembered these notes I had taken.

But I also vividly remembered *The Seduction of Ingmar Bergman*—a 2009 radio musical by the legendary duo Sparks (aka Ron and Russell Mael) and commissioned by Sveriges Radio (SR). After being broadcast in Swedish on SR and in English on BBC Radio 3, it was issued as an English-language album. But it made international headlines when the Canadian filmmaker Guy Maddin expressed interest in turning it into a film in 2011, and the Los Angeles Film Festival commissioned Maddin and Sparks to do a live preview of the film on the festival's opening night.

The plot premise is that immediately after his 1956 success at Cannes (nomination for the Palme d'Or and first prize for poetic humour) with *Smiles of a Summer Night* (1955), Bergman was enticed to Hollywood, where he was greeted by none other than Greta Garbo herself. One enthusiastic commentator wrote:

Ron and Russell Mael's yarn of the famed film director leaving Sweden for Hollywood is an [...] easily followed fable in which Bergman (Finnish actor Peter Franzén) is tempted and prodded and pushed and pulled by studio chiefs (a charmingly viscous Russell Mael), fawning fans, flacks, concierges and shapely 'welcoming committees,' all of whom would have our serious auteur bring some of that delicious Euro art-film angst to their twinkly little town [...]. Bergman spends a lot of time mulling over the possibilities; of course he also spends a lot of time agonizing over the cost of such a move. Would he sell his soul? And what is his soul, exactly? Indeed, is there a God? He can't help himself, he's sucked into the maelstrom.[1]

Set in 1956, this is obviously a fantasy: Bergman had no intention of relocating to Hollywood at that point. But fast-forward twenty years, to 1976, and there may have been more reality to the seduction scenario than we might at first think.

For at first glance, the situation in 1976 was the exact reverse of the one twenty years earlier. Rather than Hollywood beckoning Bergman in the afterglow of his triumphs in Cannes and then in Berlin, where he won the Golden Bear for *Wild Strawberries* (1957) in 1957, Bergman in 1976–1977 was at rock bottom, having had a nervous breakdown, fearing for his future as a film director, at odds with his country, even though the lawsuit was quickly dropped, while generally unmoored and uninspired by his German surroundings. What could be more natural than that he would cast his eyes elsewhere, to look towards Hollywood, rather like his somewhat younger colleagues Roman Polanski and Milos Foreman had done, or as Louis Malle was to do at about the same time: the mid-1970s saw Hollywood in crisis and in transition, but with the emergence of the so-called New Hollywood and its movie brats, it was also one of the most cinephile, experimental and innovative times in American cinema's long history.

As I try to picture this moment in time, imagining Bergman's 'last temptation' rather than his 'first seduction', and endeavour to reconstruct the narrative of Bergman's Munich years, I'm relying on these notes scribbled in 2007. When I finally sat down to transcribe them, I realized that I, too, had been concocting a fantasy, insofar as Bergman's contacts with major Hollywood figures had started much earlier, were more continuous, but were also more surprising

---

1 John Payne, *LA Weekly*, www.laweekly.com/music/live-review-sparks-the-seduction-of-ingmar-bergman-2399900 (accessed 11 March 2021).

in their twists and turns than either Sparks's and Guy Maddin's fantasy or my own musings had imagined.

Here, then, is something of a timeline, as I was able to reconstruct it, of Bergman's encounters with Hollywood, many of which centred on or were initiated by Bergman's contacts with Dino De Laurentiis, the powerful transnational producer, working out of Rome, but with long-standing interests in the Hollywood picture business.

The first relevant document in this respect dates from 9 January 1963, when De Laurentiis wrote to Bergman, inviting him to direct an episode in an omnibus film he was about to produce, called *The Bible*. De Laurentiis argues that he had already secured the co-operation of Orson Welles and Federico Fellini, as well as Robert Bresson and Luchino Visconti. He intimated that Bergman would be ideal for directing the episode of Abraham, sacrificing his son Isaac, but that he, De Laurentiis, was also open to other suggestions. Bergman's reply was a telegram, dated 24 March, which read: 'Very thankful – have no possibility to discuss your proposal, owing to my own projects.' The *Bible* film—eventually called *The Bible: In the Beginning*—was made in 1966, no longer involving any of the names mentioned by De Laurentiis but solely directed by John Huston, with a cast that included Richard Harris, Ava Gardner, George C. Scott, and Peter O'Toole.

What is intriguing is that Bergman, interviewed on SR in August 1959 about his future film plans, offered a sort of fable or parable. When asked by Torsten Jungstedt whether he might work in France, Bergman had this to say: 'With me it's like a violinist who received an offer in France. They said, you should come down here and play, but you must play on a French instrument. But the violinist didn't want to do that. It's the same with me.' This is a very perceptive remark when you think of Roman Polanski and Andrzej Wajda, not to mention more recent names such as Michael Haneke, Abbas Kiarostami, or even Aki Kaurismäki. But when Jungstedt mentions Dino De Laurentiis and *The Bible* project, 'Bergman denies any knowledge of this and referred to Dino as one of those people who "[go] to bed as Don Quixote and [get] up as Sancho Panza".'

Be this as it may, De Laurentiis was not put off by Bergman's curt reply but kept up a correspondence with him throughout the 1960s. Early in 1968, Bergman was in discussion with De Laurentiis about a two-part film project called 'Love Duet' (where Fellini was to write and direct the second part). Bergman seems to have written a script, but Fellini never did his. At a press conference in Rome on 5 January 1969, the film was announced as a co-production of De Laurentiis' DEG (De Laurentiis Entertainment Group) and Universal Studios, together with Bergman's newly founded Swiss production and distribution company Persona Film—the company that would give him so much grief with the Swedish tax authorities. Each director was to make a film based on his conception of love. A lengthy correspondence ensued—with litigation about a sum of $73,000 that was part-payment due to Bergman for his script.

Six years later, the thought of a Bergman–Fellini collaboration was revived in 1975 and discussed in early 1976, when Bergman talked about a Warner project involving his unpublished script 'The Petrified Prince'. In an interview, Bergman said: 'It's a sweet thought that Fellini and I might work together.' Could this be the project that Bergman referred to in a letter to Kohner from 7 August, 1975?

> Dear Paul... I am deeply involved in the writing about the last days of Jesus Christ. Honestly, I have a feeling that it will be very difficult to find time for the pornographic picture before the other project, but I will make my final decision in the middle of August when I have met the Italian producer from RAI.

It was in 1972 that the contacts with Hollywood began to be conducted with increasing seriousness on both sides. This is in part due to the efforts of Paul Kohner, a legendary figure, and by then a veteran Hollywood fixer, the spider in the web of several decades of transnational film relations, going back to the time of the German émigrés in the 1930s and 1940s. Of Czech-German origins, Kohner left for New York in 1920, where he worked for Carl Laemmle's Universal Pictures. He subsequently moved to Hollywood still contracted to Universal as production supervisor and casting director. In 1938, Kohner founded the Paul Kohner Talent Agency and had as his clients Marlene Dietrich, Greta Garbo, Maurice Chevalier, Billy Wilder, but also Dolores del Río, Henry Fonda, David Niven, Lana Turner, as well as John Huston. Kohner headed the agency until his death in March 1988.

Kohner made contact with Bergman because he was also the agent of Liv Ullmann, whose American career took off after she won a Golden Globe Award and a Best Actress Academy Award Nomination for her role as Kristina in Jan Troell's *The Emigrants* in 1971. It was after the success of her next—sixth—film with Bergman, *Cries and Whispers* (1972), in the USA that Kohner became seriously interested in representing Bergman, and took him on as a client.

However, on 12 January 1972 Kohner had already approached Bergman with a proposal about the possibility of producing a Broadway musical based on *Smiles of a Summer Night*. The producer was to be Harold Prince, who put on *Cabaret* in 1966 and had a string of successes collaborating with Stephen Sondheim throughout the 1970s. *Cries and Whispers* premiered in the USA in December 1972, doing very well at the box office, and garnered exuberant reviews, especially from the New York critics. Bergman kept *The New York Times* review of Sunday 15 January 1973, which says that *Cries and Whispers* is 'a film of which each and every frame could hang in an art gallery'. There was also a proposal to do a dubbed English version of *Cries and Whispers* which Bergman rejected.

Somewhat ironically, but in actual fact quite a common occurrence, it was the fame of a female star—Liv Ullmann—that opened Hollywood doors to yet another European director. This had been the case with Ernst Lubitsch in 1921, whose path to Hollywood was smoothed by the box office promise which Hollywood saw in Pola Negri; and this was the case with Mauritz Stiller, who travelled to Hollywood on the first wave of Greta Garbo mania. So the idea of having Bergman be greeted by Garbo in Sparks's *The Seduction of Ingmar Bergman* is suggestively apt.

From then on, Kohner and Bergman exchanged letters and telegrams quite frequently, including one from 18 April 1972, when Kohner asked Bergman to please drop a line to Jean Renoir, who was in poor health. On 16 June 1972, Bergman mentions his brother-in-law Paul Britten Austin, the husband of his sister Margareta. Britten Austin was an English author, translator, and broadcaster, as well as an extremely well-respected scholar of Swedish literature, who had moved to Stockholm in 1951. For some reason, Bergman fell out with him, and in this letter to Kohner he bluntly calls him 'a real idiot'. On 31 October 1973, Kohner confirmed that he was organizing the shipment of the prints that Bergman had ordered for his private film collection: Sternberg's *Shanghai Express* (1932), Hitchcock's *Psycho* (1960), Renoir's *La Grande Illusion* (1937), Chaplin's *Goldrush* (1925), Murnau's *Sunrise* (1927), and possibly *Citizen Kane* (1941), as well as Erich von Stroheim's *Merry Widow* (Mae Marsh, 1925) and DeMille's *Ten Commandments* (1956).

Perhaps by way of thank you, Bergman sent Kohner a Goethe poem from 1776 as a Christmas telegram:

Feiger Gedanken / bängliches Schwanken,
weibisches Zagen, / ängstliches Klagen

wendet kein Elend, / macht dich nicht frei.
Allen Gewalten / zum Trutz sich erhalten,
nimmer sich beugen, / kräftig sich zeigen,
rufet die Arme / der Götter herbei.

Cowardly thoughts / fearful wavering,
Womanish hesitations, / anxious lamentation
Do not end misery / nor will set you free.
Staying firm / in the face of your foes
Never bending / Displaying strength
Brings on the helping arms / of the gods.

But not everything goes smoothly in the Kohner–Bergman relation, possibly reflecting on Bergman's inexperience with the ways of Hollywood, or his mounting anxiety over money not flowing back to him. It came to a head when, in early 1973, *Scenes from a Marriage*, which was to prove an enormous success in Europe and once more featured Liv Ullmann, a bidding war started over the US distribution rights. Having upset Kohner by trying to do separate deals with Janus Film, Bergman reacted in a peevish manner and said he wanted nothing to do with the practicalities. Yet Harry Schein as well as Ingrid (Bergman's wife) also became involved, until everybody was thoroughly upset. Here is a passage from Kohner's March 1973 letter:

> My dear Ingmar,
> I had long and good talks here with Kenne Fant and Mrs. Kuhn, and [...] I could clarify my position regarding the six television segments [of *Scenes from a Marriage*]. I explained to them that I feel it detrimental to the generally very high standards which we have achieved for the Ingmar Bergman trademark, [...] that the sub-agent of Janus Film (who are not agents at all, but distributors) indicates that these segments could be bought at low prices – and is doing so at a time when he can show no prints in this country.
> [I have now] received information that the situation here had changed: namely that the sub-agent demanded $150,000.00 per segment and suggested to fly to Stockholm to look at the TV films and this of course, was a satisfactory basis, which would make stepping in unnecessary.
> Under these circumstances I feel that I have rendered an important and unselfish service in seeing to it that the actions in this country for these television films do not start out on an unreasonably low basis. And I shall be ready again to step in, should a situation develop which involves a danger of disturbing our general efforts for your

work by bargain basement competition: Ingmar Bergman against Ingmar Bergman.

In the same letter, Kohner also mentions another project, perhaps the best known of Bergman's unsuccessful Hollywood ventures: a film version of Franz Lehár's *The Merry Widow*, with Barbra Streisand in the lead role—in what would have been the fourth film version of this popular operetta. The project also connects to Dino De Laurentiis, because he seems to have been the driving force. A telegram dated 18 December 1972 opens, in typically breathless telegraph style, some rather breathtaking possibilities:

> I am pleased to tell you after two long meetings with Barbara Streisand's people together with Paul Kohner there exists the possibility of arranging a final contract stop Al Pacino does not feel himself right for Danilo and he is very unhappy that he won't have a chance this time to work with you but hopes there may be another opportunity stop Alain Delon insists he can play only Danilo stop Danny Kaye would like have a conversation with you he [is] coming to Europe near future will phone you and try come and see you stop on January 5th I will have the below the line budget and from January 5th to 13th I am in Rome stop would be delighted if you could come and spend couple of days with your wife in Rome as my guests so could meet for discussions stop if you cannot make trip then I would like arrive Stockholm Saturday January 12th for meeting with you and Kenne Fant Saturday evening to make final decisions about everything stop Merry Christmas to you and yours and very happy New Year – yours Dino.

Kenne Fant at that time was CEO of Svensk Filmindustri, and therefore a key partner in the venture, which would have been a De Laurentiis–Svensk Filmindustri co-production.

At the end of the year, on 30 December 1973, Bergman wrote to Kohner:

> 1. After Feb 1st I am ready to go to Rome or New York or anywhere else (Ingrid now says, don't promise too much).
> 2. Please tell Dino that I will never accept Alain Delon as Danilo. We must find somebody who is warm as a Vulcan and desperate as a security conference in the White House. I vote for Thommy Berggren [a favourite actor of Bo Widerberg], but if somebody could find a 'star' with his qualifications I will be ready to accept.
> 3. When you make the agreement with Mrs Streisand please tell me in advance about her conditions and rights in relation to the materialization of the picture (crossed out: i.e. I don't want her people on the set or seeing the daylies or involved in any respect).

One can sense that Bergman is anxious about the possible power relations tilting in the star's favour. A letter to Kohner from 5 February 1974 is almost offensively explicit: He calls Streisand 'that stinking little lady', but goes on to say 'I feel pity for her wonderful, extraordinary genius, that generous, beautiful genius living in a greedy, narrow and destructive mind.' However, *The Merry Widow* project was still alive on 23 March 1974, in an interview reportage in *Aftonbladet* titled 'Bergman and Streisand agree: We shall make a movie together'. There is also a note from Kohner, suggesting that Bergman should have a look at *Mary Poppins* and *The Sound of Music* to get a feel of how Hollywood does musicals. But, it seems, a month later, the project was definitely called off, and on 13 April 1974, Bergman wrote to Kenne Fant: 'Now I have finally liquidated the Widow. It was with great relief that I dismissed the troublesome lady.' He had already written to Kohner on 17 March:

> my first reason for dropping *The Widow* is an artistical one. [...] I have already lost too much creative time. I have always the feeling that my life as an artist is very short (even if I will go on until I'm 95). I always feel that I'm only in the beginning of my artistical investigations. I always feel curious to see what's going on round the corner behind the shadows in my mind, or in the workshop of my imagination. That passion is my only real treasure and I feel responsible for it in every moment.

The next challenge 'round the corner' with Hollywood came when *Scenes from a Marriage* proved Bergman's biggest box-office success in the USA, and Walter Mirish, then President, invited Bergman to become a member of the Academy of Motion Pictures. To my knowledge, Bergman did not accept; and there is another note which indicates the director's degree of ambivalence when he wrote to Kohner, on 25 September 1974, to denounce his own favourite actor Max von Sydow, for taking on 'silly pictures' that make him a lot of money, but are 'a catastrophe for his creative mind. ... This will slowly but firmly destroy him as an artist and a human being.' Presumably he was thinking of von Sydow's role in *The Exorcist* (1973).

In March 1975 Bergman visited New York to meet up with Paul Kohner and Dino De Laurentiis in order to arrange a distribution deal for *Face to Face* (1976). It proved a success, financially as well as critically, and got him an Academy Award nomination for Best Director. It also made De Laurentiis keen to have Bergman direct an English-language film for his company. This is when the possibility of *The Serpent's Egg* was first mooted, and there is a telegram from Dino, saying that he thought the script was very 'powerful'. On 9 June 1975, Bergman had renewed his contract with the Paul Kohner Agency for three years. By way of presumably ironic encouragement, Kohner sent Bergman a telegram on 1 July 1975. 'Dear Ingmar, now that your monumental chore is finished, you are fully entitled to that nervous breakdown stop let no-one deprive you of it stop I hope you enjoy it to the fullest. Fondly Paukoner.'

Three years later, on 2 October 1978, Bergman extended the contract once more with the now renamed Paul Kohner–Michael Levy Agency. This suggests that Bergman had not given up on the possibility of making a film in Hollywood, but there are other signs that he was not actively pursuing specific projects. Two incidents in particular seem noteworthy: first, Bergman and Ingrid were to spend the summer of 1976 in Los Angeles, to work on the contract details for *The Serpent's Egg*. This is how Bergman describes the visit in *The Magic Lantern*:

> The heat wave of the century had struck California. We arrived two days before mid-summer and sat in the tomb-like air-conditioned chill, watching boxing on television. We tried walking to a nearby movie theatre in the evening, and the heat hit us like a falling concrete wall. The next morning Barbra Streisand telephoned and asked whether we would like to bring our bathing gear with us for a little party by the pool. I thanked her, put down the receiver, turned to Ingrid and said: 'let's go back to Faro at once and spend the summer there. We'll just have to put up with the scorn and the laughter.' A few hours later we were on our way.[2]

The second incident came a few years later, in 1981, after a disagreement over the US distribution of *From the Life of the Marionettes* (1980). This time, Bergman did not write to Paul Kohner himself but asked Jörn Donner, then Director of the Swedish Film Institute, to do so on his behalf. This is Donner's letter to Kohner:

> I have visited Bergman at Fårö yesterday. He feels he has to cancel the US visit because commercial release of *Marionettes* has been tied to visit. The only way of having him come is to delay release until minimum two weeks *after* his departure. The only screening he has

---

2 Ingmar Bergman, *The Magic Lantern*, translated from Swedish by Joan Tate (New York and London: Penguin Books, 1988), pp. 105–106.

consented to is in LA, but even if you succeed in the above and he changes his mind, he is not going to attend the Critics luncheon because it is paid for by the distributor, nor is he going to attend the Academy presentation. Please give all this your earnest attention and telex me back soonest.

In between the two episodes is the history of *The Serpent's Egg*, in particular the struggle over finding the right male lead. The extended search, the mishaps, and the final choice are described in some detail by Bergman himself in *Images*, so I can keep it short. Bergman's preference was for Dustin Hoffman, as this telegram written to De Laurentiis on 5 May 1976, from the George V Hotel in Paris, indicates: 'Dustin Hoffman and I had a six-hour meeting Saturday I was deeply impressed by his artistic integrity and intellectual abilities; we came to an immediate emotional understanding please help me to solve if possible all the difficult technical problems.'

De Laurentiis's answer came a week later, on 12 May:

Am trying do everything possible to give you dustin hoffman for your picture but after negotiating with his agent, situation is as follows:

1) if you wish to start picture in September with dh I would have to give world wide distribution of picture to first artist warner bros, which for me is very difficult to accept but which I would do to make you happy, but even then there is yet another essential condition they insist on, and that is that picture must not cost more than 300,000 dollars. In my opinion it is impossible to make the picture with this amount.
2) Second alternative is to postpone picture to January when dustin hoffman will be free from his commitment with first artist. Please let me know your feeling, in order to enable me to answer hoffman.

In the end, Bergman had to settle for David Carradine, straight from the TV series *Kung-Fu*, whom Bergman nevertheless called 'a gift from heaven' because he reminded him of Anders Ek; but Carradine was so out of it that he regularly fell asleep during the filming. *The Serpent's Egg* was a critical and commercial disappointment, so much so that Bergman's next project, *Love without Lovers*, was turned down by both De Laurentiis and Horst Wendlandt, Bergman's German producer, whereupon Bergman cannibalized the script and made *From the Life of the Marionettes* for television and on a much more modest budget. For *The Serpent's Egg*, De Laurentiis had been able to offer him $500,000 for directing and another $250,000 for the screenplay, plus a BMW for his personal use.

In his autobiography, Bergman says relatively little about his various attempts to establish a presence in Hollywood. At the start of chapter 8 of *The Magic Lantern*—the chapter dealing with his tax troubles starting in January 1976—we find the following cryptic passage:

> Slowly and with some hesitation, I had begun to turn in the direction of America, the reason being the greater resources for myself and my company Cinematograph. The chances of producing quality films with American money, directed by others, were increasing sharply. I was extremely amused by playing film mogul, a role I now think I did not manage particularly well.[3]

After what I have tried to document, this would seem to be an understatement, but it indicates that, by the time Bergman left Sweden, and by the time he signed the contract with Dino to make *The Serpent's Egg*, the temptation of Hollywood had already receded, and Bergman seemed to know it. Although *The Serpent's Egg* was made in English, with an American actor as the male lead, and with Dino De Laurentiis's Hollywood company, Bergman considered the film not even German, but Swedish:

> *From the Life of the Marionettes* is my only German film. *The Serpent's Egg* may at first glance appear equally German. But I conceived it in Sweden [he had been working on the story since before he filmed *Face to Face*] and I wrote it at about the same time I was receiving the warning signs of my own personal catastrophe.[4]

Without going back into the archive and doing more work on the complex relations with Dino De Laurentiis which spanned at least twenty years, as well as looking into the economic benefits of his US fame and reputation, it is difficult to decide whether Bergman ever seriously considered making a film in and for Hollywood, or whether 'American money', as he calls it, was his only incentive. The parable of the violinist probably comes closest to how we may think of it. Perhaps few directors with as global a reach and as transnational an appeal to audiences as Bergman have drawn as

---

3 Bergman, *The Magic Lantern*, p. 84.
4 Ingmar Bergman, *Images: My Life in Film*, translated from Swedish by Marianne Ruuth (New York: Arcade Publishing, 1990), p. 215.

much from themselves and as little from Hollywood, and yet his commerce and correspondence with Hollywood during the 1970s casts a fascinating light on this most turbulent and for many scholars last great decade of both European and American cinema.

3
Bergman and the business: notes on the director's 'worth in the market'

Olof Hedling

Ingmar Bergman has often been described as the quintessential European auteur, implicitly dissociated from the commercial film industry in which he worked for substantial periods during his career. Even in Sweden's most commonly referenced work on the history of its national cinema, this form of committed historiography is promoted without a hint of critical reflection. Indeed, its author goes so far as to suggest that following the success of *Smiles of a Summer Night* (*Sommarnattens leende*, 1955), Bergman's 'home studio', Svensk Filmindustri (SF), and its long-serving head Carl Anders Dymling more or less presented Bergman with a blank cheque to make whatever film he wished.[1] This somewhat over-assertive assessment has been called into question in some more recent scholarship on Bergman, however.[2] For instance, it has been noted that the way Bergman's late 1960s productions were received put him in a precarious situation regarding further film financing.[3] Moreover, in the United States, United Artists' decision to end their distribution deal with regard to Bergman's films following *The Passion of Anna* (*En passion*, 1969) seemed to confirm Bergman's diminishing standing in the eyes of North American audiences.[4]

---

1 Leif Furhammar, *Filmen i Sverige: en historia i tio kapitel och en fortsättning* (Stockholm: Dialogos i samarbete med Svenska Filminstitutet, 2003), p. 264.
2 Arne Lunde, 'Ingmar's Hitchcockian Cameos: Early Bergman as Auteur Inside the Swedish Studio System', *Journal of Scandinavian Cinema* 8:1 (2018), 19–33.
3 Michael Tapper, *Ingmar Bergman's Face to Face* (London and New York: Wallflower Press, 2018), pp. 16–18. See also Maaret Koskinen, *Ingmar Bergman's The Silence, Pictures in the Typewriter, Writings on the Screen* (Seattle, WA, and Copenhagen: University of Washington Press/Museum Tusculanum Press, 2010), pp. 31–35.
4 Tino Balio, *The Foreign Film Renaissance on American Screens 1946–1973* (Madison, WI: University of Wisconsin Press, 2010), p. 284.

Another who commented on the vicissitudes of Bergman's putative value within the film industry was, obviously, Bergman himself. In his memoir entitled *The Magic Lantern*, Bergman addresses his worth in the film market and how this perceived value correlated with his ability to attract production funding during various stages of his career. One such example concerns the making of *Cries and Whispers* (1972) (*Viskningar och rop*, 1973) in the early 1970s, a period that Bergman describes as marked by difficulties in getting his film projects off the ground:

> I collected up my savings, persuaded the four main characters [three actors and the cinematographer] to invest their fees as shareholders and borrowed half a million kronor from the [Swedish] Film Institute. This caused immediate resentment among many filmmakers who complained that Bergman was taking the bread from the mouths of his poor Swedish colleagues although he could finance his films abroad. [...] After a row of semi-failures, there were no backers, either at home or abroad. Fine. I have always appreciated the honest brutality of the international film world. One need never doubt one's worth in the market. Mine was zero.[5]

Bergman's account of his situation appears exaggeratedly melodramatic. For example, it does not take into account his potential fortunes if he had shown a greater willingness to adapt and cooperate, or perhaps just to wait for offers—an unappealing position to which most filmmakers have been relegated on numerous occasions. In short, even at this time, Bergman's prospects were presumably not as dire as he would like us to believe.

This chapter examines the somewhat abstract question of Bergman's 'worth in the market'. In other words, it will consider some of the appraisals, constraints, restrictions, and forms of resistance that Bergman encountered in his interactions with industry intermediaries (such as producers, agents, censors, and distributors) as he attempted to make films with as little interference as possible and, increasingly, according to his own design; or, as he put it, in accord with his 'longing for *pure artistry*'.[6] The analysis presented here is based on studies of some of Bergman's preserved business correspondence and contracts. While not yet fully indexed or

---

5 Ingmar Bergman, *The Magic Lantern: An Autobiography*, translated from Swedish by Joan Tate (Harmondsworth: Penguin, 1988), pp. 228–229.
6 Ingmar Bergman, *Images: My Life in Film*, translated from Swedish by Marianne Ruuth (London and Boston, MA: Faber & Faber, 1995), p. 171.

searchable, this material is held in the archives of the Ingmar Bergman Foundation in Stockholm. Given the rather substantial volume of this archival material, this study has been limited to a consideration of a period of just two years, from 1959 to 1961. Bergman's North American breakthrough was imminent during this period. At the same time, these years also marked the end of the aforementioned Dymling's almost two-decade-long reign at SF. Moreover, the period arguably comprised the final years before the Swedish film industry became a state-sponsored enterprise.[7] The analysis consists of three case studies intended to illuminate a number of comparatively neglected issues while also highlighting the wide-ranging impact of Bergman's film-related activities. The first case study concerns Bergman's situation in Sweden in the late 1950s, and the second Bergman's relationship with and views on the Hollywood film industry, as reflected in his communication with his then-agents. The final case study probes the relationship Bergman gradually developed with the company that became SF's US distributor from 1958, the independent firm Janus Films, located in Boston.

Working for Svensk Filmindustri

Bergman shot three feature films in the course of just over a year, from 14 May 1959 to 16 September 1960: *The Virgin Spring* (*Jungfrukällan*, 1960), the comedy *The Devil's Eye* (*Djävulens öga*, 1960), and *Through a Glass Darkly* (*Såsom i en spegel*, 1961), all for SF. Although Bergman's relationship with SF dated back to 1944, he had made films for other producers on an intermittent basis when, on occasion and during certain periods, SF had declined his services. Bergman was fully aware of the commercial nature of the enterprise in which he was involved and of the need for relatively widespread audience approval. Accordingly, as late as 1958, in a desperate attempt to receive the green light to start production on *The Magician* (*Ansiktet*, 1958), Bergman sold the concept to Dymling on the premise that it would end up being one 'hell of an erotic comedy' (not altogether truthfully, as he later confessed).[8]

---

7 Olof Hedling and Per Vesterlund, '"Why Not Make Films for New York?": The Interaction between Cultural, Political and Commercial Perspectives in Swedish Film Policy 1963–2013', in John Hill and Nobuko Kawashima (eds), *Film Policy in a Globalised Cultural Economy* (London and New York: Routledge, 2018), pp. 57–59.

8 Bergman, *Images*, p. 167.

Judging from the preserved correspondence between Bergman and Dymling, the filmmaker's role in relation to SF seems to have been that of a prolific, reliable, increasingly international, and prestigious contributor to SF's film catalogue, rather than a consistent creator of the ever-important domestic blockbusters. In addition, Bergman's prodigious output as a writer of story concepts, treatments, and manuscripts seems to have been an asset greatly valued by SF's studio chief.

Though never credited as such in Bergman's films, Dymling repeatedly casts himself in the role of Bergman's producer in letters between the two, while also commenting on Bergman's casting, his manuscripts, the qualities of his dialogue, and his expenditure.[9] Moreover, Dymling's position as SF's chief executive meant that he was responsible for a whole range of films; he thus needed to align Bergman's projects and whims with the studio's collective output as well as with the broader industrial production context of the company's studio, Filmstaden (The Film Town).[10]

On the whole, the conversation between Bergman and Dymling was conducted in a spirit of goodwill. Nevertheless, their exchanges reveal interesting details as well as notable tensions between the two men. Perhaps unsurprisingly, their correspondence reveals complications and arguments about such issues as the quality of screening copies and the studio's sound department. At this particular point in time, Bergman seems to have harboured grave suspicions that SF had delivered a substandard copy of *The Magician* for British distribution and for a screening at the Venice Film Festival in late August/early September 1959. By Bergman's own appraisal, the copy was full of dirt and scratches, unsatisfactorily lit, and virtually impossible to screen for a paying audience.[11] Dymling would have none of Bergman's criticisms, however, even going so far as to enlist the distributor in question, one C.L. Cattermoul, to certify

---

9 See, for instance, Carl Anders Dymling, Letter to Ingmar Bergman, 13 May 1960. From this point on, the correspondence, notes, and contracts quoted are unpublished materials held by The Ingmar Bergman Foundation, Stockholm. Permission to quote from these materials has been granted by Jan Holmberg, CEO of the Ingmar Bergman Foundation. All translations from Swedish are mine.
10 Dymling, Letter to Bergman, 20 May 1959.
11 Ingmar Bergman and Sven Nykvist, Letter to Dymling and others, 8 July 1959.

the copy's excellence in a written note.¹² Bergman allegedly replied that the note was of no consequence, since, as he described him (in characteristically dramatic Bergmanesque language), Cattermoul was an 'old, alcoholic hippopotamus'. To this aspersion, Dymling replies '[y]ou really have lost your mind' and simply refuses to accept the filmmaker's verdict or to consider taking any kind of action.¹³ Instead, the studio executive—and Bergman's de facto employer—insists on having the last word, quietly asserting his authority in relation to the filmmaker.

Similarly, sound in all its forms proved to be a constant point of contention for Bergman. As evidence of this fact, Bergman disqualified SF's entire sound department during the filming of *The Virgin Spring*. He likewise dismissed the supplier of the sound system, engineering company AGA-Baltic, declaring that most of Sweden's country cinemas could achieve sound reproduction superior to what he was asked to endure in SF's screening rooms in Stockholm.¹⁴ Dymling does not appear to have been particularly concerned by this withering criticism, however. He replied, 'there are no sound systems that can satisfy your demands, since you are equipped with slightly primitive—in fact, what might be termed "animalistic"— hearing similar to that of the Norse God Heimdal, who could apparently hear the grass grow', concluding, 'there are obvious limits to what you can demand of us'.¹⁵

Amusing as this anecdote may be, it might seem insignificant viewed in relation to the wider state of affairs. Nevertheless, there were other occasions when Dymling's actions, decisions, and opinions had more far-reaching consequences for Bergman's work, as the following example from May 1960 shows: Bergman informed Dymling that he definitely wished to produce his next film in colour.¹⁶ Bergman wrote that, together with a number of his crew, he had actively participated in collaborations within the framework of Färgfilmsklubben ('The Colour Film Club') during the preceding winter in preparation for this development. Moreover, Bergman reassured Dymling that he had introduced cost-cutting measures

---

12 C.L. Cattermoul [note in support of Svensk Filmindustri with regard to the quality of the subtitled copy of *The Magician*], 2 July 1959.
13 Bergman's characterization of Cattermoul is quoted by Dymling in his response to Bergman. Dymling, Letter to Bergman, 8 July 1959.
14 Bergman, Letter to Dymling, 29 May 1959.
15 Dymling, Letter to Bergman, 3 June 1959.
16 Bergman, Letter to Dymling, 3 May 1960.

(such as limiting the cast to just four featured roles and keeping the number of filming locations down) in order to offset the increased expense that colour film would entail. At this stage, the prospective film was tentatively called *The Wallpaper* (*Tapeten*), though it was ultimately renamed *Through a Glass Darkly*.

At first, Dymling is enthusiastic about the idea of a *Kammerspiel*-type film, initially speculating about the inevitability of the eventual transition to colour. On the other hand, he is very reluctant to accept the increased costs and queries whether such a development is not perhaps still somewhat premature in Bergman's case.[17] In a letter posted a week later from the 1960 Cannes Film Festival, Dymling is even more opposed to the idea. He now suggests that the new film would actually benefit aesthetically from being shot in black and white, after indicating that it would require some particularly atmospheric photography that would be very difficult and take long hours to achieve in colour. Bergman should wait to make the transition to colour until he has a good comedy script, Dymling advises.[18]

Dymling's unwillingness to have *Through a Glass Darkly* shot in colour appears indicative of Bergman's standing with SF at the time. In 1959, 41 per cent of the twenty-seven feature films produced in Sweden were filmed in colour, whereas in 1960 this figure fell to 32 per cent of the nineteen films made.[19] This decrease reflected the prevailing decline in Swedish audiences and the increasing awareness of a state of crisis, a negative trend about which both Bergman and Dymling were increasingly concerned. Even so, as has been mentioned, SF did make colour films. In fact, Dymling approved several annually from at least 1956 onwards, on occasion even permitting the extra expense involved in using Sweden's own anamorphic widescreen process, AgaScope. It has been estimated that Swedish colour films produced during this era had budgets approximately twice the size of black and white films.[20] Consequently, the colour format was reserved for projects with major appeal to domestic audiences, usually light comedies containing song and travelogue elements and, in SF's case, starring their most bankable star, actress Sickan Carlsson. Compared to such popular cinematic fare, Bergman's films might

---

17 Dymling, Letter to Bergman, 4 May 1960.
18 Dymling, Letter to Bergman, 13 May 1960.
19 Lars Åhlander et al. (eds), *Svensk filmografi*, 9 vols (Stockholm: Svenska Filminstitutet, 1977–), vol. V (1984), pp. 733–787, and vol. VI (1977), pp. 65–85.
20 Furhammar, *Filmen i Sverige*, p. 259.

possibly have been considered too limited in their public appeal to justify the increased expense of shooting in colour, despite their international popularity. Or, as one anonymous SF employee told American writer James Baldwin when he visited Sweden in 1960: 'Bergman "wins the prizes and brings us the prestige", whereas others could be "counted on to bring in the money".'[21]

In the late summer of 1960, Bergman claimed that he had decided not to use colour in *Through a Glass Darkly* after a collective vote taken by the members of Färgfilmsklubben.[22] This statement appears suspect, however. It seems more reasonable to interpret his choice as Bergman heeding Dymling's advice and postponing the introduction of colour in his work until the comedy *All These Women* (*För att inte tala om alla dessa kvinnor*, 1964) some four years later. Indeed, extrapolating from this conclusion, the reduction in size, the pared-down chamber-play aesthetics, and the use of almost only black and white while shooting in the (increasingly outdated) Academy ratio of 1.37:1 so characteristic of Bergman's 1960s films, may be viewed as the result of a growing awareness of financial constraints and/or risk management on the director's part. In making mass-market commodities with high-art pretentions but no great general appeal, and in an increasingly difficult and shrinking market, Bergman refrained from increasing production costs simply to allow him to continue working as a comparatively independent and consistently active filmmaker.

Lessons on Hollywood

British film historian, critic, and journalist Geoffrey Macnab has on several occasions related the story of how Bergman almost came to be bankrolled by Hollywood during the late 1950s.[23] The specific project most seriously considered was an adaptation of French Nobel Laureate Albert Camus's final, brief novel *The Fall* (*La Chute*). Although the story is set in an Amsterdam bar, the film was supposed to be shot in Stockholm and at locations in either Paris or Amsterdam, financed by United Artists or Paramount, and in English. Cary Grant and Robert Ryan were proposed as the

---

21 Quoted from Balio, *The Foreign Film Renaissance*, p. 137.
22 Birgitta Steene, *Ingmar Bergman: A Reference Guide* (Amsterdam: Amsterdam University Press, 2005), p. 249.
23 Geoffrey Macnab, *Ingmar Bergman: The Life and Films of the Last Great European Director* (London and New York: I.B.Tauris, 2009), pp. 111–120.

film's presumptive stars. Furthermore, Hollywood veteran Walter Wanger (of John Ford's *Stagecoach* (1939) and Fritz Lang fame) was earmarked as a possible candidate to produce the film, since he controlled the rights to Camus's book.

Although the plans ultimately came to nothing, Macnab's account is fascinating, not least because of his source: the correspondence between Bergman and his Hollywood agent at the time. Bergman was signed to Hollywood's legendary William Morris Agency, located in Beverly Hills, California, as of 1 August 1958.[24] More specifically, he was assigned to New York University graduate Bernhard L. Wilens, who acted as his personal representative regarding possible English-language motion pictures. (In his letters to Bergman, Wilens always simply signed off as 'Bernie'. Incidentally, Wilens later became Clint Eastwood's agent.) In the resulting correspondence, almost from the start, and just under the surface, one can detect a simmering, implicit discord. This was an encounter between two individuals from essentially different cultures. Although always very polite and acting in what he believed to be Bergman's best interests, as a Hollywood type through and through, Wilens appeared not to understand why Bergman was reluctant to work in Hollywood—and according to its rules—when given the opportunity.

Bergman, on the other hand, could not quite understand Hollywood. In early December 1959, he responded to a letter from Wilens in which Wilens characteristically talked shop about various studios and powerbrokers being interested in Bergman, by asking four questions (of which two will be quoted as illuminating the character of the exchange). First, Bergman asks: 'You write that United Artists are extremely interested, but who are United Artists?'[25] Second, Bergman submits a bold proposal:

> My success depends on my making films, which I have directed and written all by myself. They have been my expressions from the beginning to the end. Is there no one of your film-bosses [...] who has got that brilliant idea simply to order a film made by me, in exactly the same way as you order a picture of a painter, without first telling him, what it is going to be like. I think that would be the best of all the ideas.

---

24 William Morris Agency, 'Extension of contract with Ingmar Bergman', 11 June 1959.
25 Bergman, Letter to Bernie Wilens, 5 December 1959. Bergman's letters in English are quoted verbatim. Though he was perfectly able to make himself understood in English, German appears to have been his preferred second language.

Having explained that 'United Artists is one of the largest distribution companies in the world' and given Bergman a mini exposé on Hollywood, Wilens elaborately, though perhaps not delicately enough, answers the filmmaker's query about Hollywood's possible willingness to assume the role of benevolent patron in support of Bergman:

> I will answer your fourth question honestly. At the present time I do not think that the major companies, and they are the only ones able to finance important pictures, will simply order a film made by you on the same basis as one orders a painting. It would be an ideal situation but this opportunity has never been afforded any of your confreres such as Kazan, Zinnemann, Mankiewicz, Wyler, Stevens etc. I disagree with one statement in this paragraph of yours. You write that your success depends upon your making films which you have written and directed yourself. I disagree with 'written'. I think that there are writers who could work with you and under your supervision and in collaboration with you. With regard to *LA CHUTE* [*The Fall*] do you wish to write it yourself? Or do you wish to explore the possibilities of a collaboration? [...] United Artists does not wish to finance a film which would appeal only to a restricted audience such as art houses attract. They would like a film which could be played in almost any theatre. Up to this point your pictures, as far as the United States is concerned, are only exhibited in art house theatres. The potential income to United Artists and the producer from the art house exhibitions would not bring them the return of their investment in the production.[26]

After Bergman had been enlightened as to the ways he was expected to adopt, and of his (as yet) limited worth in Tinseltown, the correspondence only continued for another few months, becoming increasingly half-hearted and infrequent on Bergman's part. Instead, Bergman chose to write to his newly acquired friends at Janus Films in Boston in May, inquiring as to whether he really needed an American agent.[27] Janus's Cyrus Harvey explained that agents were an inescapable fact of life in the American entertainment industry, and offered to assume the role on Bergman's behalf.[28] Bergman remained non-committal, however. Subsequently, in May 1960, *Variety* reported on Wilens' negotiations (now with Paramount)

---

26 Wilens, Letter to Bergman, 16 December 1959.
27 Bergman, Letter to Cyrus Harvey, 12 May 1960.
28 Harvey, Letter to Bergman, 16 May 1960.

and Bergman used this leak as an excuse to cancel his contract with Wilens and the William Morris Agency.[29]

Bergman's dalliances with Hollywood were not yet history, however. In the autumn of 1960, he came into contact with agent Katharine 'Kay' Brown of Lew Wasserman's MCA agency after Janus told him of the agency's prestigious reputation. Bergman eventually signed with MCA as of 1 January 1961. Brown had been an assistant to David O. Selznick and was instrumental in bringing Ingrid Bergman to Hollywood in the late 1930s. She had also visited Stockholm on several occasions. There are no hints of the friction that characterized Bergman's interaction with Wilens in the exchanges between Brown and Bergman in the early 1960s. Indeed, Bergman soon proclaimed his admiration for Brown's stately and elegant business prose.[30] Despite their rapport, nothing very concrete appears to have materialized from their communication, except Brown's suggestion concerning a possible collaboration with Ingrid Bergman, who was also her client. This idea obviously came to fruition at a much later date in *Autumn Sonata* (*Höstsonaten*, 1978).[31]

Bergman and Janus Films

American film historian Tino Balio has commented that a 'Bergman craze' hit the American art-film market in late 1959, at approximately the same time as Bergman's above-mentioned correspondence with Wilens was taking place.[32] By October of that year, no fewer than five Bergman films were being screened in New York. In the ensuing period, adulation for Bergman culminated in American reporters travelling to Sweden to cover the domestic premiere of *The Virgin Spring* in February 1960; and a couple of months later, Bergman's portrait appeared on the cover of *Time* magazine. During the years that followed (1961 and 1962), Bergman was presented with two Academy Awards for Best Foreign Film. According to Balio, much of the credit for Bergman's rise to stardom must go to Janus Films, an independent distributor founded in Boston in 1956, which was somewhat incongruously located in relation to the main American

---

29 Bergman, Letter to Wilens, 17 May 1960.
30 Bergman, Letter to Kay Brown, 25 April 1961.
31 Bergman, Letter to Brown, 25 October 1961; Brown, Letter to Bergman, 31 October 1961.
32 Balio, *The Foreign Film Renaissance*, p. 130.

film-industry clusters in Los Angeles and New York.[33] Janus struck a deal with SF in 1958 and carefully orchestrated the release of film after film, judiciously cultivating the Bergman brand. Both of the company's founders, Harvard graduates Bryant Haliday and Cyrus Harvey, similarly took the trouble to make the long trip to Stockholm to meet with Dymling and Bergman in person in March 1960. Apparently, the parties established a good rapport early on.

Although Janus Films' contract was with SF, a lively personal correspondence soon began between Bergman and Harvey, in particular, who was polite and helpful in the extreme with regard to Bergman's various queries and requests. Accordingly, Harvey supervised the process of getting Bergman's screenplays published by Simon & Schuster. For as long as their correspondence lasted, Harvey also supplied the avid film collector Bergman with 16mm copies of film classics.

This exchange became more intimate and private as time went on, particularly on Bergman's part. Soon enough, Bergman's correspondence with Harvey developed into a kind of outlet for his ill feelings, paranoia, and frustration concerning SF and Dymling. On occasion, for instance, Bergman insinuated to Harvey during the height of his American success that he was being taken advantage of financially. He was palpably frustrated that the contents of SF's ledgers were not being fully disclosed to him, and that he was being kept in the dark about the extent of the revenue paid to SF by Janus. On 15 July 1960, the second day of production for *Through a Glass Darkly* (and after having already written a long letter to Janus commenting on the publication process for his screenplay books), Bergman posted a second letter to Harvey in which he wrote:

> Of special reasons and mostly for fun I should like to know how much Janus Films Inc. has payed [sic] in to AB Svensk Filmindustri for the period January 1–April 1, 1960. I ask you to give me this message in strict confidence and I promise you not under any circumstances to use your informations [sic] for other purposes but my personal information.[34]

Bergman received no direct answer to his request, and if Harvey had chosen to disclose this information to Bergman, it might very well have constituted a breach of Janus's contract with SF. Moreover, at

---

33 Balio, *The Foreign Film Renaissance*, p. 133.
34 Bergman, Letter to Harvey, 15 July 1960.

the same time as Bergman was making financial enquiries, there are also hints that he believed Dymling to be making decisions about his films that he neither approved of nor was privy to.

Matters came to something of a head with the American premiere of *The Virgin Spring*. As mentioned previously, American journalists had been on hand to cover the film's Stockholm premiere. While there, they had reported that the film's central rape scene and subsequent retaliatory murders had created a 'great scandal'.[35] In light of this popular uproar, it was evident to Janus that screening Bergman's original cut in the USA would be impossible. At Janus's request, Dymling shipped a new, slightly edited version to America. In its turn, this version was cut by a further twenty seconds following an argument between Janus and the New York censors that lasted several days.[36] Ultimately, it was this edited version that premiered on 14 November 1960, and that went on to win an Academy Award the following spring.

As soon as Bergman became aware of these developments during the autumn, however, he began bombarding Harvey with letters.[37] Bergman wanted to postpone the premiere and demanded that the film be shown with explanatory title cards that spelled out the exact nature of the cuts and how these hurt and deprived him of his rights as an artist. In addition, Bergman claimed to have been stabbed in the back by Dymling while also asserting (somewhat paradoxically) that he did not make more of an issue of the film's handling with Dymling on account of the latter's mortal illness.

In his replies to these letters, Harvey attempted to mollify Bergman's ire. Following the film's successful premiere, Harvey went on holiday, leaving his partner, Haliday, to answer his business mail for a few weeks. Whereas Harvey, by evidence of his letters, seems to have been supremely patient and cultured with Bergman, Haliday had a self-declared 'short fuse'.[38] In defence of his partner, and to justify their collective actions, Haliday fired off a three-page, single-spaced outburst in response to Bergman's previous letters just before Christmas, from which the following excerpt is taken:

---

35 Bryant Haliday, Letter to Bergman, 20 December 1960. See also Balio, *The Foreign Film Renaissance*, p. 139.
36 Haliday, Letter to Bergman, 20 December 1960.
37 Bergman, Letters to Harvey, 22 October 1960, 25 October 1960, and 5 December 1960.
38 Haliday, Letter to Bergman, 20 December 1960.

In plain English, it was a choice between not showing the film at all or making what in all of our judgments was a small compromise. You hate compromise. I hate it too. [...] Further, I dislike our being called on the carpet like small boys at school for explanations. Contractually, we are responsible only to Svensk Filmindustri. We could, if we chose, not bother to explain anything to you. [...] Your disagreements with Dr. Dymling [are] your affair, but I do *not* think the compromise we made here was disastrous, and I *know* it was absolutely necessary. It is as much our privilege to disagree with you as you with us. I only wish we could agree with you that we were right.[39]

Bergman replied indignantly, but also admitted to being a 'prima donna'.[40] Probably at the behest of his business partner Harvey, Haliday later apologized, and even had his remorseful note translated into Swedish before sending it across the Atlantic.[41]

Conclusion

Around the time of the 'Bergman craze', American writers, critics, and reviewers attempted to establish 'the notion that Bergman the filmmaker was detached from market forces'.[42] In reality, there might have been some truth in this assessment, albeit in a quite limited sense, and above all in comparison with American commercial filmmaking of the era. To some extent, Bergman was free to choose his projects, could personally oversee casting and some of his crew, and was—in Sweden at least—successful in challenging censorship norms. On the other hand, all the apparent success, adulation, and prestigious awards bestowed on him at this time did not quite translate into what Bergman seems most to have wanted to achieve: his aforementioned quest for 'pure artistry'. His pursuit of ever-increasing, individual artistic liberty, freedom from censorship, and the freedom to decide spontaneously whether to work in colour, was, in a sense, denied him. Deep down—and contrary to many characterizations of his career—Bergman had to accept that industrial and financial logic and limitations, as well as constraints related to personal matters, would always exist, and that they were realities he would need to adapt to, and contest, as he continued his

---

39 Haliday, Letter to Bergman, 20 December 1960.
40 Bergman, Letter to Haliday, 28 December 1960.
41 Haliday, Letter to Bergman, 17 January 1961.
42 Balio, *The Foreign Film Renaissance*, p. 137.

exploration of filmmaking. Consequently, in one sense or another, Bergman's 'worth in the market' was always relative.

Acknowledgement

Thanks to Mariah Larsson and Maaret Koskinen for their comments on early drafts of this chapter.

4
Bergman, writing, and photographs: the auteur as an ekphrastic ghost

Maaret Koskinen

It is well known that Ingmar Bergman's films make ample use of photographs and that these serve various functions in his works. For example, in his article entitled 'The Holocaust in Ingmar Bergman's *Persona*: The Instability of Imagery', Peter Ohlin unravels the many uses and contexts connected with the photograph of the little boy in the Warsaw ghetto used by Bergman in the film. Similarly, Linda Haverty Rugg has shown how photographs in Bergman's films also comprise important components in his autobiographical project and 'construction of selfhood', and how they can serve as both 'portals into the Other and the past'.[1] Moreover, Rugg notes that Bergman makes use of photographs in his writings, too. In the conclusion to his autobiography *Laterna magica* (1987), for example, Bergman describes some of the photographs of his mother with 'affection and extraordinary attention to detail'. Besides, in '[r]evisiting the photographs of his parents again and again', Rugg concludes that Bergman used these as passageways to conceiving yet more narratives, namely the novels based on his parents—*Den goda viljan* (1991)/*The Best Intentions* (1992), *Söndagsbarn* (1992)/*Sunday's Children* (1994), and *Enskilda samtal/Private Confessions* (1996).[2]

The present chapter focuses on precisely this kind of detailed linguistic description of photographs in some of Bergman's writings.

---

1 Peter Ohlin, 'The Holocaust in Ingmar Bergman's *Persona*: The Instability of Imagery', *Scandinavian Studies* 77:2 (2005), 241–274; and Linda Haverty Rugg, 'Carefully I Touched the Faces of My Parents: Ingmar Bergman's Autobiographical Image', *Biography* 24:1 (Winter 2001), 72–84 (at 72–73). See also Haverty Rugg, 'Self-Projection and Still Photography in the Work of Ingmar Bergman', in Maaret Koskinen (ed.), *Ingmar Bergman Revisited: Performance, Cinema and the Arts* (London and New York: Wallflower Press, 2008), pp. 107–119.
2 Haverty Rugg, 'Carefully I Touched', 81.

In this instance, however, my aim is to demonstrate that the uses and functions of such ekphrases extend well beyond their role in imaginative conception and their organic place in the fiction of individual works.

W.J.T. Mitchell defines ekphrasis as 'a verbal representation of visual representation'; that is, typically an attempt to describe and capture an image or painting in writing. The crucial aspect, he adds, 'is that the "other" medium, the visual, graphic, or plastic object, is never made visible or tangible *except* by way of the medium of language'.[3] In thus presenting an ersatz, an ekphrasis plays with the *absence* of the image as the presence of the text and does so as if by default. This oscillation between presence and absence takes on an added dimension when considered in the light of Christine Geraghty's more general definition of adaptation, in which there is always a 'recall' (in the reader or audience) that 'positions an adaptation precisely as an adaptation'.[4] That is to say, Geraghty suggests that here one often finds a 'layering of narratives, performances, and/or settings in which one way of telling a story is set against another. Such a layering is often indicated by the foregrounding of media signifiers which invite the audience to set one media experience against another.'[5]

I will concentrate on just such invitations to media experiences or media meditations as they occur in Ingmar Bergman's writings, approaching them by way of a selection of ekphrastic descriptions of photographs, especially in two of his novels mentioned above: *The Best Intentions* and *Sunday's Children*. However, before looking more closely at Bergman's writings 'proper' (that is, at the novel-like scripts he wrote at the end of his career, which he knew he would not direct himself), it might prove useful to recall the 'opposite' phenomenon: the use and function of writing and text in Bergman's

---

3 W.J.T. Mitchell, 'There Are No Visual Media', in Oliver Grau (ed.), *MediaArtHistories* (Cambridge, MA, and London: MIT Press, 2007), pp. 395–406 (p. 402).

4 Christine Geraghty, *Now a Major Motion Picture: Film Adaptations of Literature and Drama* (Plymouth and Lanham, MD: Rowman & Littlefield Publishers, Inc., 2008), p. 4.

5 Christine Geraghty, 'Foregrounding the Media: *Atonement* (2007) as an Adaptation', *Adaptation* 2:2 (2009), 91–109 (at 95), doi: 10.1093/adaptation/app006. Also reprinted under the same title in the same title in Deborah Cartmell (ed.), *A Companion to Literature, Film, and Adaptation* (Oxford: Wiley and Blackwell, 2012), doi: 10.1002/9781118312032.ch20.

films, since these are abundant and tend to serve a similar function in foregrounding media specificities.

One particular instance of this kind is one that I have used previously as a paradigmatic example of 'intermedial overdetermination'.[6] It is a sequence at the beginning of *The Passion of Anna* (1969), in which Anna knocks on Andreas's door (played by actors Liv Ullmann and Max von Sydow, respectively) and asks to use the phone. She forgets her purse when she leaves, which prompts Andreas to open it. Finding a letter there, he cannot resist the urge to read it. Bergman employs a cut-in on the letter as he reads, so that the audience first sees it in full as we read over Andreas's shoulder, so to speak. Before long, however, a couple of sentences that speak of 'violence both mental and physical' are made to stand out in focus; and later we come to understand that the letter is from Anna's previous, now-deceased husband.

It just so happens that Anna and Andreas later move in together, and one evening Anna begins to tell Andreas about her former husband and how happy their marriage was. 'Of course, we had our conflicts', she admits, 'but the words between us were never bitter or harsh.' As she ends her story, Bergman includes a quite surprising flashback to the letter—specifically to those lines containing the words 'violence both mental and physical'. In other words, a strong sense of ambiguity is introduced here between what Anna is saying—her spoken words—and the written words in the letter, raising the question of just what we are to believe regarding her supposedly happy marriage. Our interpretation is further complicated by the fact that Bergman here shows Anna in tight close-up. Indeed, her entire, lengthy story is recounted during one long, mesmerizing take of Ullmann's face, which lasts for several minutes. Arguably, this further underlines the ambiguity between what is spoken (Anna's monologue) and what is seen (her face), if for no other reason than that the facial close-up has, with time and use, come to be interpreted as signifying 'truth' in one sense or another (at least in mainstream feature-fiction film). That is to say, as soon as something is about to be revealed, confidences

---

6 Maaret Koskinen, *Ingmar Bergman's* The Silence: *Pictures in the Typewriter, Writings on the Screen* (Seattle, WA: University of Washington Press and Copenhagen: Museum Tusculanum Press, 2010), particularly pp. 109–112. Jan Holmberg and Anna Sofia Rossholm have returned to analysing the tactile and material dimensions of the letter in this sequence in 'Screened Writing: Notes on Bergman's Hand', *Word & Image* 31:4 (2015), 459–472 (at 464 and 465), doi: 10.1080/02666286.2015.1053040.

disclosed, or someone's character unveiled, there almost invariably follows a facial close-up, which serves as a kind of visual corroboration of our somehow getting 'closer' to the truth.

It seems to me that it is precisely this associative cluster or built-in connotation of 'closeness' and 'truth' that we observe in this scene, albeit with the exact opposite intention compared with the norm—to create ambiguity rather than clarity—while at the same time calling into question the received, conventional use or putative 'nature' of the cinematic close-up. In other words, if speech and language are just as often used to hide and betray as to inform and clarify (according to Bergman's many pronouncements on the subject), in his films the face may serve as the best kind of mask, the best kind of lie. Moreover, in this particular case Bergman has the added advantage of using a facial close-up of a very good actress.[7]

It is of particular interest that the letter, too, is shown in close-up—indeed, extreme close-up—through scrutinizing pans back and forth, so that the entire screen is filled with its text. In fact, the very size of the close-up of its individual lines creates an oddly menacing, impenetrable, grid-like 'lettrification' of the image, which matches or mirrors (so to speak) the nature of the equally inscrutable facial close-up of Anna. In other words, although the letter is literally 'in our face' (or rather, precisely *because* it is in our face), it becomes inaccessible. We can barely see its words, let alone comprehend them. We cannot get at the truth, no matter how close it appears to being within our grasp. Thus, just like the facial close-up, the letter hides in plain sight owing to its conspicuous visibility. This scene constitutes an example of the cinematic spatialization of text and words as though they were spatial objects. As such, there is an intermedial overdetermination at play here too; a kind of aggressive appropriation of the image by the text, of one medium by the other.

In this context, it is worth bearing in mind that Bergman's works not only conflate various media, but often also include a kind of *uncertainty as to the choice of medium*. While this might be a result of entirely pragmatic considerations (and, later in his career, a result of his undeniably privileged position—a script by Bergman was sure to be produced in some shape or form), to me it also seems to stem from Bergman's acute awareness of the sheer abundance of media

---

7 For Bergman's comments on the subject, see numerous quotes taken from both interviews and his notebooks, in Koskinen, *Ingmar Bergman's* The Silence, pp. 68–74.

specificities at hand, not least the fact that *by default, the presence of one chosen medium entails the absence, yet lingering presence*, of another. Significantly, Bergman seems to be keenly aware that whichever medium he chooses determines what can be said; therefore, there is always another 'truth' (artistic or otherwise) that remains unreachable and unarticulated. The medium at hand is always negotiable, conditional, and tentative, as is 'Being' itself. This state of things seems to be suggested by the frequency with which Bergman 'conflated' the titles of his manuscripts, as though fully aware that if the work could not be realized in one medium, another would have to do. There are numerous examples of this practice among Bergman's titles, such as 'Trolösa. Partitur för en film/Faithless. Musical Score for Film' (manuscript dated 14 May 1997) and 'Anna. Scener för valfritt medium av Ingmar Bergman. Första versionen/Anna. Scenes for any medium by Ingmar Bergman. First version' (manuscript undated), which also remained in the typed script dated 18 September 2001.

Perhaps the best example of this hint of uncertainty or medial conflation ('scenes for any medium') is found in the script for *En själslig angelägenhet* (1980)/(*A Spiritual Matter*), which was first conceived in the form of a script for a cinematic experiment consisting entirely of close-ups. According to a telephone conversation with Bergman (14 May 2000), it was also written with Liv Ullmann in mind as the lead character; but after she declined the role as Emilie in *Fanny and Alexander* (1982), the script remained dormant for seven years before Bergman resumed work on it. However, Ullmann's part in this course of events may not have been the only factor—or even the decisive factor—in this hiatus, as it seems that the problems concerning the nature of this script existed from its inception. The initial description of the protagonist Victoria found in Bergman's notebook seems at first to be quite straightforward. However, Bergman soon experiences problems with what he calls the course or chain of events (*händelseförlopp*):

> When I try to devise a course of events for Victoria, I feel so unhappy and I just want to cry. Could it be that *something else* is more important, could it be that there is no real course of events, could it be that this whole thing is a *study*, is there something that wants to be said through this face, these hands, this voice[?]
> (Diary entry dated Thursday 22 May 1980)[8]

---

8 In Swedish: 'När jag försöker konstruera ett händelseförlopp för Victoria vill jag bara falla i gråt och känner mig olycklig. Är det så att något annat

'Could it be that there is no real course of events?' Indeed, it seems as though the story about Victoria was unsure of its own nature. That is, it seemed to want to be something other than a film. Was it a play, a television show, or perhaps even something for radio ('this voice')? As we now know, it turned out to be the latter. As Bergman himself explained in an interview with journalist Eva Ekselius in 1988: 'I've had the script since 1982. But then I looked at it again and suddenly I saw—this is a play for the radio! Then I finished it this summer.' As Ekselius rightly notes: 'The play is an example of plays that have been left unfinished because they hadn't found their proper medium.'[9]

Put another way, it seems that in Bergman's mind—and certainly in his practice—*all* media are ontologically flawed, and that there is, and always will be, a divide between that which is mediated and that which mediates. Naturally, it goes without saying that a medium can never be complete, otherwise it would conflate with the reality it tries to represent. Nonetheless, in Bergman's case it is precisely this slippage that seems to render any and every medium so very rich and attractive, but also challenging and scary—especially in relation to writing.

In fact, *A Spiritual Matter* could very well be one of the clearest manifestations of Bergman's ambivalence towards writing. After all, he began his career as a frustrated playwright who, from the very beginning, filled his film scripts not only with well-wrought dialogue but also with highly literary descriptions, notably of visual, tactile, and olfactory impressions. Then, in mid-career, Bergman attempted to retreat to puritan experiments with silences (supposedly more 'cinematographic' in nature, in his own words), only to become a willing writer again, with all that this entails. 'In the beginning was the Word', so to speak, although words were ever—and

---

är viktigare, är det så att det inte finns något verkligt händelseförlopp, är det så att det hela är en studie, är det något som vill bli sagt genom det här ansiktet, de här händerna, den här rösten. (tors. 22.5.80).' Diary no. 37/F:024:03, Ingmar Bergman Archives.

9 'Det var en sak som jag haft liggande sedan 1982. Men så tog jag fram den igen och då såg jag: detta är ju en radiopjäs! Sedan skrev jag den i somras.' Interview by Eva Ekselius, 'Ingmar Bergman om radioteatern och kulturbyråkratin: Det exklusiva är livsviktigt', *Dagens Nyheter*, 7 February 1988: 'Pjäsen är ett exempel på pjäser som blivit liggande därför att de inte hittat sitt rätta medium.' Translations mine.

acutely—present throughout Bergman's career.[10] In short, the author and wordsmith in Bergman could neither deny nor escape his fate. Ironically, the story of Victoria, a film meant to consist entirely of ('cinematographic') close-ups, turned into a monologue for radio—the quintessential medium for the speaking voice and the spoken word.

Let us now return to Bergman's writings in printed form, since 'media meditations' are also present in both his published and unpublished scripts, either through referencing or through the appropriation of one medium by another. As previously mentioned, these meditations are especially conspicuous in a number of ekphrastic descriptions of photographs and paintings found in Bergman's notebooks, drafts, and manuscripts, although ultimately only traces of them may be visible in his finished works.

In my book referenced earlier, *Ingmar Bergman's* The Silence: *Pictures in the Typewriter, Writings on the Screen*, I highlighted some examples from Bergman's notebooks regarding what have been dubbed the 'trilogy films'. One such example concerns Bergman's lengthy description of a painting by Swedish artist Axel Fridell (1894–1935) entitled *Den gamla antikvitetshandeln* ('The old antique shop'). Although Bergman describes the work in a typical ekphrasis in his notebook (and in extreme detail at that), there is no trace of it in the published script, nor in any of the three finished films. My conclusion was that this description, which runs to several pages, served as a self-imposed writing exercise more than anything else, in this case executed by someone who, at the time, claimed to be fearful of writing and of words owing to previous poor reviews by literary critics (at least according to Bergman himself).

This is precisely why it is noteworthy that Bergman retained such ekphrastic descriptions in his much-later writings, in the novel-like scripts he wrote after his final film made for the cinema theatre, *Fanny and Alexander*, knowing full well that he would not direct them. Now, why is this? After all, by this time there was hardly any

---

10 The fact that Bergman began his career as writer, and passionately desired to be accepted as such by the literary establishment, is the main argument in my book *I begynnelsen var ordet: Ingmar Bergman och hans tidiga författarskap* ['In the beginning was the word: Ingmar Bergman's early writings'] (Stockholm: Wahlström & Widstrand, 2002). In his excellent book *Författaren Ingmar Bergman* ['Ingmar Bergman the author'] (Stockholm: Norstedts, 2018), Jan Holmberg also argues that, ultimately, Bergman is likely to be remembered more as an author than as a film and theatre director.

need for 'writing exercises', given the glowing reception accorded to his autobiography, *Laterna magica* (among other written works). *Laterna magica* not only became a best-seller, but also the book that prompted critics worldwide to anoint Bergman as a master of words, of writing. That is to say, as a 'real' author, and not 'just' an auteur.

In fact, the presence and importance of photographs in and for Bergman's stories are already emphasized in the prologue to *The Best Intentions*:

> The Åkerblom family were great ones for taking photographs. After my father's and mother's deaths, I inherited a marvelous collection of albums, the earliest dating from the middle of the nineteenth century, the most recent from the beginning of the 1960s. There is undoubtedly a great deal of magic in those photographs, particularly when looked at with the help of a gigantic magnifying glass: the faces, the faces, hands, postures, clothes, jewelry, the faces, the pets, views, lighting, the faces, curtains, pictures, rugs, summer flowers, birches, rivers, coiffures, angry pimples, budding breasts, handsome mustaches—this could continue ad infinitum, so it is best to stop. But most of all the faces. I go into the photographs and touch the people in them, the ones I remember and those I know nothing about. It is almost more fun than old silent films that have lost their explanatory texts. I invent patterns of my own.[11]

First of all, the narrator makes sure to point out that these photographs do, in fact, exist, while simultaneously underlining their relationship to fiction and imagination. Unsurprisingly, Bergman returns to the photographs mentioned here later in the novel, in the form of more detailed ekphrases. One prominent example from the published novel/script is a photograph that Bergman used previously in his short film *Karin's Face* (1986), which is based entirely on pictures of his mother. Here again, the narrator emphasizes the physical existence of the photo, while at the same time stressing its connection with fiction and imagination:

> Ernst has been given a camera with a delayed action release as a birthday present, and a family photograph is to be arranged. (The photograph actually exists, though it is from a somewhat later period, probably the summer of 1912, but it fits better into this context, and anyhow this isn't a documentary.) After breakfast, the clan reassembles

---

11 Ingmar Bergman, *The Best Intentions: A Novel*, translated from Swedish by Joan Tate (New York: Arcade Publishing, 1993), 'Prologue', n.p.

in the little meadow at the edge of the forest. It is a warm, sunny day, and everyone is in light clothes. Well then [...] two chairs have been taken out. On one sits the traffic superintendent with his cane and breakfast cigar. *If you look carefully with a magnifying glass, you can see that his calm, handsome face is distorted with pain and sleeplessness.* Next to her husband sits Karin Åkerblom. *There is no doubt whatsoever* which of the two is the head of the household. The plump little person *radiates authority and possibly smiling sarcasm.* She has a stately summer hat on her well-tended hair, a kind of seal on her authority, clear eyes looking straight at the camera, and a small double chin. She has got herself into position to be photographed, but *a few seconds later, she gets up full of vitality to issue orders.*[12]

This is a true ekphrasis, in that the description also encompasses interpretations. The traffic superintendent's face is said to be distorted (which, when looking at the picture, is certainly not that obvious), whereas his wife, Bergman's grandmother, is identified as the head of the household, and so on. All this is followed by the ensuing exhortations:

Go into the photograph and recreate the following seconds and minutes! Go into the photograph as you want to so badly! Why you want to so badly is hard to make out. Perhaps it's to provide some somewhat tardy redress to that gangling young man at Ernst's side. The one with the handsome, naked, uncertain face.[13]

This imperative is multi-layered: on the one hand, it is an appeal to the narrator himself, which is of course part and parcel of the self-conscious, self-reflexive literary style, since it includes the reader as a conscious participant in the production and process of the text, as it were. As Louise Vinge and Rochelle Wright among others have pointed out, Bergman's published scripts contain many self-conscious interjections of this sort.[14] Indeed, there are numerous examples: 'Now I shall describe a quarrel that is soon to explode between Anna and Henrik. [...] Go ahead, you can browse and

---

12 Bergman, *The Best Intentions*, p. 76 (italics added).
13 Bergman, *The Best Intentions*, p. 77.
14 Rochelle Wright, 'The Imagined Past in Ingmar Bergman's *The Best Intentions*', in Roger W. Oliver (ed.), *Ingmar Bergman: An Artist's Journey: On Stage, On Screen, In Print* (New York: Arcade Publishing, 1995), pp. 116–125; and Louise Vinge, 'The Director as Writer: Some Observations on Ingmar Bergman's *Den goda viljan*', in Sara Death and Helena Forsås-Scott (eds), *A Century of Swedish Narrative: Essays in Honour of Karin Petheri* (Norwich: Norvik Press, 1994), pp. 281–293.

speculate; this is a party game' and 'Lighting? It's dramatic and full of contrasts!'[15]

The point, however, is that the photographs described in ekphrasis serve a similar function. Not least, they constitute exhortations to those who Bergman knew would turn his text into a film—both director Bille August and the actors, whom he encourages 'to go into the photograph and recreate'. Thus, these photographs function as regular stage directions, or, more precisely, as *film direction emanating from the written page*. And yet, in complete contradistinction to the self-reflexive interjections mentioned earlier, they are oddly *hidden as such*. Note, for instance, the subtle shift in tempo/tense: 'but a few seconds later, she gets up full of vitality to issue orders'. Here the narrator verbally inserts cinematic time and movement into that still image, as if anticipating the film he knew would be made from his script. In this instance, then, there is a literary and pragmatic, fruitful tension between stasis and movement—a 'still life' or a 'still in motion', as it were, pregnant with its own cinematic future.

As Swedish theatre critic Leif Zern pointed out in his review of Bergman's book: 'The director's gaze falls over the stage. It both sees and interacts with the performing shadows.'[16] The narrator thus becomes the director of the text, so to speak, his sharp gaze falling over the activity on as well as the lighting and setting of the stage. But he does so in a way that transcends the general notion according to which one can always argue that the manuscript of a film is itself a kind of direction. As James Schamus, the scriptwriter for Ang Lee's films, once wrote, it is sometimes all about 'taking ownership of the image by creating it in a dense and sensuous forest of words'.[17] In this case, the narrator does exactly and quite literally that—takes ownership of the photographs—*nota bene* by referencing a medium that arguably comes as close as is possible

---

15 Bergman, *The Best Intentions*, pp. 174–175. Oddly, however, such interjections have been excluded from the translation at times. One example is the phrase '*Nu finns det inte mer att säga om den här scenen*', which simply does not exist where it should in the translation, after the dialogue between Anna and Henrik, in Bergman, *The Best Intentions*, p. 242.
16 '*Regissörens blick faller över scenen. Den både ser och blandar sig med skuggorna som agerar.*' Leif Zern, 'Tystnad, tagning, kärleksroman', in the large Swedish tabloid *Expressen*, 2 December 1991.
17 James Schamus during a panel discussion held at Cinemateket, Film House, Stockholm, 19 March 2008.

to the film medium from a visual perspective, namely the written page. It is interesting that just after Bergman began writing the script for *The Best Intentions* in Munich in May 1988, he noted a number of historic events relevant to the story in his diary. First, he observed the intellectual mood in the Swedish university towns of Uppsala and Lund: 'Symbolism, Nietzscheanism, flaneur philosophy. People hung [pictures of] Böcklin on the walls and discussed Baudelaire and Verlaine and Stefan George.' He adds: 'In the spring of 1914, Pär Lagerkvist published his polemic *Literary Art and Pictorial Art*.'[18] This is nothing less than a reference to the classic paragone battle waged between poets and painters/image creators ever since the fifteenth century—a highly relevant detail, it would seem, at a time when Bergman the filmmaker was about to surrender to Bergman the writer.

Indeed, while busy working on this same script just a few days later, Bergman suddenly interjected in his diary that he should perhaps write a drama about Swedish silent filmmaker Georg af Klercker: 'I might as well, while I'm at it', he wrote. While at what, exactly? While writing a script that he knew he would not direct himself. In view of that, why not at least write something *directly linked to film*, something about a director who supposedly had to grapple more with moving images than with words? Ultimately, Bergman did just that in writing a 'drama' on af Klercker as well as on the circumstances and tribulations involved in making silent films.[19]

One can also find 'stage directions' emanating from the written page, similar to those in the manuscript for *The Best Intentions*, in *Sunday's Children*, which Bergman wrote a few years later. Take the following example in which the boy Pu accompanies his father, the parish parson, to a church sermon:

> He couldn't care less—the service is so boring it's almost incomprehensible. Pu looks around, and what he sees keeps him alive: the altarpiece, the stained-glass window, the murals, Jesus and the robbers in blood and torment. Mary leaning toward Saint John: 'Look upon your son, look upon your mother.' Mary Magdalene, that must be the sinner; have she and Jesus been screwing? In the west vault of

---

18 Diary, '*Den goda viljan*', no. F:025:01, date: 28 May 1988. Translation mine.

19 '*Jag tror att jag ska skriva ett sorts dialogdrama om Georg af Klercker. Det kunde jag göra medan jag ändå är i farten.*' In Bergman's diary, '*Den goda viljan*', no. F:025:01, date: 31 May 1988. Translation mine.

the church sits the Knight, loose-limbed and bowed. He's playing chess with Death: I have long been behind you. Close by, Death is sawing down the Tree of Life, a terrified jester sitting at the top, wringing his hands: 'Are there no special rules for actors?' Death leads the dance to the Dark Countries, holding the scythe like a flag, the congregation in a long line behind and the jester slinking along at the end. The demons keep things lively, the sinners falling headlong into the cauldrons [...], and the Serpent wriggling with malicious glee. The flagellants proceed along the south window, swinging their scourges and wailing with the mortal dread of sinners.[20]

This is clearly a regular ekphrasis of some details of Albertus Pictor's murals in the parish church of Täby, the most famous being 'Döden spelar schack' ('Man playing chess with Death'). Most of all, though, this is an unabashed and humorous ekphrasis of scenes from Bergman's own film *The Seventh Seal* (1957), as is evidenced by the distorted quotation taken from the film's dialogue: 'I have been walking by your side for a long time' is here rendered 'I have long been behind you', which, in the Swedish original, is both more concretely expressed and aptly childish in its formulation: '*Jag har länge funnits bakom din rygg*'/'I have long been behind your back'. In reality, this passage makes greater use of Bergman's own film than of any mural painting, as it is unlikely that Pictor ever painted a jester.[21]

The narrator and Bergman thus evoke Bergman's own iconic film in the form of a 'flashback into the future', in what is also a nod to the film's director.[22] Here, again, it appears that Bergman the director has had difficulty relinquishing control. Or, more precisely, that Bergman the author seems to have had a hard time denying the director within. In such a situation, what strategy could be more suggestive than sneaking a kind of intermediary—some sort of ersatz—into the text in the form of ekphrases, detailed descriptions

---

20 Ingmar Bergman, *Sunday's Children*, translated from Swedish by Joan Tate (New York: Arcade Publishing, 1994), pp. 136–137.
21 Pia Melin, 'Death Playing Chess with Man and Related Motifs: Painted Allegories by Albertus Pictor in some Uppland Churches', in Olle Ferm and Volker Honemann (eds), *Chess and Allegory in the Middle Ages: A Collection of Essays* (Stockholm: Sällskapet Runica et Mediævalia, Münster, Stockholm, and Uppsala Universities, 2005), pp. 9–16.
22 In fact, Bergman used the term 'flashback into the future' in this book when inserting a passage about his elderly father. Bergman, *Sunday's Children*, p. 85.

of photographs and paintings which come as close as possible to the visual aspect of film in a written text, and which function as intermediaries between pure text (author) and moving images (director) while also reminding the reader (as well as the professionals on the film set) of the director's presence in his absence? In this way, too, Bergman seems continuously to conjure forth his own biographical legend, as if to remind the reader of just who is really in charge in the context of these pages. This conclusion is supported by an analysis of the earlier (unpublished) version of the script for *The Best Intentions* vis-à-vis what has been cut from the final, published manuscript. For instance, when the female protagonist Anna is about to answer a letter, a long passage follows that was eventually cut from Bergman's script:

> Wrinkled foreheads, worried expressions! Our dramaturge has to find strength in a plastic cup of coffee and a pipe of smoke. What on earth are these excursions? Bergman should know that lengthy letters are impossible in our fast medium! And on top of that, all these descriptions. Does he really think that it is possible—practically feasible—to materialize even partially his instructions as to wallpaper, weather conditions, intonations, lighting, and expressions? For sure, he will soon start describing people's thoughts—it's only a matter of time [...] Then I will have to write a polite letter to say that, yes, of course, it's all very interesting and even somewhat gripping, but that our finances, etcetera, and all that. My defence is brief, but brilliant. I don't write for the dramaturge. I don't write for the possible viewers, although they're constantly on my mind. I don't even write for the decision-makers. I write for the actors [...], who desire material and stimulation for the imagination.
>
> A director thinks that each piece of information is important, but then shapes everything according to his own mind. The cinematographer enjoys receiving suggestions regarding the lighting, but, being a practical fellow, he knows exactly what can be done. The prop master has his preferences and knowledge, which might be much more substantial than the author's: every educated person surely knows that our city didn't get trams until 1912. [...] Not to mention the costume designer: just throw your information my way, important and unimportant, large and small, wise and inane, and we will decide ourselves what to keep and what to discard.[23]

---

23 From an early, typed version of the manuscript that includes edits made by hand, no. B: 080. Translation mine.

In effect, the narrator here *admits* to his urge to direct from the written pages, even to the extent that he anticipates the protests that are sure to be voiced by writing them into the script itself! Even so, as mentioned earlier, this passage was cut from the published version in the end, as though Bergman realized that it too readily revealed his wish to meddle in future proceedings.

In conclusion, Bergman seems to have opted for a much more elegant solution in keeping his directorial impulses in check (and yet allowing them to be present), not only through a constantly and overtly present narrative voice but also by means of ekphrastic descriptions of photographs and images that achieve their purpose in a much more covert, invisible manner. This invisible quality comes in layers. Firstly, in that the descriptions of the photographs are ekphrastic in the traditional sense: that is to say, the written-language medium captures an existing image, rendering the absent medium present in and through language only, thereby pandering to an author's medium. And yet, writing is simultaneously used to evoke a different absentee: the director and wielder of moving images, who hovers like a phantom over the textual proceedings.

It is hence evident that the ekphrastic descriptions of the photographs in Bergman's novels are scarcely employed for their documentary veracity only. Neither are they included for his own imagination's sake, nor primarily for the benefit of the actors, the latter being Bergman's own claim. The author of the text also recruits the auteur as an invisible presence, a spectre vicariously directing from the printed page.

5
The playfulness of Ingmar Bergman: screenwriting from notebooks to screenplays

Anna Sofia Rossholm

The voice: You said you wanted to 'play and fantasize'.
Bergman: We can always try.
The voice: That's what you said: 'play and fantasize'.
Bergman: Sounds good. You don't exist, yet you do.
The voice: If this venture is going to make any sense, you need to describe me. In detail, actually.
Bergman: Sit down on the chair by the window and I'll describe you.
The voice: I won't sit down unless you describe me.
Bergman: Well, then. And how do I begin? You are very attractive. Most attractive.[1]

So begins Ingmar Bergman's screenplay *Trolösa* (*Faithless*, directed by Liv Ullmann, 2000). This dialogue, which is a prologue to the story, is a playful depiction of the author's creative process in developing a fictional character. Step by step, 'the voice' in the scene is given a body, name, and characteristics. In time, she becomes the character named Marianne.

How faithfully does this scene portray Bergman's actual creative process? Obviously, it is not a literal description of what went on in Bergman's mind. The Marianne character probably did not appear as a sudden creation of the author's imagination. She is more likely to have been the result of a long mental process over the course of many years. Marianne shares traits both with real women in Bergman's life and with fictional characters from his oeuvre. Although the scene in the prologue might not constitute a wholly accurate depiction of how Marianne came into being, there is some truth in its portrayal of how Bergman developed his stories. It is an abstraction

---

1 Ingmar Bergman, *Föreställningar* (Stockholm: Norstedts, 2000), p. 9. Translation mine.

The playfulness of Ingmar Bergman 71

of his creative process and also somehow a fragment of it, a small part in the long and complex process of writing fiction. The scene's transgression of both reality and fantasy exposes the very core of fictional storytelling. It also illustrates Bergman's characteristically playful interaction with the fictional world at the moment of creation. When writing in his notebooks, Bergman sometimes conversed with himself, often in a playful, self-deprecating manner, or interacted with the fiction at the moment of creation in a way much akin to a child's make-believe game or a daydream fantasy. The question is how one should understand such 'games' and playful digressions as a feature of Bergman's writing process. What does the transgression of reality and fantasy represent in Bergman's filmmaking and screenwriting? This chapter addresses these questions and discusses the creative playfulness evident in Ingmar Bergman's writings.

Bergman's writings are examined from the perspective of genetic criticism, combined with perspectives on screenwriting as an intermediate stage-by-stage process across media. The focus is on what Jed Deppman, Daniel Ferrer, and Michel Groden in their 'Introduction to Genetic Criticism' term 'the movement of writing'—that is to say, on an examination of 'tangible documents such as writers' notes, drafts and proof corrections'—in order to understand 'the moment of writing that must be inferred from them'.[2] This perspective is not equivalent to a biographical approach—or even a psychological approach—to the creative mind of the author. Rather, it is an aesthetic approach to the way in which the subject of the author's thoughts is materialized (or, in Ferrer's words, 'produced') in the text.[3] In Bergman's case, the tangible objects in his writing process consist of notebooks, screenplay drafts, and versions of finished screenplays, from working script to shooting script, and published screenplays.

Fortunately, the Ingmar Bergman Archive, where the filmmaker's notes and screenplay drafts have been collected and digitized, facilitates just such an analysis of his writing process. The archive

---

2 Jed Deppman, Daniel Ferrer, and Michael Groden, 'Introduction to Genetic Criticism', in Jed Deppman, Daniel Ferrer, and Michael Groden (eds), *Genetic Criticism: Texts and Avant-textes* (Philadelphia, PA: University of Pennsylvania Press, 2004), p. 2.
3 Daniel Ferrer, 'Production, Invention, and Reproduction: Genetic vs. Textual Criticism', in Elizabeth Bergmann Loizeaux and Neil Fraistat (eds), *Reimagining Textuality: Textual Studies in the Late Age of Print* (Madison, WI: The University of Wisconsin Press, 2002), p. 57.

consists of donated materials comprising Bergman's personal collection of notes, drafts, letters, and other documents, both personal and professional. These documents date from his early career in the 1930s until his final productions in the early 2000s and span all relevant media and art forms.

While the archive provides unique insights into Bergman's creative process, few scholars have examined the material to date. Apart from my own previous research on the topic,[4] Jan Holmberg has published a book on Bergman as a literary author.[5] In his book, Holmberg analyses Bergman's screenplays as autonomous works of art; by contrast, my perspective highlights the process from notes to screenplays and from writing to film. Maaret Koskinen, who helped found the Ingmar Bergman Archive, has also published works on Bergman's writings. Among these, her case study of the Bergman film *Tystnaden* (*The Silence*, 1963) is of particular interest in the present context. Koskinen's study uses the notebooks and screenplay drafts involved in preparing the film as background materials in her analysis of it.[6] In contradistinction, my research constitutes the first analysis of the writing process in Bergman's filmmaking viewed as a whole. The 'playful dimension' of Bergman's writing and filmmaking as examined here refers both to his method of creative writing and to the playfulness aspect of his finished works, that is,

---

4 Anna Sofia Rossholm, *Ingmar Bergman och den lekfulla skriften: ur arkivets samlingar av anteckningar och utkast* (Stockholm and Gothenburg: Makadam förlag, 2017); 'Den lekfulla skriften: Autofiktion och minne i Ingmar Bergmans arbetsböcker och manusutkast', in Paula Henrikson and Jon Viklund (eds), *Kladd, utkast, avskrift: Studier av litterära tillkomstprocesser*, no. 68 (Uppsala: Skrifter utgivna av Avdelningen för litteratursociologi, 2015), pp. 59–80; 'Ingmar Bergman's Screenwriting', *Journal of Scandinavian Cinema* 4:2 (2014), 165–171; 'Auto-adaptation and the Movement of Writing across Media', in Jörgen Bruhn, Anne Gjelsvik, and Eirik Hanssen (eds), *Adaptation Studies: New Challenges, New Directions* (London: Bloomsbury Academic, 2013), pp. 203–222; 'Tracing the Voice of the *Auteur*: *Persona* and the Ingmar Bergman Archive', *Journal of Screenwriting* 4.2 (2013), 135–148; and, with Jon Viklund, 'Verkets förvandlingar: Ekelöf, Bergman och den genetiska kritiken', *Tidskrift för litteraturvetenskap* 1 (2011), 5–24. The research presented in this chapter has been published previously in Swedish (2015 and 2017).

5 Jan Holmberg, *Författaren Ingmar Bergman* (Stockholm: Norstedts, 2018).

6 Maaret Koskinen, *Ingmar Bergman's* The Silence: *Pictures in the Typewriter, Writings on the Screen* (Seattle, WA: University of Washington Press, 2010).

his films and screenplays. Beginning with a discussion of play and playfulness in art and creative work in general, the chapter goes on to analyse what I refer to as the 'aesthetics of play' found in Bergman's notebooks, screenplay drafts, and screenplays.

Play and artistic creation

The relationship between art and play has been conceptualized in aesthetic theory since the Romantic era, and in particular since Friedrich Schiller presented his theory on the joy of play as the driving force behind artistic creation. The correlation between art and play assumes different forms in different theoretical contexts, from psychoanalysis and the theory of creativity to theories of fiction and poststructuralist aesthetics. These various theoretical approaches share the conception of play as a positive, liberating, and transgressive activity, either in the psyche of the artist or in the artwork itself. Play provides room for the paradoxes that arise from transgressing fantasy and reality; in addition, it allows the artist to be both present in and absent from the concrete, physical space and time in which the creative act occurs.

In concrete terms, play in literary writing can be manifested in at least two different forms: as a creative driving force that generates new ideas and develops stories, or as an aesthetic dimension of the text that transgresses conceptual or narrative limits and borders.

Within the field of psychoanalysis, the concept of play is particularly central in Donald W. Winnicott's writings. In Winnicott's view, play is crucial for self-construction and its traces can be found in various activities, including artistic creation and psychoanalytical treatment.[7] Unlike Freud, Winnicott emphasizes the transgressive aspect of play, regarding it as an activity on the threshold of fantasy and reality. Play is also a key concept in Roland Barthes's and Jacques Derrida's early post-structuralism, where conceptual play destabilizes meaning and decentres the unified structure of a text.[8] Similarly, play is also central in theories pertaining to creative thinking. In this context, it generates new ideas and norm-breaking thinking,

---

7 Donald Winnicott, *Playing and Reality* (London: Routledge, 2002 [1971]).
8 Jacques Derrida, 'Structure, Sign and Play', in *Writing and Difference* (London: Routledge, 1995 [1967]), pp. 287–294; Roland Barthes, 'From Work to Text', in Stephen Heath (ed.), *Image, Music, Text* (New York: Hill and Wang, 1977), pp. 155–164.

in that it permits us to associate freely and in unexpected patterns.⁹

With regard to Bergman's creative work, playfulness is particularly evident in his notebooks, where his writing is allowed to develop spontaneously and in an open-minded manner. These notebooks serve the dual function of (1) creative diary (i.e., documenting the actual creative process) and (2) fiction (i.e., as containing early versions of the fiction that is evolving). Bergman's notebooks do not constitute a collective documentation of his personal life, but rather of the creative process of writing. Consequently, the text acquires a self-reflexive dimension, in that Bergman continuously comments on the developing fiction. This duality of reality and fiction is also found in Bergman's finished works, in particular in his screenplays' self-reflexive dimensions and in the way the 'I' of the text is articulated. The screenplay's narrating agent might be Bergman the author, or it might be a fictional character or a narrator. This ambiguity of agency in his notebooks and screenplays represents the very core of the auto-fictitious dimension of Bergman's work, in which the autobiographical is given fictitious form and the fictional is nourished from real life.

Bergman's broad and varied oeuvre is characterized by continuous renewal and the reworking of old ideas into new stories. Play is an activity driven by pleasure or joy, and it offers the freedom to create within given frames. By comparison, free play is more open-ended than games and gaming; it is an activity that transgresses and alters given frames and rules to a greater degree. Admittedly, play also involves rules and frames, although to a lesser extent.¹⁰ In playful writing, the frame might be the time-frame or the physical implements used for writing, such as pen and paper. In Bergman's case, his regimented daily routine concerning writing hours and the importance of his choices of pen and paper constitute the conditions that define the boundaries for spontaneity and freedom during the moment of writing. Bergman was a disciplined and well-organized writer: he wrote for three hours a day and selected his pen and paper with care.¹¹ Bound by rules and habits, these daily writing routines

---

9 Most notably in Edward de Bono, *Serious Creativity: Using the Power of Lateral Thinking to Create New Ideas* (London: HarperCollins, 1993 [1992]).
10 Rob Pope, *Creativity: Theory, History, Practice* (London: Routledge, 2005), pp. 119–121.
11 Mikael Timm, *Lusten och dämonerna* (Stockholm: Norstedts, 2008), p. 165.

constituted the frame for Bergman's playful writing, with its free associations, self-deprecating jokes, seemingly irrelevant comments, and playful interaction with his fictional characters.

Bergman himself compared artistic work with children's play, and the playful side of his personality has been highlighted in portraits of Bergman the auteur. Stig Björkman's documentary film *Bilder från lekstugan* (*Images from the Playhouse*, 2009) is based on the short films Bergman made while shooting his feature films, and it shows Bergman joking in front of the camera and with other members of the film crew. Marcus Lindeen's stage play *Arkivet för orealiserbara drömmar och visioner* ('The Archive of Unrealizable Dreams and Visions', Stockholms stadsteater, 2012), a work based on Bergman's rejected screenplay ideas, includes burlesque scenes and profane jokes mocking characters such as 'the king', 'the queen', and various other characters representing the artist or director. That said, the 'playful' should not be confused with the humorous or jokey. Humour and jokes are certainly playful; but play can also be a thoroughly grave, even austere, activity devoid of humour. While Bergman's humorous side is part of the playful dimension of his creative work, his writing and filmmaking encompass other aspects of playfulness as well. In the present context, Bergman's playfulness is not to be understood as existing in opposition to the serious tone, demoniac presence, or anxiety that are so manifestly present in his works.

The notebook: diary and fiction

Bergman's notebooks are creative diaries in which he reflects on the writing process while shaping the initial ideas for the fictional story that will develop in the screenplay. For the most part, his notes comprise either in-depth descriptions of characters or fragmentary scenes or situations with no clear beginning or end. Moreover, Bergman often switches focus—beginning a new story or a different line of thought—and in some cases, the fragments of a story that develop in a screenplay will produce two different screenplays in the end. Although brief sections of dialogue or a general overview of the whole story are included now and again, for the most part the fiction in Bergman's notebooks comprises fragments of scenes, descriptions, and narrative situations or character descriptions that may serve to explain a character's backstory or psychological constitution.

Bergman's notebooks not only provide unique insights into his creative process, they also reveal how much of his creative process occurs outside of his written notes. The fragmentary nature of his notebooks reveals the absences and voids in his note-taking. For Bergman, a notebook's function often seems to involve problem-solving, meaning that problems encountered in the process of developing a scene or character are more often commented on than the final outcome. Bergman's notebooks comprise a variety of purposes. One of them is to clarify thoughts in the present, or to provoke new ideas in the act of writing. Another is to create a memory for the future, to write a text that can be reread at some time when the thoughts of the present have been lost or forgotten. Each notebook entry is dated, suggesting that, at least to some extent, the notebooks are intended to be (re)read by future readers, be they Bergman himself or a reader in a future public sphere. One finds words and sentences underlined in red throughout Bergman's notebooks, which indicates that he did reread his notes. Bergman also continuously refers to his notebooks when describing his film-making process in his autobiographical book *Images: My Life in Film* (1995).[12]

The sometimes self-deprecatingly playful tone of Bergman's notebooks can be understood in terms of the author's attempt at self-distancing. For instance, when explaining in one passage that he has been invited to Hollywood, he adds the comment 'or whatever it's called, and however it's spelt'. We can of course assume that Bergman knows very well what Hollywood is and how to spell its name, but that, in jest, he wants to pretend to be someone who does not.[13] As creative diaries (in the same manner as most diaries), Bergman's notebooks are not only a tool for documentation, but also for creating a persona, perhaps with future readers in mind. It is telling that before his death, Bergman himself donated his collection of notebooks and screenplay drafts for the purpose of founding an

---

12 Ingmar Bergman, *Images: My Life in Film*, translated from Swedish by Marianne Ruuth (London: Faber & Faber, 1995).
13 Ingmar Bergman, unpublished notebook, 'Nederlaget. Experimentet. Laboratorium. Prinsen. Ormens ägg. Sju sex. Porr-film. Den förlorade försten. 48 timmar av Jesu liv', 1975 (Notebook No. 30), F:123, the Ingmar Bergman Archive. Translation mine. A selection of Bergman's notebooks was published in 2018. This chapter refers to the archival documents themselves, rather than to the published texts. My reason for doing so is not only that I have personally examined these archival documents in my research, but also because some aspects of the handwritten originals have been revised in the published texts.

The playfulness of Ingmar Bergman

archive. Bergman's writing and filmmaking always occupied a position on the threshold between the public and the intimate, and the same is true of the personal notes in his notebooks. At the same time, the text in Bergman's notebooks is far from being a fully conscious construction of the author's self, not even for himself as a future reader. It is obvious that the primary purpose of his notes is to capture thoughts in their fluid state in the present, to allow spontaneous ideas of the moment to shape the text. Coherence and context are lacking in the notebooks' fragmentary style of writing, and the notes are often cryptic. Recent research has highlighted Bergman's 'self-fashioning' and his desire to control his image in the public sphere.[14] To fully understand the complexity of Bergman's self-creation, we need to modify this image of the manipulating artist Bergman, or at least discuss the controlling side of Bergman's self-fashioning in relation to the open, searching, and spontaneous writing that opened the door for the unpredictable and the improvised.

Bergman's notebooks frequently include passages that seem to fill in gaps that are perhaps indicative of temporary creative blanks, an inability to progress, or possibly distracting procrastinations. It is significant that Bergman continues to write even when the words are seemingly meaningless in relation to the fiction he is developing; that is, that he allows room for distinctions and gaps in his writing. For instance, there are many examples in his notebooks where Bergman interrupts a story under development to reflect on the pen he is using. One such example is found in a notebook which sketches a story that is an early version of *Vargtimmen* (*Hour of the Wolf*, 1968) and, in part, also a precursor to *Persona* (1966): in the middle of a dialogue between the female protagonist (Alma) and a ghostlike creature, Bergman interrupts the fiction to describe how his pen has fallen out of the window:

'Was someone there?'
Alma nods silently. *It* was, but what was *it*?
'What did he look like?'
'I don't know', Alma says helplessly. 'It was inhuman.'
(I dropped my pen out of the window. First, I thought of leaving it there and writing with my two new pens. But now I feel that this blue pen is so alive, and its pin jumps around like crazy, so I decided to go down and get it. Now it's done.)

---

14 See, for example, Janet Staiger, 'Analysing Self-fashioning in Authoring and Reception', in Maaret Koskinen (ed.), *Ingmar Bergman Revisited: Performance, Cinema and the Arts* (London: Wallflower Press, 2008), pp. 89–106.

'Did you see anyone else?'
'No. I got scared and sneaked in. I think he's gone now.'[15]

The ambiguous function of the notebook—to document, and at the same time to develop a fictional story—is particularly evident in such passages, where there occurs an abrupt shift between the here and now of the writing situation and the fiction itself.

As material objects, the notebook and the pen with which Bergman is writing could be understood as what Winnicott calls 'transitional objects'; that is, tools that enable the transgression between the real and the imaginary.[16] Unlike a child's teddy bear, tools such as a pen and paper are not objects that move between the realms of reality and fantasy. Even so, the author's material objects do enable a transgression of reality and fantasy along similar lines: the materialization of fantasy in writing anchors the writer's thoughts in a real time and space, at the same time as they allow room for the free development of the fantastic.

The details of the material conditions of writing are important to many authors; the desk, pen, and sheets of paper can play a quasi-ritualistic role in transiting to the fictional world during the moment of creation. To Bergman, well known for his nigh-on fetishized relationship with paper materials and writing routines, these tools are of great importance. His notebooks are simple, lined notepads, and his pen was an ordinary ballpoint pen. And yet, their mundane nature does not mean that Bergman's choice of those objects lacks significance. Perhaps the simple notepad was ideal in the early phase of writing characterized by free associations, the phase during which the written words were not yet 'art' but spontaneous thoughts and reflections in the moment. Bergman's reflections on his pen and paper are certainly jokes and humorous quips with a self-deprecating twist; but they are also self-reflexive comments that can be understood in terms of media-materialist aesthetics. Bergman's spontaneous, unfettered way of writing, in which the pen follows the thought, finds parallels in the aesthetics of the finished screenplay and film. The self-reflexive modernism evident in films such as *Persona* (in which a projector is displayed and the story interrupted when the film strip burns) reveals a similar indistinctness

---

15 Ingmar Bergman, unpublished notebook, 'De skeppsbrutna', 1962–1964 (Notebook No. 21), F:114, the Ingmar Bergman Archive. Translation mine.
16 Winnicott, *Playing and Reality*, pp. 1–34.

between the here and now of the film viewing and the fictional world. Other 'distractions' from the story found in Bergman's notebooks are more readily understood as a kind of mental exhortation to simply continue writing, even when it yields no progression in thought. These exercises might be a means to dispel anxious thoughts, or to fill the gap caused by creative hiatuses or impasses. Later in the notebook quoted above, at a point when the story is developing only slowly, Bergman repeats the word *tålamod* (patience) until it degenerates into its constituent components: *tåla* (to endure, or put up with) and *mod* (courage).[17] Perhaps repeating the word 'patience', and the ensuing wordplay with its components, instils courage in the author to continue writing, and even to feel confident in ideas about which he previously had reservations. This notebook was written during a period when Bergman was taking aesthetic risks, searching for new aesthetic forms and ideas. The courage to develop new ideas may arise from the flow of the writing process itself. To use a typology coined by editorial theorist Siegfried Scheibe, Bergman could be described as a *Papierarbeiter*: an author who thinks with his pen, so to speak.[18] This categorization stands in contrast to a *Kopfarbeiter*: an author who formulates thoughts mentally before writing them down. This improvised, *Papierarbeiter* method characterized the early phase of Bergman's writing process, the time when he wrote down the reflections in his notebook.

Bergman's notebooks contain few images or illustrations. Unlike auteurs such as Stanley Kubrick, Agnès Varda, and Federico Fellini, Bergman did not prepare his films from images, but almost exclusively from words. There are sometimes doodles in the notebook margins, however, and here and there one also finds more conscious non-verbal expressions that become part of the creative process. For instance, one of Bergman's notebooks contains a line that extends across a sheet of paper and is entitled 'Exercise in Simplicity'. In this example, the seemingly irrelevant becomes a conscious method for developing aesthetic ideas beyond verbal language, something that was particularly important in Bergman's films during this period. At the same time, the associations, digressions, and detours found in the

---

17 Ingmar Bergman, unpublished notebook, 1962–1964. Translation mine.
18 Siegfried Scheibe, 'Einige grundsätzliche Vorüberlegungen zur Vereinheitlichung von Editionen', in Michael Werner and Winfried Woesler (eds), *Edition et Manuscrits: Probleme der Prosa-Edition* (Bern: Peter Lang, 1987), pp. 177–189.

notebook are spontaneous comments of the moment, and they form part of a creative method of writing fiction. In other words, Bergman's notebooks are tools for creating original and innovative stories.

In his classic work on lateral thinking, creativity theorist Edward de Bono describes how play (together with jokes and humour) is essential to any kind of creative activity. De Bono develops creative games, such as role-play, which aim to instigate a break with expected behaviour or patterns, thus opening the way for new perspectives and ideas.[19] Such deviations from the expected are characteristic of Bergman's notebooks; he might interrupt a dramatic situation or other comments to insert a reflection on his pen, or some wordplay that transforms the written, giving it new meaning. It is no coincidence that Bergman began writing his fragmentary, exploratory, creative diary during the late 1950s, a period when his artistic freedom and experimentation had increased (although it should be noted that Bergman also kept notebooks before this time).

In the example of the pen, the shift from fiction to the here and now of the writing situation is clear and unambiguous. In other cases, the transition between fiction and the author's reality is more ambiguous and transgressive. The 'I' of the text sometimes refers to both Bergman as author and to a fictional character, and Bergman sometimes speaks to himself in the third person. In one characteristic passage in a notebook, Bergman describes events from a first-person perspective, although it is unclear whether the narrator is Bergman the author, an anonymous narrating agent, or a fictional character. Suddenly, the prose is interrupted by reflections on the 'I' who is speaking. In the margins, the word 'I' (*jag* in Swedish) is written in capital letters and encircled with two arrows pointing at it from opposite directions. In the following sentence, the 'I' is transformed into 'he':

> Who is this secret 'I'? That's something to think about. I think there has to be an ambiguous fission in wishes and dreams. <u>Whole series of interesting personalities.</u> They come and go – very surprising. But this much is clear: <u>he doesn't keep very good track of his characters.</u> Now and then he loses them.[20]

This notebook is characterized by just such fissions and fusions of identities; an 'I' becomes a 'he' or a 'she', and at the same time

---

19 De Bono, *Serious Creativity*, pp. 8–17. For games as creative exercises, see pp. 77–87.
20 Bergman, unpublished notebook, 1962–1964. Translation mine.

these pronouns refer to both a fictional character and the narrating author.

In another passage in the same notebook, Bergman addresses a fictional character at the moment of its creation, a character with whom he struggles, not knowing how to shape it: 'How can I reach you? How can I feel you as real more than in brief moments? How can I experience you with emotions more than in brief instants?'[21] This marks the beginning of what later develops into the silent character Elisabet Vogler in *Persona*. Bergman's initial difficulties in creating this character later gave rise to a silent, mysterious person who chooses not to speak. This is one example of how an impasse can still drive creativity when the difficulties are expressed in writing. The passage continues with Bergman turning the focus on himself through the eyes of the fictional character: 'How do you experience me?', he asks, and continues: 'I have a feeling you know much more, are able to do much more. How can you experience me as real?'[22]

The character created by Bergman also helps define the author's own contours as materialized in the text, as though she knows things about him of which he himself is unaware. Like a child in a make-believe game, the author simulates the fiction, thereby initiating the integration of the real and the fantastic. The ambiguity of agency in this notebook, as manifested in the transgressions between author, narrator, and character, continue in Bergman's screenplays. Here, this ambiguity is no longer a creative method, but rather an aesthetic of self-reflexivity and auto-fiction. The latter undermines the autobiographical 'pact' between author and reader and negotiates the relationship between fiction and the autobiographical: the 'I' in an auto-fictitious story is sometimes identified as the author, and sometimes as a fictitious narrator or character.[23] In Bergman's case, the distinction between author, narrator, and character is constantly undermined in the screenplay—a negotiation of identity that can be traced back to the author's identification with the fiction recorded in his notebook.

---

21 Bergman, unpublished notebook, 1962–1964. Translation mine.
22 Bergman, unpublished notebook, 1962–1964. Translation mine.
23 In a study of auto-fiction from a genetic-criticism perspective, literary theorist Philippe Lejeune explains that the materialization of the author's self in the text assumes various forms and expressions. See Philippe Lejeune, 'George Perec: L'autobiographie et fiction', in Jean-Louis Jeanelle and Catherine Viollet (eds), *Genèse et autofiction* (Louvain-la-Neuve: Burylant-Academia, 2007), p. 144.

Narrator in the screenplays

To quote Steven Maras, the screenplay is an 'intermediate' text in a concrete sense of the word; that is, it is a text written to be transformed into another aesthetic form, the film.[24] At the same time, Bergman's screenwriting is anchored both in the dramaturgical conventions of industrial filmmaking of the classic period (the context in which he began his screenwriting career) and the experimental screenwriting of post-war cinematic modernism. His screenplays most often adhere to the classic three-act structure, with a development from set-up to climax; but they may also be connected with the literary screenwriting trend of the late 1950s and 1960s, of which screenplays such as Marguerite Duras's *Hiroshima mon amour* (1960) and Alain Robbe-Grillet's *L'Année dernière à Marienbad* (*Last Year at Marienbad*, 1961) are prime examples.

Bergman's screenwriting has always been regarded as 'literary' compared to most other screenwriting and, as such, also as 'autonomous' in relation to the resulting film.[25] His screenplays have been published in book form and translated into many languages. In recent years, they have also increasingly been used for stage productions. Many of Bergman's screenplays are written in a literary style which, in some ways, has more in common with the prose fiction of stage drama than with conventional screenwriting. Some of his screenplays include scene text written in the past tense and with a first-person narrator, a subjective voice that has in most cases been removed in the film adaptation. The screenplay for *Persona*, for instance, begins with the words: 'I imagine the transparent ribbon of film rushing through the projector. Washed clean of signs and pictures.'[26] In the film, the cinematic apparatus itself replaces the narrator. In this case, the images running through the projector are displayed before the eyes of the viewer, instead of being viewed by a narrator. This is one of many examples of how Bergman's screenwriting and filmmaking oscillates between transmediation and media materialism. The screenplay is written to be transformed into film,

---

24 Steven Maras, *Screenwriting: History, Theory and Practice* (London: Routledge, 2009).
25 See, for example, Birgitta Ingemanson, 'The Screenplays of Ingmar Bergman: Personification and Olfactory Detail', *Literature/Film Quarterly* 12:1 (1984), 26–33, and, more recently, in works by Jan Holmberg.
26 Ingmar Bergman, Persona *and* Shame: *The Screenplays of Ingmar Bergman* (New York: Marion Boyars Publishers Ltd., 2002), p. 23.

yet the written text includes literary dimensions that are not adapted for inclusion in the film.

In other cases, fragments of a narrating voice are retained in the film, often Bergman's own voice (e.g., a short fragment in *Persona*, the final scene in *En passion* (*The Passion of Anna*, 1969), parts of *Viskningar och rop* (*Cries and Whispers*, 1972), and the introductory parts of *Scener ur ett äktenskap* (*Scenes from a Marriage*, 1973). Nonetheless, classic, continuous narrative voice-overs are rare exceptions in the body of Bergman's filmmaking. Instead, he often gives characters a narrating role, mainly in the many long monologues describing their memories, experiences, and interpretations of events, or their personalities. The blurred boundaries between character and narrator, as well as those between showing and telling modes of representation in these monologues, can be traced in the transition from notebook to screenplay. In fact, the author's reflections on his characters' backstories in his notebooks are sometimes transformed into monologues in the screenplays. One example of this is the scene in *Scenes from a Marriage* in which Marianne (Liv Ullmann) reads her diary to her husband. The entries in the diary, which explain Marianne and her husband's backgrounds and psychological states, correspond with the author's own reflections on the characters as recorded in his notebook. The diary as the fiction functions as a *mise-en-abyme* of the notebook in the creative process—a depiction of the notebook as a space for the author's reflections on himself and others.

Shifts in the narrating subject in Bergman's work highlight a mobility of agency as well as his interest in transformations and changes across the process of creation. This suggests that it might be misleading to examine the literary qualities of Bergman's writing in terms of the artistic autonomy of each version of the story. Instead, their artistic quality is related to the intermediate process across different media forms and utterances, in the relations between notebook, screenplay, and film. In Bergman's screenplays, the 'play' evident in the transitions of the narrating 'I' is not a creative method, as it is in his notebooks, but rather an aesthetic, self-reflexive gesture that facilitates the fusion and division of narrator and characters. This aesthetic can be conceptualized according to Derrida's description of play as the presence and absence of the self in a given structure, which thereby disrupts that structure.[27]

---

27 Derrida, 'Structure, Sign and Play', p. 294.

Bergman's 'playing' with the unity of the self is especially evident in a screenplay that was never adapted for film, *Människoätarna* (*The Cannibals*, 1964), an early version of what later became *Hour of the Wolf*, which also contains elements that were subsequently rewritten into *Persona*. The story in *The Cannibals* is related by several more-or-less unreliable narrators. Most of the scene texts are quotations from a fictitious diary, while other parts are related by someone who found the diary. Bergman employs these same two narrative frames in *Hour of the Wolf*, although in this case they are only explained in the prologue, rather than being continuously integrated in the story. The storytelling as act is particularly strikingly foregrounded in a section labelled 'Alma's story', in which the narrator explains that his account is a retelling of Alma's verbal, sometimes arcane, testimony. The narrators in the frame—both the diarist and the person tracing the diarist's testimony—are to be understood as versions of Bergman as the author. This interpretation is supported by the fact that the fictitious diary's dates approximately coincide with the period when Bergman wrote the script. Just like the diarist in the fiction, Bergman dates his writing. Apart from dating his notebook entries, he also concluded his screenplays with a note on the date and location of their composition. Bergman's interplay between the fictions and actual writing in *The Cannibals* continues in the film *Hour of the Wolf*, where the diary (shown once in the images) is the same kind of lined notepad that Bergman himself usually employed for his own note-taking. As an unfilmed screenplay, *The Cannibals* constitutes a fragment of an artwork—a text that never reached an audience as a film, nor as a published book. It is also a more 'literary' text than most of Bergman's screenplays, with its multiple narrative levels and storytellers.

Writing as remembering and forgetting

Bergman's scripts were generally written and edited in three versions: (1) a handwritten draft, and (2) a typed 'working script' that was later revised into (3) the shooting script. In addition, there is also the published version, which, while not identical to any one of the script versions, most closely resembles the shooting script. Overall, the differences among these versions are relatively minor. In this regard, Bergman's screenwriting is characteristic of auteurist filmmaking in which the director has significant control over the filmmaking process and does not need to adapt the script to different readers, nor develop script versions that include technical instructions. Bergman's screenplays usually involved fewer revisions between versions and fewer alterations than screenplays used in conventional industrial filmmaking.[28] There are hardly any revisions in the phrasing, nor any stylistic changes to speak of between the first handwritten script and the later versions. Such alterations as there are mainly involve changes to content, removals, and revisions in a single scene. Bergman was obviously not an author who revised stylistic details in his scene descriptions or dialogue. This indicates that he did not necessarily 'think with his pen' when writing the screenplay. Rather, this spontaneous writing method probably primarily characterized his early note-taking. With regard to his screenplays, Bergman was a *Kopfarbeiter* rather than a *Papierarbeiter*.

Bergman's screenplays that never made it to film for one reason or another were not rewritten or changed, but instead served as inspiration for new screenplays. The rich diversity of Bergman's oeuvre is partly explained by his ability to use earlier writings in new productions. Character traits, situations, and segments of dialogue recur from one screenplay to another. The reworking of *The Cannibals* into *Hour of the Wolf* and, in part, also *Persona* is a conspicuous example of the importance of rewriting in Bergman's body of work. His entire oeuvre can be regarded as variations on certain themes, motifs, and characters. These variations moderate the autonomy of the individual artwork, since the rewriting process continues even after the seemingly final version of a story is complete. The artwork's process of becoming may instead be understood as a network with links to a variety of different texts and versions, some links being stronger than others.

Bergman's rewritings can be conceptualized in terms of the way play alters memory and experience, turning them into fantasy: each new rewriting or adaptation 'remembers' its precursor while at the same time representing something new. Koskinen aptly describes Bergman's last film *Saraband* (2003)—a retrospective that explicitly reflects on his previous works—as remembering and forgetting brought together.[29] The paradox of the remembering-forgetting

---

28 As described in Steven Price, *The Screenplay: Authorship, Theory and Criticism* (New York: Palgrave Macmillan, 2010), pp. 63–73.
29 Maaret Koskinen, '*Saraband* and the Ingmar Bergman Archive', in Maaret Koskinen (ed.), *Ingmar Bergman Revisited: Performance, Cinema and the Arts* (London: Wallflower Press, 2008), pp. 19–34.

combination that characterizes Bergman's entire oeuvre is particularly interesting in connection with depictions of violence. Here, variations in Bergman's creative process can be understood in relation to the psychosocial mechanisms of trauma, where repetition of the past event *and* its repression in the form of fantasy intersect.[30]

Violent scenes are often more explicit in Bergman's drafts, notes, and unfilmed screenplays than they are in the final versions, or in versions seen by an audience. For example, *The Cannibals* includes a cruel scene in which a woman gives birth to a premature foetus and, upon discovering that it is alive, suffocates and buries it. The scene text explicitly describes her actions with the words: 'The foetus, five months old, is lying in a mush of blood and excrement, whimpering weakly, with shivering arms and legs.' Then follows the cruel and seemingly affectless act of violence: 'She squeezes the upper part of the bundle, where the head is, with both hands, thereby stifling the snivelling noise.'[31] Later in the screenplay, we are informed that this brutal scene might have been a fantasy, a mental transformation of what was actually a miscarriage into murder. In some sense, the screenplay depicts the transformation of memory into fiction, constituting a self-reflexive image of Bergman's transformation of his past writings and memories into new stories. In his rewritings of *The Cannibals* into other screenplays, Bergman transforms portrayals of violence from the brutally explicit to the implicit. For example, *Persona* includes echoes of the scenes with the dying foetus in its monologue, in which Elisabet (through Alma's voice) confesses to the difficulties she has experienced in connection with pregnancy and motherhood. The monologue includes no descriptions of actual acts of violence, but rather fantasies and wishes regarding such violent actions. Elisabet describes her 'disgust' and 'hatred' toward her child, how she tried to induce a miscarriage, and how she wishes 'her child would die'. The brutal scene in *The Cannibals* may be viewed as the realization of Elisabet's fantasies in *Persona*.

In *Persona*, the theme of a mother's abandonment of her child is linked to the historical trauma of the Holocaust and the Second World War. In one scene, Elisabet observes the famous photograph from the Stroop Report that shows Nazi soldiers in the Warsaw

---

30 Janet Walker, *Trauma Cinema: Documenting Incest and the Holocaust* (Berkeley, CA: University of California Press, 2005).
31 Ingmar Bergman, unpublished screenplay, *Människoätarna*, 1964, B:004, the Ingmar Bergman Archive. Translation mine.

ghetto pointing their guns at a young boy raising his hands above his head. This photo of the boy is paralleled with an image of Elisabet's son, who is portrayed in a photograph that Elisabet wants to avoid seeing. The photograph of the boy in the ghetto is mentioned in Bergman's notebook, but it is not included in the resulting fiction. Instead, it is the object of his reflections on the shortcomings of art and its inability to portray reality: 'My art can't melt, transform, or forget that little boy in the picture', he writes, and continues with a reflection on how the photograph reduces his art to 'buffoonery or something indifferent', meaningful only to himself.[32] The anxiety caused by art's inability to represent the cruelty of history and reality characterizes the post-war aesthetic crisis, with the question of how to portray the Holocaust at its core. In Bergman's case, this aesthetic question concerning representation becomes an issue of the relationship between one's personal creation and its broader historico-political context; it reveals a division between the artistic creation as intimate, and historical reality as a sphere unreachable by the artist. To Bergman's mind, the photo of the boy in the Warsaw ghetto reveals both a personal anxiety and his shortcomings as an artist. At the same time, the reflections in his notebooks shed light on why violence cannot be directly represented as such, but only indirectly through mediations of it. This realization is manifested in Bergman's reworking of *The Cannibals* to become *Persona*, in the transition from a direct depiction of violence to an indirect retelling of fantasies of violent actions.

Abandoned, punished children and parents who either leave or neglect their children are recurring themes in Bergman's filmmaking. A comparison of *Persona* with *The Cannibals* shows how Bergman depicted these themes in dissimilar ways in two different screenplays. The final example in this chapter compares two versions of the same scene from Bergman's film *The Serpent's Egg* (1977), which depicts a couple living in Germany during the years before the rise of Nazism. Here, too, the rewriting effects a transition from the direct and explicit to the indirect and implicit. Likewise, historical trauma is linked to personal trauma and to the intimate in this case as well. The scene in question shows a physician's psychological experiment, displayed on a film screen, which aims to test a woman's endurance when isolated in a room together with a screaming, inconsolable infant. This 'film within a film' shows the woman's despair gradually degenerating into uncontrollable rage; in the end,

---

32 Bergman, unpublished notebook, 1962–1964. Translation mine.

she kills the infant. The German doctor who conducts the experiment represents the dehumanized ideology of Nazism. The violent act itself is neither shown in the film images nor described in detail by the doctor assisting with the projection. The projection is interrupted just prior to the killing, and the doctor explains that the apparatus is not 'in perfect condition'.

The collection of drafts and notes held at the Ingmar Bergman Archive includes an earlier version of this scene noted on some loose sheets of paper and inserted into the notebook for the film *The Silence*. It is worth observing that the event's historico-political context is not explicitly rendered in this early version. In this case, the man showing the film is not a doctor, but an amateur filmmaker who wants to demonstrate his 'hobby' to a friend. In this first draft, unlike the final version of the scene, the violent act itself is described in great detail. The scene text explains how the woman throws the infant against the wall and then stamps it to death:

> The woman lifts the screaming infant and hurls it against the wall. Her face is stony with rage. The infant screams and convulses on the floor. The woman stamps on it repeatedly until the screaming suddenly ceases in a gurgling noise. The woman's face registers the sudden silence. She sits on the bed with her hands pressed against her stomach. And with her mouth open.[33]

As in the previous examples, this scene was also rewritten in order to become a more implicit and indirect depiction of violence. In this case, the rewriting also locates the scene in a historico-political context that is absent from the early draft. In both versions, however, the film within the film contains a self-reflexive dimension that both highlights the mediation of violence and problematizes its representation. Also, in the case of *The Cannibals*, the violent scene is indirect: it is a scene that lies somewhere between nightmare fantasy and reality. While the portrayal of violence is problematized in all versions, rewriting often adds layers of the mediated, the indirect, and the implicit to its depiction.

Conclusion

Bergman develops his stories through playful, creative writing. This playfulness is first and foremost an open and spontaneous writing

---

33 Bergman, unpublished notebook, 1962–1964. Translation mine.

mode which generates a free, liberating space that transgresses reality and fantasy. This transgressive act has a good deal in common with a child's make-believe game, where the actual instance of play co-exists with the fantasy being played out. The playfulness observed in Bergman's writing sometimes also involves wordplay and ambiguous agency as he plays with the meaning of 'I' in the text. In the context of Bergman's notebooks, writing assumes the dual, simultaneous function of documenting the creative process and of developing the fiction that creates this ambiguity. In Bergman's screenplays, the roles of narrator, character, and author intersect. The evolutionary process from notebook to screenplay reveals that the author's self as a construction in the text takes on various and shifting shapes.

In his notebooks, Bergman's playfulness manifests itself in the creative method that allows for distractions, detours, and open-ended searching. In his screenplays, his playing with the absence and presence of narrators and narrative levels is less an outright method and more an aesthetic dimension of the text. The freedom that characterizes the initial entries in Bergman's notebooks lays the foundation for the creative process that generates new ideas and a variety of new, original stories. The reworking of old screenplays into new works builds on this permissiveness towards the unexpected in the screenwriting process. Notebook and screenplay represent two separate kinds of writing; and, though playful in different ways, both form part of the same creative process that ultimately generates new stories and renewed aesthetic ideas.

Spontaneity is essentially a matter of relinquishing control by allowing oneself to be surprised. The scene from *Faithless* described in the introduction to this chapter reveals the paradox inherent in what happens when an author is as it were 'surprised' by the fiction that has developed in his or her writing. From the moment he creates a fictitious character, the author becomes someone else: a fantasy or fiction that he cannot entirely control.

6
Cinema as a detour: Ingmar Bergman, writer

Jan Holmberg

Ingmar Bergman's literary output comprises dozens of books and hundreds of articles. Admittedly, this is fewer than Balzac, though considerably more than Flaubert. Despite this prodigious corpus, Bergman asserted more or less aggressively throughout his life: 'I myself have never had ambitions to be an author.'[1] Whether we believe this affirmation or not (I would advise against it), the key word here first demands a definition. The question 'What is an author?' has, of course, been famously asked—and answered— by Michel Foucault, who dates the nascence of authorship to the Renaissance as a response to the need to attribute distinctive copyright or, alternatively, to allocate personal responsibility.[2] The result was the 'author as creator', whose works began to be viewed less in their own right than as emanating from this or that individual originator.

As a creator, Ingmar Bergman has certainly benefited from this transfer of power from work to author. Officially, however, he lamented this state of affairs, aspiring to be a nameless artisan rather than a celebrated artist and identifying himself with the creators of cultural artefacts of the past, before the Renaissance elevated them to the status of artists. In an essay published in the mid-1950s, by which time Bergman was really starting to make a name for himself, he mused over the anonymity of the medieval artist:

---

1 Ingmar Bergman, 'Each Film Is My Last' [1959], translated by P. E. Burke, Lennart Swahn, and Erika Munk, *The Tulane Drama Review* 11:1 (1966), 98.
2 See Michel Foucault, 'What Is an Author?' [1969], translated by Donald F. Bouchard and Sherry Simon, in Donald F. Bouchard (ed.), *Language, Counter-Memory, Practice: Selected Essays and Interviews* (Ithaca, NY: Cornell University Press, 1977), pp. 113–138.

In former days the artist remained unknown and his work was to the glory of God. He lived and died without being more or less important than other artisans; 'eternal values', 'immortality', and 'masterpiece' were terms not applicable in his case. The ability to create was a gift. In such a world flourished invulnerable assurance and natural humility.³

The essay in question may very well be Bergman's most quoted, and I suspect that no one quoting from it has ever failed to mention the name of its author. While it is easy to jest about Bergman's false modesty—a world-famous artist yearning for anonymity—I believe his desire for obscurity to be reasonably sincere. Still, there is a paradox here: Bergman claims that anonymity is an 'invulnerable assurance' of artistic freedom; yet this freedom is, in turn, contingent on the promotion of the artist into a 'name'. Somewhere in this contradiction, we find the explanation as to why Bergman refused (or tried to refuse, or pretended to try to refuse) to be laurelled as an author.

While Bergman's aversion to being called a writer may have been sincere, I will nevertheless do my best to prove him wrong. In this chapter, I will attempt to disregard his films (or, at the very least, decline to agree with his own view) where these are the end result of a process that is rather uninteresting in itself. That is to say, instances where the written works upon which the films are based are, at best, sketches. I will instead view his writings as works in their own right. Where I have considered them at all, the films are to be regarded as interpretations. Bergman's own adaptations of his works may remain authoritative, much as when a playwright stages one of his own works to critical acclaim. Although a contemporary audience viewing such an adaptation may consider it an unsurpassable benchmark of the play in question, this too shall pass. Interpretations come and go while works remain. After all, Shakespeare's main occupation was that of theatre manager, and he probably considered his works merely a necessary means to

---

3 From among several available English-language translations of Bergman's 1954 essay 'Det att göra film' ['The making of film'], I have chosen to quote from the abridged version published as an introduction to an American collection of Bergman screenplays (the very first edition of his screenplays ever to appear in book form, in fact): 'Introduction: Bergman Discusses Film-Making', in *Four Screenplays of Ingmar Bergman*, translated by Lars Malmstrom and David Kushner (New York: Simon and Schuster, 1960), p. xxii.

attract an audience. Moreover, were we able to travel back in time to watch the Bard's own staging of *Hamlet*, we would in all probability regard it as a sub-par production with confusing direction, overdramatic acting, and poor set design (and even poorer lighting), to say nothing of the seating and the horrible audience. Media forms (be they films, stage performances, or books) are historically contingent, some more so than others. In short, my (presumably) controversial position is that Bergman the writer has a strong chance of outliving Bergman the filmmaker.

Writing for the screen

As a writer, Ingmar Bergman excelled in genres such as essays, memoirs, diaries, and letters. In this instance, however, I will limit myself to considering the bulk of his authorship—his screenplays.[4] If, indeed, that is the correct term for a form of writing that sometimes looks suspiciously like a traditional drama, sometimes like the prose of a novel, and sometimes even like poetry. Only rarely do they resemble a conventional screenplay. I would argue that the term coined by their first Swedish publisher, *filmberättelser* ('film stories' or 'film narratives'), is a more apt description, a rubric that better captures their genre-defying qualities (cf. the *ciné-romans* of Marguerite Duras or Alain Robbe-Grillet). Rather than discussing thematic features (which, in principle, do not differ from the corresponding films), I will focus on the screenplays' specifically *literary* aspects. My aim is, quite simply, to show that Bergman's film scripts, although written for the screen, are literary works rather than screenplays.

Screenplays typically adhere to a strict form in terms of dramaturgic elements, literary style, and even typography. Bergman often complained that these conventions restrained him, at least until the late 1950s. All the same, his screenwriting was considerably independent and unusually, even unnecessarily, literary from the outset. When we first meet the knight in *The Seventh Seal* (1957), he 'stares directly into the morning sun which wallows up from the misty sea like some bloated, dying fish'.[5] Even as a supposed

---

4 In my book *Författaren Ingmar Bergman* [*Ingmar Bergman, the Writer*] (Stockholm: Norstedts, 2018), I attempt to consider Bergman's authorship in its entirety, including those other genres just mentioned.
5 Ingmar Bergman, *The Seventh Seal*, translated by Lars Malmstrom and David Kushner (London: Lorrimer Publishing, 1960), p. 13.

Cinema as a detour

source of inspiration for the actor or cinematographer (which is how Bergman explained himself when writing things like this), the metaphor of the sun as a dying fish is, quite literally, too extravagant—at least for a screenplay. This passage is also addressed by Birgitta Steene, who cites it as an example of 'non-cinematic' features in Bergman's screenplays, including the early ones, in which he 'used metaphors and similes that [gave] literary significance to the text but were hardly transposable to the screen unless transformed into a piece of visual surrealism'.[6] This is a form of excess that can only be credited to the account of the writer, rather than to that of the filmmaker. It is in instances such as these that Bergman reveals himself (perhaps even *to* himself) to be an author.

While cultured people will not hesitate to assert that 'the book was better' after having seen a film based on a celebrated novel, such an opinion may seem blasphemous in the case of a Bergman film vis-à-vis its literary origin. In the case of *Hour of the Wolf* (1968), however, I stand by this assessment. As a written work, it ranks among Bergman's greatest; it is also, I submit, nigh on unsuitable for filmic adaptations—by its author or by anyone else. Above all, the text is as much a closet drama as Goethe's *Faust* or Ibsen's *Peer Gynt*. That is to say, while evidently *possible* to adapt for the screen or stage, this is first and foremost a work of *literature* belonging to the dream-play genre. *Hour of the Wolf* takes place in the twilight zone between objective and subjective, exterior and interior, waking and dreaming, reason and madness. Though this is not impossible to capture on film, text offers other and less demanding possibilities. In a work of literature, a character can interact with an unreliable outer world without the reader ever having to determine the ontological status of that world. In cinematic works, however, the filmmaker must make up the spectators' minds for them: objective reality or subjective state of mind. Indeed, even when these boundaries are blurred, as in the Bergman films *Persona* (1966) and *Cries and Whispers* (1972), we are at least *aware* that they are obscure. In *Hour of the Wolf*, even the question of obscurity is obscure; strange things happen, such as when a character walks 'up the wall to the ceiling and is standing like a fly, head downward, apparently without

---

6 Birgitta Steene, 'Chapter II: The Writer', Birgitta Steene, *Ingmar Bergman: A Reference Guide* (Amsterdam: Amsterdam University Press, 2005), p. 52.

the slightest inconvenience'.[7] Note how nimbly this peculiar state of affairs is described. On film, this same unusual course of events would be more awkward, and the scene more easily reduced to a reliance on special effects. Another reason why *Hour of the Wolf* works better in writing lies in the way it often refers to vague characters without making the reader aware of who is being mentioned—in the Swedish original, that is. Interestingly enough, the English translation makes things much 'clearer', and hence less intriguing, demanding, and original. The following passage may serve as an example: 'Then I catch sight of Johan. He is huddling behind the stump of a tree, trying to hide, but quite visible.'[8] Here, the translator has seen fit both to change the narration from the third to the first person and also to name the character behind the tree stump, Johan, although Bergman never gave him away so easily. A more faithful translation of the first sentence might instead read: 'Then she catches sight of him.'[9] Although circumstantial evidence might lead the reader to suspect that 'him' is Johan, the fact of the matter is that the text never reveals that, which is only fitting for a story about demons (or, as they are referred to in the text, 'those others'). This ambiguity is also difficult to capture on film.

Furthermore, as literary fiction *Hour of the Wolf* adds a meta-literary quality to the film, since it is a text (the book we are reading) about a text (Johan's diary, as integrated into the story). That said, it is difficult to separate one from the other at times, as the narration moves seamlessly between Johan's 'subjective' perceptions of reality, as rendered in his diary entries, and seemingly (but only seemingly) 'objective' events as retold by Alma. *Hour of the Wolf* is Bergman's version of a *récit* in the tradition of Maurice Blanchot—a narrative that is not the narration of an event, but *the event itself*.

There is a note within parentheses on the very first page of *Hour of the Wolf* that recurs throughout the manuscript: '(From here on,

---

7 Ingmar Bergman, *The Hour of the Wolf*, translated by Alan Blair, in *Four Stories by Ingmar Bergman* (Garden City, NY and New York: Anchor Press and Doubleday, 1976), p. 123.
8 Bergman, *The Hour of the Wolf*, p. 126.
9 Cf. the Swedish original: '*Så får hon syn på honom. / Han sitter hopkrupen bakom en trädrot, försöker gömma sig, men är ändå synlig.*' A lesser, though not insignificant detail ignored by the translator here as *passim* is the line break between the two sentences. It is also worth mentioning that whereas the Swedish edition of *Vargtimmen* is divided into twenty chapters (thus emphasizing the book-like quality of the work), the English translation omits these divisions.

Cinema as a detour 95

the text is to be accompanied by images *ad libitum*.)'[10] What on earth is such a note doing in a film script? Here, Bergman (who is often quoted as saying how much he distrusts language in general, and his own verbal capacity in particular), relying instead on his audio-visual gifts, is considering *images* as a supplement to the *text*, rather than the other way around. Besides, how can one possibly make a film whose images are to be decided *ad libitum*, 'at one's pleasure'? After all, the shooting of an expensive film requires somewhat more planning than that, and Bergman was not exactly known for his willingness to improvise. So what should one make of this proposed ad-libbing? The only reasonable explanation is that the Bergman who wrote *Hour of the Wolf* was writing a work of literature rather than a film. (The fact that the work was eventually adapted for cinema should not deter us from drawing this conclusion.)

It should be mentioned, however, that these notes are not included in the published English translation of *Hour of the Wolf*. In fact, this is far from the only case where translators, editors, and publishers have taken it upon themselves to 'improve' Bergman's writings by purging them of excesses and perceived semantic, syntactic, and grammatical idiosyncrasies. Their reasons are fairly obvious: if even the author himself regards these texts as mere sketches ('half-measures' is a word Bergman often used to refer to his scripts), as long as the story comes across, the philological filigree with which proper literature is ordinarily invested is simply unnecessary.

Rhythm and reduction

Moving on to another example, very different from the textual peculiarities of *Hour of the Wolf*, Bergman's *Autumn Sonata* (1968) is an example of 'pure' drama. Along with *Scenes from a Marriage*, this work is Bergman's most reduced text. It hardly includes any instructions of any kind, such as what the scenery should look like or how a character should express something, and virtually no information about what characters feel or think. It is just dialogue, pure and simple. And yet it is very consciously written. The passage below, which illustrates this feature particularly well, may give the

---

10 '(*Härifrån åtföljes texten av bilder* ad libitum.)' Ingmar Bergman, *Filmberättelser 2: Persona, Vargtimmen, Skammen, En passion* (Stockholm: PAN/Norstedts, 1973), p. 49. Translation mine.

impression of being either unfinished or an instance of stream of consciousness. Whatever the case may be, it is quite spectacular, not least when one considers (as one always should) that this is a line meant to be *heard* rather than read, even if it works well in print, too. Despite running to 207 words in total, which makes it the longest sentence in Bergman's collected prose works, the passage has a breathing rhythm that testifies to Bergman's profound understanding of performances of the written word:

> Sen plötsligt en dag stod dina resväskor nedanför trappan och du talade i telefonen på främmande språk, jag gick in i barnkammaren och bad till Gud att nånting skulle inträffa som förhindrade din resa, mormor skulle dö eller det skulle bli jordbävning eller alla flyg skulle få motorstopp, men du reste alltid, dörrarna stod öppna och det blåste genom huset och alla talade i munnen på varandra och så kom du fram till mig och omfamnade och kysste mig och kramade mig och kysste mig igen och såg på mig och log mot mig och du luktade gott och främmande och själv var du också främmande, du var redan på väg, du såg mig inte, jag tänkte nu stannar hjärtat, nu dör jag, så ont gör det, jag blir aldrig mera glad, det har bara gått fem minuter, hur ska jag uthärda att ha så ont i två månader och så grät jag i pappas knä och pappa satt alldeles orörlig med sin lilla mjuka hand på mitt huvud, han satt hur länge som helst och rökte sin gamla pipa, han omgav oss med rök, ibland sa han något: Ska vi gå på bio ikväll eller idag tror jag att det skulle smaka med glass till middagen.[11]

It is a rare treat for a Swede to be afforded the opportunity to be snobbish about his native language. Hence, I have seized the chance presented here to quote a lengthy passage in what eighteenth-century poet Esaias Tegnér called 'the language of heroes and glory'. My intent is not to embarrass readers of Bergman who are not proficient in Swedish (in fact, foreign readers have advantages over native speakers which I will address later), but to emphasize two things: (1) the rhythm of Bergman's language, and (2) the perils of translation. To illustrate these points, let us compare the beautiful Swedish sentence above with the English translation, where we read the following:

> Then suddenly one day your suitcases would be standing downstairs and you'd be talking on the phone in a foreign language. I used to go into the nursery and pray to God something would happen to

---

11 Ingmar Bergman, *Höstsonaten* (Stockholm: Norstedts, 1978), pp. 59–60.

stop you from going, that Grandma would die or that there'd be an earthquake or that all the airplanes would have engine trouble. But you always went. All the doors were open and the wind blew through the house and everyone talked at once, and you came up to me and put your arms around me and kissed me and hugged me and kissed me again and looked at me and smiled at me and you smelled nice but strange and you yourself were a stranger, you were already on the way, you didn't see me. I used to think: Now my heart will stop, I'm dying, it hurts so much, I'll never be happy again. Only five minutes have passed, how can I bear such pain for two months? And I cried in Father's lap, and he sat quite still with his soft little hand on my head. He went on and on sitting there, smoking his old pipe, puffing away till the smoke was all around us. Sometimes he'd say something: 'Let's go to a movie this evening', or 'What about ice cream for dinner today?'[12]

Although this is by far the best of the available English translations of *Autumn Sonata*, once again Bergman's language is domesticated to the brink of banality. Not only is this 'vomit' of lamentation in a single, run-on sentence broken down into several sentences, but the translator also chooses to use quotation marks where Bergman, as he often does, has left them out, thereby subtly reminding his readers to be on their guard: who is speaking? To what end? The quotation marks indicate that Eva's account is accurate. Without the quotation marks (as in the original Swedish text), the question remains more open.

While we will soon return to the minutiae of Bergman's writing, such as quotation marks, I would first like to compare *Autumn Sonata*'s clear-cut, reduced style with that of another Bergman screenplay from the same period. Whereas *Autumn Sonata* is a downsized, traditional drama, *Fanny and Alexander* (film released in 1982) is prose, and at times almost like a novel. This is especially true of the prologue, with its long descriptions of the grandmother's apartment, in which Bergman fragments Alexander's perceptual faculties by describing them one at a time. First, the narrator tells us what the protagonist is *seeing*:

From where he sat he could see into the gleaming green drawing room—green walls, carpets, furniture, curtains. There were also several palms growing in green urns. He glimpsed the naked white lady with the chopped-off arms. She stood leaning forward a little and regarding

---

12 Ingmar Bergman, *Autumn Sonata*, translated from Swedish by Alan Blair (New York: Pantheon Books, 1978), p. 50.

Alexander thoughtfully. He had seen her many times before but could never make up his mind if he was to think of her as a little bit alive and therefore frightening but at the same time attractive in some way.[13]

Note the use of the verbs *see*, *glimpse*, and *regard*: here, vision is in focus. Alexander is observing, but also sensing himself being observed by the marble statue. This passage continues for almost three pages, in visual impressions of furniture, paintings, photographs, light, darkness, and so on. Next among the sensual data is *smell*, with descriptions of olfactory impressions ranging from the odours of cabbage soup to those of the outhouse, and, not least, the various aromas of people: 'symphonies of odour' composed of sweat, tobacco, perfume, powder, soap, urine, etc. Finally, *hearing* is introduced with a call for silence—'if you stand quite still and hold your breath, you can hear the silence'[14]—followed by descriptions of clocks ticking, pens scratching, and dishes rattling, until the catalogue of sounds ends when a housekeeper fills the stove with coal, and the 'noise breaks the spell'.[15]

This well-ordered, programmatic division of the senses is reminiscent of an assignment in a creative-writing class. It may be argued that these non-cinematic descriptions (some of which are quite impossible to convey on film) serve the purpose of inspiring the actors, set designers, costume designers, cinematographer, or what have you. It is also, however (and regardless of what Bergman would say on the matter), literature. In this context, it is interesting to note that the author sometimes seems irritated by his own uneconomical style of writing, feeling the need to remind himself that he is writing a film and nothing else: 'Now, do not write things that can't be translated into images', reads a note in Bergman's work-diary for *Fanny and Alexander*. 'I'm really tired of that; it becomes a kind of semi-literary snobbery that doesn't belong anywhere.'[16] As an enthusiastic reader of Bergman, I would nonetheless argue that it does.

---

13 Ingmar Bergman, *Fanny and Alexander*, translated from Swedish by Alan Blair (London: Penguin Books, 1989), p. 15.
14 Bergman, *Fanny and Alexander*, p. 18.
15 Bergman, *Fanny and Alexander*, p. 19.
16 Work-diary entry, 5 May 1979, published in Ingmar Bergman, *Arbetsboken 1975–2001* (Stockholm: Norstedts, 2018), p. 168. Translation mine.

When the written word is spoken

There is never any doubt that the words in Bergman's works, including those spoken aloud, are *written*. This is a trait for which his films have been criticized, especially by his countrymen who hear how strange the language sounds. Bergman's alleged difficulty in hitting the right verbal notes annoyed his colleague Bo Widerberg (among others), who wondered 'to what extent Bergman's foreign translators are part of his success, if people simply talk less strangely in the American versions of his films'.[17] Similar objections are still being voiced today. But Bergman is no realist, and never has been. Spoken language in Bergman is archaic, elevated. Above all, it is a *written* language, scantily disguised as spoken words. Furthermore, Bergman evinces the utmost concern not only for the meaning of his words, but also for the way they sound. In particularly inspired moments, he combines phonetics with semantics to achieve extraordinary results. For example, consider a scene that is often misquoted, despite being Bergman's most famous scene by far. Admittedly, misquoting the dialogue is easy enough to do, since it is hard to hear what is actually being said:

> Riddaren: Vem är du?
> Döden: Jag är Döden.
> Riddaren: Kommer du för att hämta mig?
> Döden: Jag har redan länge gått vid din sida.
> Riddaren: Det vet jag.
> Döden: Är du beredd?
> Riddaren: Min kropp är rädd, inte jag själv.[18]

> Knight: Who are you?
> Death: I am Death.
> Knight: Have you come for me?
> Death: I have been walking by your side for a long time.
> Knight: That I know.
> Death: Are you prepared?
> Knight: My body is frightened, but I am not.[19]

The knight thus misinterprets Death (as, in all honesty, who does not?). To the question of whether he is prepared or not, he replies

---

17 Bo Widerberg, *Visionen i svensk film* (Stockholm: Bonniers, 1962), p. 95. Translation mine.
18 Ingmar Bergman, *Det sjunde inseglet* (*The Seventh Seal*) (Stockholm: Norstedts, 2018), p. 12.
19 Bergman, *The Seventh Seal*, p. 14.

that his body is frightened, but that he himself is not (possibly thereby demonstrating just the opposite, being so scared that he cannot even hear what is being said). These two lines convey several of Bergman's major themes: problems of communication, the split self, and truth and lies. That aside, the scene also demonstrates how *The Seventh Seal*, while being Bergman's most famous *film*, also emphasizes *writing*. In the above dialogue, Bergman plays with the quasi-homonymity of the Swedish words for 'frightened' and 'prepared' (*rädd* and *beredd*); *rädd* is pronounced in exactly the same way as the second syllable in *beredd*, which allows for a misinterpretation of Bergman's, the knight's, and, seemingly, also Death's own words (improbable though this might seem). The pun is completely lost in translation, however, and I wonder to what extent non-Swedes have pondered the knight's strange answer to the question as to whether he is prepared to die. (Although I suppose his answer may appear less strange than Death's walking around incarnate in the first place.)

In British film critic David Thomson's musings over his youth in the 1950s, and Bergman's role in it, he makes particular mention of the Swedish language 'blooming in our mouths with its gentle, pious, slightly smug closed vowels and its swallowing syllabics. We mimed the word "*Smultronstället*" from the dark as Victor Sjöström and Bibi Andersson uttered it in *Wild Strawberries* [(1957)].'[20] Further, Anthony Lane writes in the *New Yorker*:

> There is no mistaking the look of a Bergman picture, or even the sound of it. Close your eyes, or avert them from the subtitles, and you find yourself swept up afresh in the sway of his dialogue. It may be unintelligible, but, like the libretto of an opera in an unfamiliar tongue, it makes a mysterious music of its own, and the blend of clucking and lulling in the Swedish voice seems wonderfully apt to Bergman's mood.[21]

Following one of the first-ever screenings of *The Seventh Seal* in an anglophone country (in Edinburgh in 1957), a review in *The Scotsman* praised the film, including 'the excellent subtitles, suggesting that it has been written in dramatic blank verse'. The reviewer concludes that, although the film's language lacks 'the wit of

---

20 David Thomson, 'Once, the Films of the Great Swedish Director Were a Matter of Life and Death', *Independent on Sunday*, 5 January 2003.
21 Anthony Lane, 'Smorgasbord: An Ingmar Bergman Retrospective', *New Yorker*, 14 June 2004.

Shakespeare's', it is nonetheless extraordinarily apt to the subject matter of the film.[22] Although it becomes apparent on closer inspection that *The Seventh Seal* is not written in blank verse, iambic patterns frequently occur in it. In fact, it is not entirely improbable that one reason for the knight's strange reply to Death, besides that previously discussed, is metrics. Had the knight not misheard, he might have answered '*Min kropp är beredd, inte jag själv*', in which case the line would be out of rhythm. As the line is written, however, it forms four iambs (as opposed to five, as in Shakespearian pentameter):

Min kropp | är rädd, | inte | jag själv.

While *The Scotsman*'s reviewer was slightly mistaken, it seems he was still on to something that most Swedish speakers miss (as I know I did when I watched Bergman before reading him). Sometimes, not understanding a language can be an advantage in fully appreciating its distinctive characteristics. In a quarrel depicted in *Wild Strawberries*, Marianne ironically exclaims '*Stackars Evald*' ('Poor Evald'), to which he replies '*Var god stackra mig inte*' ('Please don't "poor" me').[23] Also, a little later: '*Det här livet äcklar mig till kräkningar och jag tänker inte dra på mig ett ansvar som tvingar mig att existera en dag längre än jag själv vill.*' ('This life disgusts me and I don't think that I need a responsibility which will force me to exist another day longer than I want to.')[24] Compare these words, or rather the *sounds* produced by phrases such as '*stackra mig inte*' or '*äcklar mig till kräkningar*' with '*min kropp är rädd*'. Or, for that matter, with seemingly controversial expressions found in *Saraband* (2003) and *Faithless* (2000) such as '*frukostera*' and '*nattsärk*'—archaic words for 'eating breakfast' and 'nightgown', respectively, as has been scornfully noted by Bergman's compatriots. Phonetically, these expressions are all rather similar, with the alveolar trill [r] in close connection with the voiceless velar stop [k]. In Bergman, words do not merely serve the purpose of representing this or that; he also pays the utmost attention to how they sound. Were we to *listen* to Bergman's

---

22 'Our Film Critic' (sign.), 'Stark allegory from Sweden', *The Scotsman*, 24 August 1957.
23 Ingmar Bergman, *Smultronstället* (Stockholm: Norstedts, 2018), p. 65; *Wild Strawberries*, translated by Lars Malmstrom and David Kushner (London: Lorrimer Publishing, 1970), p. 83.
24 Bergman, *Smultronstället*, p. 66; *Wild Strawberries*, p. 84.

writings (and, indeed, his films) rather than reading or watching them, and without paying too much attention to semantics, we would often hear different variations of the *krk* sound. Whether this has any significance, I cannot tell. But the notion of listening to this 'mysterious music', as Anthony Lane describes it, brings me to the topic of Bergman as poet.

Poetry in motion

Together with *Cries and Whispers*, *Faithless*, *Private Confessions* (1996), and perhaps a few other works of his, *Persona* is one example of what we might call a calculated preliminarity among Bergman's writings. This characteristic is noted by the writer himself, who opens *Persona* with the following words: 'I have not produced a film script in the normal sense. What I have written seems more like the melody line of a piece of music, which I hope with the help of my colleagues to be able to orchestrate during production.'[25] This statement is followed by the strange passage quoted below, an equivalent of which was included in the famous prologue to the film. (That said, as anyone who has seen *Persona* will confirm, the film does not follow the screenplay very carefully, and one wonders how it could have done):

> The sound establishes itself and thickens. Incoherent sounds and short fragments of words, like sparks, begin to drip from the ceiling and walls.
> From this white whiteness emerge the contours of a cloud, no a sheet of water, no it must have been a cloud, no a tree with a great leafy top, no a lunar landscape.
> The noise rises in coils and whole words (incoherent and remote) begin to emerge like the shadows of fish in deep waters.[26]

---

25 Ingmar Bergman, *Persona*, translated by Keith Bradfield, in Persona *and* Shame: *The Screen-plays of Ingmar Bergman* (New York: Grossman Publishers, 1972), p. 21.
26 Bergman, *Persona*, p. 23. I have modified this translation slightly, first in correcting an obvious error: *ljud* (meaning 'sound'), is translated as 'light'—an easy mistake to make, since 'light' is *ljus* in Swedish, and I suspect that the translator simply misread the text. (This also proves one of my aforementioned points as to the poetic peculiarities of the text—the thickening of light would perhaps be easier to understand than that of sound.) I have also made a few other alterations, including an attempt to reintroduce Bergman's own punctuation, or lack thereof.

Persona was elsewhere described by Bergman as a poem: 'not in words,' he hurries to explain, 'but in images'.[27] In fact, anyone who reads the script can testify that it is also written poetry. The images conjured verbally are of a nature that is not easily captured in literal images, as is illustrated in the following example: 'short fragments of words, like sparks, begin to drip from the ceiling and walls'—imagery that is more a case of catachresis than of metaphor, in which tenor and vehicle do not match ('fragments of words' that 'drip'?). Interestingly enough, the next 'collision' of images also deals explicitly with language, when words 'begin to emerge like the shadows of fish in deep waters'. Then comes the tentative doubtfulness: it was not a cloud but a sheet of water. Or was it a cloud after all? Or a tree, perhaps? No, a lunar landscape.

I leave it to others to decide whether this is prose, poetry, or something in between; but I think we can agree that it is not a conventional screenplay. Regardless of genre, however, Bergman's texts are always characterized by a strong sense of rhythm, drastic metaphors, and the phonetic effects of alliterations and assonances—in short, by the sensitivity to the form and colour of language that designates a poet.

Bergman devotes a passage in *The Magic Lantern* to the importance of being true to the text when staging a play. There are a couple of sentences in the original manuscript (omitted in the printed version) that I believe offer an important insight into the mind of Bergman, not only as a director but also as a writer: 'To me, interpretation is a listening to the breathing of the text: Why are these combinations of words, these commas, these hyphens *right here?*'[28] Punctuation has certain effects, not only in performed drama but also in literature (especially in literature!). Bergman often called for a system of notation for film similar to that for music. As he puts it in his essay 'Each Film Is My Last':

> I cannot use 'keys' or show an adequate indication of the tempos of the complexes involved; it is impossible to give a comprehensible idea of what puts life into a work of art. I have often sought a kind

---

27 Stig Björkman, Torsten Manns, and Jonas Sima, *Bergman on Bergman* (Cambridge, MA: Da Capo Press, 1993 [1970]), p. 198.
28 Ingmar Bergman, ['Skala lök' or 'Gycklarens Afton'], manuscript for *Laterna magica*, 1986, C:028 in the Ingmar Bergman Archives, p. 270. Translation mine.

of notation which would give me a chance of recording the shades and tones of the ideas and the inner structure of the picture.[29] Actually, such a system of notation already exists: written language. I believe that this is how we should understand Bergman's use of punctuation: as an attempt to emulate the supposedly more exact half, quarter, and sixteenth rests of music. Moreover, Bergman used every sign at his disposal to the full. By way of example, *Private Confessions* includes a pertinent conversation between Anna and her mother. Note, in particular, the various punctuation marks used after the repeated word '*och*' (Swedish for 'and'):

> –Mamma! Vet du att allt går i cirkel. Det börjar med något som vi ältade i går och i förrgår och dagen innan: hur ska en präst som har förlorat sin tro kunna predika söndag efter söndag? Och: det är mitt fel att han har förlorat sin tro. Hur kan jag ta på mitt ansvar att driva honom mot sammanbrott och utarmning? Och! Han måste genast ha ett sömnmedel. Och. Om han inte somnar så är det de onda tankarna som har gripit honom och skakar honom så att han börjar gråta. Så jag måste tända lampan. Och sedan. Och sedan?[30]

The repeated conjunction '*och*' is followed by a colon, an exclamation mark, and a full stop, in that order. Linguistically, only the first of these is uncontroversial, yet the others are scarcely mistakes. These three distinct punctuation marks render different results that are subtle, yet perceptible. The writer knows what he is doing. Now, compare the English translation:

> Mamma! You know, everything goes round in circles. It starts with something we went over yesterday, and the day before, and the day before that. How is it possible for a priest who has lost his faith to preach Sunday after Sunday? And ... it's my fault that he's lost his faith. How can I take it on as my responsibility to drive him into a breakdown and destitution? And ... if he doesn't sleep, it's because those evil thoughts have taken him over and convulse him so he starts weeping. Then I have to put out the light. And then?[31]

Translation is always difficult—some would say impossible—and too critical a scrutiny of an English version might seem unfair. Yet,

---

29 Bergman, 'Each Film Is My Last', p. 97.
30 Ingmar Bergman, *Enskilda samtal* (Stockholm: Norstedts, 1996), p. 77.
31 Ingmar Bergman, *Private Confessions*, translated from Swedish by Joan Tate (New York: Arcade Publishing, 1997), pp. 73–74.

Cinema as a detour

in this case, the translator has made too many errors for them to pass without censure. First, she misses a whole sentence: in the original, a sentence follows '[…] breakdown and destitution' that could perhaps be translated as: 'And! He must have a sleeping pill at once.' Instead, this rather significant detail is omitted entirely, which makes the ensuing sentence something of a non-sequitur. Second, the penultimate sentence in the quoted passage has Anna *putting out* the light when, at least according to Bergman, she is, in fact, *turning it on*. Third, in the Swedish original, Anna repeats the phrase '*Och sedan*' at the end of the passage, with the small but significant difference that the first sentence ends with a full stop and the second with a question mark, signifying, as I read it, resignation followed by despair. Fourth, with regard to punctuation, Bergman's idiosyncratic but stylistically logical and important ways of punctuating the three 'ands' have eluded the translator. In the two aforementioned cases (she ignored the third case altogether), she opted to insert an ellipsis; and thus, by 'correcting' Bergman's language, she effaced the nuanced shift in tone while destroying the staccato of the phrases.

Reading readings

In closing, I will offer a reading of readings in Bergman, of which there are plenty. In fact, diaries, letters, and books abound in Bergman's films (cf. Anna Sofia Rossholm's Chapter 5 in this volume), and much can be said about the following examples: Alma's reading of Elisabet's letter to the doctor in *Persona*, Johan's falling asleep while Marianne reads to him from her notebook in *Scenes from a Marriage* (1973), the book Isak reads to the children in *Fanny and Alexander*, and so on. All the same, I will focus on a book that is not just any book, but the 'book of books'. Although there are probably already too many analyses of *The Seventh Seal*, I will venture to offer one more. Despite the large number of interpretations, few critics seem to address the fact that *The Seventh Seal* is also a film about media theory, and, more specifically, about writing, as the title itself implies: the seal of what, exactly? In the Book of Revelation, we read:

> And I saw in the right hand of him that sat on the throne a book written within and on the backside, sealed with seven seals.
>
> And I saw a strong angel proclaiming with a loud voice, Who is worthy to open the book, and to loose the seals thereof? (Rev. 5:1–2)

Besides being an early example of metaliterature, the Book of Revelation is the strangest of all the books of the Bible. From a literary standpoint, it only becomes more fascinating when the scroll described so suggestively turns out to be what Alfred Hitchcock used to call a 'McGuffin'. The seven seals are broken one after the other, attended by mysterious horsemen, earthquakes, and angels blowing trumpets. Still, what is actually written in the scrolls is never revealed. Consequently, *The Seventh Seal*'s primary literary reference is to a book about a book that no one reads. As such, it is a fine example of Bergman's fundamental ambivalence towards writing, an ambivalence about which, paradoxically, he has written so eloquently. When writings are included in Bergman's works (be they texts in foreign languages, secret diaries, or private letters read by others than their addressees), they are either difficult to read, unreliable, or the mediators of unwanted information. It is hardly an accident that the heroes of *The Seventh Seal* are a band of jesters who state their business through performance rather than in writing. In all likelihood, they cannot even read.

It is my hope that this chapter has proved Ingmar Bergman's status not only as an important writer, but also as a writer who insisted on making writing itself both a major theme of and a stylistically fundamental principle in his writing. Bergman's films are good—his works of literature are great.

7
Laughing through tears: the soundscape of Ingmar Bergman's *Smiles of a Summer Night*

Alexis Luko

Aldous Huxley once said, 'We participate in a tragedy; at a comedy we only look'.[1] In 1954, Ingmar Bergman found himself on the precipice of calamity, a key participant in his own real-life tragedy. Allegedly contemplating suicide on a Swiss mountain pass, suffering from a flopped film project, a broken marriage, and a failed love affair (not to mention agonizing stomach cramps), he explained, 'I had two alternatives: write *Smiles of a Summer Night* [1955] or kill myself.'[2]

Bergman had what he termed a 'complicated' relationship with comedy, admitting that as a young boy he was accused of having no sense of humour.[3] Perhaps no one was more surprised than Bergman, therefore, when he experienced comedic success with his *Bris* soap commercials (1951), *Secrets of Women* (1952), and *A Lesson in Love* (1954).[4] These works paved the way for *Smiles of a Summer Night*, which was well received as a comedy. But given Bergman's personal struggles before shooting, it is hardly surprising

---

1 Aldous Huxley, *The Devils of Loudun* (London: Chatto and Windus, 1952), p. 324.
2 Bergman purportedly told this story to a group of students at Southern Methodist University in Dallas, Texas. In *The Magic Lantern*, he admits that the film was a success despite his being 'sick during the entire shooting' and in a 'rotten mood'; Bergman, *The Magic Lantern: An Autobiography* (*Laterna Magica*) (New York and London: Viking Penguin, 1988), p. 345.
3 The purpose of *Smiles of a Summer Night*, he explained, 'was to make money' so that he could direct *The Seventh Seal*. And money he made. The film was a huge international success, winning praise with a European Film Award and the Cannes award for Best Poetic Humor in 1956. See Bergman, *The Magic Lantern*, p. 339.
4 For *A Lesson in Love* (1954), he claims in *The Magic Lantern* that he learned to trust the comedic instincts of his actors, Eva Dahlbeck and Gunnar Björnstrand, p. 342.

that the comedy is largely driven by tragedy throughout. Bergman himself said that the film could have been a tragedy, but comedy was better for a costume film set in *fin-de-siècle* Sweden.[5]

In my book on Bergman, I examine music, sound, and silence in his more dramatic and psychologically gripping films.[6] The Bergman centenary calls for a fresh perspective. As it is a time for celebration, this chapter is dedicated to comedic Bergmanian moments driven by music. *Smiles of a Summer Night* is a suitable starting-point for such an investigation as it is, according to Arne Lunde, 'exhibit A' among his comedic films.[7]

Music in Bergman's films has long been recognized as significant and, as apparent in this centenary volume, the soundtrack continues to offer exciting new avenues for understanding Bergman's cinematic world.[8] We know from Bergman himself that music served as inspiration in his conception of *Smiles of a Summer Night*. He described it as 'a bit of Mozart' and also noted the influence of

---

5 Similarly, the Prologue of *A Lesson in Love* also states that '*Lesson* could have been a tragedy except for the kindness of the gods.' Frank Gado, *The Passion of Ingmar Bergman* (Durham, NC: Duke University Press, 1986), p. 154.

6 Alexis Luko, *Sonatas, Screams, and Silence: Music and Sound in the Films of Ingmar Bergman* (New York and London: Routledge, 2016).

7 Few scholars have grappled head-on with Bergman comedies. Exceptions are: Paisley Livingston's chapter 'The Comic Device' in his *Ingmar Bergman and the Rituals of Art* (Ithaca, NY, and London: Cornell University Press, 1982), pp. 110–142; Arne Lunde, 'Through a Laugh Darkly: Comedy in the Films of Ingmar Bergman', *Journal of Scandinavian Cinema* 4:3 (2014), 239–253; and Frank Gado, *The Passion of Ingmar Bergman* (Durham, NC: Duke University Press, 1986), pp. 149–158 and 180–188.

8 Charlotte Renaud, 'La citation musicale dans les films d'Ingmar Bergman' (unpublished PhD dissertation, Université de La Sorbonne Paris III-Censier, 2007); Maaret Koskinen, *Ingmar Bergman's The Silence* (Seattle, WA: University of Washington Press, 2010); Per F. Broman, 'Reconstructing Ingmar: The Aesthetic Purging of the Great Model', in Mark Conard and Aeon Skoble (eds), *Woody Allen and Philosophy* (Chicago and LaSalle, IL: Open Court, 2004), pp. 151–168; Per F. Broman, 'Music, Sound, and Silence in the Films of Ingmar Bergman', in J. Wierzbicki (ed.), *Music, Sound and Filmmakers: Sonic Style in Cinema* (New York: Routledge, 2012), pp. 15–31; Lawrence Kramer, 'Music, Metaphor and Metaphysics', *The Musical Times* 145 (2004), 5–18; Elsie Walker, 'An Incorrigible Music: Ingmar Bergman's *Autumn Sonata*', *Kinema* 14 (Fall 2000), 21–40; and Anyssa Neumann, 'Sound, Act, Presence: Pre-Existing Music in the Films of Ingmar Bergman' (unpublished PhD dissertation, King's College London, 2016).

Franz Lehár's *The Merry Widow*.[9] The music is rich and eclectic, drawn from the classical music canon, sacred music, and newly composed music by Erik Nordgren.[10] This chapter examines comedic moments in *Smiles of a Summer Night* and the soundscapes in which they are embedded. I explore how music intersects with three different theories on humour. First is the 'superiority theory', which accounts for humour that exists at the 'expense of characters who are particularly stupid, vain, greedy, cruel, ruthless, dirty, and [otherwise] deficient'.[11] The superiority theory walks hand-in-hand with humiliation, a common trope in Bergman's films, as expounded upon so eloquently by Paisley Livingston, who has referred to 'a form of collective brutality' that underlines the laughter in his films.[12] Second is the incongruity theory where, according to Francis Hutcheson, 'laughter arises from the view of two or more inconsistent, unsuitable, or incongruous parts or circumstances' and 'necessitates deviation from the norm ... achieved through subversion of expectation, or exaggeration of stereotypes'.[13] As we will see in the analysis below, certain musical motifs linked to individual characters in *Smiles of a Summer Night* can be better understood through this incongruity theory.

Third, and most central to this study, is another idea put forward by Livingston, who has theorized the inter-relationships in *Smiles of a Summer Night* vis-à-vis the comedic theories of Henri Bergson. Bergson wrote about how laughter arises 'in response to the

---

9 Bergman mentions that inspiration for *Smiles of a Summer Night* sprang from his Malmö staging of Franz Lehár's *The Merry Widow*; Arne Sellermark, 'Är han tyrannregissör? [and then as is]', *Veckojournalen* 41 (15 October 1955), 26–29. See Livingston, 'The Comic Device', p. 242, and Bengt Janzon, 'Bergman on Opera', *Opera News* (May 1962), 14. Also obvious is the power of Shakespeare's *A Midsummer Night's Dream*. Prior to production of *Smiles of a Summer Night*, Bergman had directed *A Midsummer Night's Dream* in 1941 at Sagoteatern and in 1942 at the Norra Latin Lyceum, and *The Merry Widow* in 1954 at the Malmö Stadsteater; Birgitta Steene, *Ingmar Bergman: A Reference Guide* (Amsterdam: Amsterdam University Press, 2005), pp. 817–820.
10 Nordgren scored thirteen films for Bergman between the years 1949 and 1964. Bergman's consistent collaboration with Nordgren was convenient because of the latter's role as the in-house composer at Svensk Filmindustri.
11 Noël Carroll, *Humour: A Very Short Introduction* (Oxford: Oxford University Press, 2014), p. 9.
12 Livingston, 'The Comic Device', p. 115.
13 Carroll, *Humour*, p. 17.

mechanical encrusted on the living', and how '[i]n comedy we are shown two or several persons who speak and act as if they were bound to each other by invisible strings'.[14] He described comedic moments in terms of mechanized childhood toy analogies: the Jack-in-the-box, the spring, the snowball, and the marionette.[15] In *Smiles of a Summer Night*, the invisible strings and the 'mechanical', I argue, are elucidated through Erik Nordgren's musical cues and, at times, even through associated sound effects and vocalizations.[16]

The first part of this chapter examines musical themes that delineate tragicomic aspects of protagonists and also demonstrates how music aids in expressing linkages and ruptures between characters. Here, music is the ultimate manifestation of the 'invisible' strings that interconnect characters. The second part includes a musical analysis of the flurry of sonic events that lead to Henrik's attempted suicide. Here, music plays a powerful role as a prime cinematic force in underlying thematic tensions regarding religion and faith as well as doubt in love. The invisible string and mechanization analogies become even more significant as Henrik is pushed and pulled back and forth like a Bergsonian spring. It is music that underscores this tension, and it is music that eventually helps move the narrative through tears towards laughter. In the end, we may indeed question Huxley's adage about only *looking* at comedy, as Bergman challenges us not only to participate but also—to *listen*.

The musical 'Life of the Marionettes'

In the manner of a Mozart opera of mixed-up lovers, *Smiles of a Summer Night* is comprised of eight people and four intertwined couples. Bergman conceived of the screenplay as a pseudo-mathematical pattern whereby all couples are initially mixed up and the equation is later sorted out on a magical midsummer night.[17]

---

14 Livingston, 'The Comic Device', pp. 117 and 119.
15 Henri Bergson, *Laughter: An Essay on the Meaning of the Comic*, translated by C. Brereton and F. Rothwell (Mineola, NY: Dover, 2005).
16 I have a holistic view of the cinematic soundtrack and am interested not only in music but also in silence, in dialogue, in sound effects, and even in vocalizations such as screams and—in the case of a comedy like *Smiles of a Summer Night*—even laughter.
17 Gado, *The Passion of Ingmar Bergman*, p. 181. These love equations include: Henrik Egerman, Petra, and Anne Egerman; Fredrik Egerman, Anne, and Desirée Armfeldt; Count Carl Magnus Malcolm, Desirée, and Countess

Henri Bergson emphasizes that 'instead of concentrating our attention on actions, comedy directs it rather to gestures ... the attitudes, the movements, and even the language by which a mental state expresses itself outwardly'.[18] For Bergson, while action is intentional, 'gesture slips out unawares, it is automatic ... an isolated part of the person is expressed'.[19] As argued below, music and sound are fundamental not only in delineating each individual's gestural language but also in revealing more complex spiritual, intellectual, or psychological interconnections between members of the cast of mixed-up lovers.

Fredrik Egerman

Fredrik Egerman, who, in operatic terms, occupies the role of the ageing buffo bass, is the butt of most jokes and is linked to the sounds of ticking clocks and women's laughter. The tick-tock that often accompanies his on-screen presence represents his position as a bureaucrat, entrenched in a realm of non-imagination; it also, as pointed out by Frank Gado, symbolizes his difficulty in coming to terms with his own ageing process.[20] As for the laughter linked to Egerman, its main point is to torture, humiliate, and emasculate. It is evinced when Desirée laughs as he falls in a puddle, when she laughs at his appearance wearing silly pyjamas, and in the hysterical prolonged laughter of Anne and Petra as they contemplate what it would be like to be a man.[21] Fredrik also has his own musical theme (see Figure 7.1), orchestrated for strings, trumpet, horns, piccolo, oboe, clarinet, bassoon, and percussion, with an initial phrase that marches arrogantly, revealing his lawyerly propensity for order and regulation. Halfway through the cue at measure 4, the music itself laughs at Fredrik as the melody in the piccolo falls over the interval of a +7th and the trumpet, horns, and bassoons ring out

---

Charlotte Malcolm; Anne, Fredrik, and Henrik; Desirée, Fredrik, and Malcolm; and Charlotte, Malcolm, and Fredrik.
18 Bergson, *Laughter*, p. 70.
19 Bergson, *Laughter*, p. 70.
20 Gado, *The Passion of Ingmar Bergman*, p. 184.
21 The laughter embroidered into the soundtrack of *Smiles of a Summer Night* might seem inconsequential; but in many cases it serves as a type of cathartic release, akin to the primal screams that figure so prominently in Bergman's more dramatic films. On screams and Bergman, see Luko, *Sonatas, Screams, and Silence*, pp. 187–196.

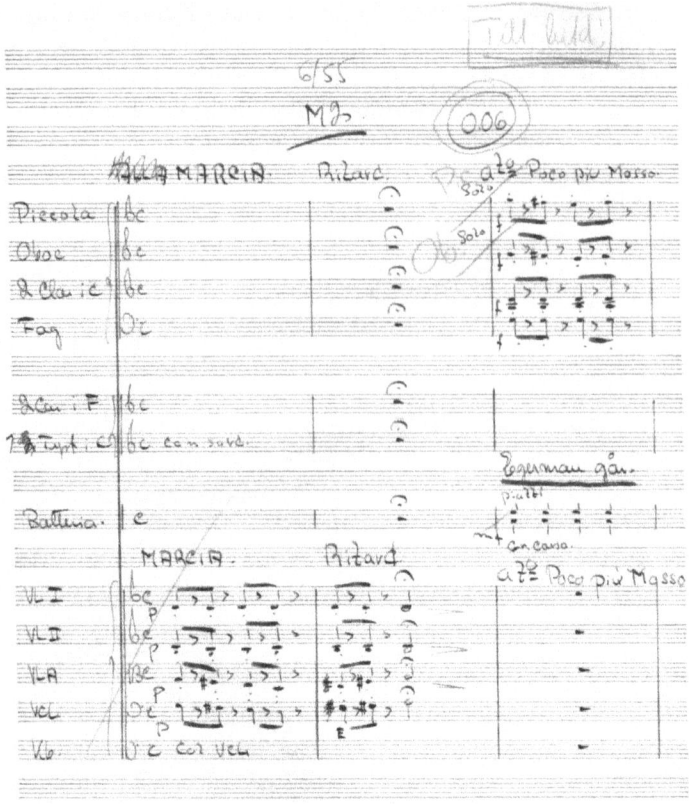

Figure 7.1a Fredrik Egerman's musical theme

with a rhythmic 'Ha-ha-ha Ha-ha-ha-ha.' Here, the incongruity theory is put to work at a musical level, with the first phrase serious (depicting how Fredrik sees himself) and the second phrase laughing (depicting how everyone else views him).

Fredrik's swagger is once again neutralized when his musical theme accompanies his departure from a shop where he has collected photos of his young trophy-wife, Anne. This time, the laughing second phrase acquires Freudian undertones as it synchronizes with the sight of blocked-up cannon, an allusion to his sexual consternation over his as-yet-unconsummated marriage.

The next time we hear Fredrik's motif, it is linked to the son of his old flame, Desirée (see Figure 7.2). His unconsummated marriage notwithstanding, it turns out that Fredrik is virile after all. But the joke is on him, as Desirée glibly refuses to admit that Fredrik

Figure 7.1b Continued

is the father. But all is revealed by the music itself, which provides the 'invisible strings' binding Fredrik and Desirée. Fredrik junior's cue unmistakably matches his father's with humorous melodic 'wrong-note' variation, the omission of the string section, and the charming addition of the triangle (!).

Anne Egerman

But what of the mechanical 'strings' between Fredrik and his young wife Anne? Near the beginning of the film, when Fredrik visits a photography studio to view his wedding pictures, the associated tune is in a flowing 6/8 metre, orchestrated for strings, flute solo, and light harp accompaniment (see Figure 7.3).

Figure 7.1c Continued

Outwardly, the musical theme sounds like a Hollywood cliché one would typically associate with the romantic female lead. But, lest we get too lulled into the comfort of the generic expectations that a romantic comedy affords, we must remind ourselves that this is, after all, a Bergman film. As we soon find out, the captured wedding images of Fredrik and Anne are not actually evidence of togetherness. He prefers admiring images of his wife (even when she is in an adjacent room) to experiencing her real love in the flesh.[22]

---

22 For Bergman, photos, letters, taped testimonials, and diary entries all figure prominently in films such as *Persona* (1966), *Saraband* (2003), *Autumn Sonata* (1978), *Hour of the Wolf* (1968), *From the Life of the Marionettes* (1980) (and the list goes on). Strangely, Bergmanian characters often express

Laughing through tears 115

Figure 7.2 Fredrik Egerman's musical theme 2

The next time we hear this theme, Fredrik describes his wife to Desirée. The motive is now distilled; it enters ever so softly, up a fifth, and is only orchestrated for strings: 'She is tender and affectionate. She likes my smoking a pipe. She likes me as if I were her father,' he says. At 'father', the cue prematurely ends mid-phrase, as if the music itself winces at the very thought of equating fatherly and spousal love (see Figure 7.4).

The music might indeed wince, but Desirée is inspired. The next time we hear the motif, Desirée arrives at her mother's, Madame Armfeldt's, house. The excerpt demonstrates how this bit of crucial information about a weakness in Fredrik's marriage is very much on her mind as she sets a plan in motion to win his heart. The motif is heard again as Desirée's mother shows love for her daughter when she says, 'one can never protect a single human being from any kind of suffering'. The next time the theme sounds, Anne looks despondently at three birds in a cage, a metaphor for being cooped up in the house in an unhappy threesome. The next time, Fredrik is once again looking at the photos of Anne. But now the motif is stripped down and accompanied by the tick-tock of a clock which fails to keep time with the musical rhythm of the cue. The sonic

---

deeper interconnectedness when beholding their loved ones in photos or reading their letters.

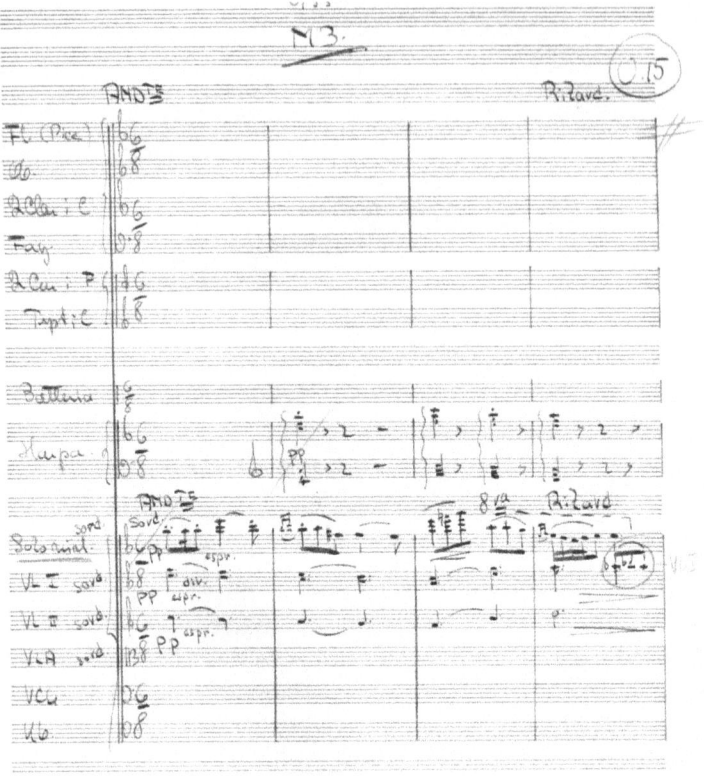

Figure 7.3a Anne Egerman example 1

disconnect plays to the detachment of Anne and Fredrik, made all the more explicit as he sadly admits, 'I understand nothing'. The cue continues to play through a cut to an idyllic pastoral scene at Madame Armfeldt's villa and the music swells to accommodate fuller orchestration (including harp accompaniment) to respond to a romantic connection, this time between Henrik and Anne, who are rowing a boat while Fredrik looks on jealously. The final sounding of the theme occurs when Henrik and Anne pronounce their love for each other.

This musical motif is thus not simply the leading theme/leitmotif of the film's heroine. It passes through several transformations, and with each repetition it underlines a different inter-relationship: Anne and Fredrik; then Anne, Fredrik, and Desirée; then Desirée and her mother; then Henrik, Desirée, and Fredrik; and finally, Henrik and Anne. It is a theme I call 'faith in love', and it suggests musical

Figure 7.3b Continued

Figure 7.4 Anne Egerman example 2

interconnection or invisible strings between different groupings of characters. The tragedy here is that the musical theme also implicitly suggests ruptures in relationships precisely by means of gradually ousting Fredrik from the mixed-up-lover equation. Indeed, his final soundscape, when he takes a last look at the photos of his beloved Anne, is distilled to merely a chiming clock.

Count Carl Magnus Malcolm

One of Fredrik Egerman's adversaries is an army officer named Count Malcolm. A caricature lacking depth, he is associated with a musical cue that accompanies his grand entrance which occurs after a witty, self-reflexive repartee between Desirée and Fredrik:

> Desirée: 'We're not on the stage, Fredrik dear!'
> Fredrik: 'But this is still a damned farce!'

Count Malcolm's theme is inherently funny (see Figure 7.5).[23] It is a pompous and militaristic march, marked *ff—double forte*—with accents, and is orchestrated for something approximating a military band. The music draws attention to Malcolm's exuberance and his propensity for violence. The extremes of register, from highest piccolo to lowest bass drum, and Nordgren's rubric, *Marcia Trioffale*

---

23 Miguel Mera, 'Is Funny Music Funny? Contexts and Case Studies of Film Music Humor', *Journal of Popular Music Studies* 14 (2002), 91–113.

Laughing through tears

Figure 7.5 Count Malcolm's theme

Grande/Triumphal Grand March, musically exaggerate Malcolm's sense of self-importance.[24] But the air quickly deflates when his tune abruptly ends mid-phrase, an affect comparable to the off-screen auteur using the proverbial 'hook', musically subduing Malcolm's hubris.

Some of Count Malcolm's statements are punctuated with musical stingers, as if underlining punchlines of jokes or imagined off-screen laughter (see Figure 7.6). Take, for example, his statement, '[m]y wife might cheat on me [...] but if anyone touches my mistress I become a tiger!' And the reverse, '[m]y mistress might cheat on me [...] but if anyone touches my wife I become a tiger!'

When Count Malcolm and Fredrik meet for the first time in Desirée's apartment, Fredrik attempts to preserve his pride—a challenging task whilst outfitted in the Count's ludicrous nightcap and pyjamas. A duel of wit, words, and music ensues as the men contrapuntally spar. While Malcolm attempts to intimidate his opponent by whistling a military tune,[25] Fredrik resorts to humiliation tactics, humming *La ci darem la mano* from Mozart's *Don Giovanni*—a

---

24 Thanks to Håkan Lundberg at Svensk Musik for providing me with Nordgren's scores, which are reproduced with kind permission of the Nordgren estate.
25 I have not yet had success in identifying this tune.

Figure 7.6 Count Malcolm's theme 2

seduction tune sung by Don Giovanni to the peasant-girl Zerlina in a brazen attempt to sleep with her before her impending marriage to Masetto. This amounts to a not-so-veiled reminder to Fredrik that he is up against an armed soldier countered by a not-so-veiled indictment of Malcolm's adulterous ways.

Countess Charlotte Malcolm

When we are introduced to Charlotte, Count Malcolm's wife, she is riding a horse in the far distance, and until she dismounts we might be under the mistaken impression that it is Count Malcolm himself. They are both linked by means of militaristic-sounding cues;

Laughing through tears

Figure 7.7 Countess Malcolm's theme

but there is a musical incongruity, as her theme is grand and much more expansive than the Count's—a sly way to further disparage him and to simultaneously suggest that she is a force to reckon with (see Figure 7.7).

Like her husband, Charlotte is also a caricature, endearing with over-the-top passions, including seething jealousy, much like Donna Elvira of *Don Giovanni* who sings 'ah, chi mi dice mai', when she discovers that Don Giovanni has been unfaithful. Charlotte spends most of the film boiling with anger. One soliloquy in particular permits full articulation of her feelings. Modernist music accompanies her hate-filled speech along with a Bergman-close-up, a cinematic fusion of sound, dialogue, and visuals representing the most frightening recesses of Charlotte's psyche: 'I hate him, I hate him, I hate him', she says. Thanks to the accompanying tritones throughout, otherwise known as 'the devil in music' or *diabolus in musica*, this

Figure 7.8 Countess Malcolm's theme 2 (*diabolus in musica*)

is music akin to what one might hear in a horror film, making for a scene that is humorously hyperbolized (see Figure 7.8).[26]

Desirée

The actress Desirée is an amalgam of Titania and Puck of Shakespeare's *A Midsummer Night's Dream* as she meddles with

---

26 See Luko, *Sonatas, Screams, and Silence*, pp. 135–175, for a discussion of the sonic world of horror in Bergman's films.

fate, generating much (but certainly not all) of the intrigue with her cunning partner-swapping plan that is enacted at her mother's summer villa. She is associated with the harp, both sonically and visually. The harp, for example, is present when she first bursts into the song, 'Go away all bitterness',[27] as she saunters through the streets with Fredrik in a charming scene that would fit seamlessly in a Hollywood musical. This 'performance' is indicative of the theatrical realm she inhabits. Harp music (particularly glissandi and arpeggios outlining 7ths and 9ths) echoes the fairy music of *A Midsummer Night's Dream* and is linked to the magic wine, pastoral shots of the lake, swans, and full moons and transitions between scenes at Madame Armfeldt's villa (itself a type of theatrical 'stage' for Desirée's plotting).

Henrik Egerman

Henrik's classical music

Henrik Egerman, Fredrik's adult son, is unable to express himself adequately either verbally or sexually. His zealous study of theology is greatly hindered by agonizing feelings of lust for the household servant Petra and, more problematically, romantic desire for his stepmother Anne. Fredrik typically turns to a romantic classical piano repertoire to seek expression for his feelings of self-pity. Fredrik is, therefore, emblematic of the Bergmanian tortured musician who uses music selfishly and misguidedly, thus further impeding any possibility for meaningful human connections.[28]

For Henrik Egerman, while words continuously fail him, music provides a mode of communication. Music, in fact, becomes a powerful agent in giving voice to his subconscious desires, waking him up to his struggles between secular love, lust, and faith, and even operates by pulling the proverbial 'strings' to control his ultimate destiny.

Early in the film, when Fredrik and his wife retire to the bedroom for an afternoon nap, Henrik works out his jealousy at the piano

---

27 The text of this song is by Bergman.
28 Examples of such characters inhabit many of Bergman's music-themed films: Stig the violinist in *To Joy* (1950), Henrik a cellist in *Saraband*, and Charlotte a concert pianist in *Autumn Sonata*. For discussions of *To Joy*, *Autumn Sonata*, and *Saraband*, see Luko, *Sonatas, Screams, and Silence*. Bergman contrasts solo musicians with those healthier and happier musicians who engage in communal music-making in orchestras or small ensembles.

in a melodramatic outpouring of Robert Schumann's *Aufschwung* from *Fantasiestücke* op. 12. In Bergman's part-autobiographical/ part-fictionalized musings on life and art in *The Magic Lantern*, he writes about being awoken by the ghost of Strindberg playing *Aufschwung* in an adjacent apartment.[29] Bergman was also familiar with Strindberg's narrative use of *Aufschwung* in his *Inferno*, where the music frightens someone away. Something similar occurs during Henrik's outburst at the piano, where music too acts as an off-screen or next-door magical presence, playing an active role in the unfolding of the plot. Henrik's choice of *Aufschwung* is noteworthy as it depicts Schumann's impetuous and passionate alter ego Florestan, a counterpart to the more careful and intellectual Eusebius—a nod to Henrik's split personality in the film, which causes him to constantly waver between faith/intellectualism and love/emotion.

The music aids in ratcheting up sexual tension, serving as an expression for Henrik's repressed sexual desires. More remarkably, however, the music also manages to break through the locked bedroom door, setting up a virtually incestuous *ménage à trois* between son, father, and stepmother.

When Henrik suddenly crashes *Aufschwung* to a standstill and sounds the first notes of Franz Liszt's *Liebesträume No 3*, music synchronizes with the visuals as Henrik shifts pieces at exactly the pivotal moment when the virginal Anne begins to respond to her husband's advances. We as audience members are left confused as to whether this is a case of chicken or egg—is the resulting synch point a *response* to the action in the bedroom or is it, rather, *influencing* the action?[30] Is Henrik intuitively *responding* to the arousal of the couple in the next room through his music? But perhaps it is *not* Fredrik who is arousing Anne at all and it is, rather, her stepson Henrik *stimulating* action by leading the seduction ritual with his music from the next room?

The plot thickens as another synch point between music and action occurs when Henrik enters the first transition section of *Liebesträume*—a cadenza specifying a change to poco agitato and

---

29 Bengt in *Music in Darkness* (1948) auditions with *Aufschwung* at a music conservatory, and Viktor in *Autumn Sonata* listens to *Aufschwung* on the radio.
30 The two poems by Uhland and the one by Freiligrath depict three different forms of love: (1) (*Hohe Liebe*): religious love; (2) (*Seliger Tod*) erotic love; and (3) (*O lieb, so lang du lieben kannst*) unconditional mature love.

marked with key-changes and a crescendo. As the music reaches a dramatic peak, Fredrik woozily calls out the name 'Desirée', thus adding a symbolic fourth person to the mix in the bedroom and revealing that his lust is not directed at Anne at all but at the subject of his dream.

The instability of the musical passage nicely reflects Anne's subsequent destabilization. Who is this woman 'Desirée'? Classical music-loving audience members may chuckle knowingly. *Liebesträume* literally means 'Love Dreams/Dreams of Love', aptly chosen as an accompaniment to Fredrik's own 'Love Dream'. The poem (by Ferdinand Freiligrath) on which *Liebesträume No. 3* is based, 'O lieb, so lang du lieben kannst', is particularly poignant in the context of the film as it serves almost as a thoughtful adage for all the lovesick characters in the film.[31] The scene comes to an end as Henrik reaches the cadenza, comprised of arpeggiated dominant 9th chords reminiscent of Desirée's realm. They have a harp-like character—and segue cogently into the next scene at the theatre, another dream world of sorts and the realm of Desirée.

This scene can be better understood through the lens of Bergson's marionette and 'dancing Jack' theory, which identifies humour when a character 'thinks he is speaking and acting freely' but 'viewed from a certain standpoint [...] appears as a mere toy in the hands of another'.[32] The synch points in this scene between music and action are so cogent that it is almost as if Henrik is providing piano accompaniment in a silent movie theatre. The music comes across as 'all-knowing', possessing an omniscience that breaks the fourth wall and reaches out to us as audience members. The music itself acts as commentator and manipulator and as a means to connect four characters, revealing their tangled inter-relationships and subconscious desires.

Henrik's (?) jealousy motif

Henrik, like Anne, is musically complex. Besides classical music he is also linked to a cue we can provisionally identify as the 'jealousy motif' (see Figure 7.9). It is first heard during the magic wine-drinking scene after he cries: 'It's too painful to be comical!!!' Like

---

31 'O love, as long as love you can/O love, as long as love you may/The time will come, the time will come/When you will stand at the grave and mourn!'
32 Bergson, *Laughter*, p. 38.

Figure 7.9 Henrik Egerman's 'jealousy motif'

his statement, the climbing, rhythmically agitated melody in the strings is melodramatic and intense and so painful it becomes funny.

The cue is heard in moments of jealousy, most notably when Anne touches Henrik's shoulder (with the 'jealousy' music perceived from the point of view of Fredrik Egerman), when Desirée spots Fredrik and Charlotte sneaking off for a secret and unscheduled rendezvous, and before Henrik attempts suicide.

Upon studying Nordgren's sketches for the magic wine-drinking scene, I found that the composer originally intended to alternate the 'jealousy motif' with the 'faith in love' theme each time a character took a drink. The original conception of the scene works beautifully in interconnecting the lovers and bringing out the main themes of faith in love and jealousy or doubt in love (see Figure 7.10).

In the end, Bergman and Nordgren opted instead for stylized harp music throughout the scene, possibly in order to underline the vital presence of magic, a favourite Bergman trope. This makes an important linkage to the fairies of *A Midsummer Night's Dream*, and it is another example of how Bergman uses music to drive the plot. The music suggests that the invisible strings are being pulled at a higher omniscient level—one involving magic and the supernatural.

Henrik-in-a-box

For the second part of this chapter, we turn to our Jack-in-the-box analogy where, as Bergson explains, 'the tension of the spring

Laughing through tears 127

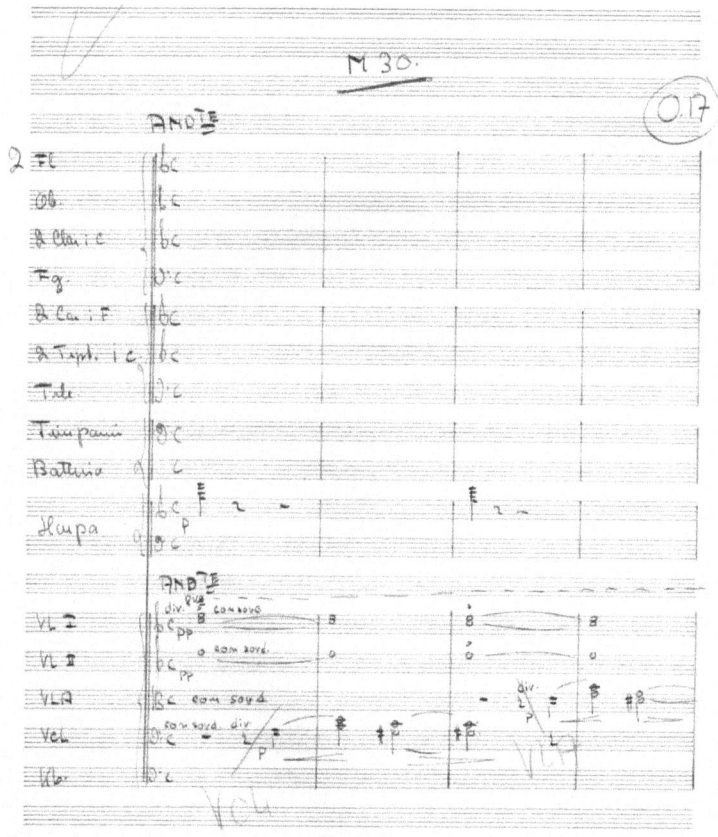

Figure 7.10a Alternating 'jealousy motif' and 'faith in love' theme

is continually being renewed and reinforced, until it at last goes off with a bang'.[33] Bergson puts this in human terms, describing a mental condition where two feelings exist 'as inelastic and unvarying elements in a ... living man, mak[ing] him oscillate from one to the other [, and the] oscillation becomes entirely mechanical'.[34] Bergson's theoretical framework beautifully captures the essence of Henrik's painful ordeal during the climax of the film as he is pushed and pulled back and forth between lust, love, and faith. What is essential to understand is that little of Henrik's internal struggle is

---

33 Bergson, *Laughter*, p. 37.
34 Bergson, *Laughter*, p. 38.

Figure 7.10b Continued

expressed in words—it is, rather, music that articulates his oscillations between different feelings.

There are two central climactic scenes in *Smiles of a Summer Night*. The first, which I have chosen not to discuss, involves the 'game' of Russian Roulette, where silence and the sound of the spinning gun chamber underscore the lead-up to the wild laughter of Count Malcolm. The other climax comprises Henrik's attempted suicide, where he accidentally trips the button for the mechanized bed that pops Anne into his bedchamber. The mechanical bed is initially introduced through the servants, Frid and Petra. This is not only a nod to comedic convention but also to opera, where nurses, maids, and servants often meddle with the lives of upper-class characters. Depressing the button for the bed pops a sleeping Anne into Henrik's bedchamber, prompting mutual avowals of love, and transforming Henrik from lovesick suicidal fool into a blissful bridegroom. The bed plays a delightful tune by Erik Nordgren orchestrated for the celesta (see Figure 7.11).

Laughing through tears 129

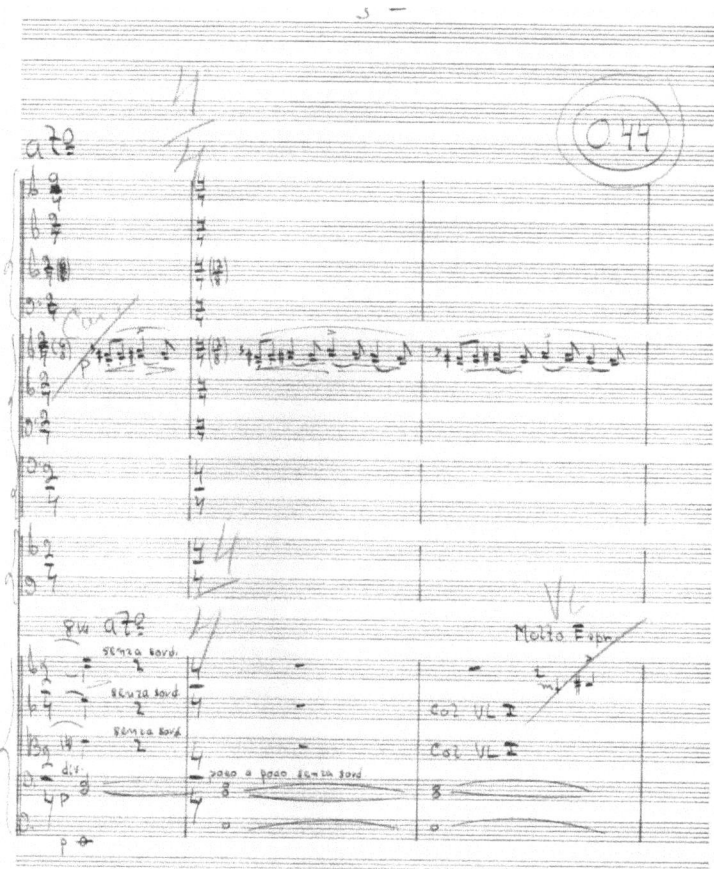

Figure 7.10c Continued

The innocent timbre, reminiscent of a child's music-box, forms a musically incongruous prelude to the more robust and seasoned notes of a trumpet, brassy and gloriously phallic in sight and sound—a musical joke made all the more explicit through the imagery of a heavenly cherub provocatively blowing a horn above a clandestine love-nest which, we are told earlier in the film, was designed to facilitate an affair for a king.

In the case of the mechanical bed, once triggered, it is a machine that operates automatically, or is 'possessed', without human control. It is an example, par excellence, of Bergson's mechanical something encrusted on the living, linking music, the mechanical, and the physical act of love at a very basic level.

Figure 7.11 Bed music

Leading up to Henrik's catharsis, Bergman forms a Bergsonian 'snowball' by structuring a semantically and sonically intertwined world with a series of overlapping and competing musical events. These events take place over almost eight minutes (without much in the way of dialogue) comprising no fewer than eleven sonic events and moments of sonic disruption, a technique I call *aural disjuncture*. *Aural disjuncture* is a term I have coined to describe sudden unexpected shifts from one sonic event to another.[35] The constant movement between one cue and the next amplifies a sense of disorientation and highlights moments where *faith in love* and *doubt in love* collide.

---

35 Alexis Luko, 'Faith, Fear, Silence, and Music in Ingmar Bergman's Medieval Vision of *The Virgin Spring* and *The Seventh Seal*', in K. Yri and S. Meyer (eds), *The Oxford Handbook of Music and Medievalism* (Oxford: Oxford University Press, 2020), pp. 636–661.

Laughing through tears

Figure 7.12 Musical climax—the gavotte

Our musical climax begins with a gavotte, composed by Nordgren with an eighteenth-century temperament, reminiscent of Mozart (see Figure 7.12). The music exudes politesse and adherence to social mores, ostensibly in denial of the extreme emotional drama that has just transpired over dinner.

The gavotte is immediately followed by Desirée's performance with harp accompaniment of *Freut euch des Lebens*.[36]

Freut euch des Lebens, referring to merriment and happiness in love, is very much out of step with a plot in which couples are torn by lust and dissatisfied in their marriages. But the music holds another layer of meaning. At the end of the nineteenth and persisting through the twentieth century, the song was transformed from one

---

36 *Freut euch des Lebens*   *Rejoice in life*
    weil noch das Lämpchen glüht   *Because the lamp is still glowing*
    Pflücket die Rose   *Pick the rose*
    eh sie verblüht!   *before it wilts!*

The song was composed in 1793 by the Swiss poet Johann Martin Usteri and composer Hans Georg Nägeli. The tune inspired Stephen Sondheim's 'Send in the Clowns' in his copycat musical, *A Little Night Music*. The discomfort of this scene is brilliantly parodied in Woody Allen's *Midsummer Night's Sex Comedy* (1982) with Leopold's hilarious performance of Schumann's *Ich grolle nicht* and a sung version of the Lord's Prayer.

with a cautionary message to one with humorous and raunchy lyrics, thus adding a naughty layer of musical meaning.[37] Had they only known, this would surely have added fuel to the censor's fire. After all, the US Legion of Decency categorized the film as 'Class-C immoral'.[38]

To this effect, could it be that the music itself has agency, playing a role in Desirée's plotting? While Desirée performs, she faces the camera rather than connecting with her audience. The general tone in the room is emotionless. This is particularly comical when viewed in the context of Bergman's oeuvre, where moments of diegetic music-listening are often deep and meaningful. Here, the audience is comically unaffected by the music. Desirée's spell is not working.

Charlotte and Fredrik stumble in late to take a seat behind the enormous harp representing the tangled web that Desirée weaves while she attempts to capture Fredrik's heart as she sings, 'One tends [...] to leave the violet unnoticed that blossoms on the path'. But her artful musical suggestion that she is a flower goes unnoticed by Fredrik. Like Henrik, Desirée expresses her emotions through music. With her professional theatre background and her elaborate plot and staging, she is making a calculated play to influence Fredrik. And it fails. In contrast, Henrik's uncontrolled passionate music is much more effective when it slips into his father's bedroom. So, music has magical power in Bergman's world; but it is tricky and unpredictable, much like Puck and his magic in *A Midsummer Night's Dream*. Near the end of Desirée's performance, an animated astronomical clock begins to chime in counterpoint with her song, both rhythmically synchronized and harmonized with the tune (see Figure 7.13).

The music of the clock is 'I himmelen, i himmelen',[39] a hymn by Laurentius Laurinus, printed in the chorale book for Sweden of

---

37 My mother grew up with this song in Switzerland and is still able to rattle off some of the more risqué verses; others I was able to find online.
38 Steene, *Ingmar Bergman*, p. 219.
39 My thanks to Jan Holmberg for bringing to my attention that Mattias Lundberg recently gave a conference paper about this hymn: Mattias Lundberg, 'Reformatorn, rektorn och regissören: Laurinus *I himmelen* som melodiskt och teologiskt tema i Bergmans *Sommarnattens leende*', 'Speglingar av Luther i Bergman och Bergman i Luther', Konferens Teologiska högskolan, 7 December 2017. In English: In heav'n above, in heav'n above, where God our Father dwells: how boundless there the blessedness! No tongue its greatness tells. There face to face, and full and free, the everliving God we see, our God, the Lord of hosts!

Figure 7.13 Desirée's performance and the astronomical clock

1697 (*Koralbok 1697*).[40] The religious text serves as a stark counterpart to the secular *Freut euch des Lebens*, perhaps acting as a moralizing force? The clock itself has a memento mori quality with its figures of a knight, princess, monk, and—most notably—the grim reaper. Astronomical clocks are usually imbued with mechanisms to predict the movements of the stars, sun, moon, and planets. Here the mechanized and musical clock, like the bed, is a Bergmanian example of mechanized motion and unmediated music (also seen in his omnipresent music boxes), devoid of human touch, perhaps suggestive of an omniscient hand at work.[41] Bergman ensures that the clock has a vital sonic presence with four separate soundings

---

40 In Nordgren's sketches for the score, he initially starts the tune in f minor, corresponding with the key in the chorale book, but eventually settles for e minor. The switch to e minor was probably made in order to ensure seamless harmonization with the end of *Freut euch des Lebens*. After all, my extensive research of Bergman's soundtracks has revealed that he typically treats the soundtrack holistically, finding interesting ways to blend sound effects and music into one harmonious tapestry. Bergman and his sound teams often looked for commonalities between music and sound so as to permit harmonization and blending.
41 As I argue in Luko, *Sonatas, Scream, and Silence*, pp. 106–134, there is a difference for Bergman between music performed by live musicians and unmediated music void of human intervention.

of the tune,[42] prompting the viewer to question: who is in control of the action? Is it Desirée Armfeldt? The magic wine? God? Frid, who becomes akin to an omniscient narrator near the end?[43] Or, are these the *machinations* of Fate itself?

The scene quickly shifts to a musical cue for harp and strings with swans, water imagery, and superimposed birdcall. Then, another shift to Henrik at the piano, lost in the romance of his own private performance of Chopin's *Fantaisie Impromptu*, op. 66. He cannot play two phrases, however, without thinking of Anne. We know this as he suddenly stops and the jealousy or 'doubt in love' motif takes over.

As Henrik reels painfully, another moment of *aural disjuncture* introduces the melodious and sensuous laughter of Petra. Then, in counterpoint with the laughter, the clock once more sounds the hymn 'I himmelen, i himmelen', yet another cautionary finger-wag from the off-screen gods, telling Henrik to halt his lustful thoughts and stay on his theological career path.

Unable to cope with the push and pull of lust, love, God, and jealousy any longer, Henrik prepares to hang himself. And then, in a moment anticipating tragedy, he trips awkwardly onto the switch for the mechanical bed. Music propels the bed with a sleeping Anne into his room, and Henrik is saved by the mysterious 'mechanism' of love.

Beyond representing individual characters, Bergman's musical cues in *Smiles of a Summer Night* have tentacles, mechanically reaching out to other characters, revealing on a musical level the invisible strings that interconnect pairs and chains of lovers.[44] For the lead-up to Henrik's attempted suicide, Bergman moves swiftly from popular song to religious tune, to romantic piano work, to a 'doubt in love' motif, to laughter, back to religious tune, to birdsong, to silence, to mechanical bed music, eventually landing on the 'faith in love' cue. These jarring musical shifts caused by *aural disjuncture* create an alienation effect that aids in underlining key thematic conflicts: the struggles of church, jealousy, lust, and romantic love occurring within Henrik's own psyche. Henrik's oscillations make

---

42 On repetition in Bergman's films, see Luko, *Sonatas, Scream, and Silence*, chapter 5.
43 Frid describes the three 'smiles' of midsummer night as three couples unite.
44 We see this in many of his subsequent dramatic films, so it is particularly interesting that we see these techniques percolating in this early comedy.

him a quintessential Bergsonian Jack-in-the-box. There is a scarcity of dialogue in the climax, which makes music and sound effects vitally important in conveying meaning. Music coils and uncoils, acting like a spring through repetitive and alternating cues, serving to unlock the secrets of Henrik's subconscious and ultimately bringing about a happy end. Incidentally, Bergman would use the same musical techniques in the flagellant scene of his next film, *The Seventh Seal* (1957), also underlining oscillations between faith and doubt—but in that case through the lens of religion.[45]

Though Bergson's theories help understand how music functions in *Smiles of a Summer Night*, the fact remains that the film treads a fine line between tragedy and comedy. As aptly put by Frank Gado, 'Bergman's best comedy reads the human condition as dismally as his most pessimistic films.'[46] In order to remind the viewer that the tragic is never far behind, Bergman emulates a Brechtian alienation or distancing effect that dizzies and destabilizes and leads viewers to question the film and the film-maker, just as the characters in the film question their beliefs in fidelity, love, and marriage.

In *Smiles of a Summer Night*, music is a powerful force which incites giggles and betrays secrets about characters, their interrelationships, and their affairs. It is used by performers like Desirée and Henrik to manipulate other characters and push the plot into new directions. Music also acts as an omniscient off-screen force—a source of magic on a midsummer night, providing a rhythmic structure to the climax of the film, mechanically swinging back and forth like a pendulum between incongruous states of laughter and tears.

---

45 Luko, 'Faith, Fear, Silence, and Music'.
46 Gado, *The Passion of Ingmar Bergman*, p. 184.

8
Sound, act, presence: classical music in the films of Ingmar Bergman—a lecture-recital

Anyssa Neumann

This chapter looks at the appearance, function, and significance of classical music in Ingmar Bergman's cinema.[1] Bergman used his love of music to fuel his films in both form and content, largely eschewing traditional soundtrack scores in favour of pre-existing music used sparingly but precisely, incorporating music into the lives of his characters, and finding artistic inspiration in the works and lives of the composers. Of the forty-two full-length films he directed between 1946 and 2003, twelve contain excerpts from Bach, while twenty-four feature other works from the classical canon; twenty-two feature music from non-classical genres, ten feature hymns, chorales, or other church music, twenty-three use an original soundtrack, and three have no music at all. Because Bergman as a source is not particularly reliable or trustworthy, I will give less weight to what he *says* about music and more to how music *sounds* in his films.[2]

A musical auteur

From lush orchestral scores to electronic music, from Swedish folk songs to the ritual chanting of the 'Dies Irae', from phrases of solo Bach to fully staged operatic productions, Bergman's film music

---

1 This is a much-reduced version of the 90-minute lecture-recital I gave at the Ingmar Bergman: 100 Years conference, in which I performed piano works drawn from Bergman's films, including pieces by Bach, Schubert, Chopin, Schumann, and Liszt. For in-depth discussions of the ideas offered in this chapter, see Anyssa Neumann, 'Sound, Act, Presence: Pre-Existing Music in the Films of Ingmar Bergman' (unpublished PhD dissertation, King's College London, 2016).
2 Bergman frequently spoke of his love for classical music, making statements like '[m]usic has all my life been just as vital as food and drink' (quoted in Lise-Lone Marker and Frederick J. Marker, *Ingmar Bergman: A Life in the*

traverses a wide range of genres and periods, both as sound and in words. Throughout his interviews and memoirs, music appears as anecdote, metaphor, description, and explanation, a mode of communication, and a glimpse into the mysterious realm beyond. In some cases music structures his films, frames the action, defines the form, or inspires the text; it can be a thematic trope, a plot device, and a vital part of the content. Music weaves itself through the film texture as a physical sound, as a presence in the lives of his characters, and also as an absence—a silence that, in Bergman's universe, reveals an inability to communicate, a spiritual void, the absence of God.

Bergman stands as one of the twentieth century's pre-eminent auteurs. In interviews and writings, he often said that he used film to communicate his artistic vision and philosophical credo as well as his personal history. But what truly distinguishes a Bergman film are its themes and recurring motifs. Bergman's obsession with religious doubt, the artist's fate, the search for meaning, and the impossibility of communication marks his films as much as their visual qualities do: the tight close-ups, bleak landscapes, and deliberate camera movements. In 2007, Claudia Gorbman introduced the idea of filmic *mélomanes*: music-loving directors who 'treat music … as a key thematic element and marker of authorial style',[3] as if it were a new development. But from his earliest films in the 1940s, Bergman does exactly this, treating music in such a way that over the course of his cinematic career, it becomes as much a part of the narrative fabric as does the technical apparatus.

Film music or music in film?

The musical soundscapes of Bergman's early films of the 1940s and 1950s reflect traditional Hollywood scoring. As a young director

---

Theater, 2nd rev. ed. (Cambridge: Cambridge University Press, 1992), p. 30), and he often referred to himself and his work in musical terms. Most of his claims have remained unchallenged, and the idea of Bergman as a so-called musical filmmaker has been widely accepted. In my work, I have closely examined some of the musical references that Bergman sprinkled throughout his autobiographical writings, using music to craft his biographical legend. I have also identified problems surrounding the film-as-music analogy, an idea Bergman frequently tossed around.

3 Claudia Gorbman, 'Auteur Music', in Daniel Goldmark, Lawrence Kramer, and Richard Leppert (eds), *Beyond the Soundtrack: Representing Music in Cinema* (Berkeley: University of California Press, 2007), p. 149.

expected to produce films for commercial success, Bergman relied on staff composers to write conventional soundtracks. Yet these scores rarely saturate the films. Much of the narrative action unfolds to sounds of everyday life—city noises, sounds of nature. Only during moments of high tension and in dream sequences does the underscore intrude on the film's diegetic soundscape, functioning to 'guide and control audience response'[4] by eliciting alarm, empathy, worry, or relief.

In several of Bergman's early films, pre-existing music surfaces as a counterpart to the soundtrack. *Music in Darkness* (1948) marks the first of many to feature classical music alongside the usual film score: heard and performed on screen, this music is a significant feature not only of the film's soundscape but also of the characters' lives. Music and musical characters populate other early films, from *Summer Interlude* (1951), featuring *Swan Lake* dance sequences from the Royal Swedish Ballet, to *Smiles of a Summer Night* (1955) featuring on-screen performances of Chopin, Schumann, and Liszt. Other films use classical music to influence the soundtrack. In *The Seventh Seal* (1957), Erik Nordgren weaves fragments of the 'Dies Irae' into his orchestral underscore. In *To Joy* (1950), Bergman takes the opposite approach, relying solely on classical music for the soundtrack, with no original cues by film composers. While these excerpts of Beethoven, Smetana, Mendelssohn, and Mozart are largely diegetic, performed by specific characters, the pre-existing music still fulfils the function of conventional film scoring—establishing setting, creating an atmosphere, underscoring key moments.

This conventional incorporation of music changed with the 1961 release of *Through a Glass Darkly*, which abandons a soundtrack score to feature fragments of the Sarabande from Bach's D minor Cello Suite, repeated four times non-diegetically. Charlotte Renaud writes:

> During the period heralded in with *Through a Glass Darkly*, music acquires a new dimension. It no longer strives to meld within the film in order to increase the drama, nor to build up the structure. Music is there for its own sake, detaching itself from the film. [...] Its presence is neither contextual nor structural, but rather metaphorical.[5]

---

4 Kathryn Kalinak, *Film Music: A Very Short Introduction* (New York: Oxford University Press, 2010), p. 14.

5 Charlotte Renaud, 'An Unrequited Love of Music', http://ingmarbergman.se/en/universe/unrequited-love-music (accessed 14 July 2015). Oddly, before this

Critics generally agree. Broadly speaking, Renaud's identification of this so-called 'new dimension' is accurate: after 1961, Bergman's music is often presented as an art-object with a history of meaning and metaphor independent of the film's narrative. Yet the foregrounding of art music, situated 'metaphorically' in Bergman's otherwise largely silent films, does not preclude music from providing context, delineating structure, or increasing drama. Nor was music in Bergman's earlier films used only to increase drama or build structure. Just as he occasionally used pre-existing music in his early films, he also continued to use soundtrack scores and non-classical genres later on. Amid the vast silences and concentrated dialogues, brief, intense moments of classical music stand alongside the occasional use of jazz, pop, hymns, cabaret songs, and modernist underscores.

Rather than viewing music in Bergman's films as a chronology of unrelated moments, I propose locating it on an ever-shifting spectrum of appearance, function, and location, not only to allow for individual nuances but also to identify differences unaccounted for by the basic binaries of classical/non-classical and diegetic/non-diegetic—the differences between music heard, music performed, and music sensed. Bergman's pre-existing music often appears diegetically; his characters listen to it, talk about it, perform it, are haunted by it. Unlike conventional film music, Bergman's pre-existing music, when placed diegetically, speaks both to his audience and also—perhaps primarily—to his characters.

Music as sound

In his essay 'Listening', Roland Barthes makes a crucial distinction. Hearing, he says, is physiological, dependent on the mechanisms of the ear. Listening, though, is a function of intelligence—a conscious choice. Barthes categorizes listening into three types: the alert, the deciphering, and the psychoanalytic;[6] but he was talking

---

statement, Renaud lists various ways in which pre-existing classical music functions in contextual and structural ways throughout Bergman's oeuvre, listing a number of examples from the post-*Through a Glass Darkly* period (by which she means 1960–2003). *Brink of Life* (1958) has no music apart from a brief clip of the Swedish national anthem, played on the radio; thus, the absence of a traditional musical score from 1961 onwards is not new, nor should it be considered shocking.

6 Roland Barthes, 'Listening' (1976), in *The Responsibility of Forms*, translated by Richard Howard (Berkeley: University of California Press, 1991), p. 245.

about listening in the real world. What about the artificial world of film, which often does not maintain the sonic fidelity of reality? Michel Chion applies Barthes's listening to the unreality of film to arrive at three types of cinematic listening: causal (alert), semantic (meaning), and reduced (pure sound).[7] Both theorists, however, are predominantly concerned with non-musical sounds. Music is generally considered a universal language; but what it communicates, and what one is supposed to understand, remains contentious. In the following examples, I have considered four aspects of cinematic musical listening: the listening subject, the musical object, the type of attention and response, and the form of mediation. This approach reveals that Bergman's portrayals of listening follow patterns discernible from his earliest work. As characters listen to music, we, the audience, listen to the same music; but we also watch them listen from a vantage point of the filmmaker's choosing.

The most immediately accessible scenes of listening are those in which the 'message' of the music either reinforces or provides ironic commentary on the narrative. Using the music's lyrics or cultural baggage to convey a message, these scenes rely on audience familiarity for maximum impact. But such an outcome is not guaranteed. In *It Rains on Our Love* (1946), former prostitute Maggie conceals her pregnancy from her boyfriend David and ignores his suggestions of marriage (the child is not his). On learning the truth, David heads to a bar, where a gramophone is playing the Bridal Chorus from Wagner's *Lohengrin*. No one seems to be actively listening to the music, but the visual emphasis on the gramophone suggests that all hear it. As David weighs his two choices, commitment or loneliness, Wagner's music draws our attention—and David's—to the idea of marriage. Whether actively shaken by the lonely drunks around him, subliminally influenced by this theme tune of matrimony, or convinced by a conversation with a man outside, who happens to be the all-knowing narrator, David returns to Maggie.

Another love-themed example occurs in *Waiting Women* (1952). Marta is nine months pregnant and waiting for her labour to start. She is also unmarried and no longer in contact with the child's father. Switching on the radio, she listens to 'Dance of the Blessed Spirits' from Gluck's *Orfeo ed Euridice* before the telephone rings; her former lover is on the other end, and Marta hangs up, refusing

---

7 Michel Chion, *Audio-Vision: Sound on Screen*, edited and translated by Claudia Gorbman (New York: Columbia University Press, 1994), pp. 25–29.

his entreaties. Bergman juxtaposes a final shot of the telephone with an image of a clock adorned with pastoral figures playing the flute and lyre, a visual prompt to Gluck's music and, of course, to Orpheus himself, a symbol of marital fidelity. While Marta succumbs to the power of music, closing her eyes in relaxed bliss, the reality of her life as an unmarried pregnant woman is a far cry from the Elysian Fields that Gluck depicts. Yet, just as Gluck gives his opera an unexpected happy ending, so too does Bergman eventually reunite Marta with her lover.

In the previous examples, the music's meaning lies in its network of reference and power of suggestion. But in other Bergman scenes, music functions as an alert, triggering action. It may still reinforce narrative themes and suggest meaning, but it also serves a more immediate purpose by drawing attention to the sound's cause and the character's reaction. Such musical alerts function as plot points, affecting the film's chain of events. In *Summer Interlude*, Marie revisits her old summer home many years after the tragic death of her first boyfriend. As she walks through what she thinks is an empty house, the sound of a piano—playing Chopin's Revolutionary Etude—startles her from reverie. She tiptoes through the house, past the grand piano, and finds her creepy 'uncle' Erland in the kitchen. In this scene, music initially functions as an alert. Startled, Marie realizes that she is not alone and understands, through a combination of sound and location, that Erland must be playing the piano. In Barthesian terms, the raw sound of Erland's playing 'reveals danger' and disturbs the 'territorial system' both of the empty house and of Marie's psychological space.[8] Years before, this man spent his summer drunkenly playing Chopin while lusting after Marie and taking advantage of her after the death of her boyfriend. Now he literally crashes back into her life in a flurry of sound. Bergman could have used more conventional methods to signal Erland's presence, a slammed door or creaking footsteps. Instead, we hear a piece laden with extra-musical reference. Still predatory and menacing, Erland uses Chopin's Etude to destroy Marie's sense of security. Here, Barthes's and Chion's first two categories combine— the alert becomes part of the narrative meaning.

Another such instance occurs in *Wild Strawberries* (1957), when Isak experiences interactive daydreams about crucial moments in his life. In one, he walks near his family's summer home and spies

---

8 Barthes, 'Listening', pp. 247–248.

his childhood sweetheart Sara playing the opening of Bach's D-sharp minor Fugue, while Isak's brother kisses her neck. While this scene contains live music-making and thus belongs to the trope of on-screen performance, we might also consider it a scene of listening. The music alerts Isak to a human presence; he then searches for its source and discovers his beloved with another man. From a narrative point of view, he understands that he is excluded from the happiness within. But this exclusion is suggested by the music *before* Isak looks through the window. While Bergman's camera stays focused on Isak, we hear the fugue subject, the countersubject, and then a slight pause as Sara starts again, repeating the opening bars before stopping completely. This particular fugue has three voices, but we only ever hear two. Listening tells Isak what seeing confirms: there is no need for a third subject or room for a third person in this closed domestic duet.

Media of transmission

Bergman's musical selections often imbue scenes with narrative-specific significance. Equally relevant, though, are his choices of musical medium, which reinforce narrative features and indicate the dynamic between listeners and their circumstances. In a few cases, Bergman directs our attention towards the listener rather than the performer, particularly in scenes of live jazz. Other scenes that privilege listener over music-maker include those with organ-grinders and accordion players on street corners, setting mood and providing context. Less anonymous than bands and buskers are performers in scenes of musical alerts, like Erland and Sara, whose identities give resonance to these scenes. Yet Bergman's cinematic and psychological focus remains on the listeners, on Marie and Isak, his main characters.

All musical experiences are mediated: between every listener and piece of music are a performer and an instrument that translate notation into sound waves. Some musical experiences are further mediated through technology. Bergman's films straddle the decades of the gramophone, radio, and tape deck; even his last two films, made during the CD era, feature only radio and gramophone. I will briefly sketch two ways that scenes of technologically mediated listening mirror the larger social and cultural codes embedded in sound media: the gramophone and the radio. The gramophone recording is a self-contained entity, mass-produced for individual purchase and consumption. Modern technology offers ways to project these recordings over loudspeakers, but in Bergman's films such music is rarely amplified beyond the capacity of simple playback devices. If, as Jacques Attali says, music articulates a space, then gramophone music articulates a closed space, a private living-room or public bar, the machine emitting a circuit of fixed sound to a small audience.[9] Characters who listen to gramophones are often similarly closed off, disconnected from the world and from one another. The bar in *It Rains on Our Love* is one example, with its drunken old men isolated and unable to interact. Wagner's Bridal Chorus not only suggests lost dreams of love; it also articulates the enclosed space of the bar and the fixity of these men's ruined lives.

If gramophones express a disconnect from outside reality, radio provides the opposite, its wireless transmission capable of covering vast spaces, linking solitary individuals in a shared listening experience. Bergman's use of the radio captures a tension between its intended communication and its unintended side-effect of increased isolation. The medium offers his characters a way of interacting with the world on their own terms, keeping it at arm's length and maintaining control. But the radio's presence nevertheless offers them a way out of their claustrophobic existences. By turning the radio on, they alleviate their alienation; by turning it off, they shut out the world. It is telling that soon after Marta in *Waiting Women* switches on the radio, the telephone rings. As a technologically mediated 'direct connection between human[s],'[10] the telephone offers Marta a channel of contact with her ex-lover. Just as she chooses to answer the phone, opening a line of communication, she also chooses to hang up, to remain alone.

In *Autumn Sonata* (1978), set in a remote corner of Norway, Viktor is listening to Schumann's *Aufschwung* on the radio when his wife Eva enters the room with an invitation she has written to her estranged mother. To enable Eva to read the letter aloud, Viktor turns off the radio, symbolically returning the household to its isolated state. In a film confined to the rooms of a house, mother and daughter later attack each other in typical Bergman dialogues that take a Kafkaesque approach to communication, as 'two

---

9 Jacques Attali, 'Noise: The Political Economy of Music' (1985), in Jonathan Sterne (ed.), *The Sound Studies Reader* (London and New York: Routledge, 2012), p. 32.
10 Catherine Covert, quoted in John Durham Peters, 'The Telephonic Uncanny and the Problem of Communication' (1999), *The Sound Studies Reader*, p. 365.

monologues that may never connect'.[11] Similarly, when Marianne listens to Brahms's first String Quartet on the radio in *Saraband* (2003) while visiting the remote country home of her ex-husband, she is interrupted by his distraught granddaughter, Karin. Switching off the radio, Marianne severs her connection to the outside world and is plunged into the world of Karin and her abusive father. In these two films, Marianne and Viktor stand just outside the films' conflicts, lending support. Their interest in the radio represents their ability to listen in general: their capacity and willingness to understand other people. Conversely, Marianne's bitter ex-husband, Johan, prefers the gramophone, listening to Bruckner's Ninth Symphony at ear-splitting decibels, hunched over the machine, his back turned towards the closed door of his study, the Scherzo so loud that he cannot hear Karin knocking, just as his festering rage shuts out any meaningful connection with others.

Listening to Bach

With one exception, I have thus far omitted a privileged space in Bergman's films—the act of listening to Bach, which Carlo Cenciarelli considers a significant trope.[12] While I agree that listening to Bach is indeed significant, I suggest that it gains this importance not from being a trope but from being the opposite: a rare occurrence. Indeed, the concentrated act of listening to Bach outside of a performance context occurs just twice, in *The Silence* (1963) and in *Persona* (1966), and only in *The Silence* is it narratively significant.

Sisters Ester and Anna, together with Anna's young son Johan, are stuck in a foreign city on the brink of war; they do not speak the language and cannot communicate with anyone there. The tense surroundings mirror the hostility between the sisters. In the evening, Ester turns on the radio to hear the 25th variation of Bach's Goldberg Variations. The door between their rooms is open—while Ester, foregrounded, contemplates Bach, Anna and Johan speak softly in the adjoining room. With a knock at the door, the maître d' enters and joins Ester in reverie, both listening intently, while a pietà-like tableau of Johan sitting on his mother's lap shines through the

---

11 Covert, *The Sound Studies Reader*, p. 367.
12 Carlo Cenciarelli, '"What Never Was Has Ended": Bach, Bergman, and the Beatles in Christopher Münch's *The Hours and Times*', *Music & Letters* 94:1 (2013), 119–137.

doorway. It turns out that the words 'music' and 'Bach' in this foreign language are the same as in Swedish. Here, for the first and only time, are recognition and communication, linguistically in the words 'music' and 'Bach' and emotionally through the sound of music. In a minor key, the 25th variation is the longest, most dissonant variation of the set and shares many similarities with the Crucifixion movements in Bach's masses. It is a painful and ruminative lament, full of suffering: this selection suggests that only in shared experiences—like this listening—are we are able to hear and understand the suffering of others.

Music as performance

When critics discuss 'music' in Bergman's films, they generally refer to his use of Bach, which can sometimes portray a '"presence," "contact," and even "grace",'[13] as Maaret Koskinen writes. Language like this is frequently used in interpretations of music as a communicative and healing tool, and such readings are reinforced by Bergman's own view of music as a 'gift', a 'comfort and consolation [...] as if someone spoke to me.'[14] Yet, as we have seen, his selection of pre-existing music is by no means limited to Bach, or to classical composers more generally. Nor is it always listened to. There is a difference between music *heard* and music *performed*. While music listened to may sometimes indicate communication and solace, music as action taps into a darker tradition based in a ritual of exposure, humiliation, and exile. As portrayed in Bergman's films, the artist-character is a figure torn by the conflict between self-expression and self-preservation; to this model belong musicians as well as other types of artists: actors, circus performers, dancers. Unlike disembodied music drifting from speakers, the musical act requires the presence of a person making music, an exposure of self to the judgement of the audience.

At the centre of such a ritual lies a shaman—the artist, in this case—who acts on behalf of a community and embodies what Paisley

---

13 Koskinen, 'Out of the Past', in Camilla Larsson (ed.), *The Ingmar Bergman Notebook: Talks and Seminars, Bergman Week 2006*, translated by Bernard Vowles (Gothenburg: Filmkonst, 2006), p. 26.
14 Ingmar Bergman, 'Sommarprat med Ingmar Bergman', by Marie Nyreröd, broadcast on 18 July 2004 (Sveriges Radio, *Sommar*, i, P1), http://sverigesradio.se/sida/artikel.aspx?programid=2071&artikel=631451 (accessed 31 July 2012), translated by Jonathan Cowell.

Livingston calls a 'mythical difference'.[15] The artist is a liminal figure, venerated as an intermediary between the real world and the beyond and castigated for his difference, unmasked, and violently expelled so that society can reinstate order and unity. The masks of difference define the artist's identity and produce belief in the artist's so-called magic. But the dissonance between mask and identity is where Bergman begins his examination of the artist's condition. If masking produces belief, unmasking shatters the illusion, an exposure and humiliation that is one of Bergman's most identifiable themes. His performing artists often live on the fringe of society, excluded from its norms. Some, like Jof and Mia in *The Seventh Seal*, travel from town to town, presenting their primitive theatre of masks and folk music to village crowds. Others, like the blind pianist Bengt in *Music in Darkness*, exist within society but live as outsiders. Bergman's cinematic treatment of musicians over five decades is remarkably consistent; his musicians are often mediocre, at best talented but unproven and at worst outright failures. In addition to dealing with a critical public, these artists also grapple with their own inadequacy.

Public performance usually takes place in urban settings: concert halls for classical music; cabarets, dance halls, or outdoor stages for popular entertainment. The spectacle of public performance relies on masks, literal or metaphorical, to maintain an illusion of the artist's role—literal like a folk-mask or metaphorical like the persona of a star violinist. Private performance generally takes place within the domestic circle, usually in a house set rurally. Among family and friends, the performer wears no literal mask; rather, his mask is metaphorical, a domestic role, such as Eva's role as devoted daughter in *Autumn Sonata*.

Music in Darkness, Bergman's first film with a musical protagonist, follows the misfortunes of Bengt, who has lost his vision, his military career, his fiancée, and the chance to study at Stockholm's Academy of Music. Destitute, he applies for a poorly paid piano job in a restaurant, auditioning for the owner. In this scene, Bengt's blindness cannot be hidden. Nor can he hide his cultured upbringing or his expectation that his talent and art will be valued. He begins with a Chopin Ballade, followed by a Chopin waltz, some high-octane dance music, and finally the schmaltzy 'Grandfather's Waltz'. If the

---

15 Paisley Livingston, *Ingmar Bergman and the Rituals of Art* (Ithaca, NY: Cornell University Press, 1982), p. 50.

musical canon is a pole, Bengt slides all the way down. The owner has no use for high art and regards Bengt as a commodity of cheap entertainment, whose only function is to play on command. Throughout the film, Bengt's talent is both exploited and denied, his dignity questioned. Yet Bergman gives the audience a happy ending: Bengt is saved by love. Ingrid, the girl he eventually marries, becomes a reflection of the film's audience; we are not encouraged to support Bengt's humiliation or collude with the society that excludes him but rather led from pity to empathy and admiration.

To Joy considers the personal and professional failures of an orchestral violinist who aspires to stardom. The friendly domestic fellowship Stig experiences while playing chamber music in his home is brutally juxtaposed with the film's climactic scene—his disastrous debut in the Mendelssohn Violin Concerto. Exposed as mediocre and humiliated in the concert hall, he retreats from all professional and personal responsibility. Portrayed as morally ambiguous, with a temper, a drinking problem, and ambition far beyond his talent, Stig suffers a fall amplified by his egotism. Eventually he is reconciled with his wife, but their happiness does not last: she and their daughter are blown up by a paraffin stove. After his musical and marital failures, Stig is faced with death and finds catharsis not through drink or stardom but through music during a rehearsal of Beethoven's Ninth Symphony. Playing in unison with others, away from the critical eyes of the public, he discovers what Bergman calls 'a joy beyond pain and boundless despair ... beyond all understanding'.[16] He experiences the desire that cellist Karin voices in *Saraband*, made 53 years later: 'I want to be surrounded by a sea of sound, in that enormous common effort. Not sit on a podium alone and exposed. I want to belong.'[17]

By the late 1970s, Bergman had experienced his own public humiliation, a tax scandal that made international headlines and triggered a nervous breakdown. Claiming he would never again work in Sweden, he spent eight years exiled in Germany. During this period he made *Autumn Sonata*, which takes place almost entirely inside the house

---

16 Bergman via Sönderby, the conductor in *To Joy*, who describes Beethoven's Ninth Symphony as such.
17 As translated and quoted in Per F. Broman, 'Music, Sound, and Silence in the Films of Ingmar Bergman', in James Wierzbicki (ed.), *Music, Sound and Filmmakers: Sonic Style in Cinema* (New York and London: Routledge, 2012), p. 28.

of frumpy, meek Eva whose estranged mother Charlotte, a concert pianist, has come to visit. The film unfolds from a double performance of Chopin's A minor Prelude. It is played first by Eva, an amateur who expects, but does not receive, her mother's artistic approval. Dissatisfied, Eva demands her mother's interpretation. Charlotte acquiesces and then translates her verbal explanation of the piece into what Lawrence Kramer calls a 'cool, controlled performance that matches her description: calm, clear, and harsh'.[18] The emotional vulnerability in this double-performance scene shows Bergman at his most sophisticated. Relying on close-ups of faces rather than hands, he emphasizes the listener over the performer—the listener as an active part of the performance dynamic. When Eva performs, we focus on Charlotte. When Charlotte performs, we focus on Eva.

Both audio versions of this prelude were recorded by Bergman's fourth wife, the concert pianist Käbi Laretei. Interestingly, the two actresses claimed they could not hear any difference between the versions.[19] By having the same professional perform both versions and trying to pass them off as two distinct, incompatible interpretations, played by two characters with vastly different experience and training (in addition to their own unique physiology), Bergman, I believe, indulged a construction too far. The credibility of this scene thus hinges on Bergman's images, not his sounds. Focusing on Eva's and Charlotte's faces and registering their every expression, Bergman controls viewer response by offering what film theorist Béla Balázs asserts: a character's facial expressions 'give an interpretation of the sounds and convey it to us',[20] so that we do not have to arrive at our own. This visual interpretation is compounded by Charlotte's spoken explanation—Bergman sets us up to hear in sounds what he has already told us in words.

Music as presence

Bergman does not limit his portrayals of musicians to fictitious characters. References to and stories of composers from Bach to

---

18 Lawrence Kramer, 'Music, Metaphor and Metaphysics', *The Musical Times* 145:1888 (Autumn 2004), 5.
19 Alexis Luko, *Sonatas, Screams, and Silence: Music and Sound in the Films of Ingmar Bergman* (London and New York: Routledge, 2016), p. 82.
20 Thomas F. Cohen, *Playing to the Camera: Musicians and Musical Performances in Documentary Cinema* (London and New York: Wallflower Press, 2012), p. 75.

Stravinsky are scattered throughout his writings and appear in his films. He often treats these figures as semi-fictionalized characters in a universal drama, attributing to them intentions and actions based only loosely on historical evidence. Particularly in Bach, Mozart, Schubert, and Chopin, he found inspiration and consolation, identifying with their struggles to such an extent that the narrative thrust of several films is underscored by their music and biography. Lacking the instrumental skill to interpret his favourite works musically, Bergman interpreted these works through cinema.

Bergman's tour de force in this regard is *In the Presence of a Clown* (1997), which weaves together a fictional tale about his real-life Uncle Carl with the music and mythology of Schubert. Typical of Bergman's mid-to-late work, the film has no soundtrack score; the only music we hear is by Schubert. Carl is an unsuccessful inventor who, while committed to a psychiatric ward, has happened upon his next great invention: a 'Live Talking Picture' that will replace silent film. He decides that his first film will be about Schubert's love affair with young countess Mizzi, who drowned herself in the Danube in 1908 (that Schubert died in 1828 is, for Carl, irrelevant). Carl himself will star as Schubert. During his hospital stay, Carl is also stalked by a clown of death. On release from the hospital, he makes his movie and takes it on tour through the Swedish hinterlands with his piano-playing fiancée Pauline.

Carl is obsessed with Schubert's life and death and haunted by the first eight bars of 'Der Leiermann', the last song of *Winterreise*, written in 1827, a year before the composer's death. As the film unfolds, the lines between reality and fantasy begin to blur, both in terms of Carl's fiction about Schubert and his own sanity. Carl begins to have auditory and visual hallucinations that no one else can hear or see—except for us, the meta-audience. Presented neither diegetically nor non-diegetically, his auditory hallucinations of 'Der Leiermann', accompanied by the presence of the clown, thus fill a subjective space that is represented by the concept of metadiegesis: 'that which is imagined or perhaps hallucinated by a character and which helps to construct the character's own reality.'[21]

Bergman noted that he feared for his life while writing this film, a fear he channelled into the character of his Uncle Carl. Like Carl, who recreated Schubert in an attempt to find comfort and solidarity

---

21 Julie Brown, 'Carnival of Souls and the Organs of Horror', in Neil Lerner (ed.), *Music in the Horror Film: Listening to Fear* (New York and London: Routledge, 2010), p. 19.

in another, Bergman recreates his uncle's past and features his own mother as a character. He endows Carl with the same mania for film and theatre that he himself often professed. Likewise, Carl's passion for music mirrors Bergman's. Carl even states that music can alleviate pain, soothe illness, dispel horrors, and connect with others who similarly suffer, offering hope and giving joy. Yet these words also recall Bergman's often-referenced belief of human connection as the purpose of art, calling into question who is actually speaking here. In a film that blurs identities as well as the line between fantasy and reality, Schubert's music transgresses boundaries of space and time, connecting fictional characters with historical figures, imagined scenarios with documented events. The presence of Schubert serves as a metaphor for artistic companionship and offers imaginative connections between sympathetic artists and audiences, connections that transcend time and space—and even death.

* * *

According to Bergman, music provided emotional and artistic stability throughout his life. To quell his fears and anxieties, he turned to music, and he often allowed his cinematic characters to do the same. Whether as a private moment or as a communicative gesture, music in Bergman's films sometimes functions as it did in his life, as a moment of grace. In other cases, it serves to enhance, underscore, comment on, or contradict the images and narrative; later, in his mature films, it stands for people, places, ideas, metaphors, and memories.

This chapter has sought to uncover some of the frameworks underlying Bergman's use of classical music by differentiating the three ways that it appears on screen—as sound, as act, and as presence—and tracing these patterns through key scenes from 1946 to 2003. As we have seen, music can be part of both the narrative fabric and the technical apparatus, functioning as structure, sound, action, content, and even a kind of philosophy; it enables us as spectators to share musical experiences and histories with on-screen characters. Bergman's films offer complex and often sophisticated insights into how cinema can explore musical interaction, opening an interpretative space within the thematic and emotional content of each film and suggesting cultural and historical implications that reach into the real world.

9
Film-musical moments in Ingmar Bergman's films

Ann-Kristin Wallengren

In recent years, scholars have been devoting more and more discussion to Ingmar Bergman's films from a musical perspective.[1] Considering that Bergman himself had a heartfelt love of music, and worked meticulously on the soundtrack of his films where music was often foregrounded as an essential conveyor of narrative information and the character's emotions, it is odd that his film music has not come in for greater attention before. Of course, this circumstance has also been noticed by other writers. Per F. Broman and Alexis Luko—the latter being the scholar who, along with Charlotte Renaud, has written the most extensive and penetrating study on Bergman's music in films and his relation to music in general—want to sort Bergman into the category of *acoustic auteur*, a label reserved for a very few notable directors such as

---

1 Charlotte Renaud, 'La Citation Musicale dans les Films d'Ingmar Bergman' (unpublished doctoral dissertation, Université de la Sorbonne Paris III-Censier, 2007); Per F. Broman, 'Music, Sound, and Silence in the Films of Ingmar Bergman', in James Wierzbicki (ed.), *Music, Sound and Filmmakers: Sonic Style in Cinema* (New York and London: Routledge, 2012), pp. 15–32; Marcos Azzam Gómez, 'Die Musik in Ingmar Bergmans Filmen', *Kieler Beiträge zur Filmmusikforschung* 11 (2014), 278–301 (originally the PhD dissertation, 'La Música en el Cine de Ingmar Bergman', Universidad de Salamanca, 2013); Alexis Luko, *Sonatas, Screams, and Silence: Music and Sound in the Films of Ingmar Bergman* (New York: Routledge, 2015); Estela Ibáñez-García, 'Music in Play on Screen: Performing Reality in Ingmar Bergman's Late Work' (PhD dissertation, University of Hong Kong, 2016), available at: http://hub.hku.hk/handle/10722/226761 (accessed 17 March 2021); Anyssa Neumann, 'Sound, Act, Presence: Pre-Existing Music in the Films of Ingmar Bergman' (PhD dissertation, King's College London, 2017), available at: https://kclpure.kcl.ac.uk/portal/en/theses/sound-act-presence(ce171b0f-b7e7-4ce2-9c49-2d465062aaba).html (accessed 17 March 2021). Several articles have been published, too, some of which I will refer to later.

Stanley Kubrick, Quentin Tarantino, and Alain Resnais.[2] The term is paraphrased from what film-music scholar Claudia Gorbman, in her article 'Auteur Music', calls *mélomane*—a word for 'music-loving directors [who] treat music not as something to farm out to the composer or even to the music supervisor, but rather as a key thematic element and a marker of authorial style'.[3] According to Gorbman's definition, Bergman may certainly join this group of acoustic auteurs, perhaps even as one of its most prominent members. The majority of writings about Bergman and music scrutinize his use of classical music, often in connection with an analysis of those of his films that depict musicians, musical performances, and music listening. Another point of interest in scholarly writings has been how musical form has inspired the organization of a film, for example the use of music to structure films into acts that correspond to specific musical forms. Hence, the music as such constitutes the point of departure for the analyses, and the music per se is in focus.

This chapter explores Bergman's use of music from a different perspective, an angle based on the notion of a *musical moment*, a theoretical and analytical concept that has gained much attention in film-music research in recent years.[4] Many writers use the term as an equivalent to musical numbers; thus, the definition of musical moments generally refers to performances of different kinds, most often song performances. Consequently, even if musical moments in this sense are supposed to appear in various genres, they are mostly found in musicals. Watching Bergman's films over the years, I have noticed a special kind of music drama that supersedes a narrative which is usually filled with dialogue. These particular scenes appear to be very prominent and significant. In Bergman's films, there are a number of instances of musical moments, even if they are not performances of songs; autonomous music and

---

2 Luko, *Sonatas, Screams, and Silence*; Broman, 'Music, Sound, and Silence'.
3 Claudia Gorbman, 'Auteur Music', in Daniel Goldmark, Lawrence Kramer, and Richard Leppert (eds), *Beyond the Soundtrack: Representing Music in Cinema* (Berkeley, CA: University of California Press, 2007), pp. 149–163.
4 Ian Conrich and Estella Tincknell (eds), *Film's Musical Moments* (Edinburgh: Edinburgh University Press, 2006); Amy Herzog, *Dreams of Difference, Songs of the Same: The Musical Moment in Film* (Minneapolis, MN: University of Minnesota Press, 2010); Phil Powrie, *Music in Contemporary French Cinema: The Crystal Song* (Cham: Palgrave Macmillan, 2017). Musical moments were the theme of the conference 'When the Music Takes Over: Musical Numbers in Film and Television' organized by the University of Salzburg, 8–10 March 2018.

Film-musical moments in Bergman's films

pre-composed music are foregrounded and, in a sense, 'take over' the scene. These kinds of musical moments are not in the focus of this chapter, though. Instead, I wish to highlight scenes that make striking use of film music, that is, music originally composed for films and music that is almost impossible to listen to as autonomous music. These film-musical moments in Bergman's films, albeit few in number, differ remarkably from the narrative and the aesthetics of the films, being distinctively transformative in that they constitute a turning point or a narrative kernel. Hence, my use of the 'musical moment' concept expands that notion from a musical number (in the form of a song) to the integrated use of film music in a transformative moment.

Scholars and writers specializing in studies of Bergman have often stated that he turned to music when verbal communication was not sufficient. An analysis based on such an assumption seems to diminish the use of music to a kind of substitution, a way of putting something else in the place of 'better' stylistic devices. On the contrary, I think that Bergman very consciously chose other modes and other styles to emphasize the scenes that are the narrative kernels in the films, moments that play a decisive role in the telling of the story. The choice to construct these critical narrative scenes as film-musical moments—moments which sometimes refer to other periods in the history of film—opens another perspective on Bergman as a cinematic narrator. A director emerges who is an acoustic auteur of considerable significance.

Musical moments: a theoretical background

Musical moments in films can be defined as moments when the music takes over, in the sense that music is no longer a mere accompaniment but foregrounded, frequently influencing editing and camera movements. Over the years, discussions on musical moments have often been based on such a definition.[5] In the growing number of studies on musical moments, scholars have in most cases derived their examples from musicals or diegetic songs in non-musical films. Sometimes this reflects an ideological standpoint, as when film scholar Phil Powrie wants to upgrade the status of

---

5 Conrich and Tincknell, *Film's Musical Moments*; Herzog, *Dreams of Difference*; Powrie, *Music in Contemporary French Cinema*.

diegetic songs as compared to symphonic non-diegetic scores.[6] He refers to James Buhler, who writes:

> Orchestral music is where the art is. The result has been a heavy interpretive bias towards the symphonic non-diegetic score [...] If non-diegetic music is opposed to diegetic, then symphonic sound is opposed to the dance band, 'classical' music to popular (jazz, or later, rock), and, therefore, high art and aesthetic values are set against low art and commercial value.[7]

Powrie wants to show that the *crystal song*—Powrie's theoretical concept of a musical moment, based on Gilles Deleuze's crystal image—can emanate from newly composed as well as pre-composed music and may, in that way, 'contest [the] cultural value' of the customary focus on classical music.[8]

Phil Powrie and Amy Herzog are the two scholars who have recently published the most extensive theories and analyses of musical moments. Media historian Amy Herzog, in her book *Dreams of Difference, Songs of the Same: The Musical Moment in Film*, focuses on the relations between the cinema and popular music; and in this endeavour, she bases her theories chiefly on Deleuze's works. Though Herzog does not want to establish 'firm distinctions between musical and nonmusical films', her work nonetheless relies more on musicals than on non-musical films.[9] The reason for this, she argues, is that musical moments 'are often most fully realized within the musical genre'.[10] In short, she defines a musical moment as a moment that 'occurs when music, typically a popular song, inverts the image-sound hierarchy to occupy the dominant position in a filmic work'.[11] It can be problematic to speak about 'dominant position' and 'hierarchy' regarding the relationship between image and sound in film, and I will return to this discussion. The formal characteristics of musical moments in Herzog's terminology are that these moments break the narrative chain and disrupt the time–space flow. Song becomes dominant in the sense that it is foregrounded, structuring and

---

6 Powrie, *Music in Contemporary French Cinema*.
7 James Buhler, 'Analytical and Interpretive Approaches to Film Music (II): Analysing Interactions of Music and Film', in K. J. Donnelly (ed.), *Film Music: Critical Approaches* (Edinburgh: Edinburgh University Press, 2001), pp. 39–62 (p. 43).
8 Powrie, *Music in Contemporary French Cinema*, p. 21.
9 Herzog, *Dreams of Difference*, pp. 2–3.
10 Herzog, *Dreams of Difference*, p. 3.
11 Herzog, *Dreams of Difference*, p. 7.

influencing time, space, and movements in the picture. Besides these formal characteristics, Herzog points to some of the moments' most essential functions, which are that they often incline towards 'aesthetic and thematic excessiveness' and thus evoke strong affective responses in the audience.[12]

The affective power of musical moments is central to Phil Powrie's discussion in his monograph *Music in Contemporary French Cinema: The Crystal Song* in which he, like Herzog, draws on the writings of Gilles Deleuze as a starting point for discussion. However, as mentioned, Powrie mostly confines himself to Deleuze's notion of the crystal image, which he transforms into the crystal song. The use of a crystal song indicates a turning point in a film (a narrative function not emphasized by Herzog); it is momentous and has high affective power, and, like a crystal, it is both confluent and centripetal, not least in the sense that different temporalities come together.[13] In general, Powrie agrees with Herzog's definition of musical moments with the exception of a couple of decisive points. First, the musical moments that Powrie defines as crystal songs appear more often in non-musical films than in musicals:

> Indeed, [the difference made by a crystal song] may well be more apparent if it does not form part of a sequence of musical numbers in a film that could be defined as a film musical, precisely because it functions as a critical fragment rather than as a part of a series closely tied to the narrative.[14]

Secondly, Powrie does not agree that we need to reveal the significance of a musical moment, as opposed to Herzog's project of laying bare the musical moment's potential as a 'disruptive force' in its tension between 'repetition' and 'difference'.[15] The moment's significance is, according to Powrie, distinct, not least because of its strong affective expression. While Herzog also discusses affective responses to musical moments, to Powrie this is a paramount characteristic which intensely and simultaneously influences both the protagonist and the audience:

> It is the moment in a film when the coming together of sound and image transports us, if only momentarily, to a different place, a place of difference, when the music takes flight, and we fly with it, whether

---

12 Herzog, *Dreams of Difference*, p. 8.
13 Powrie, *Music in Contemporary French Cinema*, pp. 2, 166–173.
14 Powrie, *Music in Contemporary French Cinema*, p. 11.
15 Herzog, *Dreams of Difference*, pp. 7, 37–38.

that flight is soaring emotion or searing insight, or, more properly for what I call the 'crystal song', a combination of the two.[16] However, Powrie asserts that for this to happen, the crystal song needs to be performed and accordingly be diegetic. The diegetic performance is central to all writers on musical moments and to the theorists to whom Powrie refers as predecessors in relation to his theory on crystal songs. Powrie claims that in performed musical numbers, and preferably with pre-composed music, the emotions experienced by both performer and audience are immediate, present, and authentic because of the embodiment by the performer.[17] In research on musical moments, these moments hence cover everything from musical numbers with minor significance for the narrative to moments in the form of crystal songs—moments which are very important to the story and emotionally intense, and which have a powerful impact on the audience. Sometimes the use of the concept is confusing as to which measure the moment serves to highlight.

When I first encountered Powrie's discussions on the crystal song, they shed much light on how I had experienced scenes in Bergman's films which struck me as extraordinary music-dramatic narratives. However, when delving more deeply into both the theory and Powrie's productive and informative analyses, it became clear that it is not possible to transfer the concept in its entirety to Bergman's transformative film-musical moments. The usefulness of the notion of crystal song is limited primarily because these moments are not songs, and they do not merge different time layers in the sense that Deleuze intended with his conception.[18] Nevertheless, other characteristics of the crystal song are valid and helpful. In Bergman's films we find musical moments of a more traditional kind: musical moments using pre-composed diegetic music and, finally, the transformative film-musical moments that are exceptional also from the perspective of film-music aesthetics in general.

Different kinds of musical moments in Bergman's films

Generally speaking, Ingmar Bergman used music in his films in ways that were highly diverse, ranging from traditional underscoring to

---

16 Powrie, *Music in Contemporary French Cinema*, p. 3.
17 I do not agree with Powrie's assertion that performance is a prerequisite for such a powerful affect to occur.
18 Gilles Deleuze, *Cinéma. 2, L'Image-Temps* (Paris: Minuit, 1985).

symphonic concert scenes, popular music, and modernistic film music. At the beginning of his career, music in Bergman's films functioned in ways that adhered to the film-musical aesthetics of the time, using extra-diegetic original music underlining actions and emotions. Even if it could be obtrusive, as in Erland von Koch's scores for wind instruments, it worked according to the functions of 'unheard' narrative film music: to bridge scenes, set emotions and moods, signal crucial actions, and follow and underline the dramaturgy.[19] As was customary for many filmmakers in Sweden during the 1940s and the 1950s, Bergman turned to Swedish art composers of the time: Erland von Koch and Erik Nordgren (as mentioned earlier) and, later on, Karl-Birger Blomdahl, Dag Wirén, and Lars-Johan Werle. Erland von Koch composed music for Bergman's first six films; he was succeeded by Erik Nordgren, who wrote music for as many as twelve of Bergman's films and was involved in two more. Even in Bergman's early films, however, the music was not subordinated in the way we usually associate with the phrase *underscoring*, or classic narrative film music. Even though the music mainly supported the flow of narrative action, it was seldom heard in combination with dialogue, nor was it audible for very long. This discrimination—this generally eclectic use of music in Bergman's films—makes scenes with music stand out as something extraordinary in the narrative.[20] There are, of course, exceptions; but it seems reasonable to claim that for the essential scenes in his films—regardless of whether those films are regarded as being of major or minor importance—he chose music as a narrative and stylistic device. Hence, all scenes with music are protrusive in some way; they are apprehended as a different level in the narrative and provide a heightened sense of experience. In this sense, music in Bergman's films often constitutes some kind of musical moment.

There are two main categories of straightforward musical moments in Bergman's films. Firstly, his films contain ample musical *numbers*, that is to say, scenes with performed orchestral numbers and songs. Musical numbers mostly occur in films that involve musicians as protagonists, for instance *To Joy* (*Till glädje*, 1950); but they also

---

19 Claudia Gorbman, *Unheard Melodies: Narrative Film Music* (Bloomington, IN: Indiana University Press, 1987).
20 This is also noted by Egil Törnqvist, 'The Role of Music in Ingmar Bergman's Films', *North-West Passage: Yearly Review of the Centre for Northern Performing Arts Studies* 8 (2011), 25–46.

appear in films not explicitly about musicians, for example in *The Devil's Eye* (*Djävulens öga*, 1960). Films containing musical numbers of varying lengths are, for instance: *Music in Darkness* (*Musik i mörker*, 1948), *Thirst* (*Törst*, 1949), *To Joy*, *Smiles of a Summer Night* (*Sommarnattens leende*, 1955), *The Seventh Seal* (*Det sjunde inseglet*, 1957), *Wild Strawberries* (*Smultronstället*, 1957), *The Magician* (*Ansiktet*, 1958), *The Silence* (*Tystnaden*, 1963), *The Devil's Eye*, *All These Women* (*För att inte tala om alla dessa kvinnor*, 1964), *Hour of the Wolf* (*Vargtimmen*, 1968), *The Serpent's Egg* (*Ormens ägg*, 1977), *In the Presence of a Clown* (*Larmar och gör sig till*, 1997), and *Saraband* (2003). The musical numbers in these films are not narratively decisive or strongly affectional, although such numbers do appear in some of these films. The musical numbers range from symphonic music, as in *To Joy*, to simple guitar songs such as Naima Wifstrand's in *The Magician* (with a text by Bergman himself), and performances of popular music as in *The Serpent's Egg*. The film *All These Women* is on the verge of being a musical because of the abundance of musical numbers. *The Devil's Eye* also contains many numbers that structure the film into narrative parts and may almost be said to 'play the film'.

Secondly, we find musical numbers that also constitute musical moments—that is to say, the moments are of narrative importance, and they have some characteristics in common with the moments defined by Herzog and Powrie in that the music 'takes over' in these scenes. These musical moments are characterized by narrative, have dramaturgic and dramatic importance, and are constituted by scenes with performances which mostly use pre-composed, diegetic music, where the music can be said to be the primary conveyor of narrative information and to influence editing, camera movements, and movements in the images to varying degrees. Examples in this category are *To Joy*, *Autumn Sonata* (*Höstsonaten*, 1978), and *Saraband*. All three films are about musicians, and they have musical titles. A brief analytical example from *To Joy* is supplied below (analyses of the use of music in the other two films are more frequent).

The dominance of music is apparent in some scenes in *To Joy*. In this film, which has much diegetic music in the soundtrack, we find at least two scenes that are typical examples of musical moments where the images adapt to the music: the pictures are edited to fit the rhythm of the film. The longest and most prominent one is when the character Stig, a violinist, is offered the chance to play the solo violin in Mendelssohn-Bartholdy's concerto for violin and orchestra, and he sees an opportunity for a breakthrough as a solo violinist.

His wife Marta nervously follows Stig's unsuccessful performance from behind the stage, and this scene marks a narrative point after which everything develops in a tragic direction. The other moment is the last scene in the film, which pictures a rehearsal of Beethoven's 'An die Freude' at which a broken Stig takes up his position in the orchestra for the first time after a long pause and the death of his wife. During the rehearsal, his young son comes to listen; and the sight of him, and the influence of the music, make Stig look towards the future with new hope.

Besides these instances of musical moments, we find something of a similar nature in three films containing scenes of dreams or hallucinations: in *Music in Darkness* (*Musik i mörker*, 1948), *Prison* (*Fängelse*, 1949), and *Waiting Women* (*Kvinnors väntan*, 1952). The dreams and hallucinations in these three films are musical moments of a kind; they comply with most of the characteristics of musical moments, even though the music is non-diegetic and does not consist in performances. However, Bergman's way of designing dreams and hallucinations in his films is quite common in cinematic narratives, indeed almost a cliché: with no dialogue, only non-diegetic music and sometimes sound, and with a different visual style from that of the surrounding scenes. Hence, these scenes do not stand out as narratively exceptional in terms of film-musical aesthetics. Conversely, more prominent sequences form the third category of musical moments in Bergman's films, that of transformative film-musical moments.

Transformative film-musical moments

Bergman's transformative film-musical moments are rare; but when they do appear, they are forceful and momentous. Here we find *Sawdust and Tinsel* (1953), *Persona* (1966), and *Hour of the Wolf* (1968). The transformative moments in these films are of an unusual length, between five minutes and over eight minutes. The length, altered style, and different mode of expression in these moments make them more like plays within the play, or rather films within the film.[21] What, then, constitutes a transformative

---

21 About Bergman's use of play within the play, see Maaret Koskinen, *Spel och speglingar: en studie i Ingmar Bergmans filmiska estetik* ('Plays and Mirrors: The Cinematic Aesthetics of Ingmar Bergman', PhD dissertation, Stockholms universitet, 1993).

film-musical moment, and what significance do such moments have in Bergman's oeuvre?

The transformative film-musical moments in Bergman's films are extraordinary experiences that have the potential to evoke strong responses and affects in the audience owing to the music and the actions in combination—moments which depict and express the characters' emotions. The transformation operates on two levels: the scenes are transformative for the lives of the characters in the film, as well as transformative for the narrative and the unfolding of the film. Besides, they offer a profound aesthetic experience, even if they are not seen in their narrative context. In Powrie's terminology, crystal songs are a combination of 'soaring emotion' and 'searing insight', a description that effectively captures Bergman's film-musical moments.[22] Scenes with intense affective power, they are, like crystal songs, momentous, forming crucial narrative moments in the film. The distinctive features of transformative film-musical moments are:

- the scene is of unusual length
- the scene is of decisive narrative importance, a turning point, and transforms the narrative and the characters
- the scene is powerfully charged with emotions
- the scene is in contrast to other scenes, fenced in with scenes in which the music is silent
- the music is originally composed for the film
- the music is non-diegetic
- the music blends with the images; there is no apparent hierarchy between the pictures and the music
- no other sound nor dialogue is heard; there is total diegetic silence. If there is any diegetic sound, it is used as a sound effect or even as a musical element
- the scenes recall silent-film aesthetics.

The scenes in the three films containing transformative film-musical moments constitute what may be labelled film-music dramas, which are narrated in a very different way compared to other parts of the film. A look at *Sawdust and Tinsel* provides an example. The scene in question is the extended flashback at the beginning of the film.[23] The episode shows the humiliation to which both the man, Frost,

---

22 Powrie, *Music in Contemporary French Cinema*, p. 3.
23 For a close analysis of the sequence, see Luko, *Sonatas, Screams, and Silence*. See also Ann-Kristin Wallengren, 'När själen spiller över', *Filmhäftet* 122 (2002), 20–25.

and the woman, Alma, are subjected, and humiliation is a recurrent motif throughout the film. The music from the opening scene is heard again later in the film when a man feels degraded because of his wife's infidelity. Bergman himself said that he regarded the film as being cast in a musical form, as a theme with variations 'both erotic and humiliating in ever-changing combinations'.[24] Karl-Birger Blomdahl wrote the music; and in a television interview called 'Ingmar Bergman och musiken' ('Ingmar Bergman and music'), Bergman tells us about how the music was composed.[25] Blomdahl and Bergman agreed that during the part where Frost carries Alma along the stony path away from the beach, only kettledrums should be heard. Apart from that, Bergman did not know how the music would sound. In an interview, he claims he met Blomdahl outside Oscarsteatern (Oscar's Theatre) in Stockholm and was invited to listen to the new composition. Blomdahl warned Bergman that the score did not include any strings, which was quite unusual at the time; but when Bergman listened to the music, played by forty wind players, he was astounded. It was a 'fabulous experience', he said. Bergman has expressed a particular delight in this sequence, which was inspired by one of his dreams.[26]

The sequence is more than eight minutes long, and the music is in a modernist style and closely connected to the images. The kettledrums in the second part of the sequence, as well as the rhythmical irregular circus-like music which creates a mocking, aggravating, and provocative expression in the first part, are very powerful in combination with the pictures. The emotive expression in the scene, as well as the presumably affectional response in the audience, is forceful and compelling. A few diegetic sounds are heard, as well as some short pieces of dialogue. However, we do not perceive the sounds at the same time as we see them being produced, which recalls the way in which sound effects in silent film could often mistakenly be performed asynchronously. This practice contributes to the disturbing experience that the actions are 'out of synch'. Like in a silent movie, we see people talk, scream, and laugh, but we do not hear their voices. The cinematography further reinforces the

---

24 Renaud, 'An Unrequited Love of Music', www.ingmarbergman.se/en/universe/unrequited-love-music (accessed 3 May 2017).
25 'Ingmar Bergman och musiken', an interview by Camilla Lundberg (SVT 2001).
26 *Bergman om Bergman*, interviews by Stig Björkman, Torsten Manns, and Jonas Sima (Stockholm: Norstedt, 1970).

silent-film aesthetic with a dissolved black-and-white colour scheme, and close-ups of faces articulating words that we cannot hear. In this scene, as well as in *Hour of the Wolf*, the actions narrated are so shocking to the persons involved, so life-changing and stigmatizing, that it seems as though they, and the film, can no longer endure sounds from reality. The shock and the psychological breakdown seem to make the characters involved switch off their normal perceptions, and they hear only the sounds that are central to their experience, that is to say, almost no sounds at all. This wipe-out of most of the realistically motivated or diegetic sounds in situations depicting the deepest of feelings could be compared to the breakdown of the filmstrip in *Persona* in the middle of the film. In her dissertation about Ingmar Bergman, Maaret Koskinen writes that at this moment in *Persona*, the film can no longer bear to show these horrible actions; the celluloid is burnt out as a result of pure panic.[27] Just as the film itself disintegrates in *Persona*, it might be possible to suggest that for the people involved, sound from reality collapses in the films containing transformative film-musical moments. The music takes over, opening another space and affording access to another dimension.[28]

The prologue in *Persona* is a transformative film-musical moment, although the musical parts are rather scant. Once more, the music is highly modernistic; Lars Johan Werle composed the scores of both *Persona* and *Hour of the Wolf*. The characters' life-transforming experiences, as narrated in the specific sequences, are as striking in these two films as the corresponding experiences in *Sawdust and Tinsel*. Especially in *Persona*, the sound composition intertwines music and natural sounds, hence blurring the border between them.[29] In the prologue, we hear dripping water, footsteps, hammer blows, the ringing of a telephone, and, as in so many of Bergman's films, church bells, as well as other sounds. Most sounds are out of synch—that is to say, we do not see the origin of the sounds; we

---

27 Koskinen, 'Spel och speglingar'.
28 Astrid Söderbergh Widding, 'Gränsbilder: det dolda rummet hos Tarkovskij' ('Liminary Images: Off Screen Space in Tarkovsky', PhD dissertation, Stockholms universitet, 1992), discusses how sound and music can afford access to other spaces in the films of Tarkovsky.
29 For a close analysis of the sound, music, and images in the prologue in *Persona*, see Michel Chion, *Audio-Vision: Sound on Screen*, translated by Claudia Gorbman (New York: Columbia University Press, 1994), pp. 198–213. The scene has been analysed by several scholars throughout the years.

only hear them. When picture and sound are suddenly in total synchronization, as when a nail is hammered through a hand, it becomes a shocking experience.

The diegetic silence, or the absence of speech, produces a kind of ghostlike atmosphere which supports the flashback narration in both *Sawdust and Tinsel* and *Hour of the Wolf*—the characters are in some way spirits from the past, disturbingly present in someone's memory and still, like ghosts, influencing life as it progresses. Eliminating dialogue and diegetic sound is a strategy that can be used to emphasize that something crucial is happening. Danijela Kulezic-Wilson writes about the practice of wiping out all diegetic noises, which could depict a state of shock.[30] She claims that *Ran* (Akira Kurosawa) from 1985 is regarded as the first film to use this strategy. Still, as we see, Bergman explored this device much earlier, and Jan Troell employed it in 1972 in his film *The New Land* (*Nybyggarna*).

In all categorization, there will be examples that do not easily fit into groups. Bergman's oeuvre offers numerous variations and idiosyncratic peculiarities, a fact which makes any organizational effort challenging. However, here I would like to mention two scenes that lie between musical moments and transformative film-musical moments. They are scenes from *Through a Glass Darkly* (*Såsom i en spegel*, 1961) and *Cries and Whispers* (*Viskningar och rop*, 1972). The music in these scenes is not made up of diegetic performances. In essence, it is non-diegetic music as in film-musical moments; but the music is pre-composed, and, most importantly, the images adapt to the music in editing and movements. The scene in *Through a Glass Darkly* is very short, about one minute; it is the scene on the boat with Minus and Karin towards the end of the film. The editing adapts to the music, 'Suite no 2 part 4 for cello' by Bach, but the form of the scene has points in common with a tableau. In *Cries and Whispers*, the relevant scene signifies a turning point.[31] The three sisters in this film are trying to deal with their life stories as one of them is dying of cancer. In this musical moment, with 'Suite no 5 for cello' by Bach, two of the sisters finally reach a moment of peace after years of hostility; it is a moment of reconciliation and intimacy. They are talking to each other; but as in the three

---

30 Danijela Kulezic-Wilson, 'The Music of Film Silence', *Music and the Moving Image* 2:3 (2009), 1–10.
31 For a close analysis of *Cries and Whispers*, see Renaud, 'An Unrequited Love of Music'.

films discussed above, there is diegetic silence, and we do not hear their words. The Bach suite for cello, together with the editing and camera work that is rhythmically coordinated with the music, and their expressive faces tell us all we need to know.

One of the crucial features of transformative film-musical moments is that they refer to silent-film aesthetics. The moving pictures and the music coalesce as stylistic equals, and this creates intensely affective film-musical magic. As I argued long ago in my dissertation, silent films could be music-dramatic works of art where music not only illustrated what happened on the screen, it also constituted an integral part of the narrative and thus contributed substantially to the film's story, mood, and meaning.[32] In film-musical moments, other characteristics evoke a silent-film aesthetic; it takes more than just the elimination of diegetic sounds and the addition of music to produce a narrative style that refers to this historical film style. In Bergman's oeuvre, we find examples of this silent-film aesthetic even in scenes that are without music. One instance is the famous scene at the beginning of *Wild Strawberries* in which Isak Borg, played by silent-film director Victor Sjöström, dreams about his death. Nonetheless, music and film without any dialogue or natural sounds create a highly poetic film language, and it seems that Bergman, as a lover of music as well as of silent film, perceived the potential of this cinematic form. In the film for television *In the Presence of a Clown*, Bergman referred explicitly to silent-film music in the scene where the piano accompaniment played in the room becomes an almost diegetic piano piece in the film. The silent movie was by necessity paired with non-diegetic music, even though the music could have a diegetic function and be understood as music in the diegetic universe. However, the profound aesthetic experience that Bergman's transformative film-musical moments offer is an experience that depends on a very close collaboration between film and music in which music works together with—rather than dominating—the visual narrative in a 'film-music-dramatic' way.

Music in film as film music

The film-musical moments in Bergman's films consist of specially composed music which we apprehend as non-diegetical. There is

---

32 Ann-Kristin Wallengren, *En afton på Röda kvarn: svensk stumfilm som musikdrama* ('An Evening at Röda Kvarn: Swedish Silent Film as Music Drama') (Lund: Lund University Press, 1998).

mostly total diegetic silence, and the music and images merge; neither is more prominent than the other. There is no inverted hierarchy, as in Herzog's definition and examples. In the musical moments in his movies, which present performances of pre-composed diegetic music, we are apt to find that the images adapt to the music in editing and movements. There are other differences between these kinds of musical moments and film-musical moments; but an essential distinction is that in the latter case, the music was originally composed. Pre-created compositions were written to be played as autonomous pieces of music and are thus differently constructed.

Original film music, on the other hand, is usually arranged in a more ruptured, fragmented, and non-melodic way (although there is of course a lot of original film music that is melodic, for example John Williams' compositions). In the transformative film-musical moments in Bergman's films, the music is of a modernist, atonal form which does not feature melody. The original compositions here are not intended to be listened to autonomously; they were written directly for the sequences. The music in *Sawdust and Tinsel* is one example; it seems impossible to listen to it without the images. Conversely, without the music, the narrative and affective power of the images would be substantially weakened. In transformative film-musical moments, pictures and music hence seem to blend; they are equivalent parameters, depending on each other without either dominating the other. I regard this as a film-musical relationship; the music becomes more of a cinematic element, a stylistic parameter like other cinematic parameters. Here Bergman adopts a narrative style that is a form of film-musical drama. If Powrie's mission was to raise the status of songs in movies, my purpose would be to re-establish the status of non-diegetic, original music that is not intended to be listened to autonomously. From a musical point of view, non-diegetic film music that underscores a film is often regarded as a minor musical form, partly because of the formal characteristics that make the music impossible or at least difficult to enjoy as autonomous unless it is reworked for listening. Non-diegetic orchestral music is frequently considered as something inferior and subordinate to the images, not as music proper, along the lines expressed in a comment in Herzog's monograph: 'Film scores exist as fragmented themes that can be woven in and out of the soundtrack as the image dictates.'[33]

---

33 Herzog, *Dreams of Difference*, p. 6.

In my opinion, discussions about hierarchy and dominance involve highly complicated matters, and it seems too facile to assert that non-diegetic film music is always supposed to be dominated or dictated by the images (to be fair, Herzog does point out that there are exceptions, such as Bernard Herrmann's scores for Hitchcock's films). In the transformative film-musical moments in Bergman's films, film and music work together in an artistic unity. The complete integration of music and images seems to transfer the music from a place outside the diegesis so that it becomes part of the diegesis instead. The distinction between diegetic and non-diegetic music can be problematic; and in instances of the kind outlined above, non-diegetic music is vital when it comes to 'producing the diegesis itself'.[34] Transformative film-musical moments, as they occur in the films discussed in this chapter, are comparatively rare in film history. Paul Schrader has, however, observed that Robert Bresson and Ozu Yasujirō both use 'a blast of music' to signal 'decisive moments' before 'decisive actions'.[35] As was mentioned at the beginning of the chapter, it is astonishing that so little research has been done on Ingmar Bergman's music in films, and that this topic has surfaced quite late in comparison to all other research on Bergman's films. Music plays a central role in many of his films, and the integration of music into the narrative and diegesis is remarkable. He was without any doubt an acoustic auteur; indeed, I would claim that he was a film-music-dramatic auteur with an unusually distinctive position and stature. Bergman often asserted that music and film were the same, and he was able to make the two art forms merge into a superbly realized wholeness.

---

34 Anahid Kassabian, *Hearing Film: Tracking Identifications in Contemporary Hollywood Film Music* (New York: Routledge, 2001), p. 42. The theory on diegetic and non-diegetic music has been problematized by several authors, for example Robyn J. Stilwell, 'The Fantastical Gap between Diegetic and Nondiegetic', in Daniel Goldmark, Lawrence Kramer, and Richard Leppert (eds), *Beyond the Soundtrack: Representing Music in Cinema* (Berkeley, CA: University of California Press, 2007), pp. 184–205; Jeff Smith, 'Bridging the Gap: Reconsidering the Border between Diegetic and Nondiegetic Music', *Music and the Moving Image* 2:1 (2009), 1–25; Ben Winters, 'The Nondiegetic Fallacy: Film, Music, and Narrative Space', *Music & Letters* 91:2 (2010), 224–244.

35 Paul Schrader, *Transcendental Style in Film: Ozu, Bresson & Dreyer* (New York: Da Capo, 1988).

10
Where does music come from? Musical meaning and musical discourse in Ingmar Bergman's films

Per F. Broman

Swedish readers of this book will be familiar with Ingmar Bergman's last major radio appearance, the 18 July 2004 edition of the talk show *Sommar* ['Summer'].[1] For those to whom this broadcast institution is unknown, *Sommar* is a long-running Swedish radio show that is aired during the summer months and features a daily almost two-hour broadcast, in which notable Swedes muse over life and select music for the programme, as typically more than half of the programme consists of music.

Bergman's talk was almost exclusively devoted to his musical interests. He began his programme by saying that there was 'much song and music in [his] parents' home'. He went on to tell a story of his first musical memory, from when he was four or five years old: a friend of his parents, an amateur violinist, performed a minor-mode Swedish folk melody from Dalecarlia. Bergman recalled having started to cry uncontrollably, as he for some reason experienced an imaginary image of his mother, lying dead in a coffin. Even at the age of eighty-six, he could recall the feeling of intense grief that this music had triggered. He recounted other anecdotes about the music in his films and about his childhood musical encounters—including how he became a Wagnerian at the tender age of thirteen. But most strikingly, for me at least, he spoke about some practical considerations during the production of *The Magic Flute* (1975), which he described as the most joyous and conflict-free production of his life thanks to everyone being immersed in Mozart's music.

Later in the programme, he provided a narrative for the beginning of the slow movement of Beethoven's fourth piano concerto. For him, there was a clearly outlined story to be told: there are two

---

[1] Available at: https://sverigesradio.se/sida/avsnitt/373942?programid=2071 (accessed 17 March 2021).

characters, the angry orchestra and the comforting piano which tries to temper the outbursts, perhaps like Johan and Alma in *Hour of the Wolf* (1968). Music for Bergman caused a wide range of reactions, from purely magical emotional ones to more or less clear-cut narrative ones; and in the case of *The Magic Flute* it served as a kind of drug, affecting the entire cast and crew.

At the end of the programme, Bergman confessed his belief that music is given to humanity as a gift—a divine one, although he did not mention God—to supply hints of realities beyond the one we can perceive, and he asked the audience two questions that had been on his mind: 'Who said that Bach plays four-hand with the Lord?' and 'Where does music come from; why are we the only animals on earth that create music?' He received close to two hundred responses, letters, postcards, and emails following the broadcast, all of which are available in the Bergman Archives.

Several listeners responded to his first question: the quotation came from Swedish poet Arne Törnqvist's (1932–2003) poem 'Till min himmelske fader' ('To my heavenly father'), from the posthumously published collection *I veka livet* (roughly translated as 'In the most vulnerable spot').[2] Written shortly before Törnqvist's death, this quasi-religious poem reminded Bergman of ungraspable aspects of music and his lifelong admiration for J.S. Bach. Bach was, of course, one of the composers that occurred most frequently in his films; and he made it a habit to try to attend a performance of the St Matthew Passion every year. His films present several striking scenes featuring Bach's music, including the two sisters' embrace in *Cries and Whispers* (1972) and the recurring theme in *Through a Glass Darkly* (1961), in both cases a Sarabande from a cello suite.

Törnqvist's poem reads (the English translation is mine):

Fader Bach	Father Bach
Du lämnar oss inte	You're not leaving us
Det är vi som lämnar dig	It is we who are leaving you
När allt detta är över	When all this is over
sitter du kvar på orgelbänken	you remain seated on the organ bench
Inte som om ingenting hänt	Not as if nothing has happened
ty fugan kommer hädanefter	since the fugue will henceforth
att sakna både kräftgång och spegelvändning	lack both retrograde and inversion

---

[2] Arne Törnqvist, *I veka livet* (Stockholm: Natur och Kultur, 2003). It is certainly possible that someone else had made the comparison, as one response letter suggested that Bergman himself had used it prior to Törnqvist's poem.

| Men du fortsätter | But you continue |
| att spela fyrhändigt med Gud | to play four-hand with God |

Bergman's first question suggested that it was the four-hand performance with God that mattered to him—that Bach's music is divine—but the cryptic lines 'the fugue will henceforth / lack both retrograde and inversion' are intriguing too, in that they suggest that the technical aspects of composition are not of overwhelming importance. When performed, music is something of a divine mode of communication, free from technical aspects. But preoccupation with technique would occur prior to performance, as Bergman pointed out on several occasions, through hard, repetitive work, which he came to experience during his marriage to pianist Käbi Laretei. Herein lies the magic: at some point the labour will turn into music. As he expressed it in *Laterna magica* after having witnessed a lesson with Laretei and her teacher: 'A phrase plucked apart into its constituent parts, practised with pedantic fingering for hours, then reassembled when the time was ripe.'[3] This distinction between labour and magic is, as we will see, prevalent in his films.

The second, more philosophical question received numerous answers, both profound and speculative, ranging from sophisticated evolutionary biological and philosophical theories to homespun speculations and statements to the effect that the human species is not alone in music-making; birdsong constitutes music, too. While none of these responses could have led Bergman to any definite answers in his quest for a final understanding of music, his radio appearance illustrates just how passionate he was about music towards the end of his life, and how integral it was to his entire existential worldview. But we do not need to take Bergman at his word on this issue, as it is evident in his output; several films explicitly deal with it. Bergman placed musical experiences in a metaphysical domain; as he stated several times, these experiences go straight to the emotional centre of perception (the Swedish noun he used was *känslocentrum*). That domain was closely integrated with religion and religious experiences, an experiential sphere that seems to have stayed with him, despite his drift toward agnosticism.

Although Bergman reminisced about a folk melody he heard as a child, in his films musical experiences are exclusively associated with Western art music from the eighteenth and nineteenth centuries.

---

3 Ingmar Bergman, *The Magic Lantern*, translated from Swedish by Joan Tate (New York and London: Penguin, 1988), p. 224.

When he briefly talked about jazz in *Sommar*, it was as a means to connect with girls in the course of a summer vacation during his teens. And when popular idioms were featured in his films, it was in the context of courtship, as Erik Hedling demonstrated so well in his aptly entitled article, 'Music, Lust and Modernity: Jazz in the Films of Ingmar Bergman'.[4]

Descriptions of music in Bergman's dialogues or monologues are often stunning. Bergman provides many musical details in his dialogues, so specific—one could almost say too specific—that only serious music aficionados would spot the references: Charlotte makes the point that the fingerings in the edition used of the Chopin prelude in *Autumn Sonata* (1978) were suggested by Alfred Cortot, the legendary Swiss pianist and pedagogue;[5] the instrument in *Saraband* is a Cahman organ from 1728, which happens to be the year when the best preserved Cahman organ, the one in Lövstabruk in Uppland, was built. While the organ in this scene is obviously not that instrument—it is an organ façade built on the set—the recording on the soundtrack was indeed made on the Lövstabruk organ.[6]

The obsession with musical detail in the performances on camera is striking, as is illustrated by the behind-the-camera and rehearsal films from *In the Presence of a Clown* (1997) and *Autumn Sonata*.[7] In the former film, the hands we see on the keyboard are those of real pianists, Käbi Laretei and Hanns Rodell; and in the latter, the actors Ingrid Bergman and Liv Ullmann received extensive training from Laretei on how to convincingly pretend to play the piano.

When I started working on music in Bergman's films almost twenty years ago, the dominant trends in film-music scholarship included narrative theories as outlined by Claudia Gorbman[8] and others, and very little attention had been given to Bergman's use of music. At that time, film-music scholarship focused primarily on traditional

---

4 Erik Hedling, 'Music, Lust and Modernity: Jazz in the Films of Ingmar Bergman', *Soundtrack* 4:2 (2011), 89–99.
5 Cortot is also mentioned in *To Joy*, as Sönderby states, 'On Thursday, Cortot arrives. There will be music.'
6 'Torvald Torén – Six Trio Sonatas', Opus 3 Records, CD 8802.
7 'I sällskap med en clown', SVT 7 November 1997. Some of the *Autumn Sonata* behind-the-scenes footage was included on the DVD made to accompany the work by Birgitta Steene, Paul Duncan, and Bengt Wanselius, *The Ingmar Bergman Archives* (Cologne: Taschen, 2008).
8 Claudia Gorbman, *Unheard Melodies: Narrative Film Music* (Bloomington, IN: Indiana University Press, 1987).

Hollywood scores by composers such as Bernard Herrmann and John Williams. I did not find that kind of research particularly helpful for Bergman's films, as so many of them used pre-composed music. Instead, the key for me became archival materials and an interview I conducted with Käbi Laretei in 2007. Since then, a number of high-quality studies have appeared, including recent ones by Alexis Luko, Anyssa Neumann, and Estela Ibáñez-García.[9] Because most of Bergman's music is pre-composed, at least in films following his international breakthrough in the late 1950s, the focus in these new studies is not on the dramatic narrative but on meaning and emotion, and on intertextual relations within Bergman's oeuvre. I have explored my fair share of such topics; but recently, I began to pay attention to dialogues about music in the films, as they provide insights into Bergman's aesthetics and create a context for how the music should be perceived. This chapter focuses on a few instances of interaction between music and dialogue in Bergman's films that resonate with his comments in the *Sommar* radio programme. These examples will illustrate different points: how music is able to communicate where words cannot (*To Joy*, 1950); how words and music interact (*Autumn Sonata*); how words about music can provide powerful metaphors and communicate central parts of the narrative (*Saraband*, 2003); and how music and the creation of music can provide the entire structure of a narrative (*In the Presence of a Clown*).

Failing words and words telling it all

Towards the end of *To Joy*, the story about two orchestral violinists named Stig and Marta, the character played by Victor Sjöström, conductor Sönderby, describes his interpretive goals in front of the orchestra, beginning a bit crudely: 'The cellos and basses should sing like hell, you see, this is about joy!' But as he continues to define this joy—'it's not about laughter, or a joy that states "I'm happy"; it's a joy so immense that it resides beyond pain and despair and beyond all comprehension'—his words falter, 'I can't explain it better.'

---

9 Anyssa Neumann, 'Sound, Act, Presence: Pre-Existing Music in the Films of Ingmar Bergman' (PhD dissertation, King's College London, 2016); Alexis Luko, *Sonatas, Screams, and Silence: Music and Sound in the Films of Ingmar Bergman* (New York: Routledge, 2015); Estela Ibáñez-García, 'Music in Play on Screen: Performing Reality in Ingmar Bergman's Late Work' (PhD dissertation, University of Hong Kong, 2016).

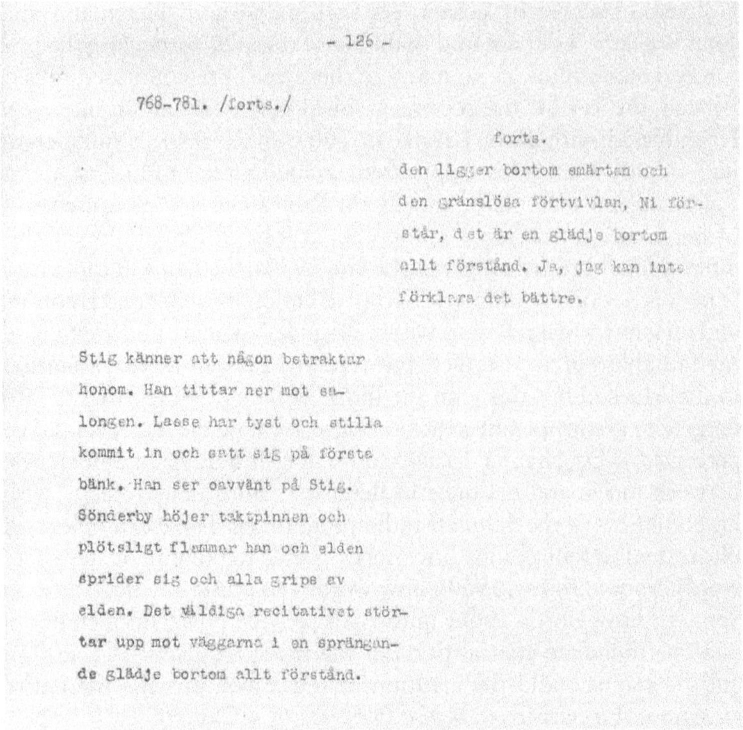

```
                                    - 126 -

     768-781. /forts./
                                          forts.
                                 den ligger bortom smärtan och
                                 den gränslösa förtvivlan, Ni för-
                                 står, det är en glädje bortom
                                 allt förstånd. Ja, jag kan inte
                                 förklara det bättre.

     Stig känner att någon betraktar
     honom. Han tittar ner mot sa-
     longen. Lasse har tyst och stilla
     kommit in och satt sig på första
     bänk. Han ser oavvänt på Stig.
     Sönderby höjer taktpinnen och
     plötsligt flammar han och elden
     sprider sig och alla gripes av
     elden. Det våldiga recitativet stör-
     tar upp mot väggarna i en sprängan-
     de glädje bortom allt förstånd.
```

Figure 10.1 Bergman's director's script (document B:010). Used with permission from The Ingmar Bergman Archives

Sönderby's deliberately awkward interpretive directions in combination with Marta's death certainly increase the impact of the music that follows, an excerpt from the last movement of Beethoven's Ninth Symphony that runs for five minutes and is accompanied by images including flashbacks and a crane panning over the orchestra and the concert hall which Stig's son Lasse, who just lost his mother, enters. The limits of language are illustrated in the script, as this long scene is only described in a few sentences.

> Stig senses someone watching him. He looks down the hall. Lasse has quietly entered and sits in the first row. He looks steadily at Stig. Sönderby raises the baton and suddenly he flames and the fire spreads and all are caught up by the fire. The huge recitative bursts up against the walls of a shattering joy beyond all comprehension.[10]

---

10 Translation mine.

Where does music come from?

It is the music that carries the scene, and together with the images it makes this ending incredibly moving (although Bergman described the ending as Beethoven's Ninth being 'shamelessly exploited').[11] One of the longest and most significant discussions of music in a Bergman film, concert pianist Charlotte's (Ingrid Bergman) monologue at the piano in *Autumn Sonata*, has been well analysed by Luko, Neumann, and others; I wrote about it in 2012.[12] Additional nuances have recently appeared in discussions of this rather complex scene, however, so it is worth revisiting. The scene is significant in that it provides a different—in fact, for Bergman, unique—application of words to music: music is described neither from a metaphysical perspective nor in terms of its emotional impact, but from the perspective of a pianist whose stern and rational views of the profession and of motherhood guide her reading of Chopin's aesthetics. The music should not sound beautiful or create associations to different worlds. Instead, she says:

> Chopin was strong in emotion, but not emotional. There is a gulf between emotion and sentimentality. The prelude you're playing speaks about restrained pain, not reverie. You have to be calm, clear, and harsh. Look at these first few bars—it hurts, but he doesn't show it. Then a brief relief. But it disappears almost immediately. Then the torment is the same—neither more nor less. The control is complete all the time.[13]

The second half of her monologue is particularly striking. It goes against more than a century of discourse on Chopin, in which Chopin has been considered weak and feminine:

> Chopin was proud, sarcastic, intense, anguished, and very masculine. So he wasn't a sentimental old woman. This second prelude has to be played in a way that's almost ugly. It must never become ingratiating. It should sound wrong, arduously or successfully struggled through. Like this.[14]

---

11 Steene, Duncan, and Wanselius, *The Ingmar Bergman Archives*, p. 72.
12 Per F. Broman, 'Silence and Sound in Ingmar Bergman's Films', in James Wierzbicki (ed.), *Music, Sound and Filmmakers: Sonic Style in Cinema* (New York: Routledge, 2012), pp. 15–21.
13 Translation mine.
14 In the Swedish original: 'Chopin var känslostark, Eva, men inte känslosam. Det är en avgrund mellan känsla och sentimentalitet. Preludiet du spelar talar om återhållen smärta. Inte om drömmerier. Du måste vara lugn, klar och kärv. Se här bara de första takterna. Det gör ont. Men han visar det inte. Sen en kort lindring. Men den förflyktigas nästan genast. Sen är plågan densamma,

In her interpretation of Charlotte's version on the soundtrack, Käbi Laretei dwells on the dissonances, making the left-hand accompaniment as important as the right hand. Her version of Eva's performance has a nervous touch to it, slowing down significantly at some phrase endings in an attempt at tempo rubato—or simply because it is too hard—along with attempts at an independent, free-flowing right hand. Eva's tempo is significantly faster (beginning with tempo 66 bpm versus Charlotte's 46 bpm, although both fluctuate a great deal throughout the piece). Eva's interpretation coincides with the historical understanding of Chopin, which was established in the nineteenth century. Jim Samson summarizes some of the descriptions:

> [They] extended beyond a generous allocation of poetic programmes to incorporate a more generalised category of the poetic, suggestive of the sublime and mysterious, distilled to intimacy. Such ideas were already current in his lifetime. 'To listen to Chopin is to read a strophe of Lamartine'; 'Chopin is a poet, and above all a tender one'; 'he is an elegiac, profound and dreamy poet of tones'; 'it is poetry in translation, but a superior translation made through sounds alone'. The implication of a hidden emotional content is clear, and it became part of the ambience of the music for later generations. It is no coincidence that one of the first French biographies was published under the title *Chopin ou le poète*.[15]

Neumann was not completely satisfied with either version: 'the melodic lines are equally clunky in both, the pedalling identical'.[16] Luko pointed out that the two versions were not distinguishable either to Ingrid Bergman or to Liv Ullmann.[17] Prompting Neumann to argue that '[i]f Laretei intended to make obvious the discrepancies in interpretation for musicians and non-musicians alike, as she claimed, she nevertheless failed to convince the two women at the heart of this scene—the women instructed to act out these

---

inte större och inte mindre. Behärskningen är hela tiden total. Chopin var stolt, sarkastisk, hetsig, plågad, och mycket manlig. Han var alltså ingen känslosam kärring. Det här andra preludiet måste spelas nästan fult. Det får aldrig bli insmickrande. Det ska låta fel. Mödosamt eller framgångsrikt genomkämpat. Så här alltså. Här ska du se.'

15 Jim Samson, 'Chopin Reception: Theory, History, Analysis', in John Rink and Jim Samson (eds), *Chopin Studies 2* (Cambridge: Cambridge University Press. 1994), p. 3.
16 Neumann, 'Sound, Act, Presence', p. 153.
17 Luko, *Sonatas, Screams, and Silence*, p. 82.

differences.'[18] And as Neumann further pointed out at the Bergman meeting in Lund in 2018, there is a lack of realism in Eva's performance: not a single note is wrong although the left hand is quite demanding, including some awkward wide-reaching stretches whose difficulty even Neumann as a professional pianist could experience.

These are all valid comments, but they call for further contextualization. During my interview with her, Laretei told me that neither Charlotte's nor Eva's version was really her own, but that she was very impressed with Bergman's script for the scene; she felt it was an antithesis of the predominant over-romanticization of Chopin by performers in Scandinavia, and she specifically mentioned Danish-Finnish pianist France Ellegaard. But even if neither version was really hers, it appears Laretei only exaggerated her own version in two different directions: On the album 'Käbi Laretei – Close-Ups – The Film Music of Ingmar Bergman'[19] that she released in 1978, the starting tempo is closer to Eva's (60 bpm), while the overall phrasing is more similar to Charlotte's; including less use of tempo rubato than Eva's, it approaches the severe mode of Charlotte's interpretation. Although, if I may speculate, it is also certainly possible that Laretei's own version was influenced by Charlotte's and Eva's, or rather by Bergman's script.

A small detail provides further insights into Laretei's interpretation. In both Bergman's director's script and the published script, after the two performances Eva's husband Viktor states: 'I think Charlotte's analysis is seductive, but Eva's interpretation is more urgent ['angelägen'].'[20] Surprisingly enough, Viktor's comment does not appear in the film. Nevertheless, Viktor is right on the money for Charlotte, as she states—'laughing happily'—'Viktor, for that remark you deserve a kiss!' and he replies 'with embarrassment', 'I only say what I think.'

Why was this brief exchange not included in the film? It certainly explains the two interpretations for those who were not able to hear the differences: the analytical versus the heartfelt. And why exactly is Charlotte happy and why would Viktor deserve a kiss? Was it because he confirmed her intentions, or because he noticed the technical deficiencies in Eva's version? The close-up of Charlotte during Eva's

---

18 Neumann, 'Sound, Act, Presence', p. 153.
19 Proprius – PROP 7829.
20 *Autumn Sonata: A Film by Ingmar Bergman*, translated by Alan Blair (New York: Pantheon Books, 1978), p. 28.

Figure 10.2 Chopin, daguerreotype by Louis-Auguste Bisson (*c*. 1849)

performance certainly suggests that she is getting emotional, and the omitted exchange would perhaps have become too obvious and might have detracted from the effect of the camerawork on Ingrid Bergman's acting. The terminology, the difference between Charlotte's *analysis* and Eva's *interpretation* is also telling, perhaps making it rather too obvious that it is a matter of words versus music—intellect versus emotion, and according to Viktor emotion won. Either way, this short exchange illustrates that Bergman's intentions are carried out in Laretei's two versions, but in a subtle way.

In the *Sommar* radio programme, Bergman mentioned an image of Chopin; it was not a youthful romanticized painting, but a severe, sad, and non-romantic daguerreotype probably taken in the year of his death. Commenting on it, Bergman focused on Chopin's hands, which he described as 'large like meat mallets' as they lay clumsily idle on his lap and seemed not to fit with the rest of his emaciated body. Bergman had been aware of this image for decades as he mentioned it in 1962, years before *Autumn Sonata*.[21] To Bergman, this portrait appears to have illustrated the point that Chopin may not have been the delicate musician he is often perceived to have been. While I do not completely agree with Bergman's meat-mallet interpretation of Chopin's hands, his reading certainly provides clues to Charlotte's monologue and performance, suggesting that the interpretation should be firmly anchored in historicist intentions combined with a spark of myth to make the narrative shine and move the audience. This image could certainly have triggered his monologue: an image turned into a model for a contrarian mode of playing Chopin, creating one of the most thoroughly analysed scenes of classical musical performance in cinematic history.

The music, the image, and the words associated with Charlotte carry the scene. The lack of significant realism in Eva's performance is not a problem: the film is a work of art, not a real-life piano lesson. Had there been any obvious errors in Eva's performance, as one would have expected from an amateur—wrong notes in particular—the scene would have been unbearable to watch. The prime example of such a scene is Stig's miserable performance of the Mendelssohn concerto in *To Joy*; it is not only the image of Stig's humiliation on stage and in the aftermath to this that makes the scene incredibly painful but the sound, as he makes an elementary error in the slow movement and plays partly out of tune and the performance has to be interrupted. The director's script is quite different from the finished film. There the problem is not Stig's performing badly, but his bad luck: the G string goes flat (as Bergman states, by 'almost a semitone') during the cadenza in the first movement. He tries to compensate, but has to stop and tune. Stig completes the concerto without enthusiasm, but nevertheless receives 'friendly

---

21 Ingmar Bergman, 'Min Pianist', *VeckoRevyn* 11 (1962), 16–18, 79.

but not overwhelming' applause.[22] In the finished film, by contrast, the scene is much crueller; the performance is a complete fiasco because of Stig's incompetence.

The unusual—and, according to Ingrid Bergman, unappealing—Chopin piece in *Autumn Sonata* can now be heard twice, in addition to the beginning when Charlotte is talking between the phrases. The audience is given an opportunity to listen carefully and compare the versions; and the perfection, the non-realism, resulting from excellent studio recordings makes a compelling contrast with *To Joy*. To make a blunt comparison: The 'duelling banjos' scene from *Deliverance* (1972) is not realistic either, yet it stands as one of the most iconic musical performances in cinematic history.

The remainder of the present chapter will be devoted to Bergman's last two films, as they both summarize his musical aesthetics and constitute a worthy finale: *In the Presence of a Clown*, an intertextual masterpiece that has long delighted Bergman fans, and *Saraband*.

Musical metaphors in *Saraband* and *In the Presence of a Clown*

In *Saraband*, the Sarabande from Bach's Fifth Cello Suite runs like a leitmotif throughout the film and serves as a point of reference for the incestuous relationship between father Henrik (Börje Ahlstedt) and daughter Karin (Julia Dufvenius), both cellists. Other diegetic classical music is plentiful, and certain works are specifically associated with different characters: the scherzo movement of Bruckner's Ninth Symphony is used for the authoritarian and severe Johan (Erland Josephson), Henrik's father; the slow movement of Brahms's String Quartet in A-minor represents the mellow Marianne (Liv Ullmann), and Bach's Trio Sonata in E-flat major is performed in the church by Henrik. The music often appears unexpectedly, but it still provides an element of coherence throughout the film. The discourse about music is also important, illustrating how Bergman used words about music as decisive metaphors in his dialogues.

A few minutes into their first meeting with Marianne, Karin initiates the story of the violent altercation with her father through her frustrations over the performance instruction for a piece she is working on. It is the piece Henrik wants her to perform at the conservatory entrance auditions, the fourth movement of Hindemith's

---

22 The director's script, document B:010, pp. 53–54, in the Bergman Archives.

Figure 10.3 Hindemith Sonata for Cello op. 25 No. 3

Sonata for Cello op. 25 No. 3, 'Lebhafte Viertel (ohne jeden Ausdruck und stets Pianissimo)'. Bergman must have realized how contradictory and frustrating this instruction would be for a cellist, or any musician for that matter: 'Lively quarter-note tempo, without any expression and pianissimo throughout' is a performance mode that no musician would ever apply to this kind of piece unless explicitly stated. In such a piece, the dynamics would be varied; and certainly there would be an attempt at expression, through building phrases dynamically and emphasizing certain notes and motifs. Karin's recollection of this piece initiates an outcry and a cry for help about her father as a teacher and human being, culminating in a flashback to the quarrel between father and daughter after which she runs away from the house. Although this piece is never heard on the soundtrack, it is used as a substitute outlet for her anger towards her sexually and emotionally disturbed and abusive father.

Saraband also includes a take on the musician's role as a mirror of society when Bergman makes Karin say, 'I do not believe in myself as a soloist. I want to become an orchestral musician. I want to be surrounded by a sea of sound, in that enormous common effort. Not sit on a podium alone and exposed. I want to live a regular life. I want to belong.' Her articulated stance is in stark contrast to Henrik's expectations of her.

This aspect would have been further emphasized in a scene that was never realized. According to the executive producer Pia Ehrnwall and assistant director Torbjörn Ehrnwall,[23] Bergman planned a scene

---

23 I interviewed them on 12 September 2016.

in which Karin would perform with the Swedish Radio Orchestra under Herbert Blomstedt during a rehearsal. The scene would have made Karin's orchestral experience come to life on screen, perhaps in a manner resembling Stig and Marta rehearsing the overture to Beethoven's *Egmont* in *To Joy*. Bergman cancelled the scene for technical reasons—the digital cameras needed could not be made available—although a deal had been negotiated with the orchestra. But let us think about it for a second: what a marvellous scene it would have been, featuring Karin surrounded by a hundred or so musicians. According to Torbjörn Ehrnwall's recollections, the scene would have started with a close-up of Karin shot from a crane; there would then have been a panning-out to a full view of the orchestra—and what a contrast it would have provided to the rest of the film, which never has more than two people in each scene.

Twenty-five years after *Autumn Sonata* and fifty-three after *To Joy*, Bergman had found a beautiful musical metaphor of music-making as a means of having a meaningful and authentic life. It is quite the opposite from the individual's struggle emphasized by Charlotte as well as by Stig's efforts to break out from the collective to gain a life of glory as a soloist (and even to have his revenge, as he says at a party at a drunken stage: 'But I will show all the bastards what it means to play the violin' ['Men jag ska visa alla djävlar vad det vill säga att spela fiol']).

One of Bergman's most remarkable but under-appreciated films, probably owing to its being made for television, is *In the Presence of a Clown*, his first cinematic production in eleven years. The title, an apparent mistranslation from the Swedish 'Larmar och gör sig till' ('Struts and frets'), is a fragment from the *Macbeth* epigraph to the film, uttered by Macbeth following the suicide of Lady Macbeth: 'Life's but a walking shadow, a poor player, / That struts and frets his hour upon the stage, / And then is heard no more: it is a tale / Told by an idiot, full of sound and fury, / Signifying nothing.' But the 'translation' is in fact quite brilliant: Erland Josephson came up with the English title, and Bergman approved.[24] The film is about life, death, and the arts, not about the clown who appears as a hallucination in the mind of the main protagonist. But the clown symbolizes death and is thus connected to the Shakespearian epigraph. The 'struts and frets' has more direct—distracting, perhaps—Shakespearian connotations.

---

24 According to Pia Ehrnwall.

The film encapsulates virtually all of Bergman's artistic themes. In Sweden in October 1925, the two protagonists—Carl Åkerblom, a character based on Bergman's uncle on his mother's side, and Osvald—have been committed to a psychiatric clinic. Upon their release, they take on a magnificent project along with Åkerblom's fiancée, Pauline (Marie Richardson), to produce and perform a silent film with live sound about Franz Schubert's final year. It is a completely made-up story, featuring Schubert's interaction with the Viennese prostitute Mizzi Veith, a non-contemporaneous historical figure, author of *The Authentic Diary of Countess Mizzi Veith* from 1908, a volume which Osvald introduces to Carl. This is a bold but dramaturgically brilliant move, replacing Countess Caroline Esterházy, Schubert's supposed love, with Mizzi Veith; and it echoes another Bergman character, Rakel in *After the Rehearsal* (1984), who argues that art is just 'shit and filth and randiness'. The two outcasts can connect with Schubert and Veith, as both are immensely suffering, abused, and maltreated servants.

The living talking picture, 'La cinématographie vivante et parlante!' as Bergman states in the script, is quite an innovative approach—creating talkies by merging film and theatre—but it comes to an abrupt end. After a fire in the fuse box, as Åkerblom short-circuited the fuses to get enough power, the film-screening has to be abandoned; instead, the group performs the story as a chamber play—Bergman's equivalent of chamber music. In the sibling-like rivalry between the art forms, theatre wins, as Algot Frövik, one the audience members (and the sexton character in *Winter Light*, 1963), put it after the performance: 'Excuse my saying so, but the play was greater than the film.'

At the end of the play, Schubert and organist Marcus Jacobi perform his Great C Major Symphony—his last and most prominent symphonic work—in a four-hand version, and Schubert receives devastating feedback: it is too long, the violin and woodwind parts are unplayable, and the last movement is too furious and repetitive. He responds with despair. Schubert 'sinks', a term that Carl Åkerblom's psychiatrist used when asked what Schubert felt after having discovered his syphilis. It is a 'sinking descending through fear, suffocation enclosed'. Music will not help; or, as he puts it, 'no notes' will help. But here, towards the end of the film, Åkerblom's identification with Schubert assumes a different direction: it is not the syphilis that is 'sinking' him, but the perception of a failed work of art. By performing the film live, Åkerblom is able to connect with his own miserable life through his proxy Franz Schubert in one of Bergman's many monologues in close-up. It is definitely one of his most moving speeches:

Schubert: The motif, the main motif, the constantly recurring motif ... is a cry... of joy! I stood here at my desk and I couldn't avoid... at every moment, I couldn't avoid feeling in my body... in my flesh, in my sex, in my nerves, in my heart ... in the terrifying racing of my heart how my illness was burrowing away... how those repulsive medicines were poisoning my nerves. Every minute, I was in hell. But God sent me that cry of joy, that cry that is so short. And it helped, it made the pain unimportant, the disease meaningless. It turned the rage of the medicines into distant echoes. I thought that... My intention was to... I thought that other people... tormented by their hellish humiliation as I am tormented... I thought I would cry out to them as to myself. And I cry out so long and so often... the pain becomes unreal and the illness a phantom.

Vogler: The large-scale form has never been your form, Schubert. You are no Beethoven. You are Franz Schubert, and that's good enough.

Schubert: What revisions should I make?

Vogler: I can only give you one single piece of advice.

Schubert: I understand.

Vogler: Forgive me.

Schubert: Don't ask for forgiveness, brother. You have done your friend the greatest of favours. You have told the truth.[25]

After Vogler leaves, Schubert looks straight into the camera and says, 'I'm sinking ... sinking.'

There is a striking difference between Charlotte's monologue and Vogler's assessment of Schubert. Charlotte's utterance is original, counter-historical, while Vogler's comments could have been quite plausible in 1828: Schubert was seen as the master of the small-scale form—short piano pieces and Lieder, in particular—as opposed to Beethoven's reputation as a symphonic composer. Schubert's Great C Major Symphony, for example, was not premiered until 1839. And contrasting Schubert's music with Beethoven's was a common trope even after Schubert's death in 1828, as feminine traits were ascribed to his music. Schubert's reputation would change: In 1840, Robert Schumann would talk about the symphony's 'heavenly length', and he expressed a sense of joy over the overall character of the

---

25 Translation mine.

work which resembles the feeling that Bergman's Schubert expressed.[26] A counter-cultural interpretation nevertheless occurs in the film when another audience member, organist Fredrik Blom—another intertextual character from *Winter Light*—expresses his gratitude for the performance of the Piano Sonata D. 960, with the caveat: 'Personally, I interpret the Schubert Sonata differently, no criticism intended. It was beautiful nevertheless, but somewhat too feminine for my taste'—again, a musician character using gendered language shedding a different kind of light on a performance.

From where did Bergman derive this dialogue and the Schubert-related threads? His sketchbooks in the Bergman Archives provide no answer, and my interview with the executive producer Pia Ehrnvall did not reveal anything—Bergman typically never talked analytically about his works during production, she told me—but given his previous intriguing comments on music in his films, he may simply have created the connection himself. The Mizzi Veith thread introduces a beautiful twist that makes artistic sense, along with fitting the intertextual elements into the film: written almost a decade later, musicologist Scott Messing mentions Mizzi Veith in the chapter 'Peter Altenberg's Schubert',[27] so the connection is not culturally outlandish in Schubert reception studies. And as Anyssa Neumann put it so well, through this plot,

> Carl is able to merge with his invented image of Schubert precisely because the character is his own invention, but we the audience, like the villagers, are never sure which aspects belong to Carl and which to Schubert, or indeed to Carl/Schubert, who simultaneously occupies Franz Schubert's Vienna between 1823 and 1828, Mizzi's 1908 Vienna, and Uncle Carl's 1926 Sweden.[28]

Add to this the sense shared by Pia Ehrnvall, along with Erland Josephson and Börje Ahlstedt, that Bergman himself was the real subject of the film, barely disguised, and we seem to have come full circle—with Bergman as Carl or as Schubert, the suffering artist being comforted by music.

Music is personal, like a drug—making the 'pain unimportant, the disease meaningless' for Schubert—but for *The Magic Flute*, it

---

26 Anthony Newcomb, 'Schumann and Late Eighteenth-Century Narrative Strategies,' *19th-Century Music*, 11:2 (Autumn 1987), 164–174.
27 Scott Messing, 'Peter Altenberg's Schubert', in *Schubert in the European Imagination*, vol. 2 (Rochester, NY: University of Rochester Press, 2007).
28 Neumann, 'Sound, Act, Presence', p. 199.

also provided universal comfort on the set. By sometimes questioning the common understanding of the classical repertoire, Bergman points to its complexities. But despite the fundamental differences in the statements across his oeuvre, they all point towards the essential metaphysical nature of music for Bergman: it may be Beethoven's Ninth overcoming death, or music as an existential motif in *Saraband* through metaphoric uses of works and modes of performance; but in the poignant words of a character who is one of Bergman's greatest human failures, Henrik in *Saraband*: 'We walk through our entire life and wonder about death and what does and does not follow, and then it is this easy: through music I can sometimes get a hint, just a hint, as in Bach.'

Acknowledgements

I am grateful for comments from a number of colleagues that inspired and improved this chapter: Anyssa Neumann, Alexis Luko, Scott Messing, Nora Engebretsen, Pia Ehrnwall, and Torbjörn Ehrnwall. Jan Holmberg and Hélène Dahl at the Bergman Archives were of great help in locating materials.

11
Bergman, Janov, and *Autumn Sonata*

Paisley Livingston

In *The Magic Lantern*, Ingmar Bergman reports that when he read Arthur Janov's *The Primal Scream* he was 'extremely stimulated and started developing a television film in four parts along Janov lines'.[1] Bergman also notes that in 1975 he visited Los Angeles and had his agent arrange a meeting with Janov. Bergman remarks that he and Janov were 'immediately on the same wavelength' and 'swiftly tried to get down to essentials'. In light of such facts, it would be unreasonable to doubt that Janov had an influence on Bergman at this stage in his career. The specific nature and extent of this influence remains difficult to identify, however. Michael Tapper offers the following conjecture on this topic in his book on *Face to Face* (1976):

> Most important to Bergman's inspiration when writing 'The Psychiatrist' was that primal therapy, like music, seemed to speak directly to the emotions. Moreover, Janov and Bergman agreed on the origins of childhood trauma, locating its causes with the truly disturbed ones in the family: the parents.[2]

Tapper also makes the following observation:

> The tarnished reputation of primary therapy undoubtedly affected *Face to Face*. Although Bergman did not make it as a propaganda piece for Janov's ideas, his public sympathies with the new-age cultural phenomenon nevertheless came to stain the work. Interestingly, Bergman never dissociated from Janov.[3]

---

1 Ingmar Bergman, *The Magic Lantern: An Autobiography*, translated from Swedish by Joan Tate (New York and London: Penguin, 1988), p. 231. Janov's work is *The Primal Scream* (London: Sphere Books, 1970).
2 Michael Tapper, *Ingmar Bergman's* Face to Face (London and New York: Wallflower, 2017), p. 116.
3 Tapper, *Ingmar Bergman's* Face to Face, p. 210.

This chapter investigates the Bergman–Janov connection with regard to *Höstsonaten* (*Autumn Sonata*, 1978). Three main approaches to the interpretation of this film will be considered. The first reads *Autumn Sonata* as a work that was, like *Face to Face*, conceived 'along Janov lines', and that consequently resonates positively with the tenets of Janov's psychology. The second and third interpretations both deny that *Autumn Sonata* is consistently Janovian. According to a first kind of 'non-Janovian' interpretation, Bergman duly accepted and worked with significant Janovian premises as he conceived of the story and characterizations for *Autumn Sonata*, just as the first interpretation holds, but adds that for various reasons, the director did not, finally, go on to make a thoroughly Janovian work. This interpretation purports, then, to identify unintentional (and indeed serendipitous) non-Janovian elements in the story conveyed by the finished audio-visual display. This is a kind of interpretation that is compatible with the idea that *Autumn Sonata* is to a significant degree ambiguous or ambivalent when it comes to Janovian doctrine. A third type of interpretation contends that even though Bergman planned to make a work 'along Janov lines', he had placed some critical distance between himself and at least some of the main tenets of Janov's psychological theory and successfully expressed these reservations in his film. According to that interpretation, then, Bergman was not thoroughly or consistently persuaded of the truth of Janov's theoretical contentions, either at the time of his initial, enthusiastic reading of *The Primal Scream* or upon subsequent reflection. Tapper could well be right that Bergman never 'dissociated' from Janov; but it does not follow that he did not become aware of shortcomings in Janov's doctrines or that he did not in one way or another distance himself from certain tenets of Janov's, at the very least when it was a matter of settling on what was meant to be fictionally true regarding the characterizations in *Autumn Sonata*.

The contest between the three interpretations of *Autumn Sonata* evoked in the previous paragraph can only be taken up once we have a sufficient understanding of what Janov's most basic and characteristic doctrines were. Very briefly, then, Janov asserts quite clearly that all neurotic individuals are troubled by repressed pain, which their various neurotic past-times prevent them from confronting, the result being any number of neurotic symptoms, physical disorders, and an overall inability to have authentic feelings. The source of this destructive repression of pain is the childhood trauma of not receiving sufficient parental love and care. As John Lennon aptly put it in a song inspired by Janov, 'Working Class Hero': 'when the pain is so great you feel nothing at all'. The parents really are the disturbed parties—as Tapper proposed above in his brief characterization of what Janov and Bergman had in common—and they pass their affliction along to their children.

As for Janov's promised remedy for neurosis, the therapy begins by setting aside all neurotic distractions and comforts so as to confront the anguish and pain that well up spontaneously when these neurotic defences are down. The therapist directs the distressed patient's thoughts towards his or her childhood and, more pointedly, to unrequited desires for parental attention and unconditional approval. Asking for mummy and daddy, the patient starts to feel her own pain, and the primal screaming begins. After many such sessions, there is supposed to be a crescendo, the moment of 'abreaction' in which the pain is finally gone and the healed patient is no longer neurotic. Once the repressed pain has been released, the patient can have authentic feelings. Janov claims that such persons find the company of neurotic individuals unpleasant, but co-exist peacefully with others who have finally confronted the infantile trauma and found emotional release from it.

Janov acknowledges that his doctrines recapitulate some very familiar psychoanalytic tenets. He was after all a practising, 'talking-cure' therapist, and one who made exorbitant and unjustifiable claims about the benefits to be had from his treatment. Unlike several of the more radical anti-psychiatric figures, he did not espouse the idea that psychotic and neurotic disorders are valuable or insightful ways of being that actually require no cure. There is no claim, for example, to the effect that in a deeply alienating and irrational society, it is the misfit, or somebody who is deemed to be abnormal, who might have a correct perspective on the way things are really going. For example, Janov notoriously deemed homosexuality a psychic disorder that was to be cured by successful primal therapy.

I turn now to the interpretations of *Autumn Sonata*, my main question being whether this is a work the psychological underpinnings of which are consistently Janovian. One might think so, first of all, because Bergman tells us that he took Janov's theory very seriously. Since he reported explicitly that *Face to Face* was conceived 'along Janov lines', it is plausible to conjecture that this could also have been true of *Autumn Sonata*, especially given that Janovian themes obviously resonate with important aspects of the story conveyed by the film. In order to assess such an interpretation, we must provide at least a sketchy account of how central elements of the story and characterizations might be understood along those lines. I shall be fairly brief, and assume that my readers have seen the film at least once.

The character played by Liv Ullmann, Eva, invites her mother Charlotte, a famous concert pianist, portrayed by Ingrid Bergman, to visit her home in Norway. They have not seen each other for seven years. Mother and daughter greet each other warmly. Yet soon tension builds. It is obvious that Eva finds her mother difficult and irritating. She is theatrical, self-absorbed, vain, at times obviously false. Eva gushes fervently to her mother about her mystical ideas; Eva believes in God and is convinced that there are countless realities. She believes that her son, who drowned when he was three years old, still lives in another world, yet is also in close contact with Eva. Charlotte is visibly sceptical and would appear to find her daughter's mystical thoughts distasteful. Later that evening, Charlotte makes the mistake of asking Eva whether she likes her, and Eva unfolds a bitter litany of complaints and accusations—what Jan Holmberg aptly calls a 'vomit of lamentations' (see Chapter 6 in this volume). She tasks her mother with having been an egotistical, cold, hypercritical, and systematically neglectful parent. Scylla was neglect, Charybdis was active disapproval and torment. Eva suffered horribly during the long periods of her mother's absence; yet when her mother returned, things only got worse, as Charlotte was overbearing and expressed constant disapproval. Eva's complaints are illustrated in flashbacks which, on this pro-Janov reading of the film, offer veridical depictions of the actual events in an implicit narrational confirmation of Eva's side of the story.

Eva becomes more and more angry as she lists what she describes as her mother's selfish, unfeeling, and hypocritical behaviours and the terrible effects they had on her. The mother's injuries, failures, and unhappiness, she repeats again and again, are passed down to the daughter. The crescendo in this lengthy string of accusations comes when Eva blames her mother for the miserable condition of Eva's younger sister, Helena, who is severely disabled and bedridden, and who must struggle to articulate even the simplest words. In a sort of primal crisis that emerges in parallel to the dispute between Eva and her mother, the wretched Helena manages to tumble out of her bed, hopelessly crying out for her mother.

Initially, the talented, world-famous pianist tries to defend herself by characterizing Eva's mounting accusations as so many wild exaggerations. Broken down finally by her daughter's emotional outbursts, Charlotte responds by explaining her very real emotional shortcomings as the product of her own miserable childhood. Without admitting that all of Eva's accusations are well-founded, she asks Eva to forgive her.

To sum up, there are reasons to think that Eva's psychologizing is consistent with Janovian doctrine, and that significant aspects of the work are designed to bring the spectator into sympathetic and empathic alignment with Eva, who effectively functions as Bergman's *porte parole*. A critic who has defended these sorts of claims in print is Robin Wood, who reads the film as implicitly endorsing Eva's accusations along with the psychological and ethical assumptions that subtend her vitriolic attack on her mother. Wood takes Bergman, or at least the film's implicit authorial persona, to be endorsing the harsh statements that Eva makes in anger to her mother, such as: 'People like you are a menace. You should be locked away so you can't do any harm.'[4] As Wood puts it, the film 'degenerates into what amounts to a hysterical diatribe against a woman who neglected her children for her career as a concert pianist'.[5] Wood contends that the film is designed to encourage the spectators to go along with the proposition that even Helena's severe physical handicap was caused by maternal neglect. It is certainly true that Eva presses this accusation, insisting with ferocity that her mother's selfish behaviour caused Helena's condition. There is a flashback illustrating an episode where Charlotte's abrupt departure, along with the related departure of her companion Leonardo, supposedly precipitates an irreversible crisis in Helena's condition.

Charlotte appears to be genuinely surprised by this accusation and asks Eva how it could be true. Eva's response, presented by her as decisive, is to ask Charlotte whether *she* can *prove* otherwise. This is a crucial moment in the dialogue, as Eva's question shifts a heavy burden of proof onto her mother's shoulders. Why, some spectators may well wonder, should Charlotte have to *prove* that her behaviour was not the cause of her daughter's severe affliction?

For those spectators who are not Janovians and who interpret the story as a matter of make-believe or imaginary events that are consistent with real-world physiological (and other) constraints, Charlotte's failures as a mother can hardly have been the sole cause

---

4 Robin Wood, *Ingmar Bergman*, 2nd edn., rev. by Barry Keith Grant (Detroit, MI: Wayne State University Press, 2013), p. 272.
5 Wood, *Ingmar Bergman*, p. 272.

of Helena's severe illness and disability. Only in an otherworldly allegory of primal scream theory could this be the aetiology of Helena's condition. Thus Robin Wood states that her condition is a 'surely physiological' degenerative disease.[6] If that is the right way to understand the story, Eva's accusation is analogous to Janov's faulty claim that poor eyesight is a product of neurosis that could be remedied by primal scream therapy. It would be reasonable, then, to protest that Charlotte does not have to shoulder the unfair burden of proof that Eva tries to impose on her; it is Eva who should have to provide evidence to support her problematic accusation that Helena's dreadful physical disability is all Charlotte's fault.

Given these strong objections to a fully fledged Janovian interpretation of the work, there is good reason to entertain the two aforementioned alternative interpretations: either Bergman had thoroughly Janovian intentions, but somehow failed to realize them in the work, or, in one way or another, his intentions were not so thoroughly Janovian, and the work was successfully designed to express that ambivalence. I turn first to some evidence that supports either of these interpretations, and then I address the question of which of these alternatives is best supported by additional evidence.

One good reason why Eva should not be taken as Bergman's *porte parole* is that when she launches her attack on her mother, she has consumed a great deal of red wine, is obviously intoxicated, and is not expressing attitudes that even she herself would endorse upon further reflection. And indeed, once Charlotte has left the house and Eva has had time to calm down, she writes her a letter in which she apologizes to her mother for having tormented her with what she herself calls an 'old soured hatred that is no longer real'. Everything she did was wrong, she adds, asking for forgiveness. That would obviously include the unjustifiable accusation regarding Charlotte's responsibility for Helena's severe disability.

Given this major inconsistency in Eva's behaviour in the course of the film, her extremely violent outbursts and hyperbolic, drunken accusations should not be read as following from anything like an accurate and comprehensive understanding of her childhood experience. These outbursts may be better understood as the expressions of a desire to assert herself and to demand her mother's attention. The film, then, has no 'moral' to the effect that the path to well-being passes through the activation of 'primal' childhood memories and

---

6 Wood, *Ingmar Bergman*, p. 272.

longings. Nor is it the case that an unrequited infantile demand for unconditional love and care is the avoidable cause of a very wide range of mental and physical disorders. Eva learns about the difficulties her mother faced as a child; and this helps her gain a broader perspective that makes it possible for her to place herself at some distance from her emotive impulses and, most importantly, from her angry judgements. After all, if the key thesis were that the symptoms are the disturbed parent's fault, this leads to a regress, since the parents' symptoms were in turn caused by the neurotic behaviour of the disturbed grandparents, and so on, *ab ovo*. Nor is there any evidence in the story of *Autumn Sonata* to support the optimistic thesis that some powerful abreactive event can bring about a full and long-lasting release from neurotic symptoms. It is at least symbolically relevant to observe that Helena's convulsive screaming at the end of film signals only more pain and confusion, not an abreactive release. On the basis of the evidence presented in the film, it would be hard to be optimistic about the prospect of Helena's being cured by some form of talking therapy.

Janov's advocate could reply that Eva is not in therapy and that a clinical setting and actual primal treatment, and not an angry encounter with the actual mother, is what she needs. Bergman's family drama cannot be expected to illustrate the more optimistic tenets of Janovian psychotherapy, and that it does not do so hardly means that the director was assuming an anti-Janov position on that topic. Yet Bergman's scenario does explore relevant factors that go uncovered in *The Primal Scream*. Eva may well have had a difficult childhood, but she has also been seriously afflicted by the loss of her child, and it is hard to see how any of the tenets of primal psychology can help her with that. The idea that Eva's mourning is pathologically prolonged or intensified by her parent-induced neurosis is hard to square with the proposition that her neurosis prevents her from having real feelings. Her mourning for her lost child certainly looks sincere and heartfelt.

More evidence running counter to a thoroughly Janovian interpretation can be found in one of the most interesting scenes in *Autumn Sonata*—the part where Eva plays a Chopin Prelude for her mother, who in turn comments on the piece and then performs her own interpretation of it. In her discussion of this sequence, Anyssa Neumann (in Chapter 8, this volume) points to shortcomings in what Charlotte has to say about this Chopin composition. Neumann argues that the gap between Käbi Laretei's two performances of the composition is not as great as the story prescribes.

As Neumann admits, these facts do not falsify the basic story premise to the effect that Charlotte's performance is that of a world-class pianist, whereas Eva's is not. The narrative context and use of reaction shots no doubt lead the average spectator to magnify perceived differences in skill across the two performances (where the actual differences, as Neumann argues, ought to have been even greater for the sake of the story). There is, in any case, no doubt that Eva is crestfallen once her mother has finished playing. For Eva this is yet another episode in a life as a victim of a selfish, unappreciative, and overbearing parent. However, such a response on her part is a mistake. Charlotte does not expect her daughter to be a brilliant pianist. She only plays and talks about the Chopin piece when Eva insists. In so doing Eva has put Charlotte in a double bind, for Charlotte must either speak dishonestly about the music or speak sincerely and disappoint her daughter's unrealistic desire. At no point does Eva express any sort of positive attitude towards the fact that her mother has a rare and precious musical talent. That Charlotte indeed has such a talent is a basic premise of this story. Nor does Eva allow that Charlotte's devotion to the art has any kind of legitimate place in the world. Instead, the brilliance of her mother's performance makes her jealous. When Charlotte speaks about how long she has worked to try to understand Chopin's preludes, Eva replies that as a child she was quickly very tired of her mother and her pianos.

I believe the evidence surveyed here suffices to establish that a fully fledged pro-Janov reading of the film is unsatisfactory, as there are too many elements in the audio-visual display that point to story propositions that are inconsistent with the pro-Janov interpretation. That leads us to the question that divides the two other alternative readings under consideration here: are the film's non-Janovian psychological insights serendipitous, or were they instead the fruit of Bergman's better intentions?

How might one argue for a reading whereby it was never Bergman's intention in the conception and making of *Autumn Sonata* to fashion a story that would serve as a consistent illustration of the tenets of Janovian psychology? One might start by appealing to a relevant counterfactual: surely if had he really wanted to, an author as talented as Bergman could have devised a story that fully meshed with Janov's theory. However, to this it might be replied that Bergman admitted to having struggled unsuccessfully with the making of *Face to Face*. He confessed that the work suffered from the 'ill-digested fruit' of his reading of Janov. A similar problem, it could be conjectured, arose in the making of *Autumn Sonata*. Whence the serendipity reading: trying to bring out a story along Janovian lines, Bergman ended up with one that manifests ways in which that doctrine is incomplete and problematic.

Some external evidence lends some tentative support to the interpretation whereby the non-Janovian elements were actually intended by the work's author. In her investigations into the Bergman–Janov connection, the Canadian musicologist Alexis Luko engaged in email communication with Janov. Luko reports that in one email to her, Janov stated that 'Bergman's chief interest in using primal therapy techniques was as a means to coach his actors on how to feel.'[7] Janov also related to Luko that 'Bergman says my ideas influenced him but I am not sure how.'[8] Both of these statements can be interpreted as casting doubt on the thesis that Bergman and Janov had a deeply theoretical meeting of minds. Had they done so, why was Janov still in the dark with regard to how Bergman understood his psychological views? Bergman, it seems, was primarily interested in ways of stirring up feelings, first in his actors and then in his audience. As Tapper put it in the passage quoted at the beginning of this chapter, it could well be the case that Bergman was at no point trying to make a work of fiction that would serve as 'propaganda' for primal scream theory.

It could be replied, however, that even if Bergman had always been somewhat agnostic about Janov's theory and was not finally interested in making a cinematic work that would take a stance on it as a hypothesis in scientific psychology, he might still have sought to recruit some of its tenets as interesting premises for an engaging psychological drama 'along Janov lines'. Here we need to draw a distinction between (1) the author's effective and final story intentions pertaining to what would be fictionally true in a film's story, and (2) whatever fervent psychological-theoretical beliefs the director might have held and would have been willing to assert. It could be a mistake to think that the items in (1) were all consistent with or informed by those in (2). And even if, with regard to (2), Bergman had a fervent belief in some Janovian proposition in psychology, it might not have been his aim to use any particular cinematic fiction, with its corresponding items in (1), to make an assertion along those lines. With this distinction in mind, it might be added that

---

7 Alexis Luko, *Sonatas, Screams, and Silence: Music and Sound in the Films of Ingmar Bergman* (New York and London: Routledge, 2016), pp. 90–91.
8 Luko, *Sonatas*, p. 91.

the object of the interpretations of *Autumn Sonata* under consideration here are the items in (1) in their relation to the finished audio-visual display. Items in (2) are relevant to such interpretations but are not their primary object.

Some of Bergman's remarks about *Autumn Sonata* in *Images: My Life in Film* appear to lend some support to the serendipity interpretation, whereby there is at least some inconsistency between Bergman's final story intentions and the meanings of the audio-visual display.[9] Apparently Bergman initially had the idea that this would be a story in which 'the child gives birth to the parent'. The thought here would be that the talented and successful concert pianist is in some sense not truly alive until her daughter's tirades bring her to acknowledge her own emotional repression and neurosis. Eva's accusatory diatribes and screams would, then, be therapeutic, not only or primarily for herself, but for her mother. Yet consider Bergman's further comment in *Images: My Life in Film* on this topic: 'There is something close to an enigma in the concept of the daughter giving birth to the mother. Therein lies an emotion that I was not able to realize and carry through to its conclusion. On the surface, the finished film resembles the outline, but actually that is not the case.'[10] Bergman goes on to say that perhaps he did not 'drill deeply' enough. It is unclear how this metaphor is to be understood: is the thought that this schematic 'giving birth' motif is psychologically superficial? The implication, then, would be that some of the key premises based on primal psychology (such as the proposition that parentally induced childhood trauma causes severe physiological disorders and degenerative disease) did not survive the process of developing a sufficiently plausible dramatization. One odd irony here is that there is nothing in Janov about a child's providing needed primal therapy for a parent, so in this regard Bergman's reasoning 'along Janov lines' is strangely non-Janovian.

Some observations about the acting in the film are relevant to the serendipity interpretation. Liv Ullmann's remarkable body language and intonations help portray an Eva who is immature and weak, at times annoyingly so. She struggles to read a letter aloud to her husband. Some of her pronouncements have a decidedly dim-witted quality. When she gets drunk and lets herself go, she

---

9 Ingmar Bergman, *Images: My Life in Film*, translated from Swedish by Marianne Ruuth (New York: Arcade Publishing, 1990).
10 Bergman, *Images*, p. 335.

obviously speaks from her heart, but she also becomes blunt and ugly. The spectator is no doubt meant to feel sorry for her, to find her somewhat sympathetic; but this does not mean that her actions and attitudes carry conviction, especially when she aggressively presses what is a highly dubious accusation against her mother. Ingrid Bergman's performance certainly brings out some of the famous pianist's vanity and self-absorption, partially re-enforcing Eva's accusations. Yet Bergman's Charlotte remains impressive; she manifests experience and intelligence. If the intention was to make a film in which the child gives birth to the parent, casting Ingrid Bergman in the role of the yet-to-be born parent was perhaps a serious blunder.

To sum up, my view is that a fully fledged pro-Janov interpretation cannot be squared with all of the available evidence. As for the choice between the two non-Janov readings of this cinematic work, it might be said with a degree of caution that the available evidence does not support a firm judgement in favour of either of them. This is the case because we lack systematic and detailed evidence into the evolution of Bergman's beliefs and artistic intentions, and also because some of the available evidence about them is fairly ambiguous. For example, the previously cited statement in *Images: My Life in Film* would appear at first glance to count in favour of the serendipity reading: Bergman identifies an important way in which the film did not turn out as planned, and we have no reason to deem him insincere in this regard. Yet this same evidence can also be interpreted as indicating that Bergman changed his mind about the Janovian premises as he made the film, in which case the story's critical distance from a Janovian perspective was, finally, the fruit of Bergman's better artistic (and other) judgements. Perhaps his final, effective artistic intentions regarding the work's themes and story were influenced by Ingrid Bergman's strong resistance to the initial characterization of Charlotte as an emotionally 'unborn' mother. In any case we may conclude that although there are certainly traces of a Janovian perspective in the story of *Autumn Sonata* (and that it is indeed very likely that Bergman at least started out with some Janov-informed story premises), the work does not finally resonate fully with a psychological doctrine according to which many or even most of the woes of the world, including physiological afflictions in the order of cerebral palsy, are the product of selfish parenting. Nor does this fiction evoke a world where people can scream their way to well-being. Bergman's *Autumn Sonata* hardly supports the idea that music, or the fine arts more generally, are a neurotic or 'narcissistic' product that the post-neurotic subject could live happily without. Bergman was no doubt interested in making artistic use of aspects of Janov's psychology and therapeutic techniques; but in the age-old rivalry between the doctors and the artists, he came down finally on the side of the artist.

A thought that may come to mind at this point is that the psychological insights of *Autumn Sonata*, at least as I have described them, are sketchy and relatively modest. Perhaps that is right, but it is also relevant to point out that the film is nonetheless thought-provoking and potentially instructive. The moving and at times very eloquent conversational exchanges, illustrated with flashbacks illustrating how things might have seemed from the character's perspective, establish a dialogical narrational pattern which suffices to cast serious doubt over the blatant simplifications of primal scream psychology. Bergman's fictional story provides an imaginary counterexample that can be taken as challenging some of the tenets of a psychological theory, the key idea being that in a case like this, an adequate diagnosis would not amount to saying that a successful and extremely talented professional woman is guilty of having single-handedly caused severe mental and physical disorders in her children. The form of the argument is simple: a particular theory says that such-and-such is what happens, and a case is imagined that does not convincingly work that way; consequently, a possible challenge to the theory has been brought to mind.

Acknowledgements

Thanks to Alexis Luko for an informative discussion of the Bergman–Janov connection based on her research at the Ingmar Bergman Archive and on her email interview with Janov.

12

Persona's penis

Daniel Humphrey

Few scholars, at least in English-language texts, have discussed the blink-and-you'll-miss-it shot—three frames, literally an eighth of a second—of the male sex in *Persona*'s (1966) pre-credit sequence (Figure 12.1). The reason for at least some of the omissions seems clear: the image simply was not visible when many spectators initially encountered Bergman's film. In a 1986 monograph, Frank Gado, having read about the image in Susan Sontag's early essay,[1] doubted its existence. He claimed he 'cannot recall having seen any such image when [...] attend[ing] the Swedish premiere of *Persona* or in two later viewings in Sweden', or when he 'examined the U.S. print on a viewer'.[2] Others probably chose to ignore the image's subsequent reappearance because they did not think it important—just another example of a censored moment in a Bergman film being restored, like *The Virgin Spring*'s (1960) rape or Anna's anal penetration by the waiter in *The Silence* (1963).

Unlike those examples, the initial loss of the risible imagery in *Persona* hardly seems a damaging excision. The film can scarcely have suffered due to the absent footage, and at least some scholars have assumed that *Persona*'s offending shot was merely an example of Bergman's many conscious provocations 'against the Swedish censorship board on Bergman's account'.[3] Upon reflection, it is clearly a visual pun; the penis takes the place of the 6 in the countdown-leader-within-the-film, situated so that the scrotum takes

---

1 Susan Sontag, 'Bergman's *Persona*' (1967), in Lloyd Michaels (ed.), *Ingmar Bergman's* Persona (Cambridge: Cambridge University Press, 2000), pp. 62–85.
2 Frank Gado, *The Passion of Ingmar Bergman* (Durham, NC: Duke University Press, 1986), p. 327n.
3 Erik Hedling, Professor of Film Studies, Lund University, personal email, 2 September 2017.

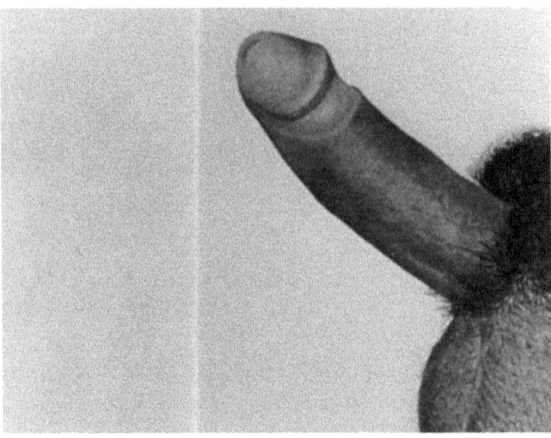

Figure 12.1 *Persona*'s penis, *Persona* (1966)

the part of the squiggle while the shaft mirrors the upper half of the glyph's stroke.

Adding to the sense that the image was a joke and yet simultaneously something more provocative, the following point should be considered: in Swedish, adopting the Latin, the word for six is 'sex'. This is a homonym for the primary word in Swedish for coitus, and if the Swedish 'sex' (in its erotic/procreative meaning) does not quite metonymically extend to explicitly referencing the *male* sex organ, it certainly raises that bit of anatomy to the surface of most people's consciousness. Admittedly, the image of the organ as a brief flash frame can almost seem a hallucination, a hallucination we might not want to admit we have had. Therefore, to borrow from Freud—the reader will soon see that this is a psychoanalytic study of Bergman's film—we may well ask if sex is sometimes simply a six? Video technology coupled with a remote control and quick reflexes has showed us that it is not. Ultimately, by transmogrifying the countdown leader's asexual 6 into the male's *sex*, *Persona* anticipates second-wave feminist film critics' key arguments by half a decade.

Sontag was surely the first Anglophone critic to mention *Persona*'s penis in writing, although she incorrectly claims that it appears *after* 'the leader flashes by', near the brief shot of the 'chase scene from a slapstick silent film', one of 'a nail being hammered into the palm of a hand', and those of 'bodies in a morgue'.[4] One should not ridicule

---

4 Sontag, 'Bergman's *Persona*', p. 74.

the mistake of a critic without the luxury of home-video technology; but claiming that the penis appears *after* the countdown leader, Sontag's error diminishes its importance. Sontag situates it within the prologue's history of cinematic representation (penis as signifier of early pornography standing in relation to the crude animation, the silent slapstick, and, finally, modernist cinema) and the bits of ephemera signifying Bergman's oeuvre (a spider in *Through a Glass Darkly* (1961), and the snow in *Winter Light* (1963)). In doing this, she misses the opportunity to connect the signifier of male sexuality to the meta-filmic imagery that concerns the basic ontology of cinema: the shutter, projector bulb, and countdown leader.

Most glibly, the image suggests that Bergman understands that his navel-gazing self-reflexivity (creating art fascinated with the meaning of art) is essentially a masturbatory state. More broadly, it posits that the cinematic apparatus gives us, or is *primed* to give us (since we are seeing a *pre-ejaculative* penis), a *male* emission, one both structurally patriarchal and corporeally impactful. It represents a certain structure of desire as being as essential to the language of the medium as mathematical formulas are to the science that makes cinematography (the film's original title) possible. Beyond this, through the suggestiveness of the shot, *Persona* can be seen as interrogating the distinction, not simply between the usual litany of binary opposites seen as fundamental to *Persona*—face/mask, image/reflection, reality/film, self/other, objectivity/subjectivity—but that between two things not often thought of as binary opposites: the penis and the phallus.

After the publication of Sontag's essay, with most prints in circulation having mysteriously lost this money shot, people could be forgiven for wondering if the American intellectual dreamed up an image now nowhere to be seen. Proving its existence, and its relationship to the broadest possible concerns of cinematic spectatorship, Hubert Cohen eventually offered a frame grab of it and compared it to the first shot in the film, one before even the faux countdown leader, one in which the glowing right electrode of a projector's carbon arc bulb resembles 'an erect penis as it emerges diagonally from the lower right'.[5] In comparing that shot (really, two shots) of the source of cinematic illumination to the image of the male member, Cohen quotes Bruce Kawin, who, in a 1978 analysis, does

---

5 Hubert I. Cohen, *Ingmar Bergman: The Art of Confession* (New York: Twayne, 1993), p. 229.

Figure 12.2 The carbon rod, *Persona* (1966)

not reference the penis but nevertheless considers the shot of the right electrode's explosive connection to the left carbon rod a visual analogue for 'intercourse' (Figure 12.2).[6] Cohen, then, with the penis as added evidence, posits the symbolization of 'what Bergman sees as a key source of his creativity – aggression and sexual energy'.[7] Like Sontag's assessment, this fecund explanation, with due respect to Cohen, also ultimately misdirects us.

One important consideration many critics seem to have missed is that the shot of the penis is not, strictly speaking, a 'motion picture' image. As brief as the rest of the prologue's shots may be (carbon arcs, slaughtered animals, piles of snow), and no matter how motionless the objects in them are, it is clear that they are *motion picture* images. The shot of the penis, on the other hand, is obviously one of a *photograph* of a penis. As such, the status of this doubly mediated image is different. Considered another way, it is the cinematographic equivalent of the word penis in quotation marks. This has both the effect of diminishing it—it is not really a flesh-and-blood penis—and emphasizing its status as a signifier: it

---

6 Bruce F. Kawin, *Mindscreen: Bergman, Godard and First-Person Film* (Princeton, NJ: Princeton University Press, 1978), p. 106.
7 Cohen, *Ingmar Bergman*, p. 229.

has become the very image of symbolic authority. In short, it has become the phallus, and a very cinematically defined one at that. Furthermore, in its comparability with the two diegetic photographs we see in the film (the photo of Elisabet's rejected son, the one Alma accuses Elisabet of wanting to have 'born dead', and the image of the Jewish boy in the ghetto) and, by extension, the moving but also doubly mediated image of the enflamed monk Elisabet sees on television, it also connects with trauma and the unbearable.[8] All this serves as evidence for why this 'gag image' does not make one laugh: instead, we gag on it. Ultimately, the grainy photo can be seen as a representation of signification as such within the traumatic logic of the castration complex.

French psychoanalyst Jacques Lacan, who married Freud's model of the psyche to the field of semiotics and, essentially, replaced the penis with the phallus in his equations, has identified three forms of the phallus: the imaginary phallus, the symbolic phallus, and the real phallus. The *real phallus* essentially references the physical organ, the penis. *Persona*'s fraction-of-a-second image can hardly be said to be introducing *that* pound of flesh to the spectator. (How could it? The semiotic real always escapes our grasp.) What we see is on screen so briefly that it seems a figment of our imagination even when we do see it. That, and the fact that it is a *cinematographic image* of a *photographic image* (and one that replaces a six and rhymes with a carbon rod) seemingly consigns the image of sex it offers to the realms of the imaginary and symbolic.

Lacan's second conception, the *imaginary phallus*, references that which is both *ev*oked and *in*voked by the castration complex—itself a concept of violence with traumatic impact; it is the 'image of the penis' as a 'partial [...] object', like the mother's breast, or the child's faeces, one implied by the 'specular image' of an imagined unified body.[9] The imaginary phallus is, in Dylan Evans' summation, 'an

---

8 Hamish Ford has pointed out that as a chronologically presented succession— erect penis + Elisabet's son + captured boy in the Warsaw Ghetto—the three photographic images connect sex to death, particularly in light of the fact that Elisabet is accused by Alma of having wanted her son to be born dead. Email exchange, 30 August 2018. As we shall see, this interpretation—sex for Elisabet leading not to renewed life but to a child she wants to have 'born dead', in Alma's disturbing accusation—rubs up against a kind of Thanatos-as-Eros that places it squarely in the realm of the most challenging forms of queer negativity.
9 Jacques Lacan, *Écrits: The First Complete Edition in English*, translated by Bruce Fink (New York: Norton, 2007), pp. 696, 693, 697 respectively. For

imaginary object [...] perceived by the child in the preoedipal phase as the object of the mother's desire, as that which she desires beyond the child'. It is also that which 'circulates between mother and child and serves to institute the first dialectic in the child's life'.[10] Understanding this, one of the implications of *Persona*'s penis becomes clear. Once we see the unnamed boy reaching towards the unstable maternal face at the end of the film's prologue, a circulation of cinematic desire is evoked as a circulation of the phallus between mother and child (and by implication between cinematic apparatus and spectator) as that phallus both illustrates and invokes the castration complex. And yet, as Lacan puts it, 'the [irregular] nature of the castration complex [...] is the sole *indication of* [...] jouissance', or the self-shattering joy of the death drive, 'in its infinitude'.[11] Therefore, in a Lacanian reading of *Persona*, the lack of a diegetic, embodied bearer of the 'real phallus' (the boy is pre-pubescent, the husband metaphorically sterile) suggests that the shot of the penis is at once a cinematic literalization of castration—*it is the cut, 'unsutured' penis*—and the marker of the unconscious force field that constitutes (traumatic) cinematic representation. This penis connects cinematic representation to negativity and death.

In its final, *symbolic* formation, the Lacanian phallus rears its head most decisively. Being in the faux countdown leader, *Persona*'s penis also proclaims its function symbolically, considering the overdetermination of numbers in relation to words in relation to images. What seems to be real, then seems to be imaginary, finally becomes symbolic. As Lacan posits,

> the [symbolic] phallus is not a fantasy [...]. Still less is it the organ [...] that it symbolizes. [...] For it is a signifier [...] destined to designate meaning effects as a whole, insofar as the signifier *conditions* them by its presence *as signifier*.[12]

This is not just a specific definition of a specific register of the phallus; it is also a compelling description of the way *Persona* works. *Persona* is a text in which its meta-cinematically articulated

---

Lacan, of course, the whole register of the 'imaginary realm' is characterized by the visual, even if ultimately it is structured by the symbolic realm. The imaginary is the seen yet unseen.

10 Dylan Evans, *An Introductory Dictionary of Lacanian Psychoanalysis* (London: Routledge, 1996), p. 142.
11 Lacan, *Écrits*, p. 696, emphasis added.
12 Lacan, *Écrits*, p. 579, emphases added.

signification-as-such is fundamental to the meanings we take from it, and it is with Lacan's formulation in mind that the phantom phallus connects with *Persona*'s basic narrative: the performer who refuses to speak.

To explain, Lacan helps us again: 'It is not man's relationship to language *as a social phenomenon* that is at issue, nor even anything [...] that derisively goes by the name of affect.' We must find, or '*re*find [...] effects that are discovered at the level of the chain of materially unstable elements that constitute language.' They 'are determinant in instituting the subject'. For Lacan,

> [the] *passion of the signifier* thus becomes a new dimension of the human condition in that it is not only man who speaks, but *in man* and *through man* that *it* speaks; in that his nature becomes woven by effects in which the structure of the language of which he becomes the material can be refound.[13]

It is *towards* this vertiginous understanding of consciousness-as-alienation that, in the film, Elisabet's doctor alludes when she diagnoses her patient in a spellbinding monologue:

> The hopeless dream of *being*. Not doing, but being [...] The feeling of dizziness [...]. Every tone of voice a lie, an act of treason. Every gesture false. Every smile a grimace. [...] Kill yourself? No – too nasty, not to be done. But you could be immobile. You can keep quiet. Then at least you're not lying.[14]

I say 'towards this understanding' because it seems clear that Elisabet's crisis is tied to duplicity *within language*, Lacan's 'language as a social phenomenon', rather than to signification per se.

And yet, this level of localized lying (Elisabet in her social world), that which Marilyn Johns Fisher and Robin Wood have looked at in feminist and queer terms, ultimately *stands for* what Lacan describes.[15] It can be seen as a metaphor for the form of alienation

---

13 Lacan, *Écrits*, p. 578, emphases added.
14 Ingmar Bergman, '*Persona*', in Persona *and* Shame: *The Screenplays of Ingmar Bergman*, translated by Keith Bradfield (London: Calder & Boyars, 1972), pp. 17–101 (p. 41), emphasis is original.
15 Marilyn Johns Blackwell, '*Persona*: The Deconstruction of Binarism and the False Mergence of Spectator and Spectacle', in *Gender and Representation in the Films of Ingmar Bergman* (Rochester, NY: Camden House, 1997), pp. 133–164; Robin Wood, '*Persona* Revisited', in *Ingmar Bergman: New Edition* (Detroit, MI: Wayne State University Press, 2013), pp. 252–274.

always-already within language itself that Lacan charts and that a number of feminists, in the years almost immediately after *Persona*'s release, dreamed of overcoming. In an oft-cited essay, dating from the year she fully embraced lesbianism, Adrianne Rich mourns that which 'is buried in the memory by the collapse of meaning under an inadequate or lying language'.[16] And if *Persona*'s Elisabet struggles against lying *in* language and by extension language *as* lying, the film in which she finds herself, like all films, threatens to perpetuate the lies despite its co-protagonist's vow of silence. However, through Bergman's deconstructive authorial voice, we witness the collapse of meaning precisely through the 'inadequate and lying language' of the cinema. Many critics have, of course, sensed these essential paradoxes within Bergman's film.

Robin Wood, in his second, more radical assessment of the film, blames Bergman for the failure of nerve represented by a film that seemed to him, in its first scenes between Elisabet and Alma in the beach house, to be moving towards a radical feminist/lesbian union between its two protagonists, only to develop into one that sees their increasing closeness homophobically.[17] To put it the way B. Ruby Rich did when comparing *Persona* unfavourably to Leontine Sagan's *Mädchen in Uniform* (1931), 'the loss of individual identity is a threat that haunts women's intimacy like a destructive specter: getting too close to another woman', ultimately, 'means losing oneself'.[18] Put simply, the self/other distinction is anchored to sexual difference; without it, according to heteronormative logic, chaos reigns in intimate relationships. This explains, for the homophobe, why same-sex unions are inherently unstable. Heterosexuality is not just written according to the structures of dualism, it is written according to the structures of dualism as anchored by the phallus. Elisabet, in a basic queer/feminist reading of the film, is attempting to move beyond an insufficient and lying language, but she is doing

---

16 Adrienne Rich, '"It Is the Lesbian within Us ..."' (1976), in *On Lies, Secrets, and Silence Selected Prose 1966–1978* (New York: Norton, 1979), pp. 199–202 (p. 199).
17 Wood, '*Persona* Revisited'. His original analysis of the film can be found in 'The World Without, The World Within', also in his *Ingmar Bergman: New Edition*, pp. 186–238.
18 B. Ruby Rich, 'From Repressive Tolerance to Erotic Liberation: *Mädchen in Uniform*', in Corey K. Creekmur and Alexander Doty (eds), *Out in Culture: Gay, Lesbian, and Queer Essays of Popular Culture* (Durham, NC: Duke University Press, 1995), pp. 137–166 (p. 149).

it through a protest made in the terms of language (since even silence is a component of speech). Similarly, Bergman, in trying to move beyond the insufficient language of classical cinema, is still, in the end, using the master's tools to tear down the master's house. As American critic Pauline Kael put it, *Persona* 'had begun to involve us in marvelous possibilities' (perhaps *lesbian* possibilities?) but Bergman 'throws [it] away'.[19] Alma becomes so attracted to her patient that she is driven mad. There can be no Sapphic happy ending.

This is, of course, a rather reductive reading of the film. Bergman did only flirt with homosexual desire in his filmmaking, despite the fact that so many of his most interesting characters were queer. But it is important to realize, according to Bergman's own admission, that it is Elisabet who should be seen as the film's queer protagonist, not the increasingly deranged Alma.[20] Elisabet offers her radical silence to Alma. Her love does not speak its name, while Alma, who tries to pull her patient back into spoken language, back to normalcy, never stops talking. The closest we get to a 'lesbian moment' in the film, one inevitably cited whenever the film is argued to be a queer classic, is a wordless one: Elisabet brushing Alma's hair out of her face in the middle of the night. But why, exactly, is it that Elisabet should be seen as the force of queer destabilization? One thing that is not mentioned often enough is the fact that although Elisabet does stop speaking, she nevertheless communicates throughout the film, via affect, action, and, most obviously, the infernal letter she writes to her doctor.

One of Jacques Derrida's key insights involves a system of so-called 'violent hierarchies' in Western thought. One of the most compelling of these hierarchies, for our inquiry here, is the one between speech

---

19 Pauline Kael, 'Swedish Summer' (1967), a review of *Persona*, in Lloyd Michaels (ed.), *Ingmar Bergman's* Persona (Cambridge: Cambridge University Press, 2000), pp. 169–171 (p. 170).
20 Bergman mentions Elisabet, along with Aman in *The Magician* (1958), Ester in *The Silence*, Tomas in *Face to Face* (1976), and Ismael in *Fanny and Alexander* (1982) (and, contextually, Johan in *Hour of the Wolf* (1968)) as representing a single (clearly queer) thematic for him. Ingmar Bergman, *Images: My Life in Film*, translated by Marianne Ruuth (New York: Arcade, 1994), pp. 28–29. I have previously discussed Bergman's comments here in my own work: Daniel Humphrey, *Queer Bergman: Sexuality, Gender, and the European Art Cinema* (Austin, TX: University of Texas Press, 2013), p. 15.

and writing. According to Derrida, '[t]he priority', in European philosophical traditions,

> of spoken language over written or silent language stems from the fact that when words are spoken the speaker and the listener are supposed to be simultaneously present to one another; they are supposed to be the same, pure unmediated presence. [...] Writing, on the other hand, is considered *subversive* in so far as it creates a [...] distance between the author and the audience; writing presupposes the absence of the author and so we can never be sure exactly what is meant by a written text; it can have many different meanings as opposed to a single unifying one.[21]

From this perspective, noting that Elisabet has only given up *spoken* language, one must consider a distinction: between her rejection of phonocentrism (and false transparency) and her continuing engagement with a destabilizing practice of inscription. If Elisabet has given up the sincerity of speech but not other, potentially duplicitous forms of communication, with what does that align her? I would posit that it places her in the position of the queer subject as defined in a major strand of queer theory advocated by Leo Bersani and Lee Edelman.[22] The latter, developing Derrida, argues that the homosexual, in the homophobic mind, takes on the position of the subversive subject who writes.[23] This threateningly duplicitous subject is explicitly contrasted to the seemingly sincere subject who *speaks*, whose self-presence is assured through false phonocentric values.

In some ways, the curious lack of academic attention to Elisabet's continuing communication—becoming increasingly more communicative throughout the film even as she maintains her refusal to speak—is a more peculiar omission than the ignored penis. The ramifications of Elisabet as a writing subject, in short (as Derrida and Edelman would argue), an 'untrustworthy' *queer* subject, may seem counterintuitive when reading *Persona* as a film about lesbianism. It is

---

21 Jacques Derrida, 'Dialogue with Jacques Derrida', in Richard Kearney (ed.), *Dialogues with Contemporary Continental Thinkers: The Phenomenological Heritage* (Manchester: Manchester University Press, 1984), pp. 105–126 (pp. 115–116), emphasis added.
22 See Leo Bersani, *Homos* (Cambridge, MA: Harvard University Press, 1995) and Lee Edelman, *No Future: Queer Theory and the Death Drive* (Durham, NC: Duke University Press, 2004).
23 Lee Edelman, 'Homographesis', in *Homographesis: Essays in Gay Literary and Cultural Theory* (New York: Routledge: 1994), pp. 3–23.

chatty Alma who seems to be in the thrall of a same-sex passion, not Elisabet, who watches her smitten caregiver from a position of bemused attachment. But despite the mini-orgy on the beach that Alma recounts, Alma in her sincerity and helpfulness must be seen as a future-orientated good citizen. She can be seen as a straight woman with something like a 'schoolgirl crush' on a famous actress. She might have bisexual urges; but unlike Elisabet, Alma is not an example of the kind of radical queer Edelman talks about when he—developing his theories beyond Derrida and towards Lacan—defines the 'sinthomosexual'.[24]

For Edelman, sinthomosexuality is a neologism that places homosexuality in relation to jouissance and the death drive; it is an unsettling, antisocial position that has been invoked by the heteronormative order to demonize the queer subject, but it can also be embraced as a position of radical power. The sinthomosexual refuses good citizenship and what Edelman calls reproductive futurity. Edelman performatively embodies this subject when he writes,

> [f]uck the social order and the Child in whose name we're collectively terrorized: fuck Annie; fuck the waif from *Les Mis*; fuck the poor, innocent kid on the Net; fuck Laws both with capital ls and with small; fuck the whole network of Symbolic relations and the future that serves as its prop.[25]

This is the queer apotheosis of the concept of radical negativity as Nietzsche and Adorno defined it long ago. Hamish Ford, adapting their definitions of negativity, has productively explored *Persona*. For him,

> [f]ollowing on from its material enactment in the prologue, negativity has in Elisabet's silence a human instigator, forcing itself into the field of social reality. [...] As Elisabet's negative subjectivity generates increasingly infectious power during the film, it is more than the troubled artist figure who stares down a very immanent crisis. [...] Through the interactions with Elisabet, [Alma] seems to become 'infected' with her patient's condition to the point where her own existential certainty is undermined.[26]

---

24 See Edelman, *No Future*, especially chapter 2: 'Sinthomosexuality', pp. 33–66.
25 See Edelman, *No Future*, p. 29.
26 Hamish Ford, *Post-War Modernist Cinema and Philosophy: Confronting Negativity and Time* (New York: Palgrave Macmillan, 2012), pp. 36, 37.

In other words, Elisabet's negativity, more specifically, her *queer* negativity has the power to contest everything Alma values: marriage, child-rearing, good citizenship. That negativity rubs off onto Alma, spectacularly, but she cannot handle it.

Elisabet's queer negativity, her sinthomosexuality, explains much more than her simple unwillingness to speak. Elisabet has rejected motherhood, marriage, and the role of a well-rewarded performer in the phallogocentric social order. Looked at this way, with Elisabet exemplifying radical queerness in contrast to the smitten if culturally conservative and future-oriented Alma, the plot developments that Robin Wood and B. Ruby Rich might have hoped for—two women falling in love, becoming lesbians, and buying their own seaside cottage—is, at best, a red herring. That would be what Lisa Duggan calls homonormativity: the good, coupled gay citizens taking their part in the social order.[27]

The radical negativity personified by Elisabet not only destabilizes Alma, it destabilizes the film in which both appear. This brings us back to *Persona*'s penis as well as to the film's phallic moorings and unmoorings. It is often said that the film's implied spectator is the boy seen in the prologue, looking up at a screen, at an image of a woman's head that also suggests Lacan's theory of the mirror phase and the cinematic fascination that is explained by it. But if a prepubescent male subject guides real spectators (us) into the film, it is one who is nevertheless doing so under the sign of the phallus, a phallus that, in its imaginary form, is circulating between himself and the maternal/anti-maternal protagonist(s) of the film. In other words, the film's phallus, visible or cloaked in darkness, is not a marker of a film's radical departure from normative logic. Rather, it stands as the normative starting point for the inevitable but perhaps productive breakdown that occurs when it vanishes. *Persona*'s invocation of the phallus, followed as it is by many more signifiers of its contested but palpable authority (from phallic female doctor to blind husband) allows the film to be destabilized by radical lesbian negativity.

On the other hand, the *evocation* of the material *penis* by the same shot suggests something else. It implies that the evocation of

---

27 See Lisa Duggan, 'The New Homonormativity: The Sexual Politics of Neoliberalism', in Russ Castronovo and Dana D. Nelson (eds), *Materializing Democracy: Toward a Revitalized Cultural Politics* (Durham, NC: Duke University Press, 2002), pp. 175–194.

same-sex eroticism in this specific film, if not in general, is a manifestation of male sexual desire (Bergman's). This raises the too-easily-dismissed spectre of lesbian sexuality as a turn-on for heterosexual men, but it can also, uncannily enough, deliver to us the possibilities of male homosexuality: same-sex sexuality is same-sex sexuality; desire for seeing one's likeness with the same is a desire for what Bersani calls 'homoness', a state promising radical non-violence and ethical engagement. Male homosexuality, of course, will be most directly expressed, in equally unstable terms, two years after *Persona*'s premiere, in *Hour of the Wolf* (1968). But *Persona* uses the penis not simply as an image of masculinity engorged by male desire, but as both a point of departure and an explanation for the *necessary* destabilization that comes after its appearance and disappearance. It is the film's disorganizing principle.

One can think of the spiralling-out-of-control that comes late in the film as disallowing the full development of homosexual desire, but only in the most reductively literal way. The queer unravelling that does take place makes a permanent Alma/Elisabet union impossible; but I think it is wrong-headed for us to assume that the takeaway is that these two characters simply go back to their previous, heterosexual lives, shaken but not stirred. They return to their careers, but they have doubtlessly been profoundly changed. The final image of Alma looking into the mirror, seeing not just herself but the possibility of herself with Elisabet, suggests that she has taken something of her patient's queer quietus with her. The film may have concluded negatively, but that is not to say that Bergman gave us an unhappy ending. Its queerness abides.

Acknowledgements

I want to thank the participants at the conference 'Ingmar Bergman: 100 Years' for their helpful responses to the original version of this chapter. It was truly a career highlight to finally meet so many of my academic heroes in Bergman Studies and hear their new work, all in the space of a few too-short days at the University of Lund. Special thanks go to Linda Haverty Rugg, Jan Holmberg, and, of course, the estimable organizer of the conference, Erik Hedling. I am also grateful for the help of John Kirk, formerly of MGM Studios, who provided me with more information on the present and absent penis in *Persona*'s various film elements than I was able, finally, to take into account, as well as Magnus Rosborn and Jon Wengström at the Swedish Film Institute who, fortunately, cleared up some errors I was about to make in this study in the last instant.

Finally, let me thank Hamish Ford for his carefully thought through comments on the original draft of this work.

13
Battlefield family: Ingmar Bergman, Henrik Ibsen, and television

Michael Tapper

The idea that Ingmar Bergman was a bourgeois film director was almost a truism in the Swedish cultural debates of the 1960s and 1970s. Maria Bergom Larsson summarized the contemporary view in the following quotation from her influential book *Ingmar Bergman and Society* of 1978: 'He is ideologically tied to a traditional puritan Protestantism and a humanism with deep roots in Western bourgeois culture.'[1] Although Bergman himself had time and again stated in personal interviews that he was a social democrat, his claims were either ignored or regarded as implicit confirmations of his bourgeois sympathies, as leading Marxist-Leninist-Maoist voices in the debate viewed Sweden's Social Democratic Party as class traitors and social fascists.[2] Likewise, Bergman's enthusiastic embrace of feminist authors such as Germaine Greer was ignored by leading Swedish feminists such as Gunilla Granath and Ebba Witt-Brattström, who regarded Bergman and his films as thoroughly reactionary.[3]

Two decades later, critic Leif Zern tried to pin down Bergman's political views in his book *Se Bergman* ('See Bergman', 1993); but this time, it was an attempt to paint the director as a critic of the social-democratic project. 'In Bergman's films, the mirror of the Swedish Welfare State is smashed', Zern declares, whereupon he asserts that the films show 'what we had repressed, what we

---

1 Maria Bergom Larsson, *Ingmar Bergman and Society* (London: The Tantivy Press, 1978), p. 8.
2 Michael Tapper, *Swedish Cops: From Sjöwall & Wahlöö to Stieg Larsson* (Bristol: Intellect, 2014), pp. 64–66.
3 Lars-Olof Löthwall, 'Väsentligt och oväsentligt', *Chaplin* 13:3 (1972), 88–99; Gunilla Granath, Annika Persson, and Ebba Witt-Brattström, 'Manligt kvinnoideal i svensk film: Gengångare från den viktorianska epoken', *Film & TV* 5–6 (1973), 1–19.

thought of as outdated and, at worst, [as] unfit to live'.[4] These sweeping statements suggest that Bergman's works conjured up the idea of a spiritual sanctuary threatened by the rationalist extermination politics of Sweden's Social Democratic Party. In fact, Bergman himself continued to emphasize his social-democratic sympathies even in interviews held long after the 1976 tax-evasion affair, and he never expressed any sympathy towards other parties or ideologies.[5] But that was of no concern to Zern. His attempt at ideological appropriation is not a unique case: against the director's explicit protests, Jan Troell's documentary *Sagolandet* (*Land of Fairy Tales*, 1988) was also used by some critics to portray a social-democratic utopia turned dystopian nightmare.[6]

These interpretations aside, yet another image of the writer-director emerges when one takes a closer look at Bergman's own works and statements. Bergman was an artist in the modernist and cultural-radicalist tradition of August Strindberg and Henrik Ibsen. This is evidenced by his attacks on social repression in those institutions with which he was most familiar: the school in *Frenzy* (*Hets*, 1944), the church in *Winter Light* (*Nattvardsgästerna*, 1963), and the bourgeois patriarchal family in *The Lie* (*Reservatet*, 1970) and *Scenes from a Marriage* (*Scener ur ett äktenskap*, 1973). If anything, these works are attacks on the bourgeois ideology, values, and class society that the social-democratic project sought to reform.

Much has been written about Strindberg's influence on Bergman, not least by Egil Törnqvist (see *Strindberg's* The Ghost Sonata, as well as other works by Törnqvist). Moreover, in interviews and other texts, Bergman himself said that he did in fact view Strindberg

---

4 Leif Zern, *Se Bergman* (Stockholm: Norstedts, 1993), p. 25. In the original Swedish text, Zern uses the word *livsodugligt* (unfit to live), which corresponds to the German *lebensunwert*, a designation for persons marked for extermination under the Nazis' *Aktion T4* euthanasia project.

5 For further information on Bergman's political leanings post-1976, see the clip from the interview 'Ingmar Bergman och politiken' ('Ingmar Bergman and politics') created by Ulf Elving for the radio programme *Efter tre* ('After three'), Sveriges Radio P3, 18 February 1988, 3.15 p.m. This clip is available at http://sverigesradio.se/sida/avsnitt/1022702?programid=1602 (accessed 8 March 2018).

6 Michael Tapper and Jon Dunås, 'Intervju: Jan Troell', *Filmhäftet* 29:1 (2001), 16–17.

as his lifelong kindred spirit.[7] From the late 1950s onwards, Henrik Ibsen joined Strindberg as a prominent source of artistic and political inspiration for Bergman.

In her award-winning book *Henrik Ibsen and the Birth of Modernism*, Toril Moi portrays the playwright as a revolutionary in opposition to the nineteenth-century hegemony of the German idealism expressed in texts such as the 1796 manifesto *Das älteste Systemprogramm des deutschen Idealismus* (*The Oldest Programme for a System of German Idealism*) by Friedrich Hölderlin.[8] Idealism fused aesthetics, ethics, and religion into a utopian vision of human perfection. It prescribed the triumph of 'humanity' over 'animality', which essentially signified the sublimation of sex. Since the idealists regarded women rather than men as the bearers of human sexuality, they stressed the importance of the idealization of female sexuality. Their view was that the spirit must rule the body, and morality and duty must trump sexual impulses. Moi asserts that Ibsen sought to deconstruct both the idealization of women and Idealism as an aesthetic theory by attacking these notions in his plays, thereby deconstructing the bourgeois patriarchal family.[9]

In my book *Ingmar Bergman's 'Face to Face'*,[10] I analyse how Ibsen's ideas correspond closely with Bergman's own artistic project, especially when Bergman sought out a mass audience by exploring the artistic possibilities of the TV medium in the late 1960s. As early as 1948, Bergman had written a screenplay adaptation of *A Doll's House* (*Et dukkehjem*, 1879), introducing it as 'a tale about the little doll wife Nora and her way out of dreams and lies to clarity and liberation'.[11] Almost a decade later, in 1957, Bergman

---

7 Stig Björkman, Torsten Manns, and Jonas Sima, *Bergman on Bergman: Interviews with Ingmar Bergman*, translated by Paul Britten Austin (New York: Simon and Schuster, 1973), p. 23.
8 Toril Moi, *Henrik Ibsen and the Birth of Modernism: Art, Theater, Philosophy*, paperback reprint (Oxford: Oxford University Press, 2012), pp. 67–104; Friedrich Hölderlin, 'The Oldest Programme for a System of German Idealism' (1796), in J.M. Bernstein (ed.), *Classic and Romantic German Aesthetics* (Cambridge: Cambridge University Press, 2003), pp. 185–187.
9 Moi, *Henrik Ibsen and the Birth of Modernism*, pp. 77–81.
10 Michael Tapper, *Ingmar Bergman's 'Face to Face'* (New York: Wallflower Press/Columbia Press, 2017).
11 Björkman, Manns, and Sima, *Bergman on Bergman*, p. 137; Birgitta Steene, *Ingmar Bergman: A Reference Guide* (Amsterdam: Amsterdam University Press, 2005), p. 80.

staged *Peer Gynt* (1867) at Malmö's municipal theatre—Malmö stadsteater. This spring production coincided with his work on the screenplay for *Wild Strawberries* (*Smultronstället*, 1957), filmed in July–August of the same year. Ibsen's critiques of bourgeois Idealism as 'living a lie' and of the patriarchal family as an 'institution of the living dead' feature prominently in *Wild Strawberries*' story of Isak Borg (played by Victor Sjöström), whose sentimental self-aggrandizement coupled with unyielding principles is reminiscent of Torvald Helmer in *A Doll's House*.

Bergman's next engagement with an Ibsen play involved staging *Hedda Gabler* (1890) at the Royal Dramatic Theatre in Stockholm in 1964. *Hedda Gabler* also became Bergman's first-ever stage production outside Scandinavia, performed at the London National Theatre in 1970. He later described the play as 'the only one of my productions that gave me any satisfaction'.[12] The play also served as a source of inspiration for Bergman's film *Persona* (1966). In his *Hedda Gabler* production, Bergman portrayed Hedda as pregnant and as feeling disgust for the result of her unwanted sexual desires—so much so that she even tries to abort the foetus with her bare hands.[13] In *Persona*, we see this same inner struggle staged as a 'dream play' set in the mind/womb of a woman split into two entities that are locked in a power struggle. Nurse Alma (played by Bibi Andersson) is the idealist woman clinging to utopian ideas about marriage and family, while modern actress Elisabet (played by Liv Ullmann) rejects the way idealist ideology defines her as a wife, mother, and woman. In the film, Alma tries to encourage Elisabet to re-enter the fold of womanhood as defined by the bourgeois hegemony, only to be confronted with her own deep-seated sentiments that are at odds with her persona. Alma's ultimate decision to return to her gender-play act and ignore her inner voice of doubt, as personified by Elisabet, exemplifies what Bergman later described as women's 'inner sabotage of themselves'.[14]

Although *Persona* represents a significant artistic achievement on Bergman's part and is a classic piece of cinema, it never reached

---

12 Ingmar Bergman, *The Magic Lantern: An Autobiography*, translated by Joan Tate (London and New York: Penguin, 1988), p. 194.
13 Maaret Koskinen, '*Allting föreställer, ingenting är*': *Filmen och teatern – en tvärestetisk studie* (Nora: Nya Doxa, 2001), p. 54.
14 Arne Sellermark, 'Kvinnor behagar med att hålla käften', *Femina* 39 (September 1974), 29, 87. Tapper, *Ingmar Bergman's 'Face to Face'*, includes a more rigorous analysis of the film *Persona*; see pp. 54–58.

Battlefield family 215

a mass audience and consequently did not have any notable social or political impact on contemporary society. However, Bergman did achieve such an impact when he turned his attention to television production in the late 1960s through his newly founded company Cinematograph. His first TV production was the provocative drama *The Rite* (*Riten*, 1969, also known as *The Ritual*); it was a *succès de scandale* and a thinly disguised allegory of his troubles with Sweden's film censorship agency and especially with Erik Skoglund, who headed the agency for many years. Bergman quickly went on to achieve his popular breakthrough in the television medium with the documentary *Fårö Document* (1970) (*Fårödokument*, 1969)—a pointedly political film about social conditions on the small, remote island that became his beloved home in 1967. Attracting an audience of 2 million viewers, the film launched Bergman as a mass-market artist and helped promote his next TV production later that year, the marital drama *The Lie: A Tragicomedy of Banality* (*Reservatet: En banaliteternas tragi-komedi*, 1970). An audience of 1.2 million Swedes viewed the first broadcast of *The Lie* on 28 October 1970. Later, as the Swedish contribution to the European Broadcasting Union's Eurovision-exchange of TV plays in 1970, it had an audience of approximately 50 million viewers in Western Europe.[15] A British version was subsequently produced by director Alan Bridges in 1971, and it was broadcast as part of the BBC drama series *Play for Today*. In addition, CBS produced a US version directed by Alex Segal in 1973.

Although the Swedish version of *The Lie* was directed by Bergman's friend and colleague, actor-director Jan Molander (who played one of the students in *Frenzy*), the media referred to it as a 'Bergman production', and not unfairly so, as it was produced under his close supervision. This ninety-one-minute TV play was only shown once, however, and it has been unavailable in any format since its premiere.[16] Although the screenplay was published in 1973, the unavailability

---

15 Figures drawn from statistics compiled by Audience & Programming Analysis, a department of Sweden's public service broadcaster, Sveriges Television. Email to the author from Department Head Thomas Lindhé, 8 December 2016. See also Lars-Olof Georgsson, 'Bergman-pjäs på "Världens största teater": Ses av 50 miljoner', *Arbetet* (a Social-Democrat broadsheet), 28 October 1970.
16 *The Lie* became available via Sveriges Television's *Öppet arkiv* streaming service while this chapter was being prepared. See www.oppetarkiv.se/video/4431171/reservatet (accessed 22 May 2018).

of a cinematic version has certainly contributed to the lack of studies of *The Lie* by Bergman scholars. For this reason, I have chosen to focus on *The Lie* rather than on *Scenes from a Marriage*, Bergman's other, better-known, and more-often-analysed marital drama made for TV.

In his autobiography entitled *Images: My Life in Film*, Bergman wrote: 'I do understand the techniques used in both melodrama and soap opera quite well. One who uses melodrama as it should be used can implement the unrestrained emotional possibilities available in the genre.'[17] The key factor in *The Lie*'s critical acclaim and public success was the ease with which Bergman merged elements of his own artistry with elements of Strindberg's play *The Father* (*Fadren*, 1887), Ibsen's *A Doll's House* and *The Wild Duck* (*Vildanden*, 1884), and melodrama in order to reach a mass audience with his portrayal of a middle-aged bourgeois couple in marital crisis.

The Lie is the first work in what I refer to as 'The Djursholm Trilogy', alongside *Scenes from a Marriage* and *Face to Face* (*Ansikte mot ansikte*, 1976). All three are contemporary melodramas that reveal the discord between individual desires (love, identity, self-fulfilment) and bourgeois conformity. They are set in the materially comfortable world of the social elite with which Bergman came into close contact while he and his fourth wife, Käbi Laretei, were living in the affluent Stockholm neighbourhood of Djursholm between 1959 and 1966.

In 2015, Professor of Business Administration Mikael Holmqvist presented an in-depth study of Djursholm in book form that attracted much attention. Subtitled *Sweden's Community of Leaders*, the book recounts Djursholm's history as a neighbourhood founded in 1889 as part of the international, utopian Garden City Movement, with the intention of becoming a patrician idyll distinctly segregated from the plebeians, that is to say, the working class. *The Lie* portrays Djursholm not only as a socio-political 'reservation', but also as a closely guarded mental sanctuary far removed from the world, its madding crowd, and its conflicts. Not only that, *The Lie*'s characters are even sheltered from themselves—from their own innermost thoughts and feelings. Theirs is a 'theatrical' society of conformist, bourgeois personas with no room for failure in either career or family life. The moments of reality that occasionally seep into the

---

17 Ingmar Bergman, *Images: My Life in Film* (London and Boston, MA: Faber & Faber, 1995), p. 278.

characters' lives cause them brief pangs of distress and awareness until the carefree sanctuary offered by creature comforts comes to their rescue, scotching any perturbing emotions.

The drama's protagonists introduce themselves in a Brechtian prologue that reveals the common origin of *The Lie* and Bergman's earlier film *A Passion* (*En passion*, 1969, also known as *The Passion of Anna*) in a draft entitled 'Annandreas' and subtitled 'Proposal for Scenes from a Marriage'.[18] The two main characters in *The Lie*, married couple Anna and Andreas Fromm (played by Gunnel Lindblom and Per Myrberg), address the camera in separate monologues, telling us their names and occupations before going on to talk about their carefree lives. They are very well aware of the privilege and security afforded them by their material wealth in a life that only rarely intersects with the outside world and its problems.

Bergman employed this same type of introduction to the protagonists in the opening scene of *Scenes from a Marriage*, this time staged as a magazine interview. In this interview, the two married protagonists again talk about themselves in a manner that suggests that they wish to convince themselves (more than the readers—or viewers) of their prudent choice of personas, setting, and narrative, thereby underlining the theatricality of their family life, just as Ibsen does in his most famous plays. Bergman concludes *Scenes from a Marriage* with an ironic twist in which Marianne (played by Liv Ullmann) thoughtfully adds, 'the very lack of problems is a serious problem'—a comment that also rings true for Anna and Andreas Fromm in *The Lie*.[19] That similarity aside, Bergman's two marital dramas involve different contexts: *Scenes from a Marriage* is a response to second-wave feminism under the artistic influence of Ibsen's *A Doll House*, which is explicitly referenced in the TV series (though not in the film version). By contrast, *The Lie* locates its marital drama in the context of contemporary social and political turmoil; its external conflicts reflect internal ones and vice versa.

Ibsen's influence is evident in the English title chosen for *Reservatet* (*The Lie*); and in fact *The Lie* premiered in between two celebrated Bergman stage productions of Ibsen's works: *Hedda Gabler* at the

---

18 Nils-Hugo Geber, '*En passion*', in Jörn Donner (ed.), *Svensk filmografi, 1960–1969* (Stockholm: Svenska Filminstitutet, 1977), p. 493; Bergman, *Images*, p. 305.

19 Ingmar Bergman, *Scener ur ett äktenskap* (Stockholm: Norstedts, 1973), p. 15.

National Theatre in London (1970) and *The Wild Duck* at the Royal Dramatic Theatre in Stockholm (1972). The latter also embarked on an international tour and went on to become one of Bergman's most successful, artistically important, and celebrated productions.[20] Bergman would later name the protagonists in *Fanny and Alexander* (*Fanny och Alexander*, 1982) after the Ekdahls in *The Wild Duck*, ironically undercutting the film's supposed celebration of bourgeois family life and values.

The political subtext in *The Lie* is more explicit than in any of Bergman's preceding or subsequent productions. To begin with, *The Lie* is set in contemporary Stockholm; the main characters live at Djursholm and work in Stockholm's city centre—Andreas as an architect at some governmental department, Anna as a lecturer in Slavic languages at the university. They have two children—Henrik, eight, and Veronica, five—and a housekeeper, Berta.[21] At an earlier point in his career in the 1960s, Bergman had deliberately chosen to avoid any references to specific times and places in his films. He wanted his works to be timeless and universal, lamenting the inclusion of any hairstyling or clothing that suggested a more specific setting and hence made the films look dated only a few years after their premiere. One notable example of Bergman criticizing himself for departing from this principle of timelessness occurred in connection with *A Passion*, in which Bibi Andersson and Liv Ullmann wear miniskirts and trendy hats in the meta-cinematic interview segments.[22]

Bergman's change of tack in this respect in connection with *The Lie* was therefore a conscious choice, and it might well have come about in response to authors Lars Forssell and Sara Lidman's criticism of his film *Shame* (*Skammen*, 1968).[23] The two writers considered

---

20 Bergman's staging of *The Wild Duck* premiered at the Royal Dramatic Theatre in Stockholm in the spring of 1972 and later went on tour to Florence, Berlin, Zurich, Oslo, Copenhagen, and London, winning both public and critical acclaim. See Steene, *Ingmar Bergman*, pp. 633–639.
21 Djursholm is only explicitly mentioned in Bergman's workbook from 1968 (see Ingmar Bergman, *Arbetsboken 1955–1974* (Stockholm: Norstedts, 2018), p. 238), but is nevertheless implied in the screenplay by the Stockholm setting, the luxurious dinner party, and the presence of a housekeeper—a vestige from the pre-welfare-state era.
22 Bergman, *Images*, p. 304.
23 Lars Forssell, 'Skammen', *BLM* 8 (1968), 605–607. Sara Lidman, 'Sara Lidman angriper Bergman – Skammen', *Aftonbladet*, 6 October 1968.

Shame to be a dangerous metaphorical abstraction of the Vietnam War, and Forssell, whose play *Show* Bergman went on to stage in 1971, thought the film misanthropic 'since all forms of commitment seemed meaningless'.[24] By contrast, *The Lie* makes lack of commitment a theme in that we are introduced to protagonists whose sole ambition is to go on living their non-committal, carefree lives, avoiding any obligation to confront the real world and the lie of the happy bourgeois family life they lead.

Bergman began working on the 'Annandreas' project in April 1968, and his notes for the screenplay soon became tinged with reflections on the murder of Martin Luther King, Jr., which affected Bergman deeply.[25] King's murder became a point of reference in the film, a sobering contrast to the 'tragicomedy of banality' presented by the mundane existential and marital problems of the wealthy protagonists. At the same time, this reference serves to remind the main characters of the real world they seek to shut out, just as they repress their true feelings about each other and about the family life they lead. From the prologue, we sense that the two protagonists are educated, intelligent people who are very well aware of the absurdity of their privileged life in a world full of social injustice. They consciously choose to avert their metaphorical gaze and to theatricalize their lives and marriage because doing so brings them comfort, even while they harbour deep-seated fears and aggressions that later rise to the surface despite their best efforts to prevent this. These repressed feelings are initially reflected in their encounters with hostile people in town, and thus outside of their physical 'sanctuary' at Djursholm. Later, in the couple's final altercation, these emotions are forced to the surface with a volcanic force that shatters their sanctuary of illusions.

Following the prologue, *The Lie*'s storyline begins on the morning of 5 April 1968, the day after the assassination of Martin Luther King, Jr. In the US, the greatest outbreak of urban violence in the nation's history has already begun, and King's murder is likewise fuelling protests and riots around the world.[26] At the Fromms's home, eight-year-old Henrik is ill; but he awakes early to the sad news of Dr King's death and is rebuffed upon seeking consolation

---

24 Forssell, '*Skammen*', 605.
25 Bergman, *Arbetsboken*, pp. 232ff.
26 Eric Foner, '*Give Me Liberty!*' *An American History*, 4th edn (New York and London: W.W. Norton, 2014 [2004]), pp. 1015–1016.

from his mother. Although Anna herself experiences one of her pangs of distress and awareness upon hearing from her son about the murder, her vexation is almost instantly expelled from her sanctuary of comfort, along with her motherly sentiments. In this way, physical violence in the outside world is mirrored in the psychological cruelties of the bourgeois family. Unlike the speech in *Fanny and Alexander* that celebrates the Ekdahl family's 'little life'—one that does not concern itself with the 'big life' of the world—the two poles are clearly connected from the outset in *The Lie*. In this instance, the cold-womb symbolism found in *Wild Strawberries* and *Persona* assumes a new, political significance, most probably owing to the influence of Bergman's close friend and former screenplay collaborator Ulla Isaksson.

Around 1970, Isaksson was working on an Ibsen-inspired novel called *Summer Paradise* (*Paradistorg*), which was subsequently published in 1973. Bergman went on to produce a film version of Isaksson's novel in 1977, directed by Gunnel Lindblom. *Summer Paradise* is the story of family lies that lead to the suicide of one of the family's children for much the same reason that Hedvig committed suicide in *The Wild Duck*. Moreover, the novel's voice of moral consciousness, social worker Emma, prophesies about the 'Aniara generation'. Inspired by both Harry Martinson's 1956 science fiction poem *Aniara*, which depicts the crew of a doomed space expedition losing all moral inhibitions, and Anthony Burgess's 1962 novel *A Clockwork Orange*, Isaksson envisions the children of post-war consumerist parents as cold, egotistical, and ruthless.[27] Bergman connects Isaksson's ideas with his own cold-womb motif in depicting the Fromm children as unloved and uncared for, as treated as if they were commodities, and, hence, as learning to seek comfort in

---

27 The concept of 'Aniara children' originated in a 1965 report on juvenile crime authored by Kristina Humble and Gitte Settergren-Carlsson, which was later published under the title 'Unga lagöverträdare: Personlighet och relationer i belysning av projektiva metoder' ('Young lawbreakers'), SOU (1974), Report No. 31. The concept migrated to the sphere of public debate in Sweden during the 1960s and 1970s and influenced novels such as Per Gunnar Evander's *Uppkomlingarna: En personundersökning* ('The Upstarts: A Personal Case Study', 1969) and films such as Jan Halldoff's *Stenansiktet* ('The Stone Face', 1973). It has much in common with historian Christopher Lasch's cultural analysis of the 'Me' generation in his seminal book *The Culture of Narcissism: American Life in the Age of Diminishing Expectations* (New York: W.W. Norton, 1979).

consumer goods, such as TV and toys, rather than in interaction with other people. In fact, we never see the children play with each other or with others; and in a moment of existential crisis, Andreas reflects on their upbringing as one of material safety but emotional coldness: 'They get all the fucking vitamins they should have, but no physical affection.'[28]

Later in the film, Anna and Andreas return from a dinner party to find Henrik asleep in front of the TV, in the sole and symbolic company of a bottle of Coca-Cola. As he goes to his bedroom, Henrik mutters about all the cruelties he has witnessed on TV—no doubt referring to the violent uprisings that followed the assassination of Martin Luther King, Jr. and to the horror-filled daily reports from the Vietnam War. His sister Veronica has enveloped herself in a sea of toys and children's books—her sanctuary. They are Aniara children in the making. Bergman revisited this motif in *Face to Face*, in which the protagonist Jenny (played by Liv Ullmann) emerges from a suicidal depression triggered by childhood trauma only to find that she herself has continued the legacy of the cold womb in her raising of her own daughter.

The Henrik and Veronica characters in *The Lie* are just two casualties of the world of war and conflict from which Anna and Andreas Fromm, like the protagonists in *Shame* before them, try so hard to escape, only to become part of—and even complicit in—its campaign of destruction. When Anna meets a less successful colleague at her university, and Andreas runs into a working-class man in the street who has witnessed his feeble attempt to abscond from a minor traffic accident, both are confronted with a naked aggression incited by what they represent: class privilege and moral indifference in an unjust world. In addition, in keeping up the façade of a happy family, Anna and Andreas are on the run from commitment to each other and to authentic life itself. Later that same day, Anna goes to visit her lover of seven years, her next-door neighbour Elis (played by Erland Josephson). Their love nest is a bland apartment located in a quiet, downtown side street, an apartment that mirrors their passionless feelings for each other. Meanwhile, Andreas experiences an attack of existential angst and goes to see his doctor, only to achieve a temporary release from his pain by having a bland

---

28 Ingmar Bergman, 'Reservatet', in Ingmar Bergman, *Filmberättelser 3: Riten/ Reservatet/Beröringen/Viskningar och rop* (Stockholm: Norstedts, 1973), p. 84.

liaison of his own with the nurse, Ester, whom he afterwards dismisses in an offhand manner. Referring to Strindberg's *Miss Julie* (*Fröken Julie*, 1888) as a play in which 'the man and the woman never stop swapping masks', Bergman claimed in an interview to 'make no special distinction between male and female'.[29] He employs this idea in the contemporary melodrama of *The Lie*, endowing it with a gender twist that truly deconstructs the idealization of women while ironically undercutting patriarchal ideology. In *The Lie*, it is Anna who is the Strindbergian 'strong one'; she wears the colloquial trousers in the family, exhibiting all the traits of a privileged male: success at work, good looks, the envy of others, and the prospect of an international career. For Anna, as for male characters in melodramas and soap operas mainly geared to female audiences, the covenant of marriage is more an arrangement of convenience than of love. Andreas, on the other hand, is weak—an aged, balding upstart whose professional career has stalled as younger men stand poised to overtake him on the ladder to success. When confronted in the street, Andreas chooses 'flight' rather than 'fight'. At home, he is at best a sexual substitute for his neighbour, Elis, who is far more skilled in satisfying Anna's sexual needs. In melodrama/soap-opera terms, Andreas is much like the classic housewife character—trusty, faithful, needy, and boring; a frail Sue Ellen to Anna's tough, cold JR.

In a moment of clarity, Andreas tries to come to grips with his situation by writing a letter to his wife—a dramatic device we recognize from previous Bergman films such as *Winter Light*. Like Nora in *A Doll's House*, Andreas is tired of the lies and the charade of the bourgeois family; he wants to break out and find a new way of life. His emotional insights go hand in hand with an awakening social consciousness:

> I think we make mistakes, somehow. Perhaps we simply live the wrong way, isolating ourselves in a small clan of people who all live a privileged life far removed from most people's reality. [...] Isn't it true that our marriage is a bloody parody of what it should be, of what it was originally intended to be? Isn't everything a wretched lie? Can we change this? Can we? Or are we stuck? Trapped in our sanctuary. Our comfortable [...][30]

---

29 Björkman, Manns, and Sima, *Bergman on Bergman*, p. 18.
30 Bergman, *Filmberättelser 3*, pp. 84–85. Translation mine.

Ultimately, he aborts his letter-writing and discards the unfinished letter. Later, when he tries to convey his thoughts to his wife during their final showdown (a no-holds-barred quarrel that might have been inspired by Edward Albee's play *Who's Afraid of Virginia Woolf?*, which Bergman staged at Stockholm's Royal Dramatic Theatre in 1963), they both agree that their marriage and their way of life has, indeed, been a tangle of lies. Nevertheless, the truth is still a more threatening proposition than falsehoods: it triggers violent emotions of shame, hurt, and hate, and calls for uncomfortable changes in their family life and social standing. While truth might set them free, comfort is what their family life has revolved around—and truth is not comfortable. Bergman leaves his protagonists at a moment of hesitation, just as the quarrel seems to end in the prospect of divorce. In an echo from Strindberg's play *The Father* (adapted for film in 1969 by Bergman's mentor, Alf Sjöberg, with Gunnel Lindblom as Laura), Anna considers leaving her husband and taking their children with her, since she is capable of taking care of herself. Then, suddenly, she stops, pained, and says: 'I don't want to. No, I don't.'[31] When Andreas asks Anna what it is that she does not want, she makes no reply.

In this final scene, Bergman leaves his protagonists on a razor's edge between their old life of lies and a possible new and uncertain life of truth. Perhaps they will return to their old ways, like Tomas the minister in *Winter Light*, who keeps writing sermons and conducting services while seriously doubting God's existence, or Alma in *Persona*, who chooses to return to her former way of life after confronting her innermost doubts about motherhood and the prospect of being a wife. If so, Anna and Andreas would join these Bergman characters in a life that consists of going through the motions without faith or a sense of purpose. That would amount to joining 'the living dead'. Whichever alternative they choose, Bergman presents the decision as a choice between ideologies: to remain within the fold of the bourgeois family would mean preserving the lies and conformity, as well as the social order and privileges inherent in the concept. The alternative would entail a jump off a cliff into the unknown. Bergman pauses at the moment of decision.

---

31 Bergman, *Filmberättelser 3*, p. 99.

14
Bergman/Birdman/Vogler: an ecocritical examination of the birds of Bergman

Linda Haverty Rugg

It is important first of all to note that this chapter will not make the claim that Ingmar Bergman was an environmental activist. The reference to ecocriticism in the title refers not to any political engagement on Bergman's part, but rather to the way in which his films create natural spaces and reflect on the non-human environment and its relation to the human. In particular, the focus is on one aspect of the non-human environment, a phenomenon that appears in almost all of his films, occasionally in obtrusive ways: the presence of birds. Looking closely at the representation of birds and their song in Bergman offers insight into the way his films frame the relationship between humans and the non-human environment, but also how they create a space for the human position within nature. Birds in Bergman's films sometimes seem to be 'merely' part of a film's *ambience*, a concept that deserves more detailed exploration, since it has special significance both in ecocriticism and in cinema. It might be argued that the ambient in a cinematic *mise-en-scène* illuminates a film's ecological position.

There are other moments in Bergman's films in which birds function not as creatures in their own right (albeit singing anonymously in the ambient background), but as part of a human symbolic language. The raven or the crow or the owl signifies disaster or death; the cuckoo sings prophetically of the potential for love or loss of love; and the song thrush (called 'night watch' in one Swedish dialect) sings in consonance with the humans in a film who sit and wait in the darkness before dawn. This human appropriation of birds and their song is the kind of practice that motivates Jacques Derrida's cry of protest in his *The Animal that Therefore I Am*, when he insists on pointing not to a symbolic cat, but the cat as subject, as individual: 'No, no, my cat, the cat that looks at me in my bedroom or bathroom, this cat that is perhaps not "my cat", or "my pussycat", does not appear here to represent, like an ambassador, the immense symbolic responsibility with which our culture has always charged the feline race.'[1] But though 'the immense symbolic responsibility' which humans impose upon animals seems to divest them of their singularity and agency, it also hints at the degree to which human translation of the world depends on human enmeshment and encounters with animals. The drive to capture animals within the net of human meaning points to a desire to draw the unknowable (the mind or the life of the animal) into a safer context of human meaning and comprehension. Thus the symbolic use of animals unveils the fact of our unknowing, but also mirrors the fact of the unknowable animal within us; humans, too, are animals, and tend to see animals as projections of our own animal essence, our desires, our fears, our prophetic suspicions. In Bergman's film *Vargtimmen* (*Hour of the Wolf*, 1968) the shadow figure of the demonic 'Birdman' encapsulates that projected unconscious image of the animal within, the figuration that has obsessed humans since prehistoric times.

In Bergman's film settings we hear birds call or sing or see them swimming or flying as they do in the natural environments that define the films' geographic space: various regions of Sweden, from the southern coast to the Stockholm archipelago. There are rooks, finches, jackdaws, gulls, swans, crows, magpies, roosters, thrushes, tits, cuckoos, owls, ravens, and many more, some visible on the screen, some only audible on the soundtrack. Because the birds we see and hear in Bergman's films define the place and time of the film's action—Sweden in the seasons of the year in which the film narratives are set—one can at first easily imagine the birds as mere elements of the film's ambience. But there is a slippage between what we might call a representation of birds as ambient nature and the use of birds as meaningful signs; Bergman's birds migrate easily from the natural realm to the human realm of signifiers. The sounds or appearances of birds in these instances are often marked in some explicit way that asks to be interpreted. Bergman's strategic use of birds and their calls reveals a thorough acquaintance with the meaning of birds as it is understood in Swedish folklore, for instance, which raises the question of how much a non-Swedish audience will comprehend. And beyond folkloric and other symbolic uses of bird imagery, there is an oblique reference to birds through Bergman's

---

1 Jacques Derrida, *The Animal that Therefore I Am* (New York: Fordham University Press, 2008), p. 9.

repeated use of the surname Vogler across several films and theatre pieces. 'Vogler' is a rare name in Sweden; it originates in German-speaking lands, where the name denotes an old profession: 'bird-catcher', which is the profession of Papageno in Mozart's *The Magic Flute*, an opera filmed and cited by Bergman. In *Hour of the Wolf*, Bergman creates an odd link between the demonic Birdman figure and Mozart's comic Papageno, which calls for further interpretation and relates to Bergman's ornithology more generally.

The first area of contact with birds is the natural realm, which invites a consideration of the concept of ambience in both cinema and ecocriticism. In cinema, I will focus on the concept of ambient *sound*, for it is in the audial realm that the birds of Bergman are most interesting. A straightforward definition appears on the website mediacollege.com: 'Ambient sound (also known as ambience, atmosphere, atmos, or background noise) means the background sounds which are present in a scene or location'.[2] But what is the sound doing there? One scholar of film sound, Budhaditya Chattopadhyay, begins to explain: 'In film and media production, ambient sound is a standard term that denotes the site-specific background sound component providing locational atmospheres and spatial information of public places.'[3] In his view, ambient sounds 'sculpt the presence of a site by producing an embodied experience of the site' and 'inject life and substance not only to what we see on the cinematic screen but also to the off-screen story-world'.[4] This is true because ambient sound can provide continuity in screened space, linking one location with another, and also reference to space that is seen neither by the film audience nor by the characters in the film, as in the space birds occupy in trees, in bushes, or in the air. In the cinematic space, the invisible overhead presence of birds (signalled by their song and calls on the soundtrack) carves out the overhead space of the world, the one occupied by unseen observers: the birds, a potential deity, and, by association, the film's viewers.

The ecocritical idea of ambience finds full and complex expression in Timothy Morton's 2007 book, *Ecology without Nature*, where

---

2 'Ambient Sound', Media College.com, www.mediacollege.com/audio/ambient/ (accessed 5 October 2018).
3 Budhaditya Chattopadhyay, 'Reconstructing Atmospheres: Ambient Sound in Film and Media Production', *Communication and the Public* 2:4 (2017), 352–364 (p. 352).
4 Chattopadhyay, 'Reconstructing Atmospheres', 352, 354.

he describes a 'poetics of ambience' that is the distinguishing feature of what he calls 'ecomimesis'. To put it simply, ecomimesis is a representational practice in literature and art which attempts to recreate the experience of nature, as when Wordsworth writes about daffodils or a film incorporates images, light, and sound to give the impression of a particular place or time in nature. Ecomimesis, writes Morton, 'involves a poetics of *ambience*. Ambience denotes a sense of a circumambient, or surrounding, *world*. It suggests something material and physical, though somewhat intangible, as if space itself had a material aspect [...] Ambience, that which surrounds on both sides, can refer to the margins of a page, the silence before and after music, the frame and walls around a picture.'[5] Here the consonance between Morton's definition and Chattopadhyay's unpacking of ambience in cinema comes into view. Morton goes on to use the term 'rendering' to describe how ecomimesis is achieved, drawing on cinema as his example: 'First and foremost, ambient poetics is a *rendering*. I mean this in the sense developed by the concrete music composer and cinema theorist Michel Chion. Rendering is technically what visual- and sonic-effect artists do to a film to generate a more or less consistent sense of atmosphere or world.'[6] So far, Morton's ecocritical definition of ambience does not differ significantly from the cinematic definition. Both ambient film sound and ambient poetics aim to conjure up an embodied world. But Morton goes on to explore the implications and challenges of creating what he calls 'a copy without an original'—that is, a representation of the natural world which is in fact a constructed aesthetic object, a construction that pretends to some degree to be natural.[7]

Ambience in film is of course not truly ambient (that is, outside the margins of the narrative), but it is part of the construction. That this is true is beautifully illustrated in Alexis Luko's book on music and sound in Bergman's films when she cites the working notes on a conversation between Bergman and a sound engineer who are putting together the rendering for *Aus dem Leben der Marionetten* (*From the Life of the Marionettes*, 1980):

> Bergman: Then here, yes. Yes, here then we have to change this. It must be quiet – a little calm.

---

5 Timothy Morton, *Ecology without Nature* (Cambridge, MA, and London: Harvard University Press, 2007), p. 34.
6 Morton, *Ecology without Nature*, p. 35.
7 Morton, *Ecology without Nature*, p. 35.

Technician:	One must hear the peep doors opening and closing … This doesn't come out in the sound at all. Door opening. Door closing.
Bergman:	Yes. A little bit calm. Mainly this one must be audible as well. But no birds? And here a little music, yes. 1:16:06. And this music. It is fantastic, beautiful. You will need to reduce the sound here.[8]

The attention to detail as the two men go over a sequence frame by frame highlights the degree to which the visual and audial dimensions of film are constructed, but what is striking about this particular exchange is Bergman's interest in including birds. Ultimately the completed film contains no birdsong at all, which is unusual among Bergman's works, but here is the evidence that if birdsong is in a film, it is not necessarily because birds happened to be singing in the background during filming: someone decided to put it there. Because ambience in film is indeed a construct, film has to use what Morton, borrowing from Derrida, calls a 're-mark' in order to try to show the viewer what is significant both in the visual frame and on the soundtrack; what are we really supposed to listen to and attend to in order to derive meaning, and what is *merely* ambient? Focusing on an object or face, lighting or camera tracking to pick out part of the screen, bringing a sound to the fore, making it part of the narrative—all of these are re-marking strategies. The answer to the question 'what is merely ambient?' is that nothing is *merely* ambient; everything carries some type of significance because it is all part of the rendering. What is in the background has the potential to be brought to the foreground, but then has to be pressed out to the margins by the narrative focus. 'Ambience', says Morton, 'can only be glimpsed as a fleeting, dissolving presence that flickers across our perception and cannot be brought front and center.'[9] Sometimes it is true, as Morton says, that the ambient sound only flickers briefly at the corner of our attention. Other times we are made more aware of what is supposedly in the background, as a sound is re-marked.

This is what happens in some of Bergman's bird sequences. Morton makes the argument for a re-marking, an awareness of the ambient as a kind of moral imperative. He declares that we must stop thinking of the ambient as something outside our margins. Quoting Bruno

---

8 Alexis Luko, *Sonatas, Screams, and Silence: Music and Sound in the Films of Ingmar Bergman* (New York and London: Routledge, 2016), p. 257.
9 Morton, *Ecology without Nature*, p. 51.

Latour, who insists that we are obliged now, in this moment of ecological crisis, 'to *internalize* the environment that [has been viewed] up to now as another world',[10] Morton argues for the re-marking of the ambient as a general practice. It is by re-marking the margins, the ambient background, as significant, at least for a flickering moment, that we become aware that the ambient carries a critical message.

We see an example of the re-marking of the ambient in *Jungfrukällan* (*The Virgin Spring*, 1960). The ambience is a Swedish summer night; the narrative focus is a father's preparation to avenge his daughter's murder. In the background we hear the persistent voice of a song thrush (*taltrast* in Swedish). That bird's call continues from the shot of the vengeful father (played by Max von Sydow) within the walls of his homestead through a brief cut to his anxious foster daughter, and it persists as he approaches a slender birch tree, which he pulls down in order to cut branches for a purifying sauna bath. Even as he falls on the tree, bringing it crashing to the ground, we can hear the voice of the bird clearly over the loud swish of moving branches and his hoarse breathing. The viewer's primary attention at that moment is in all likelihood riveted to the tall blond man and the slender white tree which, in its vulnerable isolated position against the horizon, calls to mind an association with the murdered daughter. Like the birdsong, the tree seems re-marked. The narrative at this point is intense; the father has just discovered that his daughter's murderers unwittingly arrived at his house and spent the night. At the same time, the thrush's call is persistent and striking, acting as a link between visual scenes, but also flickering into our attention, in part owing to the silence of the humans. Though there may well have been a thrush singing on site (we catch a brief glimpse of a flying bird on the screen), the song is deliberately rendered on the soundtrack to be strongly perceptible, in a way that feels obtrusive and insistent. Because we know that ambient sound is engineered, we are placed in the position of having to determine its significance if we can.

Unlike some of the birds Bergman engages in his films, the song thrush does not have a strong folkloric identity; the bird is migratory, and so its presence on the soundtrack indicates that the time of year must be spring or summer, which we already know through the narrative of the film, though the bird's voice can add to the

---

10 Morton, *Ecology without Nature*, p. 51.

sense of embodiment within time and space. A descriptive dialect name for the *taltrast* is *nattvaka*, or night watch, because the bird sings through the night. Though to non-Swedish eyes this sequence might appear to be filmed during the day, it is actually a light summer's night. Following his purifying sauna, the father will keep a vigil together with the girl's mother; they sit watching the sleeping murderers in a remarkable performance of patience, waiting for true day to come so that the father can exact his revenge when the murderers are fully awake. But a viewer's knowledge of bird lore would have to be rather extensive to associate the night watch bird with the vigil of the parents. Another, easier reading of the bird's persistent song would be its lack of correspondence to the narrative action that takes place on screen. There is a rift between the continuous vibrant presence of an active non-human world and the desperate crisis of the human figures; the bird does not know or care about the girl's murder, and non-human life continues as usual, with the human drama at the margins of the bird's world. In this way the film signals the relative insignificance of the human crisis when nested within the larger natural narrative.

The opening credit sequence of *Sommarlek* (*Summer Interlude*, 1951) is backed by both symphonic music and a birdsong medley, with a visual focus on a flowering landscape and special attention to a *prästkrage* (oxeye daisy), a flower associated with Midsummer. Summer light characterizes the flashback scenes of the film, which will stand in stark contrast to the autumnal atmosphere created through dark forest, keening wind, and crow calls that mark the present time of narration. The defining sound of the summer flashback sequences is the cuckoo's call; in Sweden the cuckoo is present only during the summer. A traditional practice is to go into the forest on Ascension Day (which normally falls in May) with a picnic in order to listen for the cuckoo's call, which was believed to prophesy marriage or a good or poor fortune in the year to come. This particular re-mark (that is, that the cuckoo has prophetic significance, particularly for a Swedish viewer) might be easy to discount as mere ambience, except that *Summer Interlude* offers additional (and more re-marked) examples of prophecy delivered by birds. One example occurs as the protagonist Marie arrives on the island to confront her past and encounters a woman who, in another scene in the film, is said to embody death. The ambience is autumn, with bare branches and a cold wind blowing on the soundtrack; but again this bird's voice, even more than the thrush in *The Virgin Spring*, is insistently re-marked, and this time the calling bird is visible, the visual focus of the frame. A flock of crows is called a murder of crows in English; similarly, in Sweden crows were believed to prophesy death. Further, in the sequence before the one in which the young male protagonist, Marie's lover Henrik, dies in an accident, Marie hears the call of a bird and is terrified. At first the mood between the two young people is cheerful and flirtatious, but then suddenly they hear the eerie call of an unseen bird, and Marie cries out 'God, how horrid! What was that?' Henrik answers, 'That was an owl; don't you recognize it?' 'God, how horrid!' she repeats. The Swedish word she uses, 'otäck', also carries some connotation of the uncanny or weird. 'Did it scare you?' asks Henrik. 'I don't know', she says. 'I just feel as if I want to cry tonight.' The bird the script identifies is a *berguv*, a horned owl. According to Swedish folk tradition, this owl's call foretold storms and accidents to such a degree that children were forbidden to imitate it.[11] And indeed, the call occurs shortly before Henrik's accident. The call on the soundtrack, however, does not belong to a horned owl; it is the voice of a *kattuggla* or brown owl, whose cry, again according to Swedish folk legend, foretells death if it is heard in the vicinity of a house.[12] It is difficult to know whether the film means to foreground the *berguv* (in the script) or the *kattuggla* (on the soundtrack), but essentially the re-mark remains the same: impending disaster linked to the voice of an owl.

In *Smultronstället* (*Wild Strawberries*, 1957), elderly protagonist Isak Borg's second nightmare opens with a remarkable flight of shrieking birds. Appearing at first superimposed on Isak's head, as if they represent his dark and overwhelming thoughts, the flock of screeching jackdaws takes flight as the first transitional image from waking into dreaming. Subsequently in the dream the object of Isak's affection appears, his cousin Sara, comforting a baby with the words, 'Don't be frightened of the jackdaws.' And indeed jackdaws, when appearing in flocks, foretell war or epidemics, particularly the plague. But in this context, they do not obviously possess that folkloric function only. Instead they indicate how what seems to be merely ambient in the natural, waking world (a flock of birds) is in fact a phenomenon from the natural world, an ambient phenomenon, which has been re-marked in Isak's dream and attached

---

11 Mats Åke Bergström and Carl-Fredrik Lundevall, *Fåglarna i Norden* (Stockholm: ICA Förlag), p. 150.
12 'Ugglor', *Nordisk familjebok*, vol. 30 (Stockholm: Nordisk familjeboksförlaget, 1904–1926), pp. 854–855.

to a meaning in Isak's dreaming consciousness. In other words, jackdaws are real, live beings that behave precisely in the way they were recorded for the film. But within the film's narrative they are also an interior projection of Isak's troubled mind. (Students in courses I have taught have misidentified the jackdaws as bats, because they associate this type of terrifying flock of creatures with bat symbolism.) Here is a way that the environment has been internalized, though perhaps not as Bruno Latour intended.

Another potential confusion of ontological space in connection with nature and birdsong occurs in *Det sjunde inseglet* (*The Seventh Seal*, 1957). When Jof, a medieval performer, leaves his wagon after waking one beautiful summer morning, he apparently sees a vision of the Virgin Mary, holding the toddler Jesus's hands as he learns to walk. Jof watches this action unfold in a sunlit glade a little distance from his wagon; before the Virgin appears, there is a medley of summer birdsong on the soundtrack. That birdsong continues as an extradiegetic music joins in, signalling the beginning of the vision. The birdsong continues, clearly audible along with the music, until Jof rubs his eyes, and both the Virgin and the music disappear. But the birdsong remains. As discussed earlier in the explanation of ambient sound, the birdsong serves to create a continuity of time and space, suggesting that the vision Jof experiences does not interrupt the sensory experiences of the natural world, but is in harmony with them. 'Vision music' and birdsong occupy the same summer space in the film.

In contrast, the examples cited from *Wild Strawberries* and *Summer Interlude*, in which birds prophesy death, point towards a demonic image of birdlife; but one might even argue that the supposedly benign representations of birds and birdsongs retain something demonic, or at least uncanny. Theodor Adorno, in his aesthetic theory, presents an unusual reading of birdsong: 'The song of birds is found beautiful by everyone; no feeling person in whom something of the European tradition survives fails to be moved by the sound of a robin after a rain shower. Yet something frightening lurks in the song of birds precisely because it is not a song but obeys the spell in which it is enmeshed.'[13] Adorno's (admittedly Eurocentric) argument seems to be staked in an understanding of birdsong as something essentially mechanical. He notes that unlike human song,

---

13 Theodor Adorno, *Aesthetic Theory*, edited and translated by Robert Hullot-Kentor (London: Athlone, 1997), p. 66.

which is produced by an individual as an act of volition, birdsong is not an act of will but a kind of mechanical response that is provoked by environmental conditions, such as the need to protect territory or find a mate.

Further, while the songs of some birds, such as the nightingale, the European blackbird, the mockingbird, and the lyrebird show amazing variation, the reason that we are able to identify species via call or song is that the sound is not unique to individuals, nor does it vary significantly. Adorno's argument runs counter to the argument implicit in Hans Christian Andersen's tale 'The Nightingale', in which a 'real' nightingale vanquishes a mechanical nightingale in a kind of contest of song because the true nightingale can vary his repertoire, while the machine repeats the same tones again and again. Perhaps more importantly, Adorno's representation of birdsong runs counter to the traditional association of 'birds' and 'freedom'. The forced repetition of the same songs again and again emphasizes nature's lack of subjective will, the deadness or machine aspect of nature. One might read the song of the thrush in *The Virgin Spring* in that way, or the endless repetition of the cuckoo at the beginning of *Summer Interlude*, a repetition that was no doubt an inspiration for the cuckoo clock.

In *Hour of the Wolf*, the artist protagonist Johan Borg shows his frightened wife a notebook in which he has drawn the demonic figures that plague him. We cannot see the notebook, but we see him point to an image, saying, 'And here: he's the worst of the lot. ... I call him the birdman. I don't know if it's a real beak or only a mask. He's so strangely quick and he's related to Papageno of *The Magic Flute*.' Later in the film we see an encounter between the artist and the demon, a man who turns into a huge raven or crow; and at the film's conclusion, the birdman again transforms into his bird shape, attacking Johan violently. It seems easy at first glance to relate the birdman to the demonic and violent flocks in Hitchcock's *The Birds*, which had come out five years earlier in 1963. But something more is happening in Bergman's evocation of birds. In Alexis Luko's book on Bergman, one chapter is entitled 'Listening to Bergman's Monsters'. In particular, Luko focuses on a concept developed by Michel Chion, the acoustic being, an entity that is heard but usually shrouded from view.[14] Chion's argument is that the sound of the unseen monster in films creates a special

---

14 Luko, *Sonatas, Screams, and Silence*, p. 137.

kind of horror. This concept can be extended to include birdsong and the calls of birds, imagining that while certain kinds of bird voices and ambient soundscapes are meant to be beautiful and evoke associations with such positive emotions as love and happiness, Bergman's birds, even in apparently positive renderings of environmental ambience, have the potential to turn into acoustic beings, unseen horrors, representations of soullessness or, as Adorno might have it, enmeshment, imprisonment. The dual possibility of the bird finds expression in Johan Borg's odd link between the demonic birdman and Papageno, the comic birdcatcher of Mozart's *Magic Flute*. How can the birdman be demonic bird and birdcatcher, *Vogelfänger*, *Vogler*, all at once?

As noted earlier, Bergman employs the surname Vogler for a number of his characters in several films. Albert Emanuel, Amanda, and Granny Vogler appear in *Ansiktet* (*The Magician*, 1958) as the leaders of a troupe of wandering magicians; Elisabet Vogler is the protagonist who falls mute in the midst of a theatre performance in Bergman's *Persona* (1966); Veronica Vogler is the demonic lover of the artist-protagonist in *Hour of the Wolf*; veteran Bergman actor Erland Josephson plays both Henrik Vogler, a theatre director in *Efter repetitionen* (*After the Rehearsal*, 1984), and Osvald Vogler, a mental patient in *Larmar och gör sig till* (*In the Presence of a Clown*, 1997). A characteristic of enmeshment or imprisonment governs several of these figures in significant ways: both Emanuel Vogler and Elisabet Vogler have elected to be (or have been forced to be) mute. This would make them voiceless mutes, the counterpart to Chion's acoustic beings: rather than being heard but not seen, they are seen but do not speak. Luko proposes that both the acoustic beings and the voiceless mutes retain the power of surveillance and observation, which is certainly one of the uncanny things about both birds as acoustic beings and Voglers as voiceless mutes. Veronica Vogler is trapped within an erotic fantasy with Johan Borg; Henrik Vogler is trapped within the structure of repetition that governs both the theatre's endless rehearsals and performances and his relationships with women. Osvald Vogler is insane, confined at one point in an asylum. The Voglers, then, cannot be associated with the free flight of birds or Papageno's easy seduction and capture of birds; they themselves reside within cages.

For a key to understanding Bergman's involvement with birds, we can return briefly to Morton, who at one point seemed to be saying that all we needed was to internalize the ambient world. He writes, 'If we could not merely figure out but actually *experience* the fact that we were embedded in our world, then we would be less likely to destroy it.'[15] But being embedded in the world is not a blissful experience of one-ness with the universe, not in Morton's view and not in Bergman's, either. As Morton notes, 'The ecological thought, the thinking of interconnectedness, has a dark side embodied not in a hippie aesthetic of life over death, or a sadistic-sentimental Bambification of sentient beings, but in a "goth" assertion of the contingent and necessarily queer idea that we want to stay with a dying world: *dark ecology*.'[16] Bergman's recurrent image of entrapment, his use of birds and birdsong as prophecies of death or as voices indifferent to the human sphere or as acoustic beings could be said to reflect a kind of dark ecology; and as in Morton's assessment of dark ecology there is a duality there, a queer representation of both beauty and terror. In an interview in 2001, Bergman said, 'I normally am afraid of birds.'[17] This is a quotation that some have linked to the negative representation of the members of the Vogler family. But he goes on to say that he had a dream of 'a large, shimmering green bird', which he took to be a message from his late wife, Ingrid. The beauty of birds, as Adorno writes, is undeniable; but the uncanniness of birds, their power of surveillance, their potential to turn into the monstrous beings of *Hour of the Wolf* or Hitchcock's *Birds*, is undeniable as well. The return of the dead as birds, as messengers from the realm of the dead, can be associated with Morton's notion of dark ecology, the desire to stay with a dying world. In Bergman's films, the birds embody both the beauty of that world and its horrors.

---

15 Morton, *Ecology without Nature*, p. 64.
16 Morton, *Ecology without Nature*, pp. 184–185.
17 Xan Brooks, 'Bergman Talks of His Dreams and Demons in Rare Interview', *Guardian* Wednesday 12 December 2001, www.theguardian.com/film/2001/dec/12/news.xanbrooks (accessed 22 May 2018).

15
Visionaries and charlatans: Ingmar Bergman's filmmaking

Laura Hubner

Over the years, Ingmar Bergman has been hailed by journalists as a visionary director, with the capacity to convey to an international audience—via films as diverse as *The Seventh Seal* (*Det sjunde inseglet*, 1956), *Persona* (1966) and *Fanny and Alexander* (*Fanny och Alexander*, 1982)—insights into the times when the films were made, as well as into more universal concerns. Myrna Oliver's headline in the *Los Angeles Times*, 'Cinema's Brooding Auteur of the Psyche: His Work Opened the Door for Foreign Film in the US', captures the essence of newspaper articles released on Bergman's death, claiming that this 'visionary' auteur redefined cinema by confronting the big questions concerning existence and God.[1] Through creative manipulation of images, sounds, and words, Bergman's films explore faith, human relationships, and communication. That Bergman died on the same day as Michelangelo Antonioni (30 July 2007) was also seen as significant. Xan Brooks from the British newspaper *The Guardian* wrote: 'It remains to be seen whether this giddy spell signals the onset of some arthouse apocalypse.'[2] A.O. Scott from *The New York Times* commented:

> [T]he simultaneity was startling. Not only because they were both great filmmakers, but more because, in their prime, Mr. Antonioni and Mr. Bergman were seen as the twin embodiments of the idea

---

1 Myrna Oliver, 'Cinema's Brooding Auteur of the Psyche: His Work Opened the Door for Foreign Film in the US', *The Los Angeles Times*, 31 July 2007, http://articles.latimes.com/2007/jul/31/local/me-bergman31 (accessed 28 August 2018).
2 Xan Brooks, 'First Ingmar Bergman, now Michelangelo Antonioni', *The Guardian*, 31 July 2007, www.theguardian.com/film/filmblog/2007/jul/31/firstingmarbergmannowmichelangeloantonioni (accessed 28 August 2018).

that a filmmaker could be, without qualification or compromise, a great artist.³

However, the label 'artist', with the expectations that it entails in terms of the ability to communicate meaningfully and to connect with the human condition, could be torturous to bear, especially as Bergman often publicly declared a desire to be perceived simply as one of many craftspeople working on a product. Throughout Bergman's career, some critics also railed against 'the visionary Bergman', often *because* of his exalted status as a supreme artist, for allegedly regurgitating the same themes, outdated symbols, or self-preoccupied fixations. Scathing criticism did not pass Bergman by unnoticed, and he was often his own worst critic; but feeding his own self-criticism back into his work led to films that scrutinize artists' relationship with their audience and reflect on the process of creating a product that can itself speak vitally to human concerns.

Bergman's films often convey the artist as a fusion of visionary and charlatan. Jof in *The Seventh Seal* has a visionary capacity as the travelling actor who can perceive a world beyond everyday reality. He sees the knight playing chess with Death; the Dance of Death is his vision. But he also fabricates and elaborates on his tales. When his wife Mia reminds him that he made up the story about the Devil painting the wheels red with his tail, he says that he did this so that she would believe in his other visions. While these are clearly 'light-touch' fabrications rather than the work of a professional charlatan, the need to make things up—to lend viability to less credible visions—opens up the notion that the visionary and the charlatan are not necessarily mutually exclusive; indeed, they often feed off each other. *The Seventh Seal* also begins to address the humiliations faced by the actor, stemming from the severe expectations an audience places on an artist, for example when Jof is made to perform like a bear. Visionaries and charlatans are not represented as straightforward opposites in Bergman's filmmaking. Not only do they merge within a single figure; they also draw on each other's energies to sustain validity and power.

However, I would like to focus on a very different figure in Bergman's filmmaking, a figure that was particularly prominent in the late 1950s. This visionary figure is someone who (in contrast to

---

3 A.O. Scott, 'Before Them, Films Were Just Movies', *The New York Times*, 1 August 2007, www.nytimes.com/2007/08/01/movies/05scot.html (accessed 28 August 2018).

Jof) is plagued by a deep-seated internal fear of being exposed as a charlatan. This condition constitutes the fear of an abrupt loss or lack—of being exposed as wanting, or suddenly bereft of a previously assumed persona, power, or skill. In *Wild Strawberries* (*Smultronstället*, 1957), we witness a figure brimming with an extraordinary visionary capacity who is also plagued by terrors of self-doubt. The film concerns the day-long journey taken by venerated seventy-eight-year-old Professor Isak Borg from Stockholm to Lund where he is to be awarded the rare accolade of 'jubilee doctor', a 'reward for both academic distinction and longevity'.[4] Following the nightmare Isak has near the start of the film, which he sees as an omen, he changes his plan to fly and decides to drive the long distance to the ceremony. As Philip and Kersti French stress, '[w]hat he has been given is a graphic intimation of imminent mortality that suggests he should revisit the scenes of his earlier life before it is too late.'[5] Along the journey he makes a number of stops, his first one at his family's former summer house beside a lake, where Isak is 'transported' back to a summer spent there in his youth with his large family. The film continues with its frequent transformations between the 'real' locations of his journey and a series of 'other worlds', built out of Isak's memories, dreams, nightmares, and visions.

When I first started thinking about this theme of charlatans and visionaries, having spent some time away from Bergman's films, there were two specific moments that kept returning in my mind with increased persistence, both from *Wild Strawberries*: 1) Isak's nightmare of the failed medical examination, and 2) the visionary ending when Isak reconjures an image of his parents across the bay where he spent his childhood. The first one, which is part of an extended dream sequence, occurs about two-thirds of the way through the film when Isak dozes off to sleep while his daughter-in-law Marianne has taken over the driving, and he is 'haunted by vivid and disturbing nightmares'.

It is pertinent that the role of Isak is played by Victor Sjöström, the esteemed actor and illustrious director from Swedish cinema's Golden Age. Isak, like Sjöström, has reached the pinnacle of his long, hard-earned career, and is at the final stage of his life. As Isak enters his childhood summer house at night-time, and hangs his

---

4 Philip French and Kersti French, *Wild Strawberries* (London: British Film Institute, 1995), p. 15.
5 French and French, *Wild Strawberries*, p. 17.

coat on the peg as he might have done many times before, the sequence's uncanniness escalates as the familiar space becomes the strange long corridor that leads to the examination room. In the auditorium sit the young hitchhikers he has picked up on his journey—Sara (played by Bibi Andersson) and the sparring young men, Viktor and Anders, who fight for Sara's affections.

Handing over his examination book, Isak is required to identify the bacterial specimen under the microscope. He sees nothing, only what appears to be his own eye: 'there seems to be something wrong', he says, but the examiner replies, 'Not with the microscope.' He cannot decipher the words on the board. When he pretends to remember the doctor's first duty and laughs towards the audience of 'friends', their expressions remain grave. Accused of 'guilt', which he is told is a serious accusation, he pleads that he is an old man with a weak heart, but his plea is rejected; there is nothing about his heart in the notes. He attempts to follow orders, using the blinding examination light to analyse the patient. But he wrongly diagnoses her as 'dead'; he is exposed as a fraud when she opens her eyes and laughs at him. The examiner's notes reveal the final verdict that he is 'incompetent'. Following this scene, Isak is taken to woods where (in what seems to be a vision constructed from memories) he witnesses his wife with another man, but the infidelity only reflects back further guilt upon himself for spending too much time on his work. However, it is the failing of the medical test that I find most poignant here because it represents the heightened terror of being exposed as a charlatan. This has a nightmarish intensity because it is the area in which he feels most secure—into which he has put so much of his energies—and from which he has so far to fall. Even the fabric of language and understanding has become alien to him, and to us. The skills and knowledge that he has devoted his life to accumulating are simply lacking, lost, or forgotten—in a world that ceases to make sense. Professional expertise is not a given.

It is important to keep this examination sequence in mind while moving on to consider the visionary ending of *Wild Strawberries*—the few encounters that occur following the evening ceremony at Lund, culminating with Isak's vision of his parents across the bay. *Wild Strawberries* helped open up new possibilities in cinema with its movement between external and internal realities, as well as across space and time. Time is a key factor. While Isak's exterior guise remains that of the frail old man, the visions are conjured via the recollection of seeing through much younger eyes. As Isak settles for bed, faint singing can be heard as though from another room, or the radio, but Isak realizes it is the young hitchhikers serenading him from just below his window. Afterwards Sara leans upwards, calling out, '[i]t's you I really love. Today, tomorrow, always.' Isak smiles, saying that he will remember. Once they are virtually out of sight, he pronounces: 'Let me hear from you.' There is both the sense that Isak knows that this is a transitory moment which the youngsters are likely to forget and the sense that at the same time Sara's sentiment—uttered in a fleeting moment—lasts a lifetime. The modern-day Sara is a mirror of his cousin and childhood sweetheart Sara, also played by Andersson in the flashbacks earlier in the film, who, we learn, ended up marrying Isak's brother because of Isak's cold detachment and naïvety. The pledge of eternal love comes as a sign to him; rather than being deluded by it, the statement itself is enough for him. It is something to hold on to against the wound of his lost childhood love.

The positioning of Isak as child (as well as old man) is made clear throughout the scene that leads into his final pre-sleep vision. Firstly, as his elderly housekeeper, Miss Agda, puts him to bed, she gives him his medicine, turns off his light, closes the curtains and asks him if he has brushed his teeth. On her way out, she declares that she will leave the door ajar, saying: 'You know where I am if you want anything.' Following this vision, Isak is partially reconciled with his son Evald, and there is an affectionate closeness with Marianne. Isak shows real concern for the well-being of their relationship. These paternal cares are significant, but so is Isak's continued and simultaneous positioning as a child. As Edward Gallafent brings to light, '[t]he final confirmation of this scenario is the appearance of Marianne, unmistakably in the role of glamorous mother figure, who arrives to show off her dancing shoes to this child for a moment, to exchange endearments and to bestow a night-time kiss.'[6] I suggest that as Isak settles, and his voice-over leads into the final visions built out of his childhood memories, these scenes that site Isak as simultaneously old and young help to frame the specific focus, and fluidity, of the final visions. The final scenes are probably not to be taken as precise memories, but rather as moments and tableaus

---

6 Edward Gallafent, 'Two Views over Water: Action and Absorption in Ingmar Bergman's *Wild Strawberries* (1957)', in Tom Brown and James Walters (eds), *Film Moments: Criticism, History, Theory* (London: British Film Institute/Palgrave Macmillan, 2010), pp. 30–33 (p. 31).

Visionaries and charlatans

Figure 15.1 Sara beckons Isak from the other side, *Wild Strawberries* (1957)

made up of fragments of the past. These are pre-sleep illusions that Isak consciously conjures as a powerful means of restoring a sense of inner calm to prevail over the inner tensions evident earlier in the film, when he falls asleep in the car. Sara's words to Isak—'There are no wild strawberries left'—have a dreamlike and symbolic quality, providing a sense that time is running out or moving on. Her directive to look for his papa, and her statement that they will sail around the island and meet him on the other side, suggests a sense of moving from one realm to another.

As Sara speaks to Isak, she almost looks the spectator in the eye. We have become placed in Isak's position. But still there seems to be a barrier between Sara and Isak, or between Sara and us. She says, 'Come, I'll help you' direct to Isak/us; but the edit from this shot to the next transforms her across to Isak's 'side', reinforcing their renewed togetherness (see Figures 15.1 and 15.2). Isak looks slightly alarmed at first, as if he is wondering if he is really up to engaging directly with her—the human contact is initially surprising. At this point, as Gallafent points out, 'a shift has taken place in Isak's relation to the figures of the past'.[7] Previously, he

---

7 Gallafent, 'Two Views', p. 32.

Figure 15.2 Sara walks into Isak's world, *Wild Strawberries* (1957)

was either invisible to the characters of his memories or there was not a positive connection. This significant edit thus helps to accentuate their closeness to each other. As Sara first takes Isak's hand and they look over to the quay, the scene is full of energy, life, and noise, as some of his family are depicted pushing one of the members into the water, splashing, squealing, and shouting. The cut back shows Isak (while still quite separate from the scene) looking over to it, happily laughing. When Sara takes Isak to see his parents across the bay, she and Isak are bathed in a balmy evening sunlight—so different from the stark midday light of the film's first nightmare sequence. The quiet is punctuated by a rising harp chord and the sounds of birds tweeting.

The vision of the parents has a tableau, painting-like, quality to it, and the couple are at first absorbed in their separate (traditionally gendered) activities: the father fishing, the mother sewing.[8] The parents break momentarily, as the mother waves and the father looks over. The cut to Isak's face shows him truly amazed. It is a child's wonder tinged with an adult's appreciation—of such a fleeting

---

8 We might recall the story Isak's ancient mother recounts to Isak and Marianne when they visit her at home just over half-way through the film—the time she spent sewing a doll's dress for Sigbritt. She remembers so clearly how Charlotta took care of the doll when Sigbritt abandoned it.

moment of the ordinary, as the parents return to their activities. The close-up on Isak's face slowly dissolves to him smiling as he turns over in bed. While the realms of dreams/imagination/memory and those of reality are on the whole carefully cued throughout *Wild Strawberries*, the film's format of interspersing dreams with the real world was nevertheless perceived as bold at the time of its release.[9] Bergman's recollection that the film's genesis was founded on the notion of moving between different spatial and temporal spheres suggests that this was something new:

> Then it struck me: supposing I make a film of someone coming along, perfectly realistically, and suddenly opening a door and walking into his childhood? And then opening another door and walking out into reality again? And then walking round the corner of the street and coming into some other period of his life, and everything still alive and going on as before? That was the real starting point for *Wild Strawberries*.[10]

The ending conveys a return visit to Isak's '*smultronstället*' (the wild-strawberry place of his childhood wonder) where it does not matter whether moments are fabricated or 'real'—where there are many layers of time and space each as real as the other. There is a hint of a shift in style at this point of time in Bergman's filmmaking, a shift that would pave the way towards expressing multiple, more fluid, perspectives.

The visionary-charlatan duality is further explored in *The Face* (*The Magician*, *Ansiktet*, 1958), this time with a focus on the figure of the artist-scientist-medic. When Doctor Vogler's Magnetic Health Theatre arrives in town, the members of the troupe are questioned by sceptical officials. Taken to task by the rationalist medical councillor, Dr Vergerus, Vogler is interrogated as a charlatan, not for his magical tricks per se but for the way they are advertised—mixed

---

9 While newspaper critics were somewhat perplexed by the film's multiple dream sequences, many praised the seamless flow between different realms, suggesting this was novel for the time. Following the London premiere, for example, C.A. Lejeune commented that the film mixed 'dream, memory and actuality so smoothly that one is only aware, at the end of it, of life as a continuing thing that touches, takes, releases and then passes on'. C.A. Lejeune, 'Review of *Wild Strawberries*, *The Observer*', in Anthony Lejeune (ed.), *The C.A. Lejeune Film Reader* (Manchester: Carcanet, 1991), p. 299.
10 Bergman, cited in Stig Björkman, Torsten Manns, and Jonas Sima, *Bergman on Bergman: Interviews with Ingmar Bergman*, translated by Paul Britten Austin (New York: Da Capo Press, 1993), p. 133.

with claims to induce visions and to possess spiritual healing powers, practising Mesmer's methods. But this is not a straightforward de-masking of the artist-illusionist. The officials in turn are exposed as fraudulent, the Police Commissioner as corrupt and abusive. While Vogler is to some degree demasked and emasculated, and the spiritual powers are mostly shown to be illusions, a number of inexplicable happenings occur through the film. Fake potions are sold; but the old woman who makes them, Granny Vogler, has considerable clairvoyant powers. Once Dr Vogler's costume is removed, so is his allure; but the issue also lies in the blind faith that others have in Vogler's life-force—in a visionary power that he never professes to possess. Vogler's young, seemingly male, assistant 'Aman' turns out to be his wife, Manda. However, it is also the case that her off-stage appearance as 'wife'—sporting the long blond hair—is as much a performance as her on-stage one, as Daniel Humphrey suggests: 'Manda's newly seen femininity appears to be as much, or even more, a costumed, culturally conditioned performance as her previous androgynous appearance.'[11] When asked by Vergerus if her husband's muteness is real, Manda replies, 'Nothing is true.' We might take this simply as a reference to the lie that they live, or—reading on another level—interpret these aspects as early indicators of the breaking of an essentialist core at the heart of Bergman's films, one that is capable of shattering the dichotomous relationship between truth and falsity, or 'visionary' and 'charlatan'. Near the start of the film, the dying actor Spegel criticizes the book Aman is reading, saying that 'the author presumes a large general truth somewhere in the backdrop – it's an illusory theory'. Aman (or Manda)—rather like an uncanny forerunner of the androgynous character Ismael in *Fanny and Alexander* (twenty-four years later)— manages to incite the inexplicable when she binds the coachman with invisible chains, a force he is unable to resist.

Figures whose visions transgress borders, time-frames, and different stages of life reappear frequently in Bergman's filmmaking and remain strong in his later work. Most prominent in this respect is *Fanny and Alexander*, which was reportedly inspired by Bergman's childhood memories of his grandmother's apartment—vivid within the imagination to the minutest detail, and brought alive as ghosts and visions encountered by the children enshroud the everyday. I suggest that

---

11 Daniel Humphrey, *Queer Bergman: Sexuality, Gender, and the European Art Cinema* (Austin, TX: University of Texas Press, 2013), p. 121.

Fanny and Alexander centres upon the vision, shared by the character Isak Jacobi, of multiple realities 'one outside the other', inspired by the thematic concerns of Bergman's 1960s and '70s films such as *Persona, Hour of the Wolf* (*Vargtimmen*, 1968), and *Cries and Whispers* (*Viskningar och rop*, 1972). *Fanny and Alexander* acknowledges the fluidity, and fragility, of identity, conveying visions, ghosts, and dreams coinciding with the everyday, breaking free to some extent from the flashback mechanisms and dream cues evident in *Wild Strawberries*. I suggest that the grand christening scene near the film's end casts a cynical eye over the comfortable, old, chauvinistic ways of the Ekdahl household, and should thus be read in a very different light from *Wild Strawberries*' final dream vision of Isak's parents, a vision denoting his harmony and inner peace. The final scene, which acts like a vital postscript or antidote to the grand Epilogue, conveys Fanny and Alexander's mother, Emilie, with their grandmother, Helena, pointing towards a new way, whereupon the women have some control (Emilie: 'It's up to us now isn't it').

Nevertheless, a particular series of events in *Fanny and Alexander* comes to mind that links back, in a single moment, to the visionary ending of *Wild Strawberries*. Helena, herself something of a visionary, is alone at home, one long rainy summer day, while the rest of the family are out on their annual excursion to Black Rock, and she senses that something is wrong with the children. Through cross-cutting (in the longer, television, version) we know that Alexander is about to be cruelly punished by his new stepfather, the Bishop, for his fantasies and the stories he tells.[12] At one point in the day, the camera sweeps over the lush, thriving plants as rain falls outside Helena's house; it tilts to observe a rusty, upturned pram, before the cut to inside—to Helena in her chair, and a close-up on her sleeping face. Her dead son, Oscar (Fanny and Alexander's father), suddenly appears by her side and pulls a chair closer to touch her cheek. As she wakes up, her first words, as though mid-conversation, are 'Yes, Oscar, that's how it is. One is old and a child at the same time.' As Maaret Koskinen writes about this moment, Helena is

---

[12] It is the longer version of *Fanny and Alexander* made for television (326 minutes) that is analysed here, not the shorter theatrical release for cinema transmission. Bergman recounted having had to remove parts that were 'vital' for the latter, stating, 'I knew with each cut I reduced the quality of my work.' Ingmar Bergman, *Images: My Life in Film* (London: Faber & Faber, 1995), p. 380.

'obviously talking just as much about herself as her son's apparition'.[13] Helena questions what happened to all the years in between. She touches Oscar's grown-man's hands, remembering them as small, and talks about her many roles in life (none perceived as fake, but nevertheless all a performance). Suddenly, Oscar's facial expression and voice become like that of an anxious boy as he confirms that he, too, is worried about the children, affirming—and perpetuating— Helena's prophetic vision. Visionary insights are represented as powerful forces in *Fanny and Alexander*.

Thus, while *Fanny and Alexander* is ideologically a very different film from *Wild Strawberries*, a testament to the different times in which they were made, it is possible to witness a striking parallel between these two moments of Isak Borg and Helena Ekdahl—at once old and seeing as though through much younger eyes—as if time between the films momentarily stands still. I suggest there is a further visionary capacity to the *performances* of Gunn Wållgren (who played Helena) and Sjöström (who played Isak), especially in the knowledge that neither was to live that long after the filming of these evocative moments. I find a particular resonance in the brief moment in *Wild Strawberries* when Sara walks Isak across the field to find his parents. For a split second, Isak (or Sjöström) stumbles and Sara (or Andersson) holds him up a little, as they continue walking.

This split second of fragility recalls a story recounted by Bergman that Sjöström did not want to carry on with the filming of this scene because the perfect sunlit evening required him to work too late in the day. Apparently, Sjöström had taken a lot of persuading by Bergman to take on *Wild Strawberries* in the first place, and one of the agreed conditions was that Sjöström would be home every day in time for his usual whisky at 4.30pm.[14] The final evening scene would entail breaking this agreement. Of course, after crossly walking off set, Sjöström did return, and when the camera ran, his face relaxed perfectly on cue to produce this time-shattering moment of elegance. It only occurred to Bergman years later that Sjöström's

---

13 Maaret Koskinen, 'Out of the Past: *Saraband* and the Ingmar Bergman Archive', in Maaret Koskinen (ed.), *Ingmar Bergman Revisited: Performance, Cinema and the Arts* (London and New York: Wallflower Press, 2008), pp. 19–34 (p. 25).
14 The anecdote is recounted in Erland Josephson, with Paul Duncan and Bengt Wanselius (eds), *The Ingmar Bergman Archives* (Hong Kong, Cologne, London, Los Angeles, Madrid, Paris, and Tokyo: Taschen, 2008), p. 215.

rage was 'nothing but an ungovernable fear of finding himself inadequate—of not being good enough'.[15] Insisting he never wanted to take it on, or that he was too old and frail, was a safety net against this exposure.

This can be related to portraits of Bergman himself. In 1998, twenty years before the Centenary Jubilee, Jörn Donner in an interview asks Bergman (who was eighty years old at this point) what he likes to imagine people would say about the figure 'Bergman' in twenty years' time. Bergman replies that future heritage is not what motivates him, and that the 'Bergman' that has become part of everyday language across multiple nations feels like someone else. The important thing, he says, is that he has a rehearsal on Tuesday, which still fills him with great fear as insomnia engulfs him: no matter that he has done it before, or that he is world famous; he thinks only, '[l]et this rehearsal go well. Let it be meaningful.'[16] Until the rehearsal gets going, he is terrified that suddenly the ability to make something living and moving will be taken away:

> The only thing that means anything when I am working is that the work should be meaningful for those who do it, and then also be alive, so that it will live its own life. That is the only thing I'm afraid of, and God knows that I'm terribly afraid of it, and that is that suddenly the ability to make something living and moving – that that will be taken away from me or I will lose it.[17]

He fears that he will no longer know how to do it, or that time will run out on him. The gaining of a lifetime's experience does not ease these anxieties. Bergman presents filmmaking as an activity built out of the striving, as a craftsman, to create a product that lives and is meaningful.

Running through Bergman's filmmaking is the drive to communicate insightful visions and scenarios that will touch lives, dissolving boundaries of space and time and between old age and childhood. The preoccupation with strict (true/false) binaries of understanding seems to break down in Bergman's work, particularly from the mid-1960s onwards, as notions of stable identities and

---

15 Josephson, Duncan, and Wanselius, *The Ingmar Bergman Archives*, p. 215.
16 *Ingmar Bergman on Life and Work / Om liv och arbete* (Jörn Donner, television documentary movie, 9 July 1998, 91 minutes); the interview is included in 'Special Features', *Wild Strawberries* DVD, The Criterion Collection (Janus Films, 2002).
17 *Ingmar Bergman on Life and Work*.

worlds begin to fracture. *Fanny and Alexander* can to some extent be seen as a celebration of multiple realms and identities, or possibilities, and in this sense as a film providing a vision that entails a liberation from some of the strict labels and masks that have traditionally governed people's lives, sometimes at the expense of happiness and well-being. In the representations of Bergman's off-screen persona, however, we also see a fear that has become engrained in his work ethic—and one that most of us might share—of not being capable. This engrained fear saw Bergman's continuing endurance—wrapped up in an unrelenting attendance to duty—that fuelled a lifelong compulsion to produce. The artist charlatan and the medical charlatan speak to the vision of the self as fraud that we see in our nightmares—of not being able, in our professions, to create or to perform—to make the deadline, to achieve the right level, to deliver what we have advertised. An empty product. This is a malady that haunts Bergman's films of the late 1950s specifically, but it also appears to have played an entrenched role as a creative force in Bergman's day-to-day working life.

16
Imagined without dialogue: *Sawdust and Tinsel* and *Dreams*

Dan Williams

When I started a PhD on the films of Ingmar Bergman in 2003, I had to select a methodology. I became interested in the theoretical work of Melanie Klein and her followers, not because this theory did away with the complexity of the films, but because of the shared themes and concerns. In particular, there is the shared focus on a bleak view of human nature, coupled with an exploration of the individual's inner world, and ultimately the possibility of an affirmative path based on the release and transformation of imagined demons.

From Kleinian theory, the concept of 'the depressive position' suggested that individual self-realization depended on concern for the 'other', from infancy to adulthood. In Bergman's films, from the outset, individual problems were played out against a background which suggested, at the very least, conflicts arising from socially constructed power relations. In the hands of different thinkers such as Richard Wollheim and Hanna Segal, Kleinian theory developed ideas about the value of art based significantly on accounts of infantile experience, while the therapy was used for child psychology, for example as part of the welfare state in the UK through the Tavistock Clinic. Although connected to modernism, Kleinian theory valued concepts of restoration and integration in therapy and in aesthetics. Meanwhile, in Bergman's films there are frequent representations of artists and performers. And through such devices as flashbacks and imaginative interludes characters confront psychic elements that become central to the possibility of resolution.

This chapter explores the parallels between Kleinian theory and two Ingmar Bergman films from the 1950s, *Gycklarnas Afton* (also known as *Sawdust and Tinsel*, 1953) and *Kvinnodröm* (known as *Dreams*, 1955).[1] Although dialogue is an enormous part of Bergman's

---

1 Birgitta Steene, *Ingmar Bergman: A Reference Guide* (Amsterdam: Amsterdam University Press), p. 205.

artistic achievement, particular attention is paid to scenes and sequences where dialogue is absent or minimal. In these segments we may detect a variety of reasons for the restriction on words. Ingmar Bergman himself explained that in *Sawdust and Tinsel*, Åke Grönberg had some difficulty remembering the lines, and that the director felt that the actor's abbreviated dialogue and moody noises worked more effectively than the original script.[2]

We know from other Bergman films the psychological intensity he invested in the dramatic impact of silence, and also that his use of silence can be related to his development of an internationally recognizable cinematic style. However, what should also be included is the influence of silent cinema, in which audiences enjoyed aural as well as visual experiences. Furthermore, the ensuing discussions focus on how dialogue is minimized but not completely absent and sound effects and music play a vital role. It is worth noting that when interviewed about the famous sequence of Alma and the troops in *Sawdust and Tinsel*, Bergman resisted the comparison with the silent classic *Battleship Potemkin*; but he stated that he was specifically inspired by some films of the thirties which were still using the techniques of pre-sound cinema.[3] This suggests an interest in a sort of in-between mode.

The idea of resisting classification is perhaps the most reliable guide to the silent-cinema aesthetic in *Sawdust and Tinsel*, with individual moments creating different associations. Consequently, this chapter begins by considering the influence of silent cinema and then moves on to key scenes, sequences, and moments from *Sawdust and Tinsel* and *Dreams* where dialogue is absent or minimal. Throughout the chapter, I will try to indicate how Kleinian theory is relevant to the way silent-cinema techniques represent psychological depth. I will finish by briefly making a comparison with some of the points raised at a recent conference in London which focused on psychotherapy and another Bergman film, *Wild Strawberries*, of 1957.

Of course, it is well known that Bergman grew up with silent cinema and paid tribute to its influence. For example, he made it clear that Ewald André Dupont's *Variety*, released in 1925, was one of his favourites, and *Sawdust and Tinsel* was a 'conscious reply'.[4]

---

2 Stig Björkman, Torsten Manns, and Jonas Sima, *Bergman on Bergman*, translated from Swedish by Paul Britten Austin (New York: Simon and Schuster, 1973 [originally published by Norstedts, 1970]), p. 95.
3 Björkman, Manns, and Sima, *Bergman on Bergman*, p. 87.
4 Björkman, Manns, and Sima, *Bergman on Bergman*, p. 82.

Bergman's subsequent assertion that his film differed significantly is not contradictory, because *Sawdust and Tinsel* picks up elements of the earlier work to fashion something completely different.[5] Other well-known silent films which fascinated the director and are directly relevant to *Sawdust and Tinsel* include Victor Sjöström's *The Phantom Carriage* (1921) and *He Who Gets Slapped* (1924), the latter made in the US. These films are great examples at a general level of how the silent cinema could explore character psychology in depth and were inspirations for Bergman's creative representation of psychology and subjectivity.

Particular concerns of Kleinian and post-Kleinian theory can be applied here because this body of theory strongly emphasizes the simultaneous engagement with external and internal realities. A feature of this psychoanalytical approach is the emphasis on the ongoing development of the patient or individual alongside an exploration of their past. Klein thus emphasized the 'epistemophilic instinct'—the desire for knowledge of external reality as a key factor alongside the other instincts identified in classical Freudian psychoanalysis.[6] Specifically from a Kleinian perspective, we might note in *The Phantom Carriage* the combination of a style directed towards enhanced realism in the use of depth of field for background detail and the representation of a psychic reality of splitting and internal trauma, expressed through the innovative use of double-exposures. With *He Who Gets Slapped* we see amazing detail in scenes such as those portraying the spectacular troupe of clowns, as well as notable use of iris shots to select and incorporate key details signifying the characters' desires and mental states.

Both these films use a wide range of sophisticated techniques to add psychological depth, including the way action is sometimes staged around doorways to signify a threshold with a range of connotations. One also thinks here of Sjöström's own appearance as Isak Borg in *Wild Strawberries* at the doorway to the dining room of his old family home. In *Sawdust and Tinsel* and *Dreams*, there are also key moments staged around doorways and when

---

5 Ingmar Bergman, *Images: My Life in Film*, translated from Swedish by Marianne Ruuth (London: Faber & Faber, 1995 [originally published by Norstedts in 1990]), p. 185.
6 For example, Klein uses this concept in 'Early Stages of the Oedipal Conflict' (1928) in Melanie Klein, *Love, Guilt and Reparation and Other Works 1921–1945* (London: Vintage, 1998 [originally published in 1975 by The Hogarth Press]), pp. 186–198.

characters look on to another's space. Specific images in both Bergman films evoke Sjöström's silent masterpieces as well as Dupont's *Variety*. The silhouetted carriage on the horizon in *The Phantom Carriage* is comparable to the way the wagons appear at the start of *Sawdust and Tinsel*. The use of specific editing patterns in *Variety* and *He Who Gets Slapped* for the purpose of intensifying the performance scenes is echoed in the way *Sawdust and Tinsel* dramatizes the circus performance, and also in the way *Dreams* brings a monotonous photo shoot to life.

We are able to trace the imprint of specific techniques and the influence of silent films favoured by Ingmar Bergman to some extent; but this is just an introduction to his continuing creative involvement in the aesthetics of the silent era. This curiosity and engagement with film history may seem surprising in a director so often understood as a modernist; but clearly modernism does not mean permanent innovation, and Bergman's awareness of the power of so-called silent cinema and its aesthetic possibilities—much of it modernistic—invests his work with a very wide range. The synthesis and integration of such an aesthetic brings to mind the emphasis on integration in Kleinian theory where elements of the past are reworked and transformed in the creative process. While Bergman drew on the language of earlier films, he also made a decisive move away from the Manichean schemes found in them.

He Who Gets Slapped may be taken as an example. This is a film in which traumatic emotions are reworked through performance by the central character in his new-found identity as a clown, but ultimately the deep need for violent revenge obliterates everything else. In contrast, the conclusions found in Bergman's films of the 1950s are more ambiguous and in some ways more mediated. In the later films of the 1950s, we have such infamously bleak conclusions as the ones delivered by *The Seventh Seal* (1957) and *The Virgin Spring* (1960). Even here, though, we have references to counterbalancing forces such as the final gaze of Jof the performer from a distance at the spectacle managed by Death, and in *The Virgin Spring* the sudden appearance of water from the earth at the place where Karin was murdered.

In *Sawdust and Tinsel* and *Dreams*, deep-rooted traumatic conflicts reverberate through the final narrative moments; but there is also a sense of temporary stability attained, a realistic acceptance that for the time being life will continue without radical external change. This is not, in my opinion, a conservative retreat, or a compromised position that was later abandoned for more challenging finales;

instead, we can see here the development of an aesthetic in which significant weight is placed on internal psychological change within the characters. This development is integrated by means of a wide array of techniques, including the continuing imagination and power in the representation of psychological reality that were found in silent cinema. To understand further how Ingmar Bergman develops this aesthetic, I will now turn in greater detail to key scenes from *Sawdust and Tinsel* and then *Dreams*.

Sawdust and Tinsel begins with a serene sequence—an episodic association of images depicting the journey of circus wagons. Silhouetted on a hillside against a towering sky, the first image appears as a forerunner of the famous depiction of figures against the skyline at the end of *The Seventh Seal* four years later; and as was mentioned above, it echoes the silhouette of the carriage on the horizon in *The Phantom Carriage*. In *Sawdust and Tinsel* the absence of dialogue enhances the expressive power of the images themselves and admits the introduction of key motifs for the story that follows—the bear, the weary dedication of the travellers, and the concern of Albert for his young girlfriend still sleeping. The absence of words allows sound effects to be more prominent—the horses' hooves on a bridge, the sound of birds and sheep, the creaking of the wagons; and the strange sound of the driver's wail-like song to the elements. Dissolves contribute to the dreamy atmosphere, which conveys the mental state of those circus performers who are still sleeping. Critical writing on the film has recognized the poetic style. John Simon, in his detailed analysis, discusses how a symbolic alternation of light and dark is established in the opening sequences;[7] and as Robin Wood notes, there is already a symbolization of breakdown in the early image of broken windmill sails.[8] Dialogue between the driver and Albert represents the intervention of storytelling, a theatrical use of speech, but also the cue for another sequence largely free of dialogue—the famous representation of Frost the clown's humiliation in a style that seems in places like a parody of silent cinema.

The sequence is largely narrated by the extraordinary music composed by a distinguished Swedish composer, Karl-Birger Blomdahl. Known for musical experimentation, including musical adaptation of Eric Lindegren's surrealistic sonnets, Blomdahl provides the

---

7 John Simon, *Ingmar Bergman Directs* (London: Davis-Poynter Limited, 1973 [originally published by Harcourt Brace Jovanovic in 1972]), pp. 68–69.
8 Robin Wood, *Ingmar Bergman* (London: Studio Vista, 1969), p. 50.

soundtrack to a series of images, which Bergman says were inspired by his own dream.[9] This use of experimental sound means that the sequence also compares with more recent experiments where silent films have been combined with unusual and innovative soundtracks.[10] Bergman's work with Blomdahl in *Sawdust and Tinsel* is significant for the meaning of the film, because the latter had an interest in negativity and human nature; but at the same time the precisely individualized sounds of the wind instruments express the rampant absurdity of circus performance. A marching brass-band sound, conveying both jolly entertainment and rising suspense, is accompanied by the noise of cannon firing.

The regiment is distracted from the firing practice by the appearance of Frost's wife, Alma, who puts on a show by bathing naked in the sea and is joined by some of the troops. In this sequence we see a close-up of an officer commanding the gunfire but hear no words, and we are jolted by the modernistic musical composition. From the carnivalesque pact between Alma and the voyeuristic troops we move to Frost's reception of the news of what is happening. The only dialogue is between Frost and the various members of the troupe, who urge him to restore his masculine pride by intervening in this humiliating situation. The style of the sequence then returns to an expressionistic pre-sound mode as the clown arrives on the scene like a desperate performer. When we see Frost call his wife but hear no sound, his powerlessness is emphasized. Finally he carries Alma, as if he is Christ bearing the cross.[11] Extreme close-ups capture the agonized emotions of Frost and Alma, but a rhythmical balance between silence and sound is created as well. One moment the troops are guffawing and the next wrapped in silent anticipation and awed fascination, with just the sound effect of the waves.

The sequence showing Frost's humiliation certainly stands out in the film as a whole. One factor here is that it has its own cinematographer. As Birgitta Steene notes, the film had three cinematographers for various reasons, with Hilding Bladh only shooting this section.[12] However, there is still a temptation to account for the

---

9 Bergman, *Images*, p. 184.
10 For instance, *He Who Gets Slapped* can be watched on the internet on the Vimeo platform with an experimental soundtrack provided by Helictite.
11 This imagery is identified and discussed in the literature about the film. For example, the imagery of the cross is discussed in Wood, *Ingmar Bergman*, pp. 52–54.
12 Steene, *Ingmar Bergman*, p. 207.

wildness of this passage as some kind of more overt moment of authorial expression. After all, the sequence conveys the theme of humiliation, a key Bergman preoccupation. The overexposed look anticipates the famous nightmare sequence of *Wild Strawberries* and the fishing sequence in *Hour of the Wolf* (1968); and yet, as with those films, we can see the integration of this passage into the wider story. Bergman himself made it clear that this sequence encapsulates the theme of the story which follows concerning Albert's humiliation. Elements of Frost's humiliation sequence return most directly in Albert's humiliation in the circus ring, but there are earlier echoes of the style used in the Frost episode when Albert and Anne's journey through the village is portrayed in parodic terms.

The emphasis on their physicality, and their exaggerated pomp, is accompanied by the brass sounds of the earlier sequence conveying the assertiveness of their mission, and also the absurdity. A sharp sense of cultural and class differences is played out as the circus performers set out to negotiate with their elitist rivals, the theatre. Consequently, a significant outcome of the film's expressive power is an engagement with a social reality, in particular a depiction of the conflicts in this social reality alongside the focus on internal conflict as experienced by Albert. The balance between a social message and an expressionistic representation of depth psychology is supported by Bergman's own account of the film's genesis, where he refers to his experience of witnessing revue performers in a hotel where he stayed, and by his acknowledgement that the character of Albert is to some extent a self-representation. Bergman puts forward this explanation as a corrective to the idea that Åke Grönberg's role was a reprise of the character played by Emil Jannings in *Variety*.[13]

In order to understand the melancholy evoked in Albert's character, we need to look more closely at the specifics of *Sawdust and Tinsel* and the range of techniques deployed. For instance, another key passage without dialogue follows the forceful assertion made by Albert's wife Agda that she will never sacrifice her freedom. These words reverberate as a series of images convey Albert's melancholic resignation, the street presence of the organ grinder, and Albert's rising anger as he spies Anne visiting the goldsmith. It is as if, at this point, the absence of dialogue reinforces our involvement in Albert's oscillating moods.

---

13 Bergman, *Images*, pp. 184–185.

Melanie Klein's writing in later years famously focused on envy, which she regarded as an inherent lifelong force to be struggled with. A significant adaption of this theory, explained by Margot Waddell, is the recognition that the confrontation with self-destructive forces is given specific form by the context in which it arises.[14] In Albert's case the envy is in bad faith, because he had just attempted betrayal. Both he and Anne are driven by an envy which is deluded because it cannot be realized owing to the reality of other characters and their motivations. The visual and musical representation of Albert's perception of Anne's betrayal expresses their emotional entanglement, laying this before the audience without linguistic explication. Waddell describes how Klein saw, with great clarity, the presence of so-called infantile emotions in the adult world and relates how Kleinian theory homes in on the movement between different mental states. Bergman is also fascinated by these oscillations.[15]

Albert's rage is wide-ranging, played out first with Anne and then with Frost as interlocutors; he mourns, and he threatens to kill those he mourns. The shift in emotions is emphasized as Frost mirrors the oscillation of sadism and sadness. Later Albert's rage will be directed into an actual mirror, and then towards the bear. In the circus-performance scene, the minimal dialogue puts the cries and wails of the clowns in the foreground while the excited laughter of the audience is the sound of happiness, recalling the mocking laughter of the soldiers in the scene where Alma bathes. This synthesis works alongside editing, which alternates between performers and audience so that an external point of view is created in which director and viewer observe this interaction. As in *Variety* and *He Who Gets Slapped*, the alternation between shots of the performers and of the audience becomes more intense as the circus performances become a direct expression of the desires and emotions of the characters. In the circus scene, rhythmical editing in conjunction with repeated and alternating close-ups anticipates the confrontation that occurs between Albert and Frans, the actor. To be sure, the theatrical speech of Sjuberg, the theatre director, formalizes the duel; but this only lends additional emphasis to the unspoken emotions of the antagonists.

We have a great deal of information from interviews with Bergman, and from his writing about the film, which shows how he drew on

---

14 Margot Waddell, *Inside Lives: Psychoanalysis and the Growth of Personality* (London: Karnac Books, 2002 [1998]).
15 Waddell, *Inside Lives*, p. 8.

personal experience for this story.[16] To my mind, the most far-reaching statements concern his feeling of connection with childhood, as when he said, 'the creative streak is [...] deeply tied up with a sort of infantility, or a left-over of the child's attitude to the world'.[17] In this interview Bergman expands on the direct relationship between being an artist and being a child, and he makes it clear that while humiliation is a key element of the artist's experience, this is part of a general pattern of dependencies which the artist experiences.[18] As mentioned before, this includes the inspiration of *Variety*, as we are plunged into the language of circus and of pre-sound cinema. While *Variety* stunned audiences with acrobatics, in Bergman's film circus and life are tenaciously interwoven through specific devices, such as the whip-pan to the clown's face, and more generally through the interweaving of different character trajectories. However, a context of collective action is ultimately a key factor. While the circus performers struggle for a material position in society, there is considerable empathy with them and fascination with their work. Taking into account the reunion of Anne and Albert, seemingly stoically resigned to their fate at the end, the film's conclusion parallels the adjustment to reality which Kleinian theory has described using the concepts of reparation and the depressive position; and this finale retains and depends on recognition of a broader social context.

A crucial point about the Kleinian theory of the depressive position, which is founded on guilt, is that it involves an active development in the recognition of emotions ranging from love to hate. It suggests a mature understanding of ambivalence and ambiguity; and Ingmar Bergman's films of the 1950s provide a parallel, specifically in the mix of comedy and tragedy. Released in 1955, *Dreams* is an apparently light tale of two women working in the world of fashion photography. In particular, I want to focus on the key scenes in which Bergman returns to the strategy of dispensing with dialogue. This strategy is discussed in the extended interview with the director where Björkman, Manns, and Sima draw attention to two such scenes—the opening, and the scene where the central character Susanne contemplates throwing herself from the train. Here Bergman offers the explanation that 'in my childhood I used to draw films, and tried to narrate what happened

---

16 For example in Bergman, *Images*, p. 185.
17 Björkman, Manns, and Sima, *Bergman on Bergman*, p. 82.
18 Björkman, Manns, and Sima, *Bergman on Bergman*, p. 83.

without using dialogue'.[19] He downplays the work as a whole, however, describing it as 'boring' and as 'a dialogue film'.[20] He seems to have a hazy memory of the whole thing, and this appears to be affected by memories of his split from the leading actress Harriet Andersson. However, a narrow auteurist reading focused on biographical explanation would once more miss the achievements of the work, including the marked use of silent-cinema techniques. There is only space here to indicate briefly some of the ways in which this approach provides entertainment whilst allowing deeper expression of psychological complexity.

The opening begins with a black screen and the sound of a ticking clock, elements familiar from other Ingmar Bergman films which introduce self-reflexivity or draw attention to time. A bold bar of light continues the elliptical representation of a photograph being anonymously developed. A woman hums a tune as we see the print dipped into the solution. The completed image showing simply a woman's lips is doubled in the reflective surface beneath the press, alongside an anonymous female hand. The hummed tune adds a gentle caress, beside the ticking clock, to the creative combination of images. Meanwhile, the title immediately introduces an imaginative realm—*Kvinnodröm*. As Birgitta Steene points out, the American title fails to note that this a film about women's dreams, while the British name *Journey into Autumn* seems even further removed from the initial intention.[21]

The credits sequence continues with the hidden hand activating the phonograph to introduce gently romantic music while photographs are looked at. Finally, one depicting a model (played by Harriet Andersson) is turned over and stamped with the name of Susanne Frank, fashion photographer. It is a smooth, beguiling introduction before we see Susanne, played by Eva Dahlbeck, observing the fashion shoot. The focus is on her intensity. Her cigarette is lit by an assistant—another initially hidden hand, as she rejects one of the photographs offered. Without dialogue, the authority of her character is established. The camera tracks to show a large man observing the shoot with fascination, and he simply endorses Susanne's decision, transfixed as he is by the model. The sequence continues, showing Doris, the young model, posing at the centre. Allied to the absence of dialogue, witty changes in composition and drily

---

19 Björkman, Manns, and Sima, *Bergman on Bergman*, p. 97.
20 Björkman, Manns, and Sima, *Bergman on Bergman*, p. 98.
21 Steene, *Ingmar Bergman*, p. 143.

observational shots with changes in the editing rhythm develop a sense of amusement as well as an underlying tension. The revelation of a slightly camp assistant's face behind the face of Doris recalls the transition from Albert's face to the clown behind him in the circus ring in *Sawdust and Tinsel*, and both moments mark an evolving fascination with juxtaposition and the overlap of facial close-ups.

Bergman later explained his fascination with such imagery where different faces appear to float in space.[22] The use of mirrors adds to this. Doris is looking into a mirror, but we do not see the reflection; moments before, Susanne's reflection appeared in the background of a shot. The repeated alternation between the tapping fingers of the fashion director and the rising tension that is evident in Susanne's expression emphasizes her private anxieties. Without explanation, Susanne abruptly removes herself to the darkroom where her gestures, the lighting, and the return of the ticking clock convey her personal crisis. The prolonged absence of dialogue contributes a comic effect, as we observe the participants on the fashion shoot from the outside. The silence is held for just long enough to overstep what we might think of as a realistic period without talk. This allows for greater attention to the humorous juxtaposition of facial expressions, but this first scene also establishes a narrative focus on Susanne's anxieties. The conjunction of inner and outer worlds so powerfully explored in some of Bergman's favourite silent films is therefore a strong aesthetic here as well.

The influence of silent cinema emerges at other points, too. The cross-cutting between Susanne and the fashion director involves rapid alternations. A similar pattern occurs again in the scene where Susanne contemplates throwing herself from the train. On this occasion, the quickened cuts are between Susanne and a warning sign on the door, and then the signs for open and close that she sees on the door. The interplay between this drama of her suicidal thoughts inside the carriage and the external sounds of the train conveys the conjunction between internal and external realities, continuing the symbolism represented by her anxiety in the darkroom. Notably, across the whole passage while Susanne is alone there is just one line of dialogue, which is Susanne's inner voice addressing her lover.

In a later scene with Susanne among suburban trees overlooking her lover's house, the sound of birds and other selected noises convey

---

22 Björkman, Manns, and Sima, *Bergman on Bergman*, p. 86.

her separation from the social world. Coming on to Doris's adventure, her initial meeting with the Consul is represented through shop window and mirror reflections in a series of shots which suggest that they are like ghosts hovering over the real world, a possible echo of the double exposures used by Sjöström. Doris's sense of abandon is accentuated in the rollercoaster and ghost-train scenes. Here, Doris's screams and the sound of the rollercoaster, alongside the spinning movement of the camera, convey her exuberance while the Consul's silence illustrates his suffering and the delusion of his flirtation. Another example of an impact achieved without dialogue is the ghostly final image of the Consul, looking out through a window in his aristocratic home—a king imprisoned in his castle. Overall, the fluency of film form in these scenes and images contributes to the lightness of tone, while the lack of speech signifies psychological turbulence.

The word 'turbulence', derived from the work of Wilfred Bion, was used as a key concept at an event I attended in London in 2018.[23] An organization providing low-cost therapy engaged their audience at this fundraising event with a screening of *Wild Strawberries*. The film provoked enormous interest in an audience predisposed to psychoanalytic themes. While Kleinian concepts like that of reparation were raised in the discussion, a strong appreciation of courage in the Sjöström character was notable. Facing up to his past was understood as heroic and as an ongoing process of development and transformation. The way the narrative of *Wild Strawberries* provided a container for disparate and challenging psychic content was fully appreciated. In *Sawdust and Tinsel* and in *Dreams*, there is also a sense of inner turbulence. I hope that I have conveyed how turbulence or psychic conflict is skilfully woven into the narratives of these films, as well as the contribution made by silent cinema to this achievement.

---

23 Good Life, a conference at University College London, organized by the Camden Psychotherapy Unit, 21 April 2018.

17
The ghost in the machine: *Saraband*

Lars Gustaf Andersson

In December 2003, the Swedish Public Service corporation Sveriges Television (SVT) screened *Saraband*, Ingmar Bergman's last film, with a cast that included Liv Ullmann and Erland Josephson. This production may be regarded as a summary of Bergman's experiences as an author and director. By way of names, allusions, and direct quotations, the film is also connected to several other works in the Bergman universe, such as *Wild Strawberries* (*Smultronstället*, 1957), *The Magician* (*Ansiktet*, 1958), *Persona* (1966), *Cries and Whispers* (*Viskningar och rop*, 1972), and *Scenes from a Marriage* (*Scener ur ett äktenskap*, 1973).

Saraband has the structure of a chamber play, with a small group of characters meeting in diverse combinations, with only two of them in each scene. This mathematical structure reminds us, as Jan Holmberg has pointed out, of the art of Johann Sebastian Bach, a constant point of reference for Bergman.[1] The dramatis personae visible on the screen are represented by a mere five actors: Johan (Erland Josephson) is an old retired professor, living in the countryside in splendid isolation; Marianne (Liv Ullmann) is his former wife, a lawyer by profession, who visits him in his remote home; Henrik (Börje Ahlstedt), Johan's son from his first marriage, is visiting Johan, staying in a small guest cottage along with his own daughter, Karin (Julia Dufvenius); and Karin is a young musician who, aided by her father, is preparing her application to study at the Academy of Music.

The fifth character is only present in one brief sequence in the epilogue. This is one of the daughters of Johan and Marianne, Martha (Gunnel Fred), a long-time patient in a nursing home. There

---

1 Jan Holmberg, *Författaren Ingmar Bergman* (Stockholm: Norstedts, 2018), p. 253.

are in fact some other characters, but they are never visible on screen: the woman who helps Johan with cooking and cleaning has vital functions in the film, but most important of all is Anna, the wife of Henrik and the mother of Karin. Anna is dead, but she is constantly referred to; a letter of hers is quoted, and her portrait is visible on a couple of occasions.

The plot is organized into ten scenes, framed by a prologue as well as an epilogue. They are both presented by Marianne, who addresses the audience directly. In the prologue, she sits in front of a big table covered with black-and-white photographs. She tells us about her divorced husband Johan, saying that he retired from his work at the university as he inherited a lot of money. He now lives in a remote place in the countryside. Marianne goes on to tell us that she has very little contact with their two daughters: Sara, who is happily married to a lawyer and lives in Australia, and Martha, who is isolated in a nursing home owing to some kind of mental illness. And Marianne has herself had no contact with Johan for many years. The prologue is quite dreamlike, with an abundance of photographs spread out on the table in front of Marianne.

In the first scene, Marianne is reunited with Johan. This expository scene confirms the circumstances supplied in the prologue. Johan tells us more about his son Henrik and granddaughter Karin, who are staying with him at the moment. In the second scene Marianne and Karin meet, and Karin reveals her problematic relationship with her father, who wants her to be a great musician. Marianne contributes a description of her unhappy marriage to Johan. Karin also speaks about an incident in the morning when she did not want to rehearse with her father and they began to quarrel, the row ending with her running away from him. In the next scene, Karin returns to her father. After a brief conversation, she goes to bed (it is obvious that father and daughter sleep in the same bed). Henrik follows her and tells his daughter about his marriage to Anna, in which he felt subordinated and feared that his wife would leave him. Henrik returns in the fourth scene, visiting his father, trying to ask him for a loan in order to buy a cello for Karin. Johan is in his library, reading Søren Kierkegaard and taking notes. After a long discussion in which they humiliate each other, Johan eventually promises to think it over, but provokes his son to an outburst in the course of which Henrik sweeps a lamp from the table. In the fifth scene, entitled 'Bach', Marianne meets Henrik by chance in a country church she is visiting, where Henrik is practising on the organ. He opens his heart to her, talking about his love for Karin and his longing for his dead wife, his hatred of his father Johan, and his thoughts of death. One moment he is amiable and gentle towards Marianne, and the next moment he is full of contempt and scorn. She seems quite shocked. He leaves her and she stays in the church, staring at the altarpiece.

In the following scene, Karin in turn visits Johan, who tells her that a famous Russian conductor wants to help her with her career—in order to save her from her mediocre father. The conductor invites her to St Petersburg. Karin supplies an answer to this offer in next scene, the seventh, where she once again meets Marianne. She explains that she cannot leave her father; he needs her. She lets Marianne read a letter that Anna, her mother, wrote to Henrik a few days before she died. In the letter she utters a warning to Henrik, afraid that he will keep Karin so close to him that he will suffocate her.

The eighth scene contains the final dialogue between Karin and her father. This scene has often been discussed by critics and film scholars. Henrik is enthusiastic and wants Karin to rehearse the cello suites by Bach with him for a concert he has planned, but after a while he realizes that something is wrong. Karin shows Henrik the letter from Anna that she has read, and he feels betrayed. Karin is very tender towards him at first; they even kiss, but then she pushes him away and tells him that she has other plans. She explains that she does not want to be a solo artist and that she has changed her mind about the Academy of Music. Instead she plans to go to Germany with some friends and join a programme for young musicians. Karin says:

> Father! I don't want to. Really. I don't look upon myself as a solo artist. I want to play in an orchestra. I want to live enclosed in the body of sound, in an enormous, common effort. Not sit alone on a stage, lonely and vulnerable. I don't want others to tell me I'm not good enough. I want to decide my own future. I want to live a simple, ordinary life. I want to feel that I belong. And live an ordinary life. Not as a bad substitute for my mother. Which you repay with vague utterances about something that I am not and do not have. It must end. And now it has come to an end.[2]

Karin is in tears. Henrik asks her once again to play Bach's *Sarabande* to him, which she does.

---

[2] This English translation from the film as well as the ensuing ones were made by the author.

The ninth scene implies that some time has passed. Karin is on her way to Germany. Johan and Marianne learn that Henrik has tried to commit suicide, and they reproach each other. The last scene is at night. Marianne tries to sleep, and Johan visits her bedroom. He tells her that he suffers from great anxiety and is afraid of death. They both undress, and she allows him to get into her bed.

In the epilogue we meet Marianne, who addresses the audience for the last time and explains that the relationship between her and Johan faded out after the related episodes. Marianne then remembers a visit she made to her daughter Martha, saying, 'I thought about the enigmatic fact that I, for the first time in our shared existence, realized, *sensed*, that I am touching my daughter, *my child*.'

As is clear from this summary, *Saraband* offers a field day for all Bergman interpreters. It invites associations to all the dysfunctional families whose members are unable to communicate with one another—here are the harsh fathers, acting as judges, and the forgiving mothers; here are the allusions to music and musical composition; and, most notably, here is the fear of death and the fear of life. Some key scenes that are easy to relate to other Bergman films are the final scene between Henrik and Karin and the meeting between Marianne and Martha. In *Autumn Sonata* (*Höstsonaten*, 1978), Liv Ullmann played the daughter of a very dominant mother, a famous concert pianist. Besides the Ullmann character, there was also a disabled sister whom the mother did not want to see. The alienated or even aborted child is a recurrent figure in the Bergman universe, for example in *Persona*. What happens in *Saraband*, however, is that communication is in fact established—or re-established—between mother and daughter. Marianne's final words are reminiscent of what the boy Minus says in *Through a Glass Darkly* (*Såsom i en spegel*, 1961): 'Daddy spoke to me!' A new line for this minimalistic dialogue is thus delivered more than four decades later in *Saraband*.

The war between the generations is another important motif in Bergman's work. Most notably, ever since *Frenzy* (*Hets*, 1945), many of the protagonists have been young people struggling with a hard and unsympathetic world of adults. When Karin in *Saraband* escapes the suffocating love of her father, a full circle is concluded. And her words about her desire to be an ordinary human being, working together with others, echoes the famous essay about the snakeskin that Bergman wrote in the 1960s, where he claimed that he wanted to be an anonymous builder of a cathedral, along with other anonymous workers.[3]

Here the intertextual relations to other works by Bergman are mixed with allusions to works by a number of other artists, most of them old acquaintances in the Bergman universe. Since music is an important topic in *Saraband*, names of composers—including Paul Hindemith, Anton Bruckner, and Zoltán Kodály—are mentioned; but the most important one is Bach.

Strindberg is another recurrent intertext in the films of Ingmar Bergman, and although the allusions are never explicit in *Saraband*, there are some notable connections. The chamber-play formula and the discussion of guilt and forgiveness that we recognize from the later stages of Strindberg's oeuvre are apparent. A more subtle reference to Strindberg is the interior design of Johan's home. The design is a blend of bourgeois fin-de-siècle and a rural style, a blend which we can recognize from several stage productions of Strindberg from the beginning of the twentieth century onwards. The kitchen, a crucial meeting point for the characters in this drama, is old-fashioned, and there is a pantry door that is taken directly from Strindberg's drama *Dreamplay*; also, the ventilation hole in the shape of a four-leaf clover is one of Bergman's ways of establishing contact with his mentor. The name August Strindberg is never mentioned, however. The only authors named are Freud—Johan has quit smoking to avoid developing cancer like Sigmund Freud—and Kierkegaard. The latter is not mentioned in the dialogue; but his name is highlighted in that Johan reads one of his works, *Either—Or* (*Enten—Eller* in the original Danish), in the scene where Henrik asks for a loan. We are allowed to see a close-up of the title of the book and the name of the author.

A vital reference that is explicit in the published script, but is not articulated in the actual film, is Swedish mystic and scholar Emanuel Swedenborg. In the first scene of the film, Johan tells Marianne that he sometimes thinks he is already dead, living in hell (a similar thought is formulated by Henrik in his conversation with Marianne in the church). In the published script, Johan refers to Swedenborg and his vision of how we reside in the world of spirits after death. Johan says, 'most of them do not notice the difference and cannot see that they are in hell. They are in fact quite happy

---

3 Ingmar Bergman, 'Ormskinnet', first published in *Expressen*, 1 August 1965. There is an English translation by Keith Bradfield, 'The Snakeskin', www.ingmarbergman.se/en/production/snakeskin (accessed 1 October 2018).

with their existence. Some of them live deep down among their own excrements, eating them, sleeping among them.'

The theology of Emanuel Swedenborg offers one way of entering into the cinema of Ingmar Bergman, at least when it comes to the Swedenborg vision of spirits and the world as a transitional space where we humans wander before entering the real world, whether it is heaven or hell. Here, Bergman joins the Strindberg of *Inferno* and *The Blue Book*, as well as an impressive line of artists and thinkers including Ralph Waldo Emerson, Honoré de Balzac, Charles Baudelaire, Jorge Luis Borges, and Czesław Miłosz. Like his predecessors, Bergman does not follow the Swedenborg theological system in any detail. It is the fascinating thought of unclear borders between life and death that invites an interpretation influenced by Swedenborg, as does the idea of correspondences (something which also fascinated Baudelaire, for example). A well-known hymn by Swedish hymnologist Johan Olof Wallin—'Where Is the Friend I Seek?'—was quoted in extenso in *Wild Strawberries*, in the scene where Isak Borg rests at a wayfarers' inn during his peregrination towards Lund for his jubilee-doctor ceremony; and in *Saraband*, Johan quotes some of these lines again. Bergman said in a late interview that this hymn is 'Swedenborgian', since it deals with correspondences—i.e. the idea that the world we see has to be deciphered.[4] Beyond the material world is the true home of God, heaven. The hymn enquires into the correspondence between the beauty that we see and the beauty that awaits us when we reach God. The hymn is in fact also present in the fifth scene of the film, where Marianne visits the country church. A board on the wall announces the hymns for today's service. There is only one number this time, No. 305, which is the number of this particular hymn in the Swedish hymnal.

When Johan reflects upon the world as being inhabited by the dead, or when his son Henrik tells us about his own feeling of being dead already, they witness a stage of liminality. They are not the only ones to have such an experience, and the liminalities that are developed through the film are diverse. Johan is reflecting upon his age and the fact that he is walking towards death, and Henrik seeks his own death through suicide, though he fails. They are the living who walk towards death; but we also have a dead individual walking towards life, though she can never break through the wall completely:

---

4 The documentary 'I Bergmans regi' ('As Directed by Bergman') (2003), by Arne Carlsson and Marie Nyreröd, part of the DVD edition of *Saraband*, Sveriges Television.

I am thinking of Anna, who is constantly referred to as the one who knows the other characters best and whose picture is visible on some occasions. One might even say that the protagonists of *Saraband* try to raise Anna from death, to make her live again, giving vivid descriptions of her, quoting her words—for example from the letter to Henrik that Karin has read. Anna's vital role has been thoroughly discussed by Maaret Koskinen and Anna Sofia Rossholm.[5] Johan's remote estate is in fact a kind of transitional space for movements, not only between the spheres of life and death but across other borders as well. The war between generations and the lack of communication are challenged by Johan's understanding of Karin, and maybe even more intriguingly by the way Marianne feels that she can finally communicate with her daughter Martha. These experiences may be said to transcend the fate of parents, losing contact with their children, that recurs throughout Bergman's oeuvre. Another instance of transcendence, or rather transgression, is Henrik's implicit attempt to break the taboo of incest—we know that he sleeps in the same bed as his daughter and that he kisses her, and she herself describes her relation to him as that of a substitute for Anna, his dead wife. Karin manages to break out of this relationship; and like Marianne, she evades the seemingly set relationships in this dysfunctional family. But the breaking of the incest taboo reminds us that a state of liminality is not necessarily free or liberating in itself; it may also be a state bordering on violent desire and abuse.

One of the basic elements of Kierkegaard's philosophy is the idea of life as a succession of stages—the aesthetic, the ethical, and the religious—and all of the characters in *Saraband* may be seen as aiming or waiting for transgression and thus looking to attain a new stage in life, even if it is not necessarily possible to trace these aims back to the Kierkegaard matrix. As was pointed out above, the Kierkegaard book that Johan reads in the film is *Enten—Eller*, whose very title constitutes an interpretation of a liminal situation: 'Either or'.

The main character in the film, and to a certain extent the narrator of the story it presents, is Marianne. In the prologue, she introduces herself and talks to us, the audience, speaking in the present tense.

---

5 Maaret Koskinen, '"Ett förtvivlans kanske" – Om gudars skändlighet och människans helighet hos Ingmar Bergman', in Tomas Axelson and Ola Sigurdson (eds), *Film och religion: Livstolkning på vita duken* (Örebro: Cordia, 2005), pp. 151–174; Anna Sofia Rossholm, *Ingmar Bergman och den lekfulla skriften* (Gothenburg and Stockholm: Makadam, 2017), pp. 71–75.

Then, in the first scene, she is in Johan's living room, unseen by him but seen by us, and she talks to us again, giggling over the situation as if it is some kind of joke. She transgresses a taboo when entering into Johan's house, interacting with the audience as well as with the cinematographic apparatus. A door is suddenly closed as if by an invisible hand, like the magic enacted in the attic in *The Magician*; a wall clock chimes; there are traces of a machine, something that makes the world go round. She looks around, but nobody is there.

On the spur of the moment, Marianne decides to visit Johan after many years, and suddenly things start to happen. When the narration of the film ends, Karin has left her father, Henrik has tried to kill himself, Johan has momentarily been awakened from his misanthropic existence, and Johan and Marianne have broken the long silence that has existed between them. And Marianne has the feeling of being in touch with her silent child, Martha, after all those years. But Marianne is not omniscient; she cannot make things move without interaction with the apparatus: the camera and the projection. And there are areas about which the camera knows more than she does.

When Marianne visits the country church where Henrik plays the organ, she visits another transitory space, a sacred room which in itself encloses liminalities of all sorts, but mainly the transition between life and death, which is underscored by the conversation with Henrik: Henrik says that he thinks of death all the time, and that he feels that he is already dead, as he can sometimes see his dead beloved Anna so clearly. He then offends Marianne, and in a way transgresses the line between sanity and insanity. Suddenly he becomes paranoid, asking if she 'fucks the old man' and if she is there to get his money. When he leaves, Marianne walks slowly towards the altar, and non-diegetic music is played, a cello suite. She looks at the altarpiece and the picture of Christ, and a ray of light is projected from the church window. She looks intensely at the Christ figure and then closes her eyes, as if in prayer. She then looks up, and even smiles slightly, and the scene fades to black. The intervention of the non-diegetic music and the light from the window emanate from the same source as the closing of doors in the first scene, *by an invisible hand*—that is: the camera, the light, the montage, the cinematographic apparatus, the vehicle of language in whatever form, and all correspondences between Man and God in the film. There would be no world at all in *Saraband* if there was no camera. That is a truism, to be sure; but the trivial truth becomes meaningful with the small hints that Bergman gives us about the different levels of narration and consciousness. It is not as ostentatious as in *Persona*, but with a subtlety that comes from an old master, well aware of his own liminalities.

An ironic comment is made in the ninth scene, where Marianne and Johan learn that Henrik has tried to commit suicide. Marianne tells Johan that a woman found Henrik lying naked in the cottage, covered in blood, having tried to cut his throat. A photographic still of Henrik is inserted, as a reminder of the presence of the apparatus. In the conversation between Marianne and Johan, they reproach each other, and she says to him: 'Sometimes I think that you behave like a character in some old, forgotten movie. A very silly movie. You are in fact not a real person. …' And she is right, of course; Johan is not a real person, he is a construction of light and sound in a movie, conditioned by the technology of film.

In the epilogue, Marianne asks us, the viewers, if we want to know how everything turned out. She shows us a black-and-white photograph of her and Johan in her bed, a frozen still from their last night together. This picture once again marks the non-diegetic presence of the apparatus. She tells the story of how her relationship with Johan faded out, and how the silence between them returned. She then talks about Anna and meditates upon her, before she tells us about her meeting with Martha. In a flashback, we see the interiors of the nursing home, bleak and grey, like in a much older film. Marianne touches Martha and removes her spectacles. All of a sudden, their eyes meet and the same cello music is heard as in the scene before the altarpiece. The last words of the film are 'My child'.

The machine is still working.

Acknowledgements

I am grateful for the rewarding discussions I have had with Patrik Fridlund, Reader and Senior Lecturer at the Centre for Theology and Religious Studies, Lund University, concerning this interpretation of *Saraband*.

18
Return to the bourgeoisie:
Fanny and Alexander in Swedish politics

Erik Hedling

The political climate in Sweden was somewhat tumultuous at the time of Bergman's writing *Fanny and Alexander* in 1979. The oil crisis of 1973 had impaired the strong Swedish economy, which had been growing steadily since the late 1940s. In 1976, several factors caused Sweden's ruling Social Democratic Party to lose the general election for the first time in forty years, and the international scandal surrounding tax evasion charges brought against Bergman was one of them.[1] Despite their election promises, Sweden's newly elected government (consisting of three non-socialist parties, from liberals to conservatives) continued to follow the same Keynesian economic policies that had held sway in Sweden for half a century, and the economic decline continued.[2]

---

1 For an account of the tax scandal, see Erik Hedling, 'Bergmans bortgång: Realpolitiska reflektioner', in Erik Hedling and Ann-Kristin Wallengren (eds), *Den nya svenska filmen: Kultur, kriminalitet & kakofoni* (Stockholm: Atlantis, 2014), pp. 329–352.
2 Many Swedish historians have recounted and analysed domestic events of the late 1970s and early 1980s. I have chosen to base my account on two popular histories distributed by mainstream publishers and widely read in Sweden: Göran Hägg, *Välfärdsåren: svensk historia 1945–1986* (Stockholm: Wahlström & Widstrand, 2005) and Kjell Östberg, *När vinden vände: Olof Palme 1969–1986* (Stockholm: Leopard, 2009 [2012]). Both authors can be loosely affiliated with a general Social Democratic outlook—that is to say, with Sweden's dominant political party of the twentieth century—and both have published regularly in the tabloid *Aftonbladet*, Sweden's main Social Democratic newspaper. This does not mean that I consider them biased, however. Since I interpret Bergman's politics at this particular time (although certainly not always, since he was a self-confessed Social Democrat for many years) as being in opposition to the Social Democrats, I consider this to be a reasonable approach.

The Islamic Revolution in Iran in March 1979 caused a second oil crisis in Sweden. What some critics perceived to be the disadvantages of the Swedish Model Welfare State (high taxes, a huge and expensive public sector, and low mobility in the labour market) were now singled out as the major reasons for Sweden's limited economic growth and high inflation. This led the post-1976, non-socialist government to introduce some very unpopular changes from 1980 onwards, namely restrictions to welfare policies; cuts were made in the state budget that would have been unthinkable during the decades of Social Democratic rule. As Swedish historian Kjell Östberg puts it, 'Keynes was dead and Sweden had taken its first steps towards market-orientated politics.'[3] Östberg also describes the years that followed as being characterized by neoliberalism—a distinct right-wing wave—and by a decline in the leftist values that had permeated rather significant areas in Swedish media and culture during the 1970s.[4]

In this context, it is important to differentiate between the various layers of Swedish left-wing politics. On the one hand, there was (and still is) the 'Establishment Left', characterized by the powerful Social Democratic Party (which has governed Sweden for sixty-nine of the last eighty-six years), and the trade unions. On the other hand, there was the (albeit much smaller) 'Anti-establishment Left', comprised of a number of Marxist fractions which began to emerge with Sweden's anti-Vietnam War movement in the mid-1960s.[5] By 1980, however, these latter groups had begun to lose some of their former media clout. While the Establishment Left and the Anti-establishment Left had very little sympathy for each other, some semantic problems arose from the fact that they both described themselves as 'Socialist'.

Swedish culture also underwent change during this period. Young literary critics began to attack Sweden's former predilection for left-wing politics, a penchant that was replaced by a philosophical approach and a more modernist-elitist aesthetic. Or, as historian

---

3 Östberg, *När vinden vände*, p. 279. Here and elsewhere in this chapter, quotations from works originally in Swedish have been translated by the author.
4 Östberg, *När vinden vände*, pp. 275–279.
5 For a thorough general account of this process, see Kim Salomon, *Rebeller i takt med tiden: FNL-rörelsen och 60-talets politiska ritualer* (Stockholm: Rabén Prisma, 1996).

Göran Hägg describes it in his outspoken history of the Swedish Model welfare state:

> it was a process where the arts sector as a whole changed its stripes—most often silently—from a routine leftist engagement to 'postmodernism' or other vaguely apolitical ideas. Some leading arts personalities even went so far as to express right-wing or neoliberal political sympathies, which would have been inconceivable only a few years before.[6]

Nobody knows how Bergman was affected, if at all, by these vicissitudes in Sweden's cultural, economic, and political climate. The only overtly political comment I can find in the numerous interviews he gave to the Swedish press at the time pertains to a discussion of Sweden's upcoming referendum on nuclear power in March 1980. Theatre critic Arne Ruth conducted the interview on behalf of Sweden's liberal *Expressen* tabloid, one of the major newspapers to support Bergman throughout his tax scandal trauma four years before.[7]

Bergman typically—and provocatively—claimed that Sweden had exchanged debating religion for discussing nuclear power, just as it had done earlier with the Vietnam War and the furore over Stockholm's elm trees, to mention two examples. Ironically, the latter instance referred to a violent public demonstration organized by the Anti-establishment Left against the felling of trees in Stockholm's inner city in 1971. Bergman also declared himself to be opposed to nuclear power: 'Although I will get into trouble for saying so, I am a passionate opponent of nuclear power. At the same time, my position on this matter makes me feel ridiculous.'[8] This latter comment was probably connected to Bergman's juxtaposition of religion and nuclear power. However, his anti-nuclear stance was not shared by the Social Democrats, the very party Bergman himself claimed he had long voted for. That said, according to various accounts his support for the Social Democrats waned after the tax scandal of 1976.[9]

---

6 Hägg, *Välfärdsåren*, p. 376.
7 Arne Ruth, '"Svenskarna pratar om kärnkraft istället för Gud"', *Expressen*, 15 March 1980, Arts section.
8 Ruth, '"Svenskarna pratar om kärnkraft"'.
9 While Bergman might have retained his sympathy for Social Democratic ideology, a few things indicate that he changed his vote. One of Bergman's personal friends, Finnish-Swedish film director and author Jörn Donner,

Bergman's politics

Bergman made the following comment to a Swedish weekly in an interview published in 1956, shortly after completing his film *The Seventh Seal* (1957):

> I have not turned bourgeois in my old age [Bergman was thirty-eight at the time]. I have always been bourgeois, conservative, reactionary— or whatever you wish to call it.[10]

In spite of his self-confessed lack of interest in politics,[11] in so far as Bergman was referring to an actual political stance he might have inherited this outlook from his upper-middle-class upbringing in the 1920s and 1930s. By the 1950s, however, Sweden was very heavily influenced by the Social Democratic Party and the impact of its—at that time—successful implementation of the Swedish Model Welfare State. Although the Social Democrats were originally a workers' party, they also attracted members of the middle class as well as many intellectuals. The fact that Bergman eventually joined the Social Democratic ranks might be considered something of a surprise given both his background and the nature of his films produced up until the mid-1960s, which espouse a world-view far removed from that championed by the Social Democrats. It was a world-view focused on spirituality rather than science and progress, human tragedy rather than social optimism, humiliation rather than material prosperity, and—albeit inconsistently—conservatism rather than modernity.[12] Bergman biographer Michael Timm describes this aspect of Bergman as follows: 'For decades he had opposed official Sweden, not in political statements, but like [...] the neorealists[, in] presenting counter-images to official ideology

---

claims to know that Bergman voted for Sweden's liberal party (Folkpartiet) in the 1990s. See Jörn Donner, 'Ett långsamt farväl till Ingmar Bergman', *Svenska Dagbladet*, 14 July 2018, Arts section.

10 Ingmar Bergman, *Artiklar, Essäer, Föredrag*, edited by Håkan Bravinger, Christo Burman, Jan Holmberg, Maaret Koskinen, Per Stam, and Astrid Söderbergh Widding (Stockholm: Norstedts, 2018), p. 239.

11 Stig Björkman, Torsten Manns, and Jonas Sima, *Bergman om Bergman* (Stockholm: P.A. Norstedt & Söners förlag, 1970), p. 15.

12 See also Erik Hedling, 'The Welfare State Depicted: Post-Utopian Landscapes in Ingmar Bergman's Films', in Maaret Koskinen (ed.), *Ingmar Bergman Revisited: Performance, Cinema and the Arts* (London and New York: Wallflower Press, 2008), pp. 180–193.

[implicitly, Social Democratic ideology].'[13] I have chosen to single out an article by socialist film critic Jonas Sima from among the writings of many critics and scholars who have recognized this aspect of Bergman's views. The article is a review of *From the Life of the Marionettes* from 1981, published in the Social Democratic Party newsletter *Aktuellt i politiken*. In it, Sima describes Bergman's counter-images in bourgeois terms:

> Ingmar Bergman is a bourgeois artist. His films are most often bourgeois melodramas set in upper-class surroundings (preferably stucco-decorated Östermalm apartments [that is to say, in a distinctly upper-class neighbourhood in central Stockholm]), among well-educated people with solid bank accounts and respectable family trees.
>
> By his own account, Bergman claimed to have voted for the Social Democrats up until his 'exile' in Germany.[14]

This does not amount to saying that I personally believe that Bergman's films can be squeezed into a definite ideological framework: sometimes the narrative perspective is clearly conservative, as in some of his early films, and sometimes it is surprisingly radical. That was how Bergman functioned as an artist.

If such a change ever actually occurred, perhaps Bergman's shift in ideological outlook—his conversion to Social Democracy—might have taken place, at least in part, when Sweden's Social Democratic government began to show him open support. Bergman himself claimed that his 'mistrust of politics' lasted until the mid-1960s.[15] In January 1963, Bergman received a phone call from Sweden's then-minister of culture and education, Social Democrat Ragnar Edenman, in which Edenman offered him the position of head of the Royal Dramatic Theatre in Stockholm, one of Sweden's most important administrative positions for a man of the arts.[16] Later that same year, Edenman also personally proposed to Bergman that he submit his new film *The Silence* (1963), with its provocative display of sexuality, to the state's film censorship authority for

---

13 Michael Timm, *Lusten och dämonerna: Boken om Bergman* (Stockholm: Norstedts, 2008), p. 461.
14 Jonas Sima, 'Bergman – angår han oss', *Aktuellt i politiken*, 12 February 1981, 33.
15 See Maria Bergom Larsson, *Ingmar Bergman och den borgerliga ideologin* (Stockholm: Bokförlaget PAN/Norstedts, 1976), p. 26.
16 Timm, *Lusten och dämonerna*, p. 352.

approval while its notoriously strict censor Erik Skoglund was taking his annual holiday. Unsurprisingly, the film passed inspection without cuts, and in the fierce debate that followed—even reaching the Swedish Parliament—Edenman, who was no friend of film censorship, proved to be a staunch supporter of Bergman.[17] Regarding the liberalization of sexual politics during the 1960s, Bergman's views and the Social Democrats' visions most certainly coincided.[18]

As head of the Royal Dramatic Theatre, and following the founding of the Swedish Film Institute in 1963, Bergman presumably became convinced that the arts (particularly the elite culture that he represented, especially through the theatre) needed strong state support to survive in a capitalist economy. Thus, I believe he was at least partly referring to himself when he wrote in his private notes concerning the film *Shame* in 1967 that the two leading roles, artists Jan and Eva (played by Max von Sydow and Liv Ullmann), should be named Rosenberg. As he wrote, 'they are sprung from the same rose', the red rose being the traditional symbol of the Socialist movement and, since 1969, also the official symbol of the Swedish Social Democratic Workers' Party. Bergman goes on to specify: 'They are Social Democrats[.] They have always supported the Social Democrats, as that party supports the arts.'[19]

Bergman went on to declare his support for Sweden's Social Democratic Party in a series of interviews, ranging from the classic interview book *Bergman om Bergman* (1970)[20] to an especially candid interview with British critic and poet Alfred Alvarez. This interview was published in *The New York Times* just weeks before the start of the rift between Bergman and the Social Democrats over the infamous 1976 tax scandal. In it, Bergman openly praised the social revolution in his homeland—that is to say, the implementation of the Swedish Model Welfare State—and was taken seriously

---

17 Timm, *Lusten och dämonerna*, pp. 362–363.
18 See Erik Hedling, 'Breaking the Swedish Sex Barrier: Painful Lustfulness in Ingmar Bergman's *The Silence*', *Film International* 6 (2008), 17–27.
19 Ingmar Bergman, *Arbetsboken 1955–1974*, edited by Håkan Bravinger, Christo Burman, Jan Holmberg, Maaret Koskinen, Per Stam, and Astrid Söderbergh Widding (Stockholm: Norstedts, 2018), p. 217. I also believe that the name 'Rosenberg' has a connection to the famous American spy couple, Ethel and Julius Rosenberg, who were executed for espionage in 1953. I believe that, to Bergman, the name signified his protagonists' status as victims of an oppressive state apparatus.
20 Björkman, Manns, and Sima, *Bergman on Bergman*, especially pp. 19 and 192.

by Alvarez on political matters in a manner that differed from that of Swedish critics, who were somewhat condescending in their approach to Bergman where politics was concerned:[21]

> But you must remember that 50 years ago Sweden was an extraordinarily poor country—people were starving and life [was] generally hard. Then this almost completely unbloody revolution happened in a mere 50 years. This, in my opinion, is remarkable.[22]

Even so, Bergman was less enthusiastic the next time he commented on his commitment to Social Democracy. The remark coincided with his self-imposed exile in Germany after he was charged (wrongly, as it was later proven) with tax evasion in January 1976, an event that echoed throughout the Western world. Many years later, Sweden's Social Democratic government would apologize officially to Bergman for this error.[23] Just before leaving Sweden, in April of the same year, Bergman wrote a farewell letter published in the Swedish newspaper *Expressen* in which he lamented:

> I have been a convinced Social Democrat. With genuine passion have I believed in this ideology of grey compromise. I thought my country the best in the world, and if I continue to think so, it is perhaps because I have seen so very little of other lands. My awakening was a shock, partly because of my unbearable humiliation, partly because I saw that anyone in this country, whenever and however, can be attacked and abased by a special kind of bureaucracy that grows like a galloping cancer [...] and to which society has given powers exercised by individuals who are in no way mature enough to handle them.[24]

---

21 Regarding *Bergman on Bergman* by Björkman, Manns, and Sima, Bergman would later state explicitly: 'My young interviewers were the bearers of the one and only true political conviction. They also knew that I had been left behind by the times, demeaned and scorned by the new aesthetics of the younger generation. [...] What I did not realize during our sessions was that they were little by little reconstructing a dinosaur piece by piece with the kind assistance of the monster himself.' Ingmar Bergman, *Images: My Life in Film*, translated from Swedish by Marianne Ruuth (New York: Arcade Publishing, 1990), p. 11.
22 Alfred Alvarez, 'A Visit with Ingmar Bergman', *The New York Times*, 7 December 1975.
23 See Birgitta Steene, *Ingmar Bergman: A Reference Guide* (Amsterdam: Amsterdam University Press, 2005), p. 46.
24 Ingmar Bergman, *Artiklar, Essäer, Föredrag*, p. 295. The English translation is from Frank Gado, *The Passion of Ingmar Bergman* (Durham, NC: Duke University Press, 1986), p. 468.

These sentiments might have epitomized Bergman's mood when he wrote *Fanny and Alexander* three years later. Bergman himself wrote of this film:

> I conceived *Fanny and Alexander* during the fall of 1978, a time when everything around me left me in darkest despair. But I wrote the screenplay during the spring of 1979, and by that time many things had eased up. *Autumn Sonata* had a successful premiere, and the whole tax business had dissolved into thin air.[25]

This development marked something of an end to Bergman's public relationship with the Swedish political faction I have termed the 'Establishment Left'. That aside, something remains to be said about the relationship which he was simultaneously developing with the Anti-establishment Left, a relationship which might also have had some bearing on his work on *Fanny and Alexander*.

The Anti-establishment Left attacked Bergman vigorously from the late 1960s onwards, even going so far as to organize demonstrations outside cinemas in connection with the release of Bergman's pacifist film *Shame* in September 1968.[26] The protesters objected that in reality, Bergman was acting as an errand boy for American imperialism by suggesting that the two opposing sides were equally guilty of atrocities during war, particularly since he told reporters that his film was about the Vietnam War. Conversely, the Anti-establishment Left advocated a firm commitment to the Vietnamese people, as represented by North Vietnam and the South Vietnamese Communist guerrilla force, or Viet Cong (a stance often challenged by contemporary historical research on the Vietnam War).[27]

This strong anti-Bergman sentiment, including harsh accusations of his being a bourgeois artist with no relevance for the working class, persisted into the 1970s, and it is summarized in Maria Bergom

---

25 Bergman, *Images*, p. 370.
26 For an account of the fierce debate regarding *Shame*, see Erik Hedling, '*Shame*: Ingmar Bergman's Vietnam War', *Nordicom* 29:2 (2008), 245–259.
27 See, for example, Max Hastings, *Vietnam: An Epic Tragedy, 1945–1975* (London: HarperCollins, 2018). Without defending the American intervention in the slightest, Hastings also points to the appalling atrocities committed against the common people by both the North Vietnamese army and the Viet Cong. He likewise draws attention to the brutal and deadly dictatorship imposed on Vietnam after the American withdrawal in 1975. In Hastings's view, this was a conflict that nobody deserved to win, an understanding of the war that coincides with that portrayed in Bergman's *Shame* in 1968.

Larsson's book *Ingmar Bergman och den borgerliga ideologin*.[28] Some film critics continued to view Bergman in this light even up until the 1980s, as is exemplified by Jonas Sima's defence of Bergman in the quotation below, in spite of his aforementioned review of *From the Life of the Marionettes*:

> I think that Bergman's films can teach us Socialists something about life itself, for example. [...] I don't view Bergman as being a particularly bourgeois person. But he does drill into something that he knows very well: the bourgeois society, the sacred family, and [...] good manners. He transcends taboos[;] in the end he is showing us the inside of the soul. There are several good artists [who] provide us with a picture of the dark side of society. [...] The bourgeoisie is a carcass. Nevertheless[,] it moves. Sometimes Bergman's gluttonous approach to this rotten social body feels rather necrophiliac.[29]

This kind of discussion of Bergman's films was common within left-wing circles, sometimes with favourable connotations, as in this example. Most often, however, the opposite was true.

Bergman's own ultimate opinion of Sweden's Anti-establishment Left proved to be scathing. In his autobiography *The Magic Lantern* (1987), published a few years after *Fanny and Alexander*'s release, he writes:

> It is possible some brave researcher will one day investigate just how much damage was done to our cultural life by the 1968 movement. [...] Today, frustrated revolutionaries still cling to their desks in editorial offices and talk bitterly about 'the renewal that stopped short'. They do not see (and how could they!) that their contribution was a deadly slashing blow at an evolution that must never be separated from its roots. In other countries where varied ideas are allowed to flourish at the same time, tradition and education were not destroyed. Only in China and Sweden were artists and teachers scorned.[30]

As is further demonstrated in the twenty-two pages of *The Magic Lantern* dedicated to the subject, Bergman was deeply affected by the tax scandal of 1976, and he indirectly laid the blame for the wrongful charges levelled against him at the feet of the Social Democrats and their charismatic prime minister, Olof Palme.[31]

---

28 Bergom Larsson, *Ingmar Bergman*.
29 Sima, 'Bergman – angår han oss', 33.
30 Ingmar Bergman, *The Magic Lantern*, translated from Swedish by Joan Tate (New York and London: Penguin, 1988), p. 199.
31 Bergman, *The Magic Lantern*, pp. 84–106.

Fanny and Alexander revisited

At the time of its release, most critics viewed *Fanny and Alexander* as a celebration of what could be loosely termed 'bourgeois values'. This was certainly the case in Sweden, albeit without the negative connotations such a designation would have entailed in the two decades prior. Thus, while Bergman himself remained unaffected by the changes in the zeitgeist, the opposite is true of *Fanny and Alexander*'s reception. Historian Göran Hägg explicitly refers to *Fanny and Alexander* as a parable of the troubled nature of the era:

> Ingmar Bergman returned to his native Sweden after his exile in the aftermath of the tax scandal of 1976. *Fanny and Alexander* (1982) met with enormous success as a series on Sweden's then-dominant public-service TV network (still a state monopoly at the time), and afterwards as a film all over the world. [Hägg gets the chronology of events wrong here, since the film came before the series.] When the first episode was broadcast, some critics interpreted its lavish Christmas party as a satire depicting a depraved upper class. However, it was soon revealed that on the contrary, it was in fact a paean to the Oscarian bourgeoisie [named after Sweden's King Oscar II, who reigned in the late nineteenth and early twentieth centuries] as a life form, and to the virtues of the 'little world,' and was thus far from any moralism or social posing. In this regard, the film was highly typical of the new ideological climate.[32]

In a caption, Hägg adds regarding *Fanny and Alexander*: 'A vanished bourgeoisie is suddenly portrayed with the same kind of nostalgia as was reserved for the working class in the 1960s, and the peasants in the 1970s.'[33]

One could even apply a neoliberal understanding to *Fanny and Alexander*, although many film scholars would shudder at the mere suggestion. The 'little world' famously hailed by Gustaf Adolf Ekdahl (played by Jarl Kulle) in the film's concluding speech could be understood to represent the Ekdahl family's capitalist enterprises, the theatre and other small companies he obviously ran with great financial success, though the theatre experiences a (presumably) brief hiatus in its operations when its star actress, Emilie Ekdahl (played by Eva Fröling), temporarily ends her career to marry the bigot Bishop Edvard Vergérus (played by Jan Malmsjö). Here, the

---

32 Hägg, *Välfärdsåren*, p. 409.
33 Hägg, *Välfärdsåren*, p. 409.

little world is portrayed as the antithesis of a broken monolith, the state-run Church of Sweden, as represented by the morally and financially destitute Bishop.

Swedish film scholar Mats Rohdin has studied the theatre–church dichotomy in *Fanny and Alexander* as an interplay between the profane and the sacred, the new and the old. Rohdin notes: 'what separates *Fanny and Alexander* from earlier Bergman films, such as *Sawdust and Tinsel* (1953) and *The Magician* (1958), is that the bourgeoisie (read: the Ekdahl family) has this time formed an alliance with representatives of the theatrical arts, instead of oppressing and humiliating them.'[34] To this could be added the purely economic juxtaposition of the Ekdahl family businesses (representing healthy commercial private ventures) with the church (representing an outdated and stale public sector).

Things become even more complex in connection with the depiction of the main villain of the piece, the Bishop. The Bishop is named Vergérus, a character who has appeared in several Bergman films since *The Magician* in 1958. This name might be derived from the Latin verb *vergo/vergere*, which, among other things, means 'to lie'. In other words, Vergérus is a liar. Vergérus is most often depicted as an arch-rationalist, a man of science who is thoroughly aware of his superior point of view, as in the case of his debut in *The Magician*. In that instance, Gunnar Björnstrand plays Vergérus in the role of a particularly arrogant and conceited medical doctor. As the Vergérus character developed over the years, he came to take on the physical appearance and personality traits (already evident in *The Magician*) of famous Uppsala Professor of Philosophy Ingemar Hedenius. Hedenius was well known in Sweden in the 1950s and 1960s both as a major contributor to Stockholm's biggest broadsheet, *Dagens Nyheter*, and as a keen critic of various conservative institutions.[35] As an introducer of Anglo-Saxon analytical philosophy in Sweden, Hedenius was recognized as a fierce and highly eloquent atheist, and even as something of a nemesis of the state-run church during the social and political upheavals of the 1950s. In their fascinating comparison of Hedenius and Bergman as critics of religion, Maria Bergom Larsson and Bengt Kristensson Uggla maintain: 'The

---

34 Maaret Koskinen and Mats Rohdin, *Fanny och Alexander: Ur Ingmar Bergmans arkiv och hemliga gömmor* (Stockholm: Wahlström & Widstrand, 2005), p. 125.

35 See Svante Nordin, *Ingemar Hedenius: En filosof och hans tid* (Stockholm: Natur & Kultur, 2004).

rationalistic mode of thought represented by Hedenius' philosophy characterized both Sweden's Modern Project and the social-engineering process that would build the new state [*folkhemmet* ('the people's home'), according to Social Democratic phraseology].'[36] Hedenius's book *Tro och vetande* (*Belief and Knowledge*), published in 1949,[37] sparked a huge debate in Sweden, as is elegantly summarized by Bergman in the dialogue between the medical and theology students during lunch at the inn Gyllene uttern in *Wild Strawberries* (1957). Kristensson Uggla and Bergom Larsson highlight this scene as a comic critique of just how abstract and theoretical the debate triggered by Hedenius could be.[38] Hedenius was also identified as an occasional Social Democrat, in this case representing the strong scientific and educational bent found in official party policy.

The physical representation of Hedenius in Vergérus is particularly striking in German actor Heinz Bennent's appearance in *The Serpent's Egg* (1977). Here, Bennent plays the diabolical Dr Hans Vergérus who conducts scientific experiments on humans in 1920s Berlin, often with fatal consequences.

Although exaggerated scientific rigour is exchanged for religious bigotry in *Fanny and Alexander*, the phenomenon works in similar ways. Hedenius is invoked by Bishop Vergérus (incarnated by Jan Malmsjö) in what Mats Rohdin has described as 'his idealistically elevated search for purity, free from all kinds of human misery, penury, and decay'.[39] In this instance, a passion for science has developed into a particularly austere and grim version of Lutheranism. Hedenius was also famous for his love of classical music and was known as a master flautist, even performing for live audiences. In order to make the connection between Vergérus and Hedenius in *Fanny and Alexander*, Bergman made the Bishop a devoted flute player.

While I am speculating about Bergman's use of names, I cannot resist the urge to mention that Bishop Edvard Vergérus also bears the given names Henrik—which Bergman famously used to depict

---

36 Maria Bergom Larsson and Bengt Kristensson Uggla, 'Film som religiöst språk: Hedenius och Ingmar Bergman i livsåskådningsdebatten', in Maria Bergom Larsson, Stina Hammar, and Bengt Kristensson Uggla (eds), *Nedstigningar i modern film – hos Bergman, Wenders, Adlon, Tarkovskij* (Delsbo: Åsak, 1992), p. 9.
37 Ingemar Hedenius, *Tro och vetande* (Stockholm: Bonnier, 1949).
38 Bergom Larsson and Kristensson Uggla, 'Film som religiöst språk', p. 12.
39 Koskinen and Rohdin, *Fanny och Alexander*, p. 146.

his father, Erik Bergman—and Olof, which he shares with the most famous of Sweden's Social Democratic politicians, former Prime Minister Olof Palme, a man whom Bergman 'despised', according to his own testimony in relation to the tax scandal in *The Magic Lantern*.[40] According to Michael Timm, the ire Bergman felt towards Palme lasted until his death.[41] On the other hand, 'Olof' might also refer to Olof Lagercrantz, the powerful editor-in-chief of Swedish daily newspaper *Dagens Nyheter*, a person whom Bergman regarded as an enemy from time to time.[42]

That aside, the Vergérus persona also embodies several more of Hedenius's character traits, such as were often gossiped about among his many adversaries: his smug sense of self-importance, his contempt for others, and his appeal to a higher power. For Hedenius personally, and for some of the other Vergéruses in Bergman's films, the latter was represented by scientific discourse. For the man of religion in *Fanny and Alexander* (such as he purports to be), a similar line of thought creates 'an atmosphere of purity and austerity'. Moreover, his clearly neurotic sister is allowed to add regarding the Bishop's Palace that 'punctuality, cleanliness, and order rule in this house', to the great dismay of the children, Fanny and Alexander. We also discern that blatant anti-Semitism infects the Bishop's Palace.

Of course, it would be highly ironic of Bergman to model this religious bigot, the arch-villain of the film, and the obvious criticism of the Church that he embodies, on Ingemar Hedenius, the harshest and best-known critic of Christianity in modern Swedish history. What is more, Bergman would not be Bergman if there was not a catch somewhere, something that would foil overly narrow interpretations of his work. This anticipated catch appears towards the end of the film, in the masterful scene in which the Ekdahl brothers finally confront the Bishop.[43] Surprisingly, the Bishop somehow has

---

40 Bergman, *The Magic Lantern*, p. 95.
41 Timm, *Lusten och dämonerna*, p. 470.
42 Jan Holmberg describes Lagercrantz, a major critic and one of two editors-in-chief at *Dagens Nyheter*, as Bergman's 'Nemesis'. See Jan Holmberg, *Författaren Ingmar Bergman* (Stockholm: Norstedts, 2018), p. 47. While Lagercrantz was often critical of Bergman, he could also be highly supportive of the filmmaker, as in the debate regarding *The Silence*. See Hedling, 'Breaking the Swedish Sex Barrier', pp. 24–25.
43 It should be noted that this masterful scene is only included in the complete, five-hour version, which is the version that was aired on Swedish television and elsewhere and released on DVD by Artificial Eye.

the last word, concluding the discussion by saying that Gustaf Adolf Ekdahl 'believes that everything can be bought and sold'. He then adds: 'Director Ekdahl is the son of one of the greatest actresses in the land. Despite this, he has grasped little or nothing [...] of the mind's unlimited power over matter.' This, I would suggest, is a typical Bergman twist on the film's general sentiment.

The Bishop is thus allowed to deliver the counter-argument, dismissing such capitalist practices as buying and selling and arguing that mind comes before matter. His words constitute a solid critique of a neoliberal ethos, thus harmonizing with the general tenor found universally in Bergman's oeuvre, where economic gain counts for very little and where mind always seems to triumph over matter.

Naturally, the film also contains other minor ambiguities, such as the Ekdahl family name which is a reference to Ibsen's play *The Wild Duck*, in which the Ekdals (a variant spelling of the same name) are characterized by a lifelong deception regarding their own existence.[44] Bergman was once asked in an interview: 'Is it a coincidence that [the family in *Fanny and Alexander*] bears the same surname as the family in Ibsen's *The Wild Duck*, which also defends the "life-lie"?' To which he replied:

> No, it [was a] highly conscious [choice], but I didn't think it would be noticed [...] many serious people would now attack me for defending our need for a life-lie, for escapism. [We're] all supposed to be so committed [to contemporary society]. [I'm] just not sure that everybody is [cut out] to be that [way].[45]

Thus, paradoxically, the Bishop in *Fanny and Alexander* seeks an oppressive and limiting 'truth', while the Ekdahls relax behind their life-affirming 'lie'.

To summarize, one could at least partly interpret *Fanny and Alexander* as a film embodying Bergman's reconciliation with his upper-middle-class background. In calling attention to the favourable aspects of a bourgeois way of life, Bergman might also have intended an implicit critique of Sweden's Social Democratic Party's policies, in spite of that party's irrefutable contribution to the progress made by post-war Swedish society—policies that Bergman himself had openly supported. In one way, it was also Bergman's revenge: he

---

44 Henrik Ibsen's influence on Bergman is particularly emphasized in Michael Tapper's book *Ingmar Bergman's Face to Face* (London and New York: Wallflower Press, 2017).
45 Christina Palmgren, 'En gobeläng om barndomen', *Vi* 15:5 (1975), 40.

was given the opportunity to return to Sweden for one last major film production and, seizing the chance, he triumphed, getting away with a piece that can be viewed as propaganda in support of his own social class. Although the film presented both Sweden's Establishment Left and Anti-establishment Left with an enormous, obvious target at which to take aim, everyone was happy. In a sense, this was a sign of the changes that had occurred with respect to ideological attitudes in Sweden by the early 1980s.

Post scriptum

I have read all the reviews of *Fanny and Alexander* printed in Sweden's major newspapers. I have not quoted from them, however, as they are all predictably affirmative—even laudatory—and enthusiastic. There is one minor exception to this rule: Jan Aghed, a distinguished Swedish critic with a consistently left-wing view. Aghed wrote for the Malmö daily *Sydsvenska Dagbladet* before he died in 2018. While Aghed praised Bergman's filmmaking in *Fanny and Alexander*, he typically complained about the lack of social analysis included in the depiction of the patriarchal, sexist world of the film, and about its celebration of the bourgeoisie. Aghed wrote a substantial review of books by Peter Cowie and Paisley Livingston[46] for the Swedish film journal *Chaplin* in 1983, in which he continued his political critique of *Fanny and Alexander* despite his admiration for the film. In it, Aghed compared the film's lyrical setting with the grim realities of Swedish society at the time (just prior to the First World War), characterized as it was by an unstable labour market, the fight for universal suffrage, and violent class struggles:

> I do not wish to imply by this that the spectacular variance between the film's idealization of the bourgeoisie and the reality of an exploitative, besieged, and aggressive bourgeois class, together with its objectively uncalled-for optimism and creation of a truly idyllic space, diminishes *Fanny and Alexander*, which I consider to be a great cinematic work.[47]

In reality, Aghed was just about the only person to express any such reservations.

---

46 Peter Cowie, *Ingmar Bergman: A Critical Biography* (London: Secker & Warburg, 1982) and Paisley Livingston, *Ingmar Bergman and the Rituals of Art* (Ithaca, NY: Cornell University Press, 1982).
47 Jan Aghed, 'Konstnären som gammal valp', *Chaplin* 189:6 (1983), 265. Translation mine.

Index

Whenever a name or a work title occurs both in the running text and in a footnote on the same page, references to the latter have been omitted. Titles refer to works by Ingmar Bergman unless otherwise stated.

A Lesson in Love 107, 108n5
A Ship Bound for India 18
Adorno, Theodor 207, 232–233, 234, 235
After the Rehearsal 181, 234
Aghed, Jan 284
Åhlander, Lars 47n19
Ahlstedt, Börje 178, 183, 261
Åkerblom, Karin 64
Albee, Edward 223
All These Women 48, 158
Allen, Woody 26, 27, 108n8, 131n36
Altenberg, Peter 183
Alvarez, Alfred 275–276
Andersen, Hans-Christian 233
Anderson, Lindsay 24
Andersson, Bibi 12, 19, 25, 26, 27, 100, 214, 218, 239, 240, 246
Andersson, Harriet 27, 258
Andersson, Lars Gustaf 14, 261
Antonioni, Michelangelo 24, 28, 236
Attali, Jacques 143
August, Bille 65
Austin, Paul Britten, *see* Britten Austin

Autumn Sonata 10, 11, 12, 22, 51, 95, 96, 97, 108, 114n22, 123n28, 124n29, 143, 146, 147, 158, 170, 171, 173–177, 178, 180, 182, 185–196, 264, 277
Axelson, Tomas 267n5

Bach, Johann Sebastian 11, 14, 136, 138, 142, 144, 145, 148, 149, 163, 164, 168, 169, 178, 184, 261, 262, 263, 265
Bálazs, Béla 148
Baldwin, James 48
Balio, Tino 42n4, 48n21, 51, 52n33, 53n35, 54n42
Balzac, Honoré de 90, 266
Barthes, Roland 73, 139–140, 141
Baudelaire, Charles 266
Bazin, André 18
Beethoven, Ludwig van 11, 138, 147, 159, 167–168, 172–173, 180, 182, 184
Belafonte, Harry 19
Bennent, Heinz 281
Béranger, Jean 3, 18n4
Berggren, Thommy 36
Bergman, Erik 19, 282

Bergman, Ingrid (actress) 12, 51, 170, 173, 174, 176, 178, 188, 195
Bergman, Ingrid (wife) 35
Bergman, Margareta 34
Bergmann Loizeaux, Elizabeth 71n3
Bergom Larsson, Maria 211, 274n15, 277–278, 280–281
Bergson, Henri 109, 110, 111, 125, 126, 127, 129, 130, 135
Bergström, Mats Åke 231n11
Bernstein, J. M. (Jay) 213n8
Bersani, Leo 206, 209
Bion, Wilfred 260
Bisson, Louis-Auguste 176, 177
Björkman, Stig 75, 103n27, 161n26, 213n7, 222n29, 243n10, 250n2–4, 257–258, 259n22, 273n11, 275n20, 276n21
Björnstrand, Gunnar 27, 107n4, 280
Bladh, Hilding 254
Blair, Alan 94n7, 97n12, 98n13, 175n20
Blake, Richard Aloysius 4
Blanchot, Maurice 94
Blomdahl, Karl-Birger 11, 157, 161, 253–254
Blomstedt, Herbert 180
Bono, Edward de *see* de Bono
Boorman, John 26
Borges, Jorge Luis 266
Bouchard, Donald F. 90n2
Bradfield, Keith 102n25, 265n3
Brahms, Johannes 144, 178
Bravinger, Håkan 273n10, 275n19
Brecht, Bertolt 135, 217
Breillat, Catherine 8, 26
Brereton, Cloudesley 110n15
Bresson, Robert 28, 32, 166
Bridges, Alan 215
Brink of Life 139n5
 see also *So Close to Life*
Britten Austin, Paul 34, 213n7

Broman, Per F. 11, 108n8, 147n17, 151, 152, 167, 173n12
Brooks, Xan 235n17, 236
Brown, Julie 149n21
Brown, Katharine (Kay) 51
Brown, Tom 240n6
Bruckner, Anton 144, 178, 265
Bruhn, Jörgen 72n4
Buhler, James 154
Burgess, Anthony 220
Burke, P. E. 90n1
Burman, Christo 6, 7n20, 273n10, 275n19

Camus, Albert 9, 48, 50
Cariou, Len 27
Carlsson, Arne 266n4
Carlsson, Sickan 47
Carradine, David 39
Carroll, Noël 109n11 and 13
Cartmell, Deborah 57n5
Cassavetes, John 24
Castronovo, Russ 208n27
Cattermoul, C. L. 45, 46
Cenciarelli, Carlo 144
Chaplin, Charles 18, 34
Chattopadhyay, Budhaditya 226, 227
Chevalier, Maurice 33
Chion, Michel 140, 141, 162n29, 227, 233–234
Chopin, Frédéric 10, 11, 134, 136n1, 138, 141, 146, 148, 149, 170, 173–174, 178, 191, 192
Cohen, Hubert 199–200
Cohen, Thomas F. 148n20
Conard, Mark 108n8
Conrich, Ian 152n4, 153n5
Cortot, Alfred 170
Covert, Catherine 143n10, 144n11
Cowell, Jonathan 145n14
Cowie, Peter 8, 17, 18n2, 21n9, 25n18, 284

Index

Creekmur, Corey K. 204n18
Cries and Whispers 26, 33, 34, 43, 83, 93, 102, 163, 168, 245, 261
Crouse, Lindsay 26
Crowther, Bosley 23

Dahlbeck, Eva 19, 26–27, 107n4, 258
Dano, Royal 26
de Bono, Edward 74n9, 80
de Gaulle, Charles 24
De Laurentiis, Dino 8, 21, 30, 32, 33, 36, 37, 39, 40
Death, Sara 64n14
Del Río, Dolores 33
Deleuze, Gilles 154, 156
Delon, Alain 36
DeMille, Cecil B. 34
Denis, Claire 25–26
Depmann, Jed 71
Derrida, Jacques 73, 83, 205–206, 207, 224–225, 228
Desplechin, Arnaud 25
Dietrich, Marlene 33
Donnelly, Kevin J. 154n7
Donner, Jörn 4, 22, 38–39, 217n18, 247, 272–273n9
Doty, Alexander 204n18
Dreams 13, 249, 250, 251–252, 253, 257–260
Dreyer, Carl Theodor 28, 166
Dufvenius, Julia 178, 261
Duggan, Lisa 208
Dunås, Jon 212n6
Duncan, Paul 170n7, 173n11, 246n14, 247n15
Dupont, E. A. (Ewald André) 14, 250, 252
Duras, Marguerite 82, 92
Dymling, Carl Anders 8, 9, 42, 44, 45, 46, 47, 48, 52, 53, 54

Eastwood, Clint 49
Edelman, Lee 206, 207
Edenman, Ragnar 274–275

Ehrnwall, Pia 179–180, 183
Ehrnwall, Torbjörn 179–180
Eisenhower, Dwight D. 24
Ek, Anders 39
Ekelöf, Gunnar 72n4
Ekselius, Eva 61
Ellegaard, France 175
Elsaesser, Thomas 8, 30
Elving, Ulf 212n5
Emerson, Ralph Waldo 266
Enhörning, Magnus 21
Erikson, Erik H. 3
Erlander, Tage 24
Esterházy, Caroline 181
Eurovision exchange of TV plays, European Broadcasting Union 215
Evander, Per Gunnar 220n27
Evans, Dylan 201–202

Face to Face 1, 4, 12, 21, 22, 37, 40, 42, 185, 186, 187, 192, 205n20, 213, 214, 216, 221, 283
Faithless 60, 70, 89, 101, 102
Fanny and Alexander 4, 13, 14, 22, 27, 60, 62, 97, 98, 105, 205n20, 218, 220, 236, 244–246, 248, 270, 277, 278, 279–284
Fant, Kenne 28, 35, 36, 37
Fårö Document 215
Fellini, Federico 17, 21, 24, 28, 32, 33
Ferm, Olle 67n21
Ferrer, Daniel 71
Fink, Bruce 201n9
Fisher (formerly Blackwell), Marilyn Johns 203
Flaubert, Gustave 90
Fonda, Henry 33
Foner, Eric 219n26
Ford, Hamish 201n8, 207
Ford, John 49
Föreställningar 70

Forman, Milos 31
Forsås-Scott, Helena 64n14
Forssell, Lars 218–219
Foucault, Michel 90
Fraistat, Neil 71n3
Franzén, Peter 31
Fred, Gunnel 261
Fredericksen, Don 4
Freiligrath, Ferdinand 124n30, 125
French, Kersti 238
French, Philip 238
Frenzy (film by Alf Sjöberg) 14, 18, 212, 215, 264
Freud, Sigmund 73, 112, 198, 201, 251, 265
Fridell, Axel 62
From the Life of the Marionettes 22, 38, 39, 40, 114n22, 227, 274, 278
Furhammar, Leif 42n1, 47n20

Gado, Frank 4, 108n5 and 7, 110n17, 111, 135, 197, 276n24
Gallafent, Edward 240, 241
Garbo, Greta 30, 33, 34
Gardner, Ava 32
Geber, Nils-Hugo 217n18
Georgsson, Lars-Olof 215n15
Geraghty, Christine 57
Gervais, Marc 4
Gillett, John 19
Gilliam, Terry 26
Gjelsvik, Anne 72n4
Gluck, Christoph Willibald 140–141
Godard, Jean-Luc 2, 3, 17, 25, 28, 200
Goethe, Johann Wolfgang von 34–35
Goldmark, Daniel 137n3, 152n3, 166n34
Gómez, Marcos Azzam 151n1
Gorbman, Claudia 137, 140, 152, 157n19, 162n29, 166, 170

Grade, Lew 22
Granath, Gunilla 211
Grant, Barry Keith 3n6, 189n4
Grant, Cary 48
Grau, Oliver 57
Grede, Kjell 21
Greer, Germaine 211
Groden, Michel 71
Grönberg, Åke 250, 255

Hägg, Göran 270n2, 272, 279
Haliday, Bryant 52, 53, 54
Halldoff, Jan 220n27
Hammar, Stina 281n36
Haneke, Michael 32
Hansen-Løve, Mia 28
Hanssen, Eirik 72n4
Hardy, Forsyth 18
Harris, Richard 32
Harvey, Cyrus 9, 19, 50, 52, 53, 54
Hastings, Max 277n27
Haverty Rugg, Linda 13, 56, 209, 224
Heath, Stephen 73n8
Hedenius, Ingemar 280–281, 282
Hedling, Erik 1, 14, 30, 170, 197n3, 270, 273n12, 275n18, 277n26, 282n42
Hedling, Olof 8, 9, 42, 44n7
Henrikson, Paula 72n4
Herrmann, Bernard 166, 171
Herzog, Amy 152n4, 153n5, 154–155, 158, 165, 166
Hill, John 44n7
Hindemith, Paul 178–179, 265
Hitchcock, Alfred 233, 235
Hoffman, Dustin 39
Hölderlin, Friedrich 213
Holmberg, Jan 1n1, 6, 10, 15, 16n26, 45n9, 58n6, 62n10, 72, 82n25, 90, 132n39, 188, 261, 273n11, 275n19, 282n42
Holmqvist, Mikael 216
Honemann, Volker 67n21

Hour of the Wolf 9, 10, 13, 20, 77, 84, 85, 93, 94, 95, 114n22, 158, 159, 162, 163, 168, 205n20, 209, 225, 226, 233, 234, 235, 245, 255
Hubner, Laura 3, 7, 13, 236
Hullot-Kentor, Robert 232n13
Humble, Kristina 220n27
Humphrey, Daniel 7, 12, 197, 205n20, 244
Huston, John 32, 33
Hutcheson, Francis 109
Huxley, Aldous 107, 110

Ibáñez-García, Estela 151n1, 171
Ibsen, Henrik 13, 17, 18, 211, 212–213, 214, 216, 217–218, 220, 283
Images: My Life in Film 5, 40, 43, 76, 194, 195, 205, 216, 218, 245, 255, 251n5, 254, 257n16, 277
In the Presence of a Clown 11, 149, 158, 164, 170, 171, 178, 180–182, 234
Iñárittu, Alejandro González 28
Ingemanson, Birgitta 82n25
Isaksson, Ulla 220
It Rains on Our Love 140, 143

Jannings, Emil 255
Janov, Arthur 4, 12, 185–196
Janzon, Bengt 109n9
Jeanelle, Jean-Louis 81n23
Johns Fisher, Marilyn *see* Fisher
Josephson, Erland 27, 178, 180, 183, 221, 234, 246n14, 247n15, 261
Journey into Autumn see Dreams
Jungstedt, Torsten 32

Kael, Pauline 205
Kalinak, Kathryn 138n4
Karin's Face 63–64

Kassabian, Anahid 166n34
Kaufman, Philip (*The Right Stuff*) 27
Kaurismäki, Aki 32
Kawashima, Nobuko 44n7
Kawin, Bruce 199–200
Kaye, Danny 36
Kearney, Richard 206n21
Kennedy, John F. 24
Keynes, John Maynard 270, 271
Kiarostami, Abbas 32
Kierkegaard, Søren 262, 265, 267
Kilday, Gregg 26n24
King, Martin Luther, Jr. 219–220, 221
Klein, Melanie 14, 249, 250, 251, 252, 256, 257, 260
Klercker, Georg af 17, 66
Kodály, Zoltán 265
Kohner, Paul 8, 30, 33–38
Koskinen, Maaret 2, 5, 6, 9, 42n3, 56, 58n6, 59n7, 72, 77, 85, 108n8, 145, 159n21, 162, 214n13, 245–246, 267, 273n10 and 12, 275n19, 280n34, 281n39
Kramer, Lawrence 108n8, 137n3, 148, 152n3, 166n34
Krieps, Vicky 28
Kristensson Uggla, Bengt 280–281
Krook, Caroline 4n11
Kubrick, Stanley 8, 25, 152
Kulezic-Wilson, Danijela 163
Kulle, Jarl 279
Kurosawa, Akira 17, 28, 163
Kushner, David 91n3, 92n5, 101n23

Lacan, Jacques 12, 201–204, 207, 208
Laemmle, Carl 33
Lagercrantz, Olof 282
Lagerkvist, Pär 66
Lamartine, Alphonse de 174

Lane, Anthony 100, 102
Lang, Fritz 49
Laretei, Käbi 148, 169, 170, 171, 174, 175, 177, 191, 216
Larsson, Camilla 145n13
Larsson, Maria Bergom see Bergom Larsson
Larsson, Stieg 211n2
Lasch, Christopher 220n27
Laterna magica 56, 63, 103n28, 169
see also *The Magic Lantern*
Latour, Bruno 228–229, 232
Lauder, Robert E. 4
Laurinus, Laurentius 132
Lehár, Franz 8, 36, 109
Lejeune, Anthony 243n9
Lejeune, C. A. (Caroline Alice) 243n9
Lejeune, Philippe 81n23
Lennon, John 186–187
Leppert, Richard 137n3, 152n3, 166n34
Lerner, Neil 149n21
Levy, Michael 38
Lidman, Sara 218–219
Lindblom, Gunnel 21, 217, 220, 223
Lindeen, Marcus 75
Lindegren, Erik 253
Lindhé, Thomas 215n15
Liszt, Franz 10, 124–125, 136n1, 138
Livingston, Paisley 3, 11, 12, 108n7, 109, 110n14, 145–146, 185, 284
Loman, Rikard 2n3
Löthwall, Lars-Olof 211n3
Lubitsch, Ernst 34
Luko, Alexis 7, 10, 107, 108n6, 111n21, 122n26, 123n28, 130n35, 133n41, 134n42, 135n45, 148n19, 151, 152n2, 160n23, 171, 173, 174, 193, 196, 227–228, 233–234

Lundberg, Camilla 161n25
Lundberg, Håkan 119n24
Lundberg, Mattias 132n39
Lundbergh, Holger 4
Lunde, Arne 42n2, 108
Lundevall, Carl-Fredrik 231n11
Luther, Martin 132n39
Lynch, David 26

Macnab, Geoffrey 48, 49
Maddin, Guy 30, 32
Mael, Ron 30, 31
Mael, Russell 30, 31
Magnusson, Jane 26n23
Malle, Louis 27, 31
Malmsjö, Jan 279, 281
Malmstrom, Lars 91n3, 92n5, 101n23
Mamet, David 26
Människoätarna 84, 86n31
see also *The Cannibals*
Manns, Torsten 103n27, 161n26, 213n7, 222n29, 243n10, 250n2–4, 257–258, 259n22, 273n11, 275n20, 276n21
Maras, Steven 82
Marker, Frederick J. 2n3, 136n2
Marker, Lise-Lone 2n3, 136n2
Marmstedt, Lorens 18
Marsh, Mae 34
Martinson, Harry 220
Mattsson, Arne 19
Melin, Pia 67n21
Mendelssohn-Bartholdy, Felix 138, 147, 158, 177
Mera, Miguel 118n23
Mesmer, Franz Anton 244
Messing, Scott 183
Meyer, Stephen 130n35
Michaels, Lloyd 197n1, 205n19
Milne, Tom 25n20
Miłosz, Czesław 266
Mitchell, W.J.T. (William John Thomas) 57

Index

Moi, Toril 213
Molander, Jan 12, 215
Morton, Timothy 13, 226–227, 228–229, 234–235
Mosley, Philip 3
Mozart, Wolfgang Amadeus 10, 21, 108, 110, 119, 131, 138, 149, 167, 226, 233, 234
Münch, Christopher 144n12
Munk, Erika 90n1
Murnau, Friedrich 34
Music in Darkness 11, 18, 124n29, 138, 146, 158, 159
Myrberg, Per 217

Nägeli, Hans Georg 131n36
Negri, Pola 34
Nelson, Dana D. 208n27
Neumann, Anyssa 10, 11, 108n8, 136, 151n1, 171, 173, 174–175, 183, 191, 192
Newcomb, Anthony 183n26
Nietzsche, Friedrich 207
Niven, David 33
Nordgren, Erik 10, 11, 109, 110, 111–135, 138, 157
Nordin, Svante 280n35
Nykvist, Sven 21, 27, 45n11
Nyreröd, Marie 145n14, 266n4
Nystedt, Hans 4n11

O'Toole, Peter 32
Ohlin, Peter 56
Oliver, Myrna 236
Oliver, Roger W. 64n14
Orff, Carl 11
Östberg, Kjell 270n2, 271
Ozu, Yasujirô 166

Pacino, Al 36
Pallas, Hynek 26n23
Palme, Olof 270, 278, 282
Palmgren, Christina 283n45
Park, Chan-wook 26

Payne, John 31
Persona 4, 10, 12, 20, 26, 27, 56, 72, 77, 78, 81, 82, 83, 84, 85, 86, 87, 93, 94, 95n10, 102, 103, 105, 114n22, 144, 159, 162, 197–209, 214, 220, 223, 234, 236, 245, 261, 264, 269
Persson, Annika 211n3
Peters, John Durham 143n10
Petheri, Karin 64n14
Peyrefitte, Alain 20
Pictor, Albertus 67
Polanski, Roman 31, 32
Pope, Rob 74n10
Powell, Dilys 23
Powrie, Phil 152n4, 153–154, 155–156, 158, 160, 165
Price, Steven 85n28
Prince, Harold 27, 34
Prison 159
Private Confessions 56, 102, 104
Pushkin, Alexander 19

Rafaelson, Bob 27
Reisz, Karel 24
Renaud, Charlotte 108n8, 138, 139, 151, 161n24, 163n31
Renoir, Jean 34
Resnais, Alain 152
Revelation, Book of 105–106
Rich, Adrienne 204
Rich, B. Ruby 204, 208
Richardson, Marie 181
Richardson, Tony 24
Rink, John 174n15
Robbe-Grillet, Alain 82, 92
Rodell, Hanns 170
Rohdin, Mats 280, 281
Rosenbaum, Jonathan 16n27, 28
Rosenberg, Ethel 275n19
Rosenberg, Julius 275n19
Rosenberg, Ulrika 22
Rossholm, Anna Sofia 1n1, 6, 9, 58n6, 70, 72n4, 105, 267

Roth, Tim 28
Rothwell, Fred 110n15
Rugg, Linda Haverty *see* Haverty Rugg
Ruth, Arne 272
Ruuth, Marianne 5n14, 205n20, 251n5, 276n21
Ryan, Robert 48

Sagan, Leontine 204
Salomon, Kim 271n5
Samson, Jim 174
Saraband 11, 14, 85, 101, 114n22, 123n28, 144, 147, 158, 170, 171, 178–180, 184, 246n13, 261–269
Saura, Carlos 24
Sawdust and Tinsel 1, 11, 13, 14, 18, 24, 26, 159, 160, 162, 163, 165, 249, 250–255, 259, 260, 280
Scenes from a Marriage 1, 12, 14, 20, 21, 27, 35, 37, 83, 95, 105, 212, 216, 217, 261
Schamus, James 65
Scheibe, Siegfried 79
Schein, Harry 35
Schiller, Friedrich (von) 73
Schlesinger, John 24
Schrader, Paul 166
Schubert, Franz 136n1, 149, 150, 181, 182, 183
Schumann, Robert 10, 124, 131n36, 136n1, 138, 143, 182–183
Scott, A. O. (Anthony Oliver) 236–237
Scott, George C. 32
Secrets of Women 107
Segal, Alex 215
Segal, Hanna 249
Sellermark, Arne 109n9, 214n14
Selznick, David O. 18, 51
Settergren-Carlsson, Gitte 220n27

Shakespeare, William 2, 10, 26, 29, 91–92, 101, 109n9, 122–123, 126, 132, 180
Shame 20, 82n26, 102n25, 203n14, 218–219, 221, 275, 277n26 and 27
Sibelius, Jean 17
Siclier, Jacques 3
Sigurdson, Ola 267n5
Sima, Jonas 103n27, 161n26, 213n7 and 11, 222n29, 243n10, 250n2–4, 257–258, 259n22, 273n11, 274, 275n20, 276n21, 278
Simon, John 253
Simon, Sherry 90n2
Singer, Irving 3
Sjöberg, Alf 14, 18, 19, 223
Sjöström, Victor 14, 17, 25, 100, 164, 171, 214, 238, 246–247, 251, 252
Sjöwall, Maj 211n2
Skoble, Aeon 108n8
Skoglund, Erik 215, 275
Smetana, Bedřich 138
Smiles of a Summer Night 10, 19, 24, 26, 27, 30, 34, 42, 107–135, 138, 158
Smith, Jeff 166n34
So Close to Life (British title) 19 *see also Brink of Life*
Söderbergh Widding, Astrid 162n28, 273n10, 275n19
Sondheim, Stephen 27, 34, 131n36
Sontag, Susan 197, 198–199, 200
Staiger, Janet 77n14
Stam, Per 273n10, 275n19
Steene, Birgitta 5–6, 48n22, 93, 109n9, 132n38, 170n7, 173n11, 213n11, 218n20, 249n1, 254, 258, 276n23
Sterne, Jonathan 143n9
Stiller, Mauritz 17, 34

Index

Stilwell, Robyn J. 166n34
Stravinsky, Igor 149
Streisand, Barbra 8, 21, 36, 37, 38
Strindberg, August 5, 13, 14, 17, 124, 212–213, 216, 222, 223, 265, 266
Stroop, Jürgen 86
Summer Interlude 13, 18, 138, 141, 230, 232, 233
Summer with Monika 24, 25
Sunday's Children 9, 56, 57, 66–67
Swahn, Lennart 90n1
Swedenborg, Emanuel 14, 265–266

Tapper, Michael 1n1, 4, 6, 12, 13, 42n3, 185, 186, 187, 193, 211, 212n6, 213, 214n14, 283n44
Tarantino, Quentin 152
Tarkovsky, Andrei 26, 27, 162n28
Tate, Joan 5n14, 63n11, 67n20, 104n31
Tavernier, Bertrand 25
Taylor, Elizabeth 27
Tegnér, Esaias 96
The Best Intentions 9, 56, 57, 63, 64–65, 66, 68
The Cannibals 84, 85, 86, 87, 88
The Devil's Eye 44, 158
The Face 19, 24, 243
   see also *The Magician*
The Lie 12, 212, 215–222
The Magic Flute (production) 21, 167, 168, 183–184
The Magic Lantern 5, 40, 43, 103, 107n2–4, 124, 169, 185, 214, 278
   see also *Laterna magica*
The Magician 13, 19, 24, 26, 44, 45, 46, 158, 205n20, 234, 243, 261, 268, 280
   see also *The Face*
The Passion of Anna 20, 42, 58, 83, 217, 218
The Rite 20, 215, 221n28
The Serpent's Egg 8, 21, 30, 38, 39, 40, 87, 158, 281
The Seventh Seal 4, 10, 11, 13, 19, 23, 24, 25, 26, 67, 92n5, 99n18 and 19, 100, 101, 105, 106, 107n3, 130, 135, 138, 146, 158, 232, 236, 237, 252, 253, 273
The Silence 6, 20, 24, 42, 58n6, 59n7, 62, 72, 88, 144, 158, 197, 205n20, 274, 275n18, 282n42
'The Snakeskin' 264–265
The Touch 20, 221n28
The Virgin Spring 13, 19, 24, 44, 46, 51, 53, 130, 197, 229–230, 233, 252
Theunissen, Gert H. 20n7
Thirst 158
Thomson, David 100
Through a Glass Darkly 4, 19, 26, 44, 47, 48, 52, 138, 139, 163, 168, 199, 264
Thulin, Ingrid 19, 27
Timm, Mikael 5, 28–29, 74n11, 273–274, 275n17, 282
Tincknell, Estella 152n4, 153n5
To Joy 11, 123n28, 138, 147, 157, 158, 170n5, 171–173, 177, 178, 180
Torén, Torvald 170n6
Törnqvist, Arne 168–169
Törnqvist, Egil 157n20, 212
Troell, Jan 33, 163, 212
Truffaut, François 2
Turgenev, Ivan 18
Turner, Lana 33

Uhland, Ludwig 124n30
Ullmann, Liv 12, 20, 27, 33, 34, 35, 58, 60, 70, 83, 170, 174, 178, 188, 194–195, 214, 217, 218, 221, 261, 264, 275

Usteri, Johann Martin 131n36
Ustinov, Peter 18

Vadim, Roger 24
Veith, Mizzi 181, 183
Verhoeven, Paul 25
Vesterlund, Per 44n7
Vietnam War 219, 221, 272, 277
Viklund, Jon 72n4
Vinge, Louise 64
Viollet, Catherine 81n23
Visconti, Luchino 24, 32
von Koch, Erland 157
von Sternberg, Joseph 34
von Stroheim, Erich 34
von Sydow, Max 24, 25, 27, 37, 58, 229, 275
von Trotta, Margarethe 28
Vowles, Bernard 145n13

Waddell, Margot 256
Wagner, Richard 11, 140, 143, 167
Wahlöö, Per 211n2
Waiting Women 18, 140, 143, 159
Wajda, Andrzej 32
Walker, Elsie 108n8
Walker, Janet 86n30
Wallengren, Ann-Kristin 11, 151, 160, 164, 270n1
Wållgren, Gunn 246
Wallin, Johan Olof 266
Walters, James 240n6
Wanger, Walter 49
Wanselius, Bengt 170n7, 173n11, 246n14, 247n15
Wasikowska, Mia 28

Wasserman, Lew 51
Welles, Orson 28, 32
Wendlandt, Horst 39
Werle, Lars-Johan 157, 162
Werner, Michael 79n18
Widding, Astrid Söderbergh *see* Söderbergh Widding
Widerberg, Bo 36, 99
Wierzbicki, James 108n8, 147n17, 151n1, 173n12
Wifstrand, Naima 158
Wild Strawberries 3, 13, 19, 23, 25, 26, 31, 100, 101, 141, 158, 164, 214, 220, 231–243, 245, 246, 247n16, 250, 251, 255, 260, 261, 266, 281
Wilder, Billy 33
Wilens, Bernhard L. 8, 49, 50, 51
Williams, Dan 3, 7, 13, 14, 249
Williams, John 165, 171
Winnicott, Donald W. 73, 78
Winter Light 1, 4, 19, 24, 181, 183, 199, 212, 222, 223
Winters, Ben 166n34
Wirén, Dag 157
Witt-Brattström, Ebba 211
Woesler, Winfried 79n18
Wollheim, Richard 249
Wood, Robin 3, 189, 190, 203, 204, 208, 253, 254n11
Wordsworth, William 227
Wright, Rochelle 64

Yri, Kirsten 130n35

Zanussi, Krzysztof 25
Zern, Leif 65, 211–212

EU authorised representative for GPSR:
Easy Access System Europe, Mustamäe tee 50,
10621 Tallinn, Estonia
gpsr.requests@easproject.com

www.ingramcontent.com/pod-product-compliance
Ingram Content Group UK Ltd.
Pitfield, Milton Keynes, MK11 3LW, UK
UKHW021824140426
5217IPUK00004B/79